CONTENTS

Published in Great Britain in 2005 by Philip's,
a division of Octopus Publishing Group Limited,
2–4 Heron Quays, London E14 4JP

Copyright © 2005 Philip's

Cartography by Philip's

CITY PLANS
Page 29, Dublin: The town plan of Dublin is based on
Ordnance Survey Ireland by permission of the Government
Permit Number 7978. © Ordnance Survey Ireland and
Government of Ireland.

 Page 31, London: This product
includes mapping data licensed
from Ordnance Survey® with
the permission of the Controller of Her Majesty's Stationery
Office. © Crown copyright 2005. All rights reserved.
Licence number 100011710.

Vector data: Courtesy of Gräfe and Unser Verlag GmbH,
München, Germany (city-centre maps of Bangkok,
Cape Town, Mexico City, Singapore, Sydney and Tokyo).

ISBN-13 978–0–540–08874–4
ISBN-10 0–540–08874–9

A CIP catalogue record for this book is available from the
British Library.

Printed in Hong Kong

Details of other Philip's titles and services can be found
on our website at: www.philips-maps.co.uk

Philip's World Atlases are published in association
with The Royal Geographical Society (with The
Institute of British Geographers).
    The Society was founded in 1830 and given a
Royal Charter in 1859 for 'the advancement of
geographical science'. Today it is a leading world
centre for geographical learning – supporting
education, teaching, research and expeditions, and
promoting public understanding of the subject.
    Further information about the Society and how to
join may be found on its website at: www.rgs.org

WORLD STATISTICS

4–7	Countries
8–9	Cities
10–11	Time zones
12–13	Flight paths
14–15	Distance table
16–19	World climate
20	Conversion chart

CITY PLANS

21	City plans – legend
22	Amsterdam
23	Athens
24	Bangkok
25	Berlin
26	Brussels
27	Cape Town
28	Chicago
29	Dublin
30	Hong Kong
31	London
32	Madrid
33	Mexico City
34	Moscow
35	New York
36	Paris
37	Prague
38	Rio de Janeiro
39	Rome
40	San Francisco
41	Singapore
42	Sydney
43	Tokyo
44	Toronto
45	Vienna

GAZETTEER OF NATIONS

46–47	Gazetteer of Nations – contents
48–72	Country-by-country profiles

NOTE:
For reasons of safety or politics, there may be times
when it is not advisable, or desirable, to visit one
or more of the countries described in the Gazetteer
of Nations section. If in doubt, please check with the
Foreign Office (www.fco.gov.uk).

WORLD MAPS

1	World Maps – general reference
2–3	Northern hemisphere 1:133.3M
4–5	Southern hemisphere 1:133.3M

EUROPE

6–7	Europe 1:26.7M
8–9	Scandinavia and the Baltic Lands 1:13.3M
10–11	British Isles 1:6.7M
12–13	France 1:6.7M
14–15	Germany and Benelux 1:6.7M
16–17	Central Europe 1:6.7M
18–19	Spain and Portugal 1:6.7M
20–21	Italy and the Adriatic 1:6.7M
22–23	Greece and the Balkans 1:6.7M
24–25	Eastern Europe 1:13.3M

ASIA

26–27	Asia 1:67M
28–29	Western Russia and Central Asia 1:26.7M
30–31	Eastern Siberia 1:26.7M
32–33	Japan 1:8.5M
34–35	China 1:26.7M
36–37	Philippines and Eastern Indonesia 1:16.7M
38–39	South-east Asia 1:16.7M
40–41	Eastern India, Bangladesh and Burma 1:13.3M
42–43	Western India and Pakistan 1:13.3M
44–45	Iran, the Gulf and Afghanistan 1:13.3M
46–47	The Middle East and Turkey 1:13.3M
48–49	Arabia and the Horn of Africa 1:20M

AFRICA

| **50–51** | Africa 1:56M |

52–53	North-west Africa 1:20M
54–55	North-east Africa 1:20M
56–57	Central Africa 1:20M
58–59	Southern Africa 1:20M

AUSTRALASIA

60–61	Australia 1:26.7M
62–63	South-east Australia 1:10.7M
64–65	New Zealand 1:8M
	Central and South-west Pacific

NORTH AMERICA

66–67	North America 1:46.7M
68–69	Western Canada 1:20M
70–71	Eastern Canada 1:20M
72–73	North-west USA 1:8M
74–75	North-central USA 1:8M
76–77	North-east USA 1:8M
78–79	South-west USA 1:8M
80–81	Southern USA 1:8M
82–83	South-east USA 1:8M
84–85	Mexico 1:20M
86–87	Caribbean and Central America 1:20M

SOUTH AMERICA

88–89	South America 1:46.7M
90–91	South America – North-west 1:21.3M
92–93	South America – North-east 1:21.3M
94–95	South America – South 1:21.3M

POLAR REGIONS

| **96** | Antarctica 1:46.7M |

INDEX

| **97–160** | Index to World Maps |

Country/Territory	Area (1,000 sq km)	Area (1,000 sq mi)	Population (1,000s)	Capital City	Annual Income US$
Afghanistan	652	252	28,514	Kabul	700
Albania	28.7	11.1	3,545	Tirana	4,400
Algeria	2,382	920	32,129	Algiers	5,400
American Samoa (US)	0.20	0.08	58	Pago Pago	8,000
Andorra	0.47	0.18	70	Andorra La Vella	19,000
Angola	1,247	481	10,979	Luanda	1,700
Anguilla (UK)	0.10	0.04	13	The Valley	8,600
Antigua & Barbuda	0.44	0.17	68	St John's	11,000
Argentina	2,780	1,074	39,145	Buenos Aires	10,500
Armenia	29.8	11.5	2,991	Yerevan	3,600
Aruba (Netherlands)	0.19	0.07	71	Oranjestad	28,000
Australia	7,741	2,989	19,913	Canberra	26,900
Austria	83.9	32.4	8,175	Vienna	27,900
Azerbaijan	86.6	33.4	7,868	Baku	3,700
Azores (Portugal)	2.2	0.86	236	Ponta Delgada	15,000
Bahamas	13.9	5.4	300	Nassau	15,300
Bahrain	0.69	0.27	678	Manama	15,100
Bangladesh	144	55.6	141,340	Dhaka	1,800
Barbados	0.43	0.17	278	Bridgetown	15,000
Belarus	208	80.2	10,311	Minsk	8,700
Belgium	30.5	11.8	10,348	Brussels	29,200
Belize	23.0	8.9	273	Belmopan	4,900
Benin	113	43.5	7,250	Porto-Novo	1,100
Bermuda (UK)	0.05	0.02	65	Hamilton	35,200
Bhutan	47.0	18.1	2,186	Thimphu	1,300
Bolivia	1,099	424	8,724	La Paz/Sucre	2,500
Bosnia-Herzegovina	51.2	19.8	4,008	Sarajevo	1,900
Botswana	582	225	1,562	Gaborone	8,500
Brazil	8,514	3,287	184,101	Brasília	7,600
Brunei	5.8	2.2	365	Bandar Seri Begawan	18,600
Bulgaria	111	42.8	7,518	Sofia	6,500
Burkina Faso	274	106	13,575	Ouagadougou	1,100
Burma (= Myanmar)	677	261	42,720	Rangoon	1,700
Burundi	27.8	10.7	6,231	Bujumbura	500
Cambodia	181	69.9	13,363	Phnom Penh	1,600
Cameroon	475	184	16,064	Yaoundé	1,700
Canada	9,971	3,850	32,508	Ottawa	29,300
Canary Is. (Spain)	7.2	2.8	1,682	Las Palmas/Santa Cruz	19,900
Cape Verde Is.	4.0	1.6	415	Praia	1,400
Cayman Is. (UK)	0.26	0.10	43	George Town	35,000
Central African Republic	623	241	3,742	Bangui	1,200
Chad	1,284	496	9,539	Ndjaména	1,000
Chile	757	292	15,824	Santiago	10,100
China	9,597	3,705	1,298,848	Beijing	4,700
Colombia	1,139	440	42,311	Bogotá	6,100
Comoros	2.2	0.86	652	Moroni	700
Congo	342	132	2,998	Brazzaville	900
Congo (Dem. Rep. of the)	2,345	905	58,318	Kinshasa	600
Cook Is. (NZ)	0.24	0.09	21	Avarua	5,000
Costa Rica	51.1	19.7	3,957	San José	8,300
Croatia	56.5	21.8	4,497	Zagreb	9,800
Cuba	111	42.8	11,309	Havana	2,700
Cyprus	9.3	3.6	776	Nicosia	13,200
Czech Republic	78.9	30.5	10,246	Prague	15,300
Denmark	43.1	16.6	5,413	Copenhagen	28,900

Listed above are the principal countries and territories of the world. If a territory is not completely independent, then the country it is associated with is named. The area figures give the total area of land, inland water and ice. The population figures are 2004 estimates. The annual income is the Gross Domestic Product per capita in US dollars. [Gross Domestic Product per capita has been measured

Country/Territory	Area (1,000 sq km)	Area (1,000 sq ml)	Population (1,000s)	Capital City	Annual Income US$
Djibouti	23.2	9.0	467	Djibouti	1,300
Dominica	0.75	0.29	69	Roseau	5,400
Dominican Republic	48.5	18.7	8,834	Santo Domingo	6,300
East Timor	14.9	5.7	1,019	Dili	500
Ecuador	284	109	13,213	Quito	3,200
Egypt	1,001	387	76,117	Cairo	4,000
El Salvador	21.0	8.1	6,588	San Salvador	4,600
Equatorial Guinea	28.1	10.8	523	Malabo	2,700
Eritrea	118	45.4	4,447	Asmara	700
Estonia	45.1	17.4	1,342	Tallinn	11,000
Ethiopia	1,104	426	67,851	Addis Ababa	700
Faroe Is. (Denmark)	1.4	0.54	47	Tórshavn	22,000
Fiji	18.3	7.1	881	Suva	5,600
Finland	338	131	5,215	Helsinki	25,800
France	552	213	60,424	Paris	26,000
French Guiana (France)	90.0	34.7	191	Cayenne	14,400
French Polynesia (France)	4.0	1.5	266	Papeete	5,000
Gabon	268	103	1,355	Libreville	6,500
Gambia, The	11.3	4.4	1,547	Banjul	1,800
Gaza Strip (OPT)*	0.36	0.14	1,325	–	600
Georgia	69.7	26.9	4,694	Tbilisi	3,200
Germany	357	138	82,425	Berlin	26,200
Ghana	239	92.1	20,757	Accra	2,000
Gibraltar (UK)	0.006	0.002	28	Gibraltar Town	17,500
Greece	132	50.9	10,648	Athens	19,100
Greenland (Denmark)	2,176	840	56	Nuuk (Godthåb)	20,000
Grenada	0.34	0.13	89	St George's	5,000
Guadeloupe (France)	1.7	0.66	445	Basse-Terre	9,000
Guam (US)	0.55	0.21	166	Agana	21,000
Guatemala	109	42.0	14,281	Guatemala City	3,900
Guinea	246	94.9	9,246	Conakry	2,100
Guinea-Bissau	36.1	13.9	1,388	Bissau	700
Guyana	215	83.0	706	Georgetown	3,800
Haiti	27.8	10.7	7,656	Port-au-Prince	1,400
Honduras	112	43.3	6,824	Tegucigalpa	2,500
Hong Kong (China)	1.1	0.42	6,855	–	27,200
Hungary	93.0	35.9	10,032	Budapest	13,300
Iceland	103	39.8	294	Reykjavik	30,200
India	3,287	1,269	1,065,071	New Delhi	2,600
Indonesia	1,905	735	238,453	Jakarta	3,100
Iran	1,648	636	69,019	Tehran	6,800
Iraq	438	169	25,375	Baghdad	2,400
Ireland	70.3	27.1	3,970	Dublin	29,300
Israel	20.6	8.0	6,199	Jerusalem	19,500
Italy	301	116	58,057	Rome	25,100
Ivory Coast (= Côte d'Ivoire)	322	125	17,328	Yamoussoukro	1,400
Jamaica	11.0	4.2	2,713	Kingston	3,800
Japan	378	146	127,333	Tokyo	28,700
Jordan	89.3	34.5	5,611	Amman	4,300
Kazakhstan	2,725	1,052	15,144	Astana	7,200
Kenya	580	224	32,022	Nairobi	1,100
Kiribati	0.73	0.28	101	Tarawa	800
Korea, North	121	46.5	22,698	Pyŏngyang	1,000
Korea, South	99.3	38.3	48,598	Seoul	19,600
Kuwait	17.8	6.9	2,258	Kuwait City	17,500

using the purchasing power parity method. This enables comparisons to be made between countries through their purchasing power (in US dollars), showing real price levels of goods and services rather than using currency exchange rates.] The figures are the latest available, usually 2002 estimates. *OPT = Occupied Palestinian Territory; N/A = Not available.

Country/Territory	Area (1,000 sq km)	Area (1,000 sq m)	Population (1,000s)	Capital City	Annual Income US$
Kyrgyzstan	200	77.2	5,081	Bishkek	2,900
Laos	237	91.4	6,068	Vientiane	1,800
Latvia	64.6	24.9	2,306	Riga	8,900
Lebanon	10.4	4.0	3,777	Beirut	4,800
Lesotho	30.4	11.7	1,865	Maseru	2,700
Liberia	111	43.0	3,391	Monrovia	1,000
Libya	1,760	679	5,632	Tripoli	6,200
Liechtenstein	0.16	0.06	33	Vaduz	25,000
Lithuania	65.2	25.2	3,608	Vilnius	8,400
Luxembourg	2.6	1.0	463	Luxembourg	48,900
Macau (China)	0.02	0.007	445	–	18,500
Macedonia (FYROM)	25.7	9.9	2,071	Skopje	5,100
Madagascar	587	227	17,502	Antananarivo	800
Madeira (Portugal)	0.78	0.30	241	Funchal	22,700
Malawi	118	45.7	11,907	Lilongwe	600
Malaysia	330	127	23,522	Kuala Lumpur/Putrajaya	8,800
Maldives	0.30	0.12	339	Malé	3,900
Mali	1,240	479	11,957	Bamako	900
Malta	0.32	0.12	397	Valletta	17,200
Marshall Is.	0.18	0.07	58	Majuro	1,600
Martinique (France)	1.1	0.43	430	Fort-de-France	10,700
Mauritania	1,026	396	2,999	Nouakchott	1,700
Mauritius	2.0	0.79	1,220	Port Louis	10,100
Mayotte (France)	0.37	0.14	186	Mamoundzou	600
Mexico	1,958	756	104,960	Mexico City	8,900
Micronesia, Fed. States of	0.70	0.27	108	Palikir	2,000
Moldova	33.9	13.1	4,446	Chişinău	2,600
Monaco	0.001	0.0004	32	Monaco	27,000
Mongolia	1,567	605	2,751	Ulan Bator	1,900
Montserrat (UK)	0.10	0.04	9	Plymouth	3,400
Morocco	447	172	32,209	Rabat	3,900
Mozambique	802	309	18,812	Maputo	1,100
Namibia	824	318	1,954	Windhoek	6,900
Nauru	0.02	0.008	13	Yaren District	5,000
Nepal	147	56.8	27,071	Katmandu	1,400
Netherlands	41.5	16.0	16,318	Amsterdam/The Hague	27,200
Netherlands Antilles (Neths)	0.80	0.31	218	Willemstad	11,400
New Caledonia (France)	18.6	7.2	214	Nouméa	14,000
New Zealand	271	104	3,994	Wellington	20,100
Nicaragua	130	50.2	5,360	Managua	2,200
Niger	1,267	489	11,361	Niamey	800
Nigeria	924	357	137,253	Abuja	900
Northern Mariana Is. (US)	0.46	0.18	78	Saipan	12,500
Norway	324	125	4,575	Oslo	33,000
Oman	310	119	2,903	Muscat	8,300
Pakistan	796	307	159,196	Islamabad	2,000
Palau	0.46	0.18	20	Koror	9,000
Panama	75.5	29.2	3,000	Panamá	6,200
Papua New Guinea	463	179	5,420	Port Moresby	2,100
Paraguay	407	157	6,191	Asunción	4,300
Peru	1,285	496	27,544	Lima	5,000
Philippines	300	116	86,242	Manila	4,600
Poland	323	125	38,626	Warsaw	9,700
Portugal	88.8	34.3	10,524	Lisbon	19,400
Puerto Rico (US)	8.9	3.4	3,898	San Juan	11,100
Qatar	11.0	4.2	840	Doha	20,100
Réunion (France)	2.5	0.97	766	St-Denis	5,600
Romania	238	92.0	22,356	Bucharest	7,600

Country/Territory	Area (1,000 sq km)	Area (1,000 sq m)	Population (1,000s)	Capital City	Annual Income US$
Russia	17,075	6,593	143,782	Moscow	9,700
Rwanda	26.3	10.2	7,954	Kigali	1,200
St Kitts & Nevis	0.26	0.10	39	Basseterre	8,800
St Lucia	0.54	0.21	164	Castries	5,400
St Vincent & Grenadines	0.39	0.15	117	Kingstown	2,900
Samoa	2.8	1.1	178	Apia	5,600
San Marino	0.06	0.02	29	San Marino	34,600
São Tomé & Príncipe	0.96	0.37	182	São Tomé	1,200
Saudi Arabia	2,150	830	25,796	Riyadh	11,400
Senegal	197	76.0	10,852	Dakar	1,500
Serbia & Montenegro	102	39.4	10,826	Belgrade	2,200
Seychelles	0.46	0.18	81	Victoria	7,800
Sierra Leone	71.7	27.7	5,884	Freetown	500
Singapore	0.68	0.26	4,354	Singapore City	25,200
Slovak Republic	49.0	18.9	5,424	Bratislava	12,400
Slovenia	20.3	7.8	2,011	Ljubljana	19,200
Solomon Is.	28.9	11.2	524	Honiara	1,700
Somalia	638	246	8,305	Mogadishu	600
South Africa	1,221	471	42,719	Cape Town/Pretoria/Bloemfontein	10,000
Spain	498	192	40,281	Madrid	21,200
Sri Lanka	65.6	25.3	19,905	Colombo	3,700
Sudan	2,506	967	39,148	Khartoum	1,400
Suriname	163	63.0	437	Paramaribo	3,400
Swaziland	17.4	6.7	1,169	Mbabane	4,800
Sweden	450	174	8,986	Stockholm	26,000
Switzerland	41.3	15.9	7,451	Bern	32,000
Syria	185	71.5	18,017	Damascus	3,700
Taiwan	36.0	13.9	22,750	Taipei	18,000
Tajikistan	143	55.3	7,012	Dushanbe	1,300
Tanzania	945	365	36,588	Dodoma	600
Thailand	513	198	64,866	Bangkok	7,000
Togo	56.8	21.9	5,557	Lomé	1,400
Tonga	0.65	0.25	110	Nuku'alofa	2,200
Trinidad & Tobago	5.1	2.0	1,097	Port of Spain	10,000
Tunisia	164	63.2	9,975	Tunis	6,800
Turkey	775	299	68,894	Ankara	7,300
Turkmenistan	488	188	4,863	Ashkhabad	6,700
Turks & Caicos Is. (UK)	0.43	0.17	20	Cockburn Town	9,600
Tuvalu	0.03	0.01	11	Fongafale	1,100
Uganda	241	93.1	26,405	Kampala	1,200
Ukraine	604	233	47,732	Kiev	4,500
United Arab Emirates	83.6	32.3	2,524	Abu Dhabi	22,100
United Kingdom	242	93.4	60,271	London	25,500
United States of America	9,629	3,718	293,028	Washington, DC	36,300
Uruguay	175	67.6	3,399	Montevideo	7,900
Uzbekistan	447	173	26,410	Tashkent	2,600
Vanuatu	12.2	4.7	203	Port-Vila	2,900
Vatican City	0.0004	0.0002	1	Vatican City	N/A
Venezuela	912	352	25,017	Caracas	5,400
Vietnam	332	128	82,690	Hanoi	2,300
Virgin Is. (UK)	0.15	0.06	22	Road Town	16,000
Virgin Is. (US)	0.35	0.13	109	Charlotte Amalie	19,000
Wallis & Futuna Is. (France)	0.20	0.08	16	Mata-Utu	2,000
West Bank (OPT)*	5.9	2.3	2,311	–	800
Western Sahara	266	103	267	El Aaiún	N/A
Yemen	528	204	20,025	Sana'	800
Zambia	753	291	10,462	Lusaka	800
Zimbabwe	391	151	12,672	Harare	2,100

	Population (1,000s)		Population (1,000s)		Population (1,000s)		Population (1,000s)
Afghanistan		Beijing	10,839	Yixing	1,108	**Georgia**	
Kabul	2,602	Tianjin	9,156	Yongzhou	1,097	Tbilisi	1,406
Algeria		Hong Kong	6,860	Chifeng	1,087	**Germany**	
Algiers	1,722	Wuhan	5,169	Huzhou	1,077	Berlin	3,387
Angola		Chongqing	4,900	Daqing	1,076	Hamburg	1,705
Luanda	2,697	Shenyang	4,828	Zigong	1,072	Munich	1,195
Argentina		Guangzhou	3,893	Mianyang	1,065	Cologne	963
Buenos Aires	12,024	Chengdu	3,294	Nanchong	1,055	**Ghana**	
Córdoba	1,368	Xi'an	3,123	Fuyu	1,025	Accra	1,868
Rosario	1,279	Changchun	3,093	Jining, Shandong	1,019	**Greece**	
Mendoza	934	Harbin	2,928	Hohhot	978	Athens	3,116
Armenia		Nanjing	2,740	Xinyi, Guangdong	973	**Guatemala**	
Yerevan	1,407	Zibo	2,675	Benxi	957	Guatemala City	3,242
Australia		Dalian	2,628	Jixi	949	**Guinea**	
Sydney	4,086	Jinan	2,568	Liuzhou	928	Conakry	1,232
Melbourne	3,466	Guiyang	2,533	Xiangxiang	908	**Haiti**	
Brisbane	1,627	Linyi	2,498	Yichun, Heilongjiang	904	Port-au-Prince	1,769
Perth	1,381	Taiyuan	2,415	Xianyang	896	**Honduras**	
Adelaide	1,096	Qingdao	2,316	Linqing	891	Tegucigalpa	949
Austria		Zhengzhou	2,070	Changzhou	886	**Hungary**	
Vienna	1,807	Zaozhuang	2,048	Zhangjiagang	886	Budapest	1,819
Azerbaijan		Liupanshui	2,023	Zhangjiakou	880	**India**	
Baku	1,792	Handan	1,996	Jiamusi	874	Mumbai	16,086
Bangladesh		Jinxi	1,821	Yichun, Jiangxi	871	Kolkata	13,058
Dhaka	12,519	Lu'an	1,818	Zhaotong	851	Delhi	12,441
Chittagong	3,651	Hangzhou	1,780	Yuyao	848	Chennai	6,353
Khulna	1,442	Tianmen	1,779	Jinzhou	834	Bangalore	5,567
Rajshahi	1,035	Changsha	1,775	Xuanzhou	823	Hyderabad	5,445
Belarus		Wanxian	1,759	Huaibei	814	Ahmedabad	4,427
Minsk	1,717	Lanzhou	1,730	Xinyu	808	Pune	3,655
Belgium		Nanchang	1,722	Mudanjiang	801	Surat	2,699
Brussels	964	Kunming	1,701	**Colombia**		Kanpur	2,641
Bolivia		Yantai	1,681	Bogotá	6,771	Jaipur	2,259
La Paz	1,487	Tangshan	1,671	Medellín	2,866	Lucknow	2,221
Santa Cruz	1,035	Xuzhou	1,636	Cali	2,233	Nagpur	2,089
Brazil		Xiantao	1,614	Barranquilla	1,683	Patna	1,658
São Paulo	17,962	Shijiazhuang	1,603	Bucaramanga	937	Indore	1,597
Rio de Janeiro	10,652	Heze	1,600	Cartagena	845	Vadodara	1,465
Belo Horizonte	4,224	Yancheng	1,562	**Congo**		Bhopal	1,425
Pôrto Alegre	3,757	Yulin	1,558	Brazzaville	1,306	Coimbatore	1,420
Recife	3,346	Xinghua	1,556	**Congo (Democratic**		Ludhiana	1,368
Salvador	3,238	Tai'an	1,503	**Republic of the)**		Cochin	1,340
Fortaleza	3,066	Pingxiang	1,502	Kinshasa	5,054	Visakhapatnam	1,309
Curitiba	2,562	Anshan	1,453	Lubumbashi	965	Agra	1,293
Brasília	2,051	Luoyang	1,451	Mbuji-Mayi	806	Varanasi	1,199
Belém	1,658	Jilin	1,435	**Costa Rica**		Madurai	1,187
Manaus	1,467	Qiqihar	1,435	San José	961	Meerut	1,143
Campinas	1,434	Suining, Sichuan	1,428	**Croatia**		Nashik	1,117
Santos	1,270	Ürümqi	1,415	Zagreb	1,067	Jabalpur	1,100
Goiânia	1,117	Fushun	1,413	**Cuba**		Jamshedpur	1,081
São José dos Campos	972	Fuzhou	1,397	Havana	2,256	Asansol	1,065
São Luís	968	Neijiang	1,393	**Czech Republic**		Bhilainagar-Durg	1,049
Maceió	886	Changde	1,374	Prague	1,203	Dhanbad	1,046
Teresina	848	Zhanjiang	1,368	**Denmark**		Allahabad	1,035
Campo Grande	821	Huaian	1,354	Copenhagen	1,332	Faridabad	1,018
Natal	806	Yiyang	1,343	**Dominican Republic**		Vijayawada	999
Bulgaria		Xintai	1,325	Santo Domingo	2,563	Rajkot	974
Sofia	1,187	Baotou	1,319	Santiago de los		Amritsar	955
Burkina Faso		Dongguan	1,319	Caballeros	804	Srinagar	954
Ouagadougou	831	Nanning	1,311	**Ecuador**		Ghaziabad	928
Burma (= Myanmar)		Weifang	1,287	Guayaquil	2,118	Trivandrum	885
Rangoon	4,393	Wenzhou	1,269	Quito	1,616	Calicut	875
Cambodia		Hefei	1,242	**Egypt**		Aurangabad	868
Phnom Penh	1,070	Huaian	1,232	Cairo	9,462	Gwalior	855
Cameroon		Yueyang	1,213	Alexandria	3,506	Solapur	853
Douala	1,642	Suqian	1,189	Shubrâ el Kheima	937	Ranchi	844
Yaoundé	1,420	Tianshui	1,187	**El Salvador**		Tiruchirapalli	837
Canada		Suzhou	1,183	San Salvador	1,341	Jodhpur	833
Toronto	4,881	Shantou	1,176	**Ethiopia**		**Indonesia**	
Montréal	3,511	Ningbo	1,173	Addis Ababa	2,645	Jakarta	11,018
Vancouver	2,079	Yuzhou	1,173	**Finland**		Bandung	3,409
Ottawa	1,107	Datong	1,165	Helsinki	937	Surabaya	2,461
Calgary	972	Jingmen	1,153	**France**		Medan	1,879
Edmonton	957	Leshan	1,137	Paris	9,630	Palembang	1,422
Chile		Shenzhen	1,131	Lyons	1,353	Ujung Pandang	1,051
Santiago	5,467	Wuxi	1,127	Marseilles	1,290	Bandar Lampung	915
China		Xiaoshan	1,124	Lille	991	**Iran**	
Shanghai	12,887	Zaoyang	1,121	Nice	889	Tehran	6,979

	Population (1,000s)		Population (1,000s)		Population (1,000s)		Population (1,000s)
Mashhad	1,990	**Mexico**		Voronezh	918	Los Angeles	11,789
Esfahan	1,381	Mexico City	18,066	Saratov	881	Chicago	8,308
Tabriz	1,274	Guadalajara	3,697	Simbirsk	864	Philadelphia	5,149
Karaj	1,200	Monterrey	3,267	Krasnoyarsk	840	Miami	4,919
Shiraz	1,124	Puebla	1,888	**Saudi Arabia**		Dallas–Fort Worth	4,146
Qom	888	Toluca	1,455	Riyadh	3,180	Boston	4,032
Ahvaz	871	Tijuana	1,297	Jedda	1,490	Washington	3,934
Iraq		León	1,293	**Senegal**		Detroit	3,903
Baghdad	4,865	Ciudad Juárez	1,239	Dakar	2,078	Houston	3,823
Basra	1,338	Torreón	1,012	**Serbia & Montenegro**		Atlanta	3,500
Mosul	1,131	San Luis Potosí	857	Belgrade	1,673	San Francisco	3,229
Irbil	840	Mérida	849	**Sierra Leone**		Phoenix	2,907
Ireland		**Morocco**		Freetown	822	Seattle	2,712
Dublin	985	Casablanca	3,357	**Singapore**		San Diego	2,674
Israel		Rabat	1,616	Singapore City	4,131	Minneapolis–St Paul	2,389
Tel Aviv-Yafo	2,001	Fès	907	**Somalia**		St Louis	2,078
Italy		Marrakesh	822	Mogadishu	1,162	Baltimore	2,076
Rome	2,649	**Mozambique**		**South Africa**		Tampa–St Petersburg	2,062
Milan	1,183	Maputo	1,094	Johannesburg	2,950	Denver	1,985
Naples	993	**Nepal**		Cape Town	2,930	Cleveland	1,787
Turin	857	Katmandu	1,176	Durban / eThekwini	2,391	Pittsburgh	1,753
Ivory Coast		**Netherlands**		Pretoria / Tshwane	1,590	Portland	1,583
(= Côte d'Ivoire)		Amsterdam	1,105	Port Elizabeth	1,006	San Jose	1,538
Abidjan	3,790	Rotterdam	1,078	**Spain**		San Bernardino	1,507
Japan		**New Zealand**		Madrid	3,017	Cincinnati	1,503
Tokyo	12,064	Auckland	1,102	Barcelona	1,527	Norfolk–Virginia Beach	1,394
Yokohama	6,427	**Nicaragua**		**Sudan**		Sacramento	1,393
Osaka	2,599	Managua	1,009	Khartoum	2,742	Kansas City	1,362
Nagoya	2,172	**Nigeria**		**Sweden**		San Antonio	1,328
Sapporo	1,922	Lagos	8,665	Stockholm	1,612	Las Vegas	1,314
Kobe	1,493	Ibadan	1,549	**Switzerland**		Milwaukee	1,309
Kyoto	1,468	Ogbomosho	809	Zürich	939	Indianapolis	1,219
Fukuoka	1,341	**Pakistan**		**Syria**		Providence	1,175
Kawasaki	1,250	Karachi	10,032	Aleppo	2,229	Orlando	1,157
Hiroshima	1,126	Lahore	5,452	Damascus	2,144	Columbus	1,133
Kitakyushu	1,011	Faisalabad	2,142	Homs	811	New Orleans	1,009
Sendai	1,008	Rawalpindi	1,521	**Taiwan**		Buffalo	977
Chiba	887	Gujranwala	1,325	Taipei	2,550	Memphis	972
Jordan		Multan	1,263	Kaohsiung	1,463	Austin	902
Amman	1,148	Hyderabad	1,221	T'aichung	950	Stamford	889
Kazakhstan		Peshawar	1,066	**Tanzania**		Salt Lake City	888
Almaty	1,130	**Panama**		Dar es Salaam	2,115	Jacksonville	882
Kenya		Panamá	1,173	**Thailand**		Louisville	864
Nairobi	2,233	**Paraguay**		Bangkok	7,372	Hartford	852
Korea, North		Asunción	1,262	**Tunisia**		Richmond	819
Pyŏngyang	3,124	**Peru**		Tunis	1,892	**Uruguay**	
Hamhung	821	Lima	7,443	**Turkey**		Montevideo	1,324
Korea, South		**Philippines**		Istanbul	8,953	**Uzbekistan**	
Seoul	9,888	Manila	9,950	Ankara	3,203	Tashkent	2,148
Pusan	3,830	Davao	1,146	Izmir	2,250	**Venezuela**	
Inch'on	2,884	**Poland**		Bursa	1,184	Caracas	3,153
Taegu	2,675	Warsaw	1,626	Adana	1,133	Maracaibo	1,901
Taejŏn	1,522	Lódz	815	Gaziantep	862	Valencia	1,893
Kwangju	1,379	**Portugal**		**Uganda**		Maracay	1,100
Sŏngnam	1,353	Lisbon	3,861	Kampala	1,213	Ciudad Guayana	966
Ulsan	1,340	Porto	1,940	**Ukraine**		Barquisimeto	923
Ansan	984	**Puerto Rico**		Kiev	2,621	**Vietnam**	
Puch'on	900	San Juan	2,217	Kharkov	1,521	Ho Chi Minh City	4,619
Suwŏn	876	**Romania**		Dnepropetrovsk	1,122	Hanoi	3,751
Kuwait		Bucharest	2,001	Donetsk	1,065	Haiphong	1,676
Kuwait City	879	**Russia**		Odessa	1,027	**Yemen**	
Latvia		Moscow	8,367	Zaporozhye	863	Sana'	1,327
Riga	811	Saint Petersburg	4,635	**United Arab Emirates**		**Zambia**	
Lebanon		Nizhni Novgorod	1,332	Abu Dhabi	928	Lusaka	1,653
Beirut	2,070	Novosibirsk	1,321	Dubai	886	**Zimbabwe**	
Libya		Yekaterinburg	1,218	**United Kingdom**		Harare	1,791
Tripoli	1,733	Omsk	1,174	London	8,089	Bulawayo	824
Benghazi	829	Samara	1,132	Birmingham	2,373		
Madagascar		Ufa	1,102	Manchester	2,353		
Antananarivo	1,603	Kazan	1,063	Liverpool	852		
Malaysia		Chelyabinsk	1,045	Glasgow	832		
Kuala Lumpur	1,379	Perm	1,014	**United States of**			
Mali		Rostov	1,012	**America**			
Bamako	1,114	Volgograd	1,000	New York	17,800		

Listed above are the principal cities with more than 800,000 inhabitants. The figures are taken from the most recent census or estimate available (usually 2000), and as far as possible are for the metropolitan area or urban agglomeration.

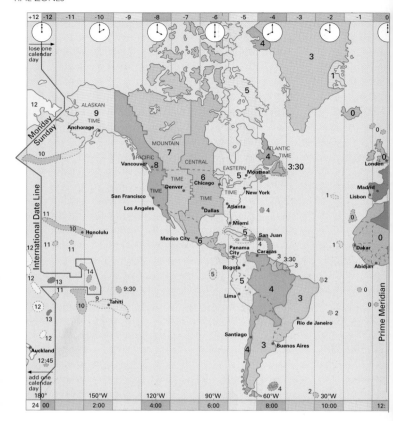

The world is divided into 24 time zones, each centred on meridians at 15° intervals, which is the longitudinal distance the Sun travels every hour. The Prime Meridian running through Greenwich in London, England, passes through the middle of the first time zone. Zones to the east of Greenwich are ahead of Greenwich Mean Time (GMT) by one hour for every 15° of longitude, while zones to the west are behind GMT by one hour.

When it is 12 noon at the Greenwich meridian, 180° east it is midnight of the same day, while at 180° west the day is only just beginning. To overcome this, the International Date Line was established in 1883 – an imaginary line which approximately follows the 180th meridian. Therefore, if one travelled eastwards from Japan (140° East) towards Samoa (170° West), one would pass from Sunday night straight into Sunday morning.

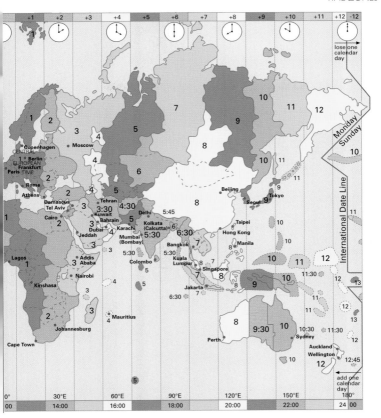

TIME DIFFERENCES FROM GMT (LONDON)

BEIJING	+8	BANGKOK	+7
CHICAGO	−6	DELHI	+5.30
JO'BURG	+2	LAGOS	+1
LOS ANGELES	−8	MEXICO CITY	−6
MOSCOW	+3	NEW YORK	−5
PARIS	+1	ROME	+1
SYDNEY	+10	TEHRAN	+3.30
TOKYO	+9	TORONTO	−5

KEY TO TIME ZONES MAP

10	Hours slow or fast of UT or Co-ordinated Universal Time		Zones ahead of UT (GMT)
	Zones using UT (GMT)		Half-hour zones
	Zones behind UT (GMT)	—	Time zone boundaries
- - -	International boundaries	—	International Date Line

Actual solar time, when time at Greenwich is 12:00 (noon)

Note: Certain time zones are affected by the incidence of daylight saving time in countries where it is adopted.

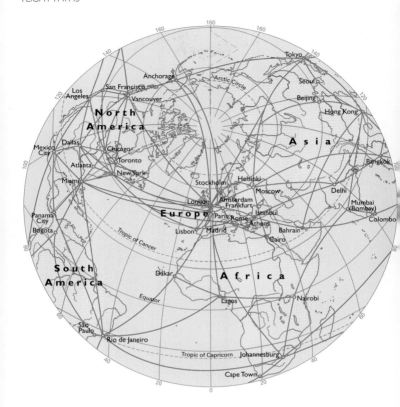

WORLD'S BUSIEST AIRPORTS

TOTAL NUMBER OF PASSENGERS IN MILLIONS (2004)

ATLANTA HARTSFIELD INTL. (ATL)	**83.6**
CHICAGO O'HARE INTL. (ORD)	**75.4**
LONDON HEATHROW (LHR)	**67.3**
TOKYO HANEDA (HND)	**62.3**
LOS ANGELES INTL. (LAX)	**60.7**
DALLAS/FORT WORTH INTL. (DFW)	**59.4**
FRANKFURT INTL. (FRA)	**51.1**
PARIS CHARLES DE GAULLE (CDG)	**50.9**
AMSTERDAM SCHIPHOL (AMS)	**42.5**

The flight paths shown on the maps above usually follow the shortest, most direct route from A to B, known as the *great-circle route*. A great circle is any circle that divides the globe into equal halves. Aircraft do not always fly along great-circle routes, however. Lack of search and rescue and emergency landing provisions, together with limits on fuel consumption and minimum flying altitudes, mean that commercial aircraft do not usually fly across Antarctica.

FLIGHT TIMES FROM LONDON

ATHENS	4hrs 05mins
AUCKLAND	24hrs 20mins
BANGKOK	14hrs 30mins
BUENOS AIRES	14hrs 20mins
HONG KONG	14hrs 10mins
LOS ANGELES	12hrs 00mins
MOSCOW	3hrs 50mins
MUMBAI (BOMBAY)	11hrs 15mins
NEW YORK	6hrs 50mins

FLIGHT TIMES FROM NEW YORK

FRANKFURT	8hrs 35mins
JOHANNESBURG	17hrs 45mins
MEXICO CITY	5hrs 45mins
PARIS	8hrs 15mins
ROME	9hrs 35mins
SANTIAGO	12hrs 55mins
SINGAPORE	23hrs 10mins
TOKYO	14hrs 35mins
VANCOUVER	7hrs 25mins

Kms

	Beijing	Bombay (Mumbai)	Buenos Aires	Cairo	Calcutta (Kolkata)	Caracas	Chicago	Hong Kong	Honolulu	Johannesburg	Lagos	London
Beijing		2956	11972	4688	2031	8947	6588	1220	5070	7276	7119	5057
Bombay (Mumbai)	4757		9275	2706	1034	9024	8048	2683	8024	4334	4730	4467
Buenos Aires	19268	14925		7341	10268	3167	5599	11481	7558	5025	4919	6917
Cairo	7544	4355	11814		3541	6340	6127	5064	8838	3894	2432	2180
Calcutta (Kolkata)	3269	1664	16524	5699		9609	7978	1653	7048	5256	5727	4946
Caracas	14399	14522	5096	10203	15464		2502	10166	6009	6847	4810	4664
Chicago	10603	12953	9011	3206	12839	4027		7783	4247	8689	5973	3949
Hong Kong	1963	4317	18478	8150	2659	16360	12526		5543	6669	7360	5980
Honolulu	8160	12914	12164	14223	11343	9670	6836	8921		11934	10133	7228
Johannesburg	11710	6974	8088	6267	8459	11019	13984	10732	19206		2799	5637
Lagos	11457	7612	7916	3915	9216	7741	9612	11845	16308	4505		3118
London	8138	7190	11131	3508	7961	7507	6356	9623	11632	9071	5017	
Los Angeles	10060	14000	9852	12200	13120	5812	2804	11639	4117	16676	12414	8758
Mexico City	12460	15656	7389	12372	15280	3586	2726	14122	6085	14585	11071	8936
Moscow	5794	5031	13477	2902	5534	9938	8000	7144	11323	9161	6254	2498
Nairobi	9216	4532	10402	3536	6179	11544	12883	8776	17282	2927	3807	6819
New York	10988	12541	8526	9020	12747	3430	1145	12950	7980	12841	8477	5572
Paris	8217	7010	11051	3210	7858	7625	6650	9630	11968	8732	4714	342
Rio de Janeiro	17338	13409	1953	9896	15073	4546	8547	17704	13342	7113	6035	9299
Rome	8126	6175	11151	2133	7219	8363	7739	9284	12916	7743	4039	1431
Singapore	4478	3914	15879	8267	2897	18359	15078	2599	10816	8660	11145	10852
Sydney	8949	10160	11800	14418	9138	15343	14875	7374	8168	11040	15519	16992
Tokyo	2099	6742	18362	9571	5141	14164	10137	2874	6202	13547	13480	9562
Wellington	10782	12370	9981	16524	11354	13122	13451	9427	7513	11761	16050	18814

The table above shows air distances in miles and kilometres between 30 major cities.

Known as 'great-circle' distances, these measure the shortest routes between the cities.

The table below gives great-circle distances. The upper-right half (above the diagonal of city names) is in **Miles**; the lower-left half (below the diagonal) is in kilometres.

Los Angeles	Mexico City	Moscow	Nairobi	New York	Paris	Rio de Janeiro	Rome	Singapore	Sydney	Tokyo	Wellington	
6251	7742	3600	5727	6828	5106	10773	5049	2783	5561	1304	6700	**Beijing**
8700	9728	3126	2816	7793	4356	8332	3837	2432	6313	4189	7686	**Bombay (Mumbai)**
6122	4591	8374	6463	5298	6867	1214	6929	9867	7332	11410	6202	**Buenos Aires**
7580	7687	1803	2197	5605	1994	6149	1325	5137	8959	5947	10268	**Cairo**
8152	9494	3438	3839	7921	4883	9366	4486	1800	5678	3195	7055	**Calcutta (Kolkata)**
3612	2228	6175	7173	2131	4738	2825	5196	11407	9534	8801	8154	**Caracas**
1742	1694	4971	8005	711	4132	5311	4809	9369	9243	6299	8358	**Chicago**
7232	8775	4439	5453	8047	5984	11001	5769	1615	4582	1786	5857	**Hong Kong**
2558	3781	7036	10739	4958	7437	8290	8026	6721	5075	3854	4669	**Honolulu**
10362	9063	5692	1818	7979	5426	4420	4811	5381	6860	8418	7308	**Johannesburg**
7713	6879	3886	2366	5268	2929	3750	2510	6925	9643	8376	9973	**Lagos**
5442	5552	1552	4237	3463	212	5778	889	6743	10558	5942	11691	**London**
Los Angeles	1549	6070	9659	2446	5645	6310	6331	8776	7502	5475	6719	**Los Angeles**
2493	*Mexico City*	6664	9207	2090	5717	4780	6365	10321	8058	7024	6897	**Mexico City**
9769	10724	*Moscow*	3942	4666	1545	7184	1477	5237	9008	4651	10283	**Moscow**
15544	14818	6344	*Nairobi*	7358	4029	5548	3350	4635	7552	6996	8490	**Nairobi**
3936	3264	7510	11842	*New York*	3626	4832	4280	9531	9935	6741	8951	**New York**
9085	9200	2486	6485	5836	*Paris*	5708	687	6671	10539	6038	11798	**Paris**
10155	7693	11562	8928	7777	9187	*Rio de Janeiro*	5725	9763	8389	11551	7367	**Rio de Janeiro**
10188	10243	2376	5391	6888	1105	9214	*Rome*	6229	10143	6127	11523	**Rome**
14123	16610	8428	7460	15339	10737	15712	10025	*Singapore*	3915	3306	5298	**Singapore**
12073	12969	14497	12153	15989	16962	13501	16324	6300	*Sydney*	4861	1383	**Sydney**
8811	11304	7485	11260	10849	9718	18589	9861	5321	7823	*Tokyo*	5762	**Tokyo**
10814	11100	16549	13664	14405	18987	11855	18545	8526	2226	9273	*Wellington*	**Wellington**

Miles

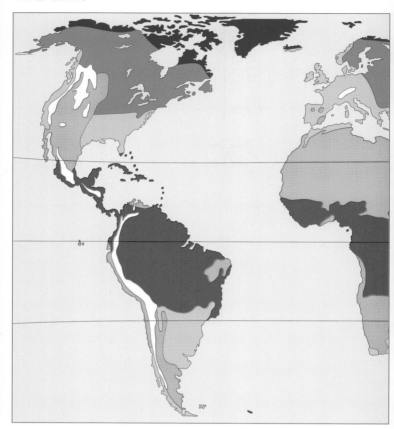

Climate is weather in the long term: the seasonal pattern of temperature and precipitation averaged over a period of time. Temperature roughly follows latitude, and is warmest near the equator and coldest near the poles. The interplay of various factors, however, namely the differential heating of land and sea, the influence of landmasses and mountain ranges on winds and ocean currents, and the effect of vegetation, all combine to add complexity. Thus New York and Naples share almost the same latitude, but their resulting climates are quite different. Most scientists are now in agreement that the world's climate is changing, due partly to atmospheric pollution. By the year 2050, average world temperatures are predicted to rise by between 1.5°C and 2.8°C to make the climate hotter than it has been at any time during the last 120,000 years. Climate statistics for 18 cities are given on pages 18 and 19.

16

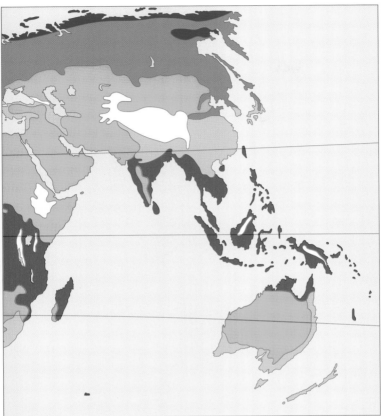

SEASONAL WEATHER EXTREMES

- **Caribbean**
  Hurricanes – August to October
- **Northern Latitudes**
  Blizzards – November to March
- **Southern Asia**
  Cyclones and typhoons – June to November
- **Southern Asia**
  Monsoon rains – July to October

CLIMATIC REGIONS

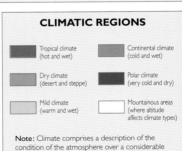

Tropical climate (hot and wet)

Dry climate (desert and steppe)

Mild climate (warm and wet)

Continental climate (cold and wet)

Polar climate (very cold and dry)

Mountainous areas (where altitude affects climate types)

Note: Climate comprises a description of the condition of the atmosphere over a considerable area for a long time (at least 30 years).

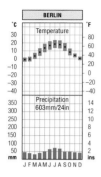

BERLIN — Temperature — Precipitation 603mm/24in

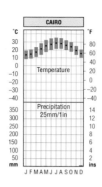

CAIRO — Temperature — Precipitation 25mm/1in

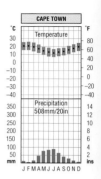

CAPE TOWN — Temperature — Precipitation 508mm/20in

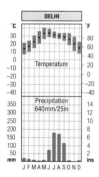

DELHI — Temperature — Precipitation 640mm/25in

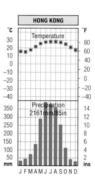

HONG KONG — Temperature — Precipitation 2161mm/85in

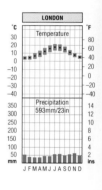

LONDON — Temperature — Precipitation 593mm/23in

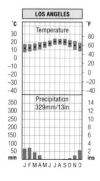

LOS ANGELES — Temperature — Precipitation 329mm/13in

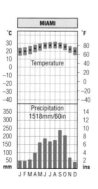

MIAMI — Temperature — Precipitation 1518mm/60in

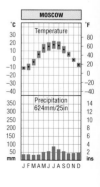

MOSCOW — Temperature — Precipitation 624mm/25in

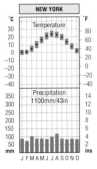

NEW YORK
Temperature
Precipitation
1100mm/43in
J F M A M J J A S O N D

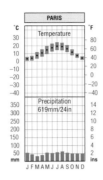

PARIS
Temperature
Precipitation
619mm/24in
J F M A M J J A S O N D

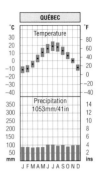

QUÉBEC
Temperature
Precipitation
1053mm/41in
J F M A M J J A S O N D

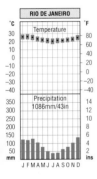

RIO DE JANEIRO
Temperature
Precipitation
1086mm/43in
J F M A M J J A S O N D

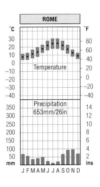

ROME
Temperature
Precipitation
653mm/26in
J F M A M J J A S O N D

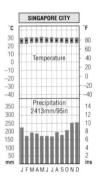

SINGAPORE CITY
Temperature
Precipitation
2413mm/95in
J F M A M J J A S O N D

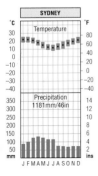

SYDNEY
Temperature
Precipitation
1181mm/46in
J F M A M J J A S O N D

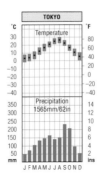

TOKYO
Temperature
Precipitation
1565mm/62in
J F M A M J J A S O N D

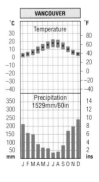

VANCOUVER
Temperature
Precipitation
1529mm/60in
J F M A M J J A S O N D

TO CONVERT	INTO	MULTIPLY BY
Length		
Centimetres	Inches	0.394
Feet	Metres	0.305
Inches	Centimetres	2.540
Inches	Millimetres	25.400
Kilometres	Miles	0.621
Metres	Feet	3.281
Metres	Yards	1.094
Miles	Kilometres	1.609
Millimetres	Inches	0.039
Yards	Metres	0.914
Area		
Acres	Hectares	0.405
Hectares	Acres	2.471
Square centimetres	Square inches	0.155
Square feet	Square metres	0.093
Square inches	Square centimetres	6.452
Square kilometres	Square miles	0.388
Square metres	Square feet	10.764
Square miles	Square yards	1.195
Square yards	Square metres	0.836
Volume		
Cubic centimetres	Cubic inches	0.61
Cubic feet	Cubic metres	0.028
Cubic metres	Cubic feet	35.315
Cubic inches	Cubic centimetres	16.387
Cubic metres	Cubic yards	1.308
Cubic yards	Cubic metres	0.785
Gallons (Imperial)	Litres	4.506
Gallons (US)	Litres	3.785
Litres	Gallons (Imperial)	0.220
Litres	Gallons (US)	0.264
Litres	Ounces (fluid)	33.814
Litres	Pints	2.113
Litres	Quarts	1.057
Millilitres (cc)	Ounces (fluid)	0.034
Ounces (fluid)	Millilitres (cc)	29.573
Pints	Litres	0.473
Quarts	Litres	0.946
Weight		
Grams	Ounces	0.35
Kilograms	Pounds	2.205
Ounces	Grams	28.350
Pounds	Kilograms	0.454
Tons (2,000 lbs)	Tons metric	0.907
Tons metric	Tons (2,000 lbs)	1.102

CITY PLANS

22 Amsterdam   **34** Moscow

23 Athens   **35** New York

24 Bangkok   **36** Paris

25 Berlin   **37** Prague

26 Brussels   **38** Rio de Janeiro

27 Cape Town   **39** Rome

28 Chicago   **40** San Francisco

29 Dublin   **41** Singapore

30 Hong Kong   **42** Sydney

31 London   **43** Tokyo

32 Madrid   **44** Toronto

33 Mexico City   **45** Vienna

LEGEND TO CITY PLANS

Motorway	Abbey/cathedral
Through route	Church of interest
Secondary road	Hospital
Other road	Mosque
Limited access / pedestrian road	Shrine
Railway	Synagogue
Tramway/monorail	Temple
Rail/bus station	Tourist information centre
Underground/Metro station	Public building
Ferry route/destination	Place of interest

0   km   2

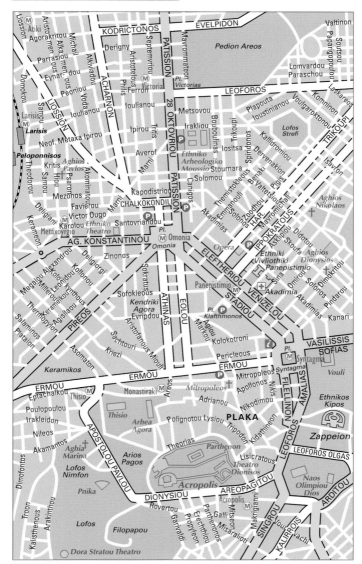

0   km   1

COPYRIGHT PHILIP'S

0   km   2

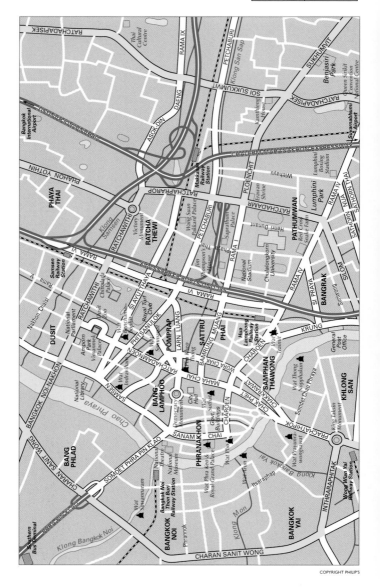

COPYRIGHT PHILIP'S

0 km 1

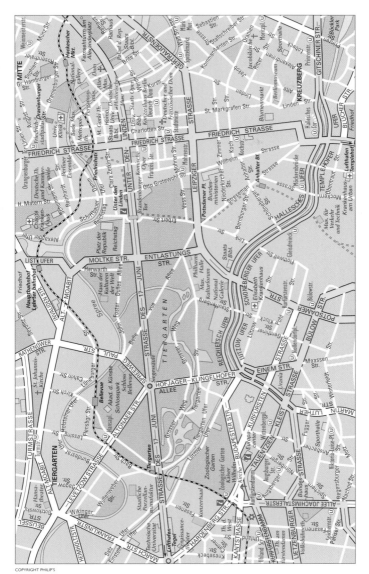

COPYRIGHT PHILIP'S

0   km   1

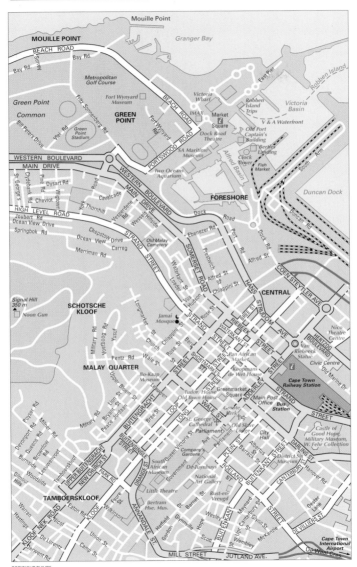

Mouille Point

MOUILLE POINT

Granger Bay

BEACH ROAD

Bay Rd.

Bay Rd.

Surrey

Green Point Common

Metropolitan Golf Course

Fort Wynyard Museum

GREEN POINT

Fritz Sonnenberg Rd.

BEACH ROAD

Fort Wynyard Rd.

PORTSWOOD ROAD

Bill Peters Drive

Vlei Rd.

Green Point Stadium

Victoria Wharf

IMAX

Market Square

Robben Island Trips

East Pier

Robben Island

Victoria Basin

V & A Waterfront

Dock Road Theatre

Old Port Captain's Building

Berth of Landing

WESTERN BOULEVARD

MAIN DRIVE

SA Maritime Museum

Alfred Basin

Clock Tower

Fish Market

South Arm

Duncan Arm

St. George's

Clydebank Rd.

Pine Rd.

Dysart Rd.

Cheviot Rd.

Wigtown

York

Cavalcade

Thornhill

WESTERN BOULEVARD

MAIN DRIVE

Vesperdene

Wessel Hill Ave.

Vos

Two Oceans Aquarium

FORESHORE

Duncan Dock

HIGH LEVEL ROAD

Joubert Rd.

Ocean View Drive

Springbok Rd.

Chepstow Drive

Ocean View

Carreg

Merriman Rd.

STRAND STREET

Old Malay Cemetery

Ebenezer Rd.

Prestwich St.

Dock

Road

Port Rd.

Dock Rd.

Duncan Rd.

Alfred St.

Somerset Rd.

Waterkant St.

Loader St.

Alfred St.

Chiappini St.

CENTRAL

COEN STEYTLER AVE.

Signal Hill 350 m

Noon Gun

SCHOTSCHE KLOOF

Longmarket St.

Jamai Mosque

STRAND

Hudson

Rose St.

BREE STREET

BREE STREET

LOOP

STRAND

HERTZOG BOULEVARD

Nico Theatre Centre

Van Riebeeck Statue

Civic Centre

Old Marine Dr.

Military Rd.

Voetboog

Yusuf

Pentz Rd.

MALAY QUARTER

Bo-Kaap Museum

Church St.

Wale St.

Chiappini St.

Rose St.

Bend

SHORTMARKET

WATERKANT

Pan African Market

Koopmans de Wet House

Main Post Office

Bus Station

ADDERLEY STREET

STRAND

Cape Town Railway Station

Upper Bloem St.

Lion St.

Bryant St.

Pearce Jordaan

BUITENGRACHT

LOOP

Bree St.

LONG

WALE

St. George's Cathedral

Tudor Hse.

Old Town House

Greenmarket Square

Groote Kerk

Old Slave Lodge

City Hall

Castle of Good Hope, Military Museum, W. Fehr Collection

Devonport Rd.

Poyer Rd.

Queens Rd.

Milner Rd.

Brownlow Rd.

Burnside

Woodside

Leeuwenvoet

Tamboerskloof

UPPER BUITENGRACHT

NEW CHURCH RD

PARK RD

ORANGE ST.

Parliament

Queen Victoria

Company's Gardens

Government Ave.

De Tuynhuys

Parliament St.

PLEIN

Barrack St.

BUITENKANT

Albertus

District Six Museum

DARLING ST.

Hanover Rd.

Canterbury Rd.

Gilmour Hills

Warren

Hastings

TAMBOERSKLOOF

KLOOF NEK ROAD

ANNANDALE ST.

Frere Rd.

Wilkinson

South African Museum

Little Theatre

Bertram Hse. Mus.

National Art Gallery

Rust-en-Vreugd

Barnet

Hope

Wesley

ROELAND

BUITENKANT

STRAND

Canterbury

Chni St.

McKenzie

DE VILLIERS ST.

Oester Laan

Nicol

Da Lorentz

Eaton Rd.

Union St.

Camp St.

Watfield

Glynnville

Scott

Maynard

Wembley

Gilmour

Derwent Rd.

MILL STREET

JUTLAND AVE.

Cape Town International Airport

Du Wind Dam

COPYRIGHT PHILIP'S

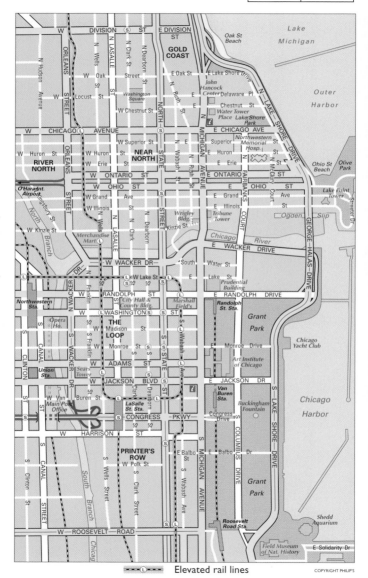

0   km   0.5

Elevated rail lines

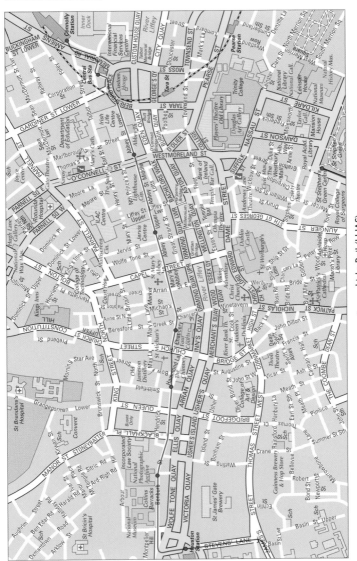

0   km   0.5

Light Rail (LUAS)

COPYRIGHT PHILIP'S

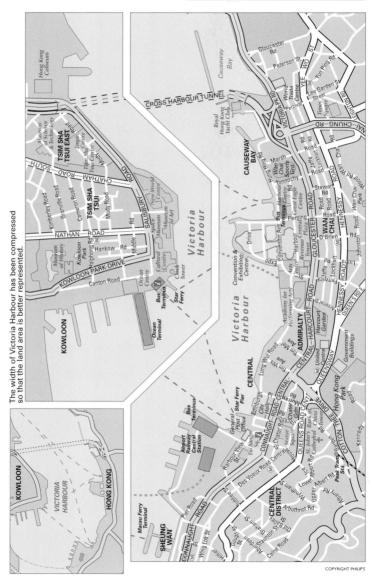

The width of Victoria Harbour has been compressed so that the land area is better represented.

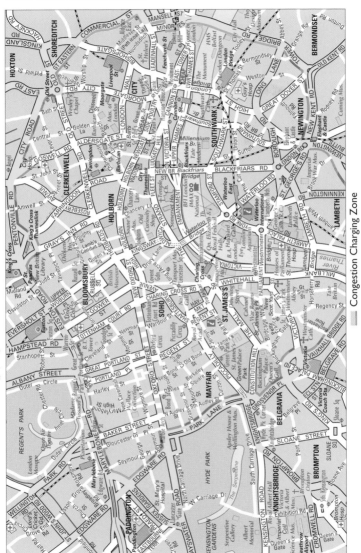

0   km   2

Congestion Charging Zone

COPYRIGHT PHILIP'S

31

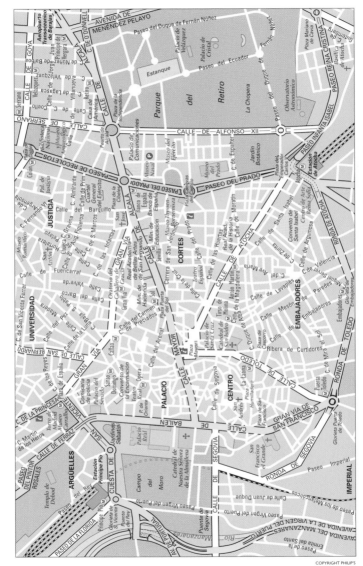

0   km   1

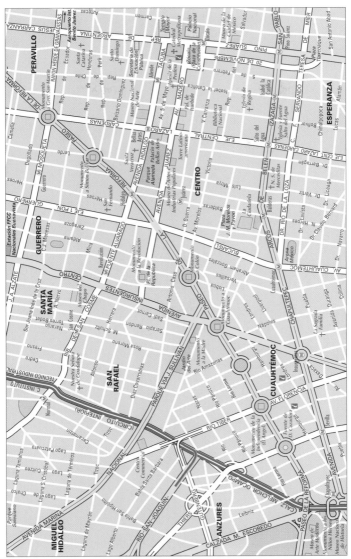

PERAVILLO

JESÚS CARRANZA

Aztecas

Aeropuerto Int.
Benito Juárez

RAYÓN HÉROE DE GRANADITAS

ARGENTINA

Carmen

DE LA REFORMA

Monumento
a San Martín

Ecuador

Santa
Catarina

Santo
Domingo

Perú

REP.

Rep.

Chile

DE

TACUBA

Templo
Mayor

Palacio
Nacional

Catedral

Moneda

Museo de la
Ciudad de
México

SAN PABLO

MIER

Secretaría de
Educación
Pública

Honduras

Rep.

Palacio
de la
Provincia

Zócalo
(Plaza de la
Constitución)

Allende

Febrero

SAN SUÁREZ

PINO SUÁREZ

Plaza
Tlaxcoaque

San Antonio Abad

Bolívar

Rep.

Museo Nacional
de Arte

AV. MADERO

Bessarión Domínguez

Pal. de
Iturbide

Av. 5 de Mayo

V. Carranza

Isabel la
Católica

Iglesia de
la Profesa

ESPERANZA

20 DE NOVIEMBRE

Rep.

CÁRDENAS

LÁZARO

Biblioteca
Nacional

Iglesia de
Regina

ZARAGOZA

Altamir

PASEO

Monumento a
Simón Bolívar

AVENIDA HIDALGO

JUÁREZ

Palacio de
Bellas Artes

Museo de Artes
e Industrias
Populares

Torre Latino-
americana

AV.

Iglesia y Fuente
Salto del Agua

EJE CENT. LÁZARO CÁRDENAS

Chimalpopoca

Lucas

Museo
Veracruz

REFORMA

San
Fernando

Parque
Alameda

CENTRO

Balderas

D. Guerra

Av. Morelos

Salto del
Agua

N.S. de
Mercedes

SERVANDO

TERESA

Monumento
Gral. San Martín

GUERRERO

EJE 1 PON

Camelia

Héroes

Degollado

Zaragoza

C.J. Menезas

Aldama

Mina

Luis Moya

Victoria

Plaza
J.M. Morelos
y Pavón

La Ciudadela

Balderas

Barragán

DR. RÍO DE LA LOZA

DE

Dr. Vértiz

Dr. Lavista

N. Barreda

Dr. Lucio

Dr. Liceaga

ARCOS

Dr. Claudio Bernard

Dr. Navarro

AV. CUAUHTÉMOC

Arena
México

SANTA
MARÍA

CENTRO

J.A. ALZATE

Sor Juana Inés de la Cruz

A Nervo

Museo del
Chopo

Naranjo

San Cosme

Serapio Rendón

BUCARELI

Abraham González

Versalles

Lisboa

Cuauhtémoc

Liverpool

Puebla

Durango

Colima

Monumento
a la Revolución

Pl. de la
República

Antonio Caso

Monumento
Colón

La Sagrada
Familia

SAN RAFAEL

Nuestra Señora
de Guadalupe

Fresno

Pedro

Alfonso

Sadi Carnot

M Schultz

Rosa Moreno

Herrera

DE

AVENIDA

INSURGENTES

Monumento a
Cuauhtémoc

PASEO

Monumento a
la Mujer

Nápoles

CHAPULTEPEC

La Sagrada
Familia

Oaxaca

CUAUHTÉMOC

TÉCNICO INDUSTRIAL

MIGUEL
HIDALGO

C INSTITUTO

Normal A.

Paramatía

Laguna Tamiahua

Laguna S. Cristóbal

Lago Cuitzeo

Lago de
Chalco

Parque
Salesiano

AVENIDA MARINA

Laguna de Mayrán

Laguna de Términos

Lago Pátzcuaro

Lago Alberto

RÍO SAN-JOAQUÍN

RÍO TIBER

Bahía Santa Bárbara

Bahía San Juan

Central
Commercial

Diaz Covarrubias

PARQUE VÍA J. SULLIVAN

Jardín
del Arte

Monumento
del Arte

Río Amazonas

Río Nazas

Río Pánuco

Río Rhin

Río Lerma

Monumento de la
Independencia
(El Ángel)

Fuente de
D. Cazadores

AV. FLORENCIA

Londres

Hamburgo

Liverpool

Génova

Reforma

Sevilla

AVENIDA

Puebla

MELCHOR OCAMPO

ANZURES

M. ESCOBEDO

CALZADA M. ESCOBEDO

THIERS

GUTENBERG

Leibniz

Kant

PASEO DE LA REFORMA

Chapultepec

Museo de
Arte Moderno

Monumento a los
Niños Héroes

Museo Nacional
de Historia

CALZ. MELCHOR OCAMPO

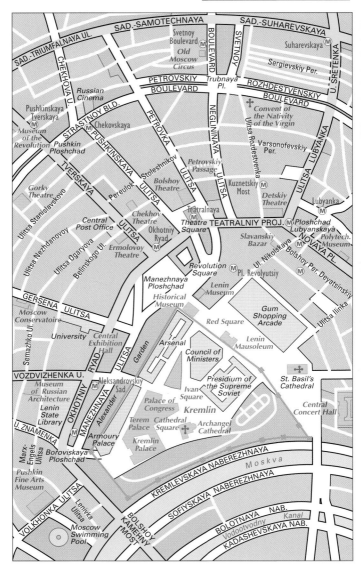

0   km   1

34

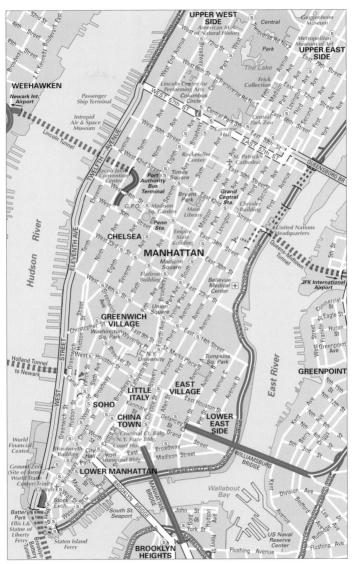

0   km   2

UPPER WEST SIDE

Central

Guggenheim Museum

52nd St

46th Street

45th Street

American Mus of Natural History

West 79th Street

Metropolitan Museum of Art

UPPER EAST SIDE

West 66th Street

Park

East 79th Street

J.F. Kennedy Boulevard East

West End Avenue

Broadway

Lincoln Center for Performing Arts

Central Transverse Rd No 2

The Lake

East 72nd Street

Frick Collection

WEEHAWKEN

Passenger Ship Terminal

Columbus Circle

Central Transverse Rd No 1

Amsterdam Ave

East 66th Street

Madison Ave

Park Ave

Lexington Ave

Second Ave

First Ave

Newark Int. Airport

WEST 57TH ST

Central Park South

EAST 57TH ST

Intrepid Air & Space Museum

West 50th Street

Broadway

Carnegie Hall

Central Park Zoo

Lincoln Tunnel

Ninth Ave

Rockefeller Center

St. Patrick's Cathedral

East 50th Streets

Fifth

Third

QUEENSBORO BR

TWELFTH AVENUE

West 42nd Street

Times Square

East 42nd Street

Chrysler Building

Eleventh Ave

Port Authority Bus Terminal

Bryant Park

Grand Central Sta.

Tenth Ave

Jacob Javits Convention Center

West 30th

G.P.O.

Madison Sq. Garden

Main Library

Madison Ave

Park Ave

United Nations Headquarters

Penn Sta.

Empire State Building

East 34th Street

Queens-Midtown Tunnel

Hudson River

CHELSEA

West 23rd

Seventh Ave

MANHATTAN

Madison Square

East 30th Street

JFK International Airport

ELEVENTH AVE

Tenth

Flatiron Building

Bellevue Medical Center

West 14th St

Sixth

Broadway

Fifth

Park

East 23rd Street

WEST STREET

Greenwich

Union Square

Irving Place

East 14th Street

Hudson

GREENWICH VILLAGE

East 8th Street

Third

First

Avenue C

Christopher St

Washington Sq. Park

Waverley Pl.

Fourth

St Marks Place

Tompkins Sq. Park

Holland Tunnel to Newark

West

Houston St

Bleecker St

N.Y. University

Second

Avenue D

GREENPOINT

Canal St

Broadway

Lafayette

Bowery

East Houston St

Nth 15th St

Nth 12th St

Kent Ave

Commercial St

Eagle St

Franklin St

Huron St

Greenpoint Ave

Greenwich St

LITTLE ITALY

EAST VILLAGE

Allen St

Berry

5th

4th

3rd

Driggs

East River

SOHO

Kenmare St

Chrystie St

LOWER EAST SIDE

Church St

Worth St

CHINA TOWN

Grand

Delancey St

Hudson St

Woolworth Building

Criminal Ct. Bldg.

N.Y. State Bldg.

Court Ho.

Broadway

Street

WILLIAMSBURG BRIDGE

Kent

5th 2nd St

World Financial Center

City Hall Park

Row

Municipal Bldg.

Madison Street

FRANKLIN D ROOSEVELT

Wallabout Bay

Bedford

Division Ave

Ground Zero (Site of former World Trade Center) Trinity Church

LOWER MANHATTAN

BROOKLYN BRIDGE

MANHATTAN BRIDGE

John St

Gold

Hudson Ave

US Naval Reserve Center

Lee

Rutledge

Flushing Ave

Battery Park Ellis I.& Statue of Liberty Ferry

Stock Exch.

Wall St

Maiden La

Water St

South St Seaport

York St

Front St

QUEENS

Staten Island Ferry

Brooklyn-Battery Tunnel

BROOKLYN HEIGHTS

Flushing

Flushing Avenue

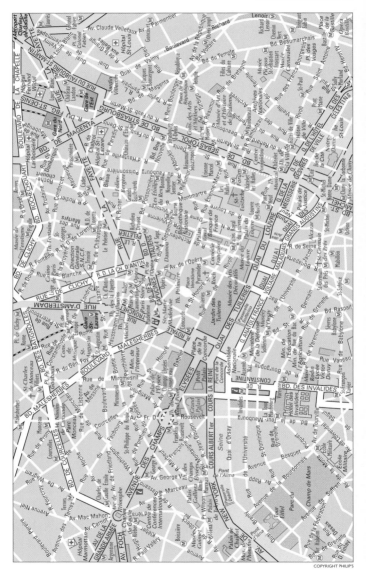

0   km   0.5

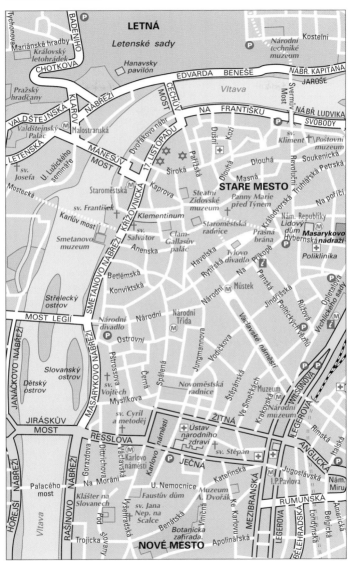

LETNÁ

Letenské sady

Tychonova

Mariánské hradby

Královský
letohrádek

BADENIHO

CHOTKOVA

Hanavsky
pavilón

Pražský
hradčany

EDVARDA BENEŠE

Národní
technické
muzeum

Kostelní

NABŘ. KAPITÁNA
JAROŠE

Vltava

Svermův
Most

NÁBŘ LUDVÍKA
SVOBODY

KLÁROV

NÁBŘEŽÍ

NA FRANTIŠKU

VALDŠTEJNSKÁ

Valdštejnský
Palác

Malostranská

MANESŮV
MOST

Dvořákovo nábř.

17. LISTOPADU

Dušní

Kozí

sv.
Kliment

Poštovní
muzeum

Soukenická

LETENSKÁ

sv.
Josefa

U. Lužického
semináře

Mostecká

sv. František

Karlův most

Smetanovo
muzeum

Staroměstská

KŘIŽOVNICKÁ

Kaprova

Pařížská

Široká

Dlouhá

Dlouhá

Masná

Revoluční

Truhlářská Petrská

Na poříčí

Státní
Zidovské
muzeum

Klementinum

sv.
Salvátor

Clam-
Gallasův
palác

Anenska

SMETANOVO NÁBŘEŽÍ

Betlémská

Konviktská

Střelecký
ostrov

MOST LEGII

Národní
divadlo

JANÁČKOVO NÁBŘEŽÍ

Slovanský
ostrov

Dětský
ostrov

JIRÁSKŮV
MOST

MASARYKOVO NÁBŘEŽÍ

Ostrovní

Petrossova

RESSLOVA

Gorazdova

Dittrichova

Václavská

NÁBŘEŽÍ

RAŠÍNOVO NÁBŘEŽÍ

Palackého
most

Staroměstská
radnice

Havelska

Rytířská

Tylovo
divadlo

STARE MESTO

Panny Marie
před Týnem

Prašná
brána

Na příkopě

Nám. Republiky

Lidový
dům

Hybernská

Masarykovo
nádraží

Poliklinika

Na

Panská

Jindřišská

Politických

Václavské náměstí

Ružova

Opletalova

Vrchlického sady

Müstek

Národní

Národní
Třída

Jungmannova

Národní

Černá

sv.
Vojtěch

Myslíkova

sv. Cyril
a metoděj

Karlovo
náměstí

Karlovo
náměstí

Na Moráni

Klášter na
Slovanech

Vltava

Trojicka

Slovany

Všehradská

sv. Jana
Nep. na
Scalce

Faustův dům

Vyšehradská

Benátská

Vodičkova

Spálená

Novoměstská
radnice

náměstí

Štěpánská

Ve Smečkách

Krakovská

ŽITNÁ

Ústav
národního
zdraví

JEČNÁ

Kateřinská

Viničná

Botanická
zahrada.

Apolinářská

NOVÉ MESTO

sv. Štěpán

U. Nemocnice

Muzeum
A. Dvořák

MEZIBRANSKÁ

Muzeum

Národní
muzeum

WILSONOVA

LEGEROVA

ANGLICKÁ

Jugoslávská

I.P.Pavlova

Ke Karlovu

RUMUNSKÁ

LEGEROVA

BĚLEHRADSKÁ

Rímská

Halská

Náto.
Miru

Jablonského

Americká

Belgická

Londýnská

0   km   0.5

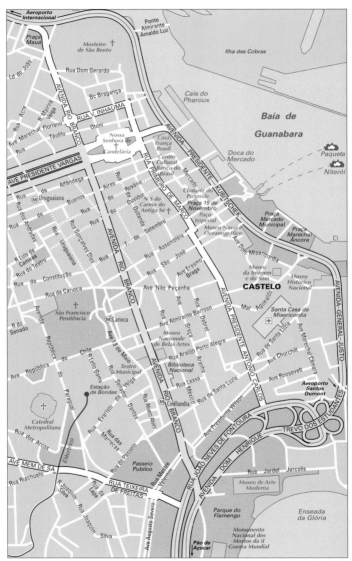

Aeroporto Internacional

Praça Mauá

Mosteiro de São Bento

Ponte Almirante Arnaldo Luz

Ilha das Cobras

Ld do João

Rua Dom Gerardo

Bc Bragança

Cais do Pharoux

Baía de Guanabara

Rua Acre

Rua Mairink Veiga

AVENIDA RIO BRANCO

Otoni

RUA V. INHAUMA

Ave Marechal Floriano

Téofilo

Rua

Nossa Senhora de Candelária

AVENIDA PRESIDENTE KUBITSCHEK

Casa França Brasil

Doca do Mercado

Paquetá

Niterói

AVE PRESIDENTE VARGAS

Centro Cultural Banco do Brasil

Rua da Alfândega

Aires

Rosário

Chafariz da Pirâmide

Praça 15 de Novembro

Praça Mercado Municipal

Rua das Andradas

M Uruguaiana

Buenos

do

Ouvidor

N S do Carmo da Antiga Sé

Praça Marechal Âncora

RUA PRIMEIRO DE MARÇO

AVENIDA MERCADO

Paço Imperial

Rua Uruguaiana

Rua Gonçalves Dias

Rua

Clarinda

7 de Setembro

Museu Naval e Oceanográfico

AVENIDA DOM

Misericórdia

R Luís de Camões

Rua do Teatro

Rua Assembléia

Rua São José

Ave Erasmo Braga

Museu da Imagem e do Som

Museu Histórico Nacional

Rua da Constituição

AVENIDA RIO BRANCO

CASTELO

Rua da Carioca

Ave Nilo Peçanha

Ave

Rua Barroso

Mal Aguinaldo

Santa Casa da Misericórdia

AVENIDA GENERAL JUSTO

São Francisco Penitência

M Carioca

Ave Almirante Barroso

Graça

R do Senado

Avenida

M

Museu Nacionale de Belas Artes

Rua Araújo Porto Alegre

Rua de Santa Lúcia

Ave Marechal Câmara

Ave República

do

Chile

R Leite Gama

Ave 13 de Maio

AVENIDA PRESIDENTE ANTONIO CARLOS

Ave Churchill

Teatro Municipal

Biblioteca Nacional

Aranha

Rua Lessa

Rua México

Ave Roosevelt

Ave

do

Paraguai

República

Rua Senador Dantas

Estação de Bondes

Rua Álvaro Alvim

M Cinelândia

Rua de Santa Luzia

Aeroporto Santos Dumont

Catedral Metropolitana

Eletrônica

Rua Evaristo da Veiga

Rua das Marrecas

Ave Presidente Wilson

TREVO DOS ESTUDANTES

Rua dos Arcos

AVE MEM DE SÁ

Passeio Público

AVENIDA DOM HENRIQUE

AVENIDA JOÃO NEVES DE FONTOURA

Rua Riachuelo

R Joaquim Silva

Rua da Lapa

Rua Joaquim

RUA TEIXEIRA DE FREITAS

Rua Mestre Valentim

Rua Jardel

Jercolis

Museu de Arte Moderna

Silva

Ave Augusto Severo

Pão de Açúcar

Parque do Flamengo

Enseada da Glória

Monumento Nacional dos Mortos da II Guerra Mundial

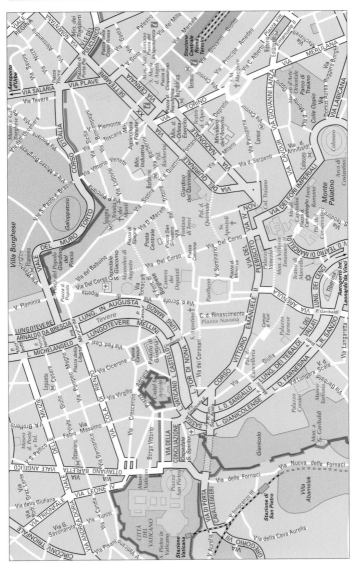

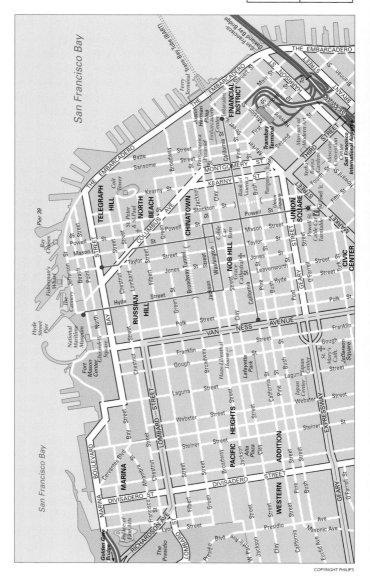

0   km   0.5

San Francisco Bay

San Francisco Bay

THE EMBARCADERO

San Francisco–Oakland Bay Bridge

Ferry Terminal
Ferry Building

FINANCIAL DISTRICT

Justin Herman Plaza

Embarcadero Center

Transbay Terminal

Museum of Modern Art

San Francisco International Airport

Moscone Convention Center

Yerba Buena Gardens

THE EMBARCADERO

Pier 39

Bay Cruises

Fisherman's Wharf

The Cannery

National Maritime Museum

Hyde Street Pier

Fort Mason Center

Palace of Fine Arts

Golden Gate Bridge

The Presidio

TELEGRAPH HILL

Coit Tower

St Peter & St Paul

NORTH BEACH

Transamerica Pyramid

Batte Street

Sansome Street

Broadway

MONTGOMERY ST

KEARNY

Bank of America

Union Square

Cable Car Turntable

Grace Cathedral

CHINATOWN

NOB HILL

RUSSIAN HILL

COLUMBUS AVE

Broadway Tunnel

UNION SQUARE

CIVIC CENTER

VAN NESS AVENUE

Lafayette Park

Haas–Lilienthal House

Japan Center

Japan Center

St Mary's Cath.

Jefferson Square

GEARY

MARINA

MARINA BOULEVARD

LOMBARD STREET

DIVISADERO ST

PACIFIC HEIGHTS

Alta Plaza

WESTERN ADDITION

EXPRESSWAY

DIVISADERO STREET

GEARY

RICHARDSON AVE

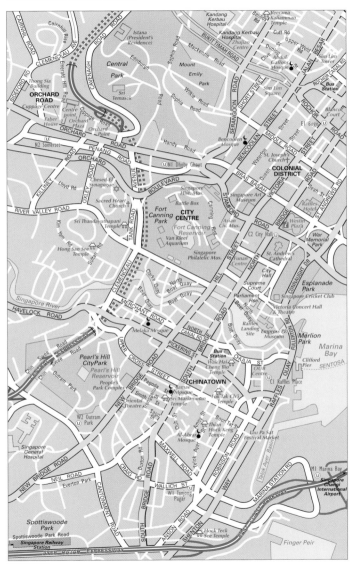

0   km   1

Cairnhill Rise
CAIRNHILL ROAD
Cairnhill Rise
BIDEFORD RD
CLEMENCEAU AVE
Emerald Hill Road
CAVENAGH ROAD
Istana (President's Residence)
Kandang Kerbau Hospital
Kandang Kerbau Hospital
Zhujiao Centre
BUKIT TIMAH ROAD
Mackenzie Road
Sophia Road
Bellit Josi Rd
Veerama Kaliamman Temple
Cuff Rd
Upper Weld Rd
Dunlop
Abdul Gafoor Mosque
ALLAN RD
JALAN BESAR
Sim Lim Tower
ROCHOR CANAL RD
Edinburgh Road
Central Park
Mount Emily Park
White Road
Sophia Road
Sim Lim Square
SERANGOON ROAD
SHORT STREET
Sim Lim Square
STREET
ROCHOR
ROAD
Bus Station
Blancou Court
Thong Sia Building
ORCHARD ROAD
Cuppage Centre
Centrepoint
Cuppage Road
Orchard Plaza
Orchard Point
Faber House
Sri Temasek
ORCHARD ROAD
Handy Road
Handy Road
BENCOOLEN STREET
Bencoolen Mosque
Waterloo
Street
St. Joseph's Church
COLONIAL DISTRICT
El Bogo
MIDDLE ROAD
VICTORIA STREET
Seah St
Raffles Hotel
PENANG ROAD
ORCHARD ROAD
KILLINEY ROAD
Lloyd Rd
Chesed-El Synagogue
OXLEY ROAD
Sacred Heart Church
N2 Somerset
PENANG ROAD
ORCHARD ROAD
AVENUE
BOULEVARD
U N1 Dhoby Ghaut
Singapore Hist. Mus.
Singapore Art Museum
STAMFORD ROAD
BRAS BASAH ROAD
ST ANDREW'S RD
Westin Plaza
Raffles City
C2 City Hall
RIVER VALLEY ROAD
Sri Thandayuthapani Temple
TANK ROAD
Fort Canning Park
Fort Canning Reservoir
CITY CENTRE
Asian Civ. Mus.
Kim Yam Rd
Hong San See Temple
Sultan St
Van Kleef Aquarium
Battle Box
CANNING
Singapore Philatelic Mus.
STAMFORD
HILL STREET
NORTH BRIDGE ROAD
War Memorial Park
St. Andrew's Cathedral
City Hall
Supreme Court
Parliament Hall
Hunan Centre
CLEMENCEAU AVENUE
HAVELOCK ROAD
Singapore River
Clarke Quay
North Boat Quay
Boat Quay
South Boat Quay
MERCHANT ROAD
Melaka Mosque
NORTH CANAL ROAD
Raffles Landing Site
Empress Pl. Museum
Victoria Concert Hall & Theatre
Singapore Cricket Club
Esplanade Park
CONNAUGHT Dr
Merlion Park
Marina Bay
PICKERING STREET
Bus Station
Wak Hai Cheng Bio Temple
CHULIA ST
OUB Centre
Clifford Pier
SENTOSA
Pearl's Hill CityPark
Pearl's Hill Reservoir
People's Park Complex
UPPER CROSS STREET
NEW BRIDGE ROAD
Chin Swee Road
Chin Swee
EXPRESSWAY
Chin Swee
Outram Park
SOUTH BRIDGE ROAD
Smith St
Oriental Theatre
CHINATOWN
Jamae Mosque
Sri Mariamman Temple
Temple St
Pagoda St
Sago St
Trengganu St
Tuk Tak Chi Temple
C1 Raffles Place
RAFFLES QUAY
W2 Outram Park
Amoy St
Boon Tat St
Thian Hock Keng Temple
Al-Abrar Mosque
Telok Ayer
Lau Pa Sat Festival Market
ROBINSON ROAD
MARINA STATION RD
Singapore General Hospital
NEW BRIDGE ROAD
NEIL ROAD
Everton Park
CRAIG ROAD
Duxton Rd
CANTONMENT ROAD
MAXWELL ROAD
SOUTH BRIDGE
WALLICH ST
W1 Tanjong Pagar
SHENTON WAY
Teluk Ayer Basin
M1 Marina Bay
U Singapore Changi International Airport
Spottiswoode Park
Spottiswoode Park Road
ANSON ROAD
Hock Teck See Temple
EXPRESSWAY
Finger Peir
Singapore Railway Station
AYER RAJAH EXPRESSWAY

COPYRIGHT PHILIP'S

41

0   km   1

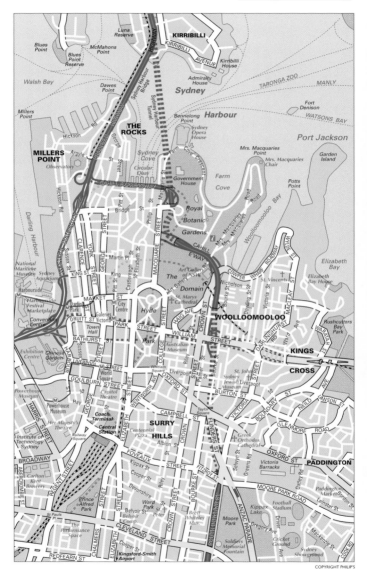

COPYRIGHT PHILIPS

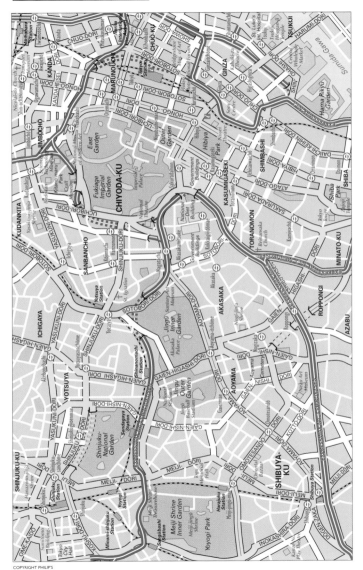

0   km   2

COPYRIGHT PHILIP'S

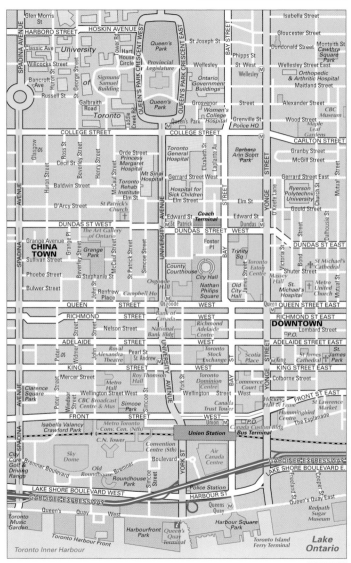

0   km   1

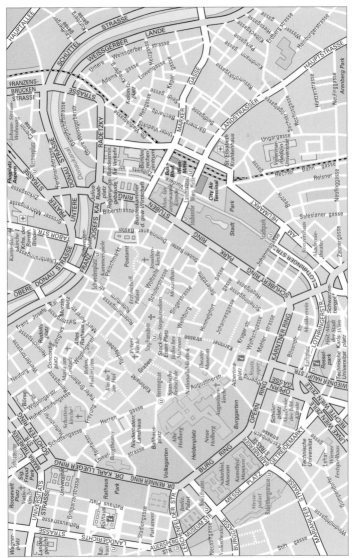

COPYRIGHT PHILIP'S

45

GAZETTEER OF NATIONS

48 Afghanistan
Albania
Algeria
American Samoa
Andorra
Angola

49 Anguilla
Antigua & Barbuda
Argentina
Armenia
Aruba
Australia

50 Austria
Azerbaijan
Azores
Bahamas
Bahrain
Bangladesh

51 Barbados
Belarus
Belgium
Belize
Benin
Bermuda

52 Bolivia
Bosnia-Herzegovina
Botswana
Brazil
Bulgaria
Burma (= Myanmar)

53 Cambodia
Canada
Canary Islands
Cape Verde
Cayman Islands
Chad

54 Chile
China
Colombia
Comoros
Costa Rica
Croatia

55 Cuba
Cyprus
Czech Republic
Denmark
Dominica
Dominican Republic

56 Ecuador
Egypt
El Salvador
Estonia
Ethiopia
Fiji Islands

57 Finland
France
French Polynesia
Gambia, The
Georgia
Germany

58 Gibraltar
Greece
Grenada
Guadeloupe
Hong Kong
Hungary

59 Iceland
India
Indonesia
Iran
Ireland
Israel

60 Italy
Jamaica
Japan
Jordan
Kenya
Korea, South

61 Kuwait
Latvia
Lebanon
Libya
Liechtenstein
Lithuania

62 Luxembourg
Madagascar
Malawi
Malaysia
Maldives
Malta

63 Martinique
Mauritius
Mexico
Monaco
Mongolia
Morocco

64 Namibia
Nepal
Netherlands
Netherlands Antilles
New Zealand
Nigeria

65 Norway
Oman
Pakistan
Paraguay
Peru
Philippines

66 Poland
Portugal
Puerto Rico

Qatar
Réunion
Romania

67 Russia
St Kitts & Nevis
St Lucia
St Vincent & the Grenadines
Samoa
Saudi Arabia

68 Serbia & Montenegro
Seychelles
Singapore
Slovak Republic
Slovenia
South Africa

69 Spain
Sri Lanka
Sweden
Switzerland
Syria
Taiwan

70 Tanzania
Thailand
Trinidad & Tobago
Tunisia
Turkey
Uganda

71 Ukraine
United Arab Emirates
United Kingdom
United States of America
Uruguay
Venezuela

72 Vietnam
Virgin Islands, British
Virgin Islands, US
Yemen
Zambia
Zimbabwe

AFGHANISTAN

GOVERNMENT Transitional
LANGUAGES Pashtu, Dari/Persian, Uzbek
CURRENCY Afghani = 100 puls
MEDICAL Visitors should protect against yellow fever, polio, typhoid and malaria
TRAVEL Most governments currently advise against all travel to Afghanistan. The security situation remains serious, with danger away from main roads from mines and unexploded ordnance
WEATHER Jun to Aug very hot; Dec to Mar very cold; Jun to Sep scanty rainfall; mild at other times
BANKING 0800–1200 and 1300–1630 Sat to Wed; 0830–1330 Thu. However, at the time of writing, many banks are closed
EMERGENCY Unavailable
TIME ZONE GMT +4.30
INTERNATIONAL DIALLING CODE Unavailable

ALGERIA

GOVERNMENT Socialist republic
LANGUAGES Arabic and Berber (both official), French
CURRENCY Algerian dinar = 100 centimes
MEDICAL There is a risk of yellow fever, malaria, hepatitis A, typhoid and polio
TRAVEL Most governments currently advise against all tourist and non-essential travel to Algeria. Travel by public transport should be avoided and only secure accommodation used
WEATHER Jun to Sep in the north is usually hot with high humidity along the coast; Oct to Feb wet and mild
BANKING 0900–1630 Sun to Thu
EMERGENCY Unavailable
TIME ZONE GMT +1
INTERNATIONAL DIALLING CODE 213

ANDORRA

GOVERNMENT Parliamentary co-princedom
LANGUAGES Catalan, Spanish, French
CURRENCY Euro = 100 cents
MEDICAL There are no specific health risks
TRAVEL In Andorra, visitors will find some of the most stunning scenery and the best skiing in the Pyrenees. Shopping around, prices may often be up to 30% below those in France and Spain
WEATHER Jun to Sep warm and pleasant; Dec to Apr sunny but cold with abundant snow; rain falls throughout the year; snow often remains on the peaks of mountains until July
BANKING 0900–1300 and 1500–1700 Mon to Fri; 0900–1200 Sat
EMERGENCY Police 110; Fire/Ambulance 118
TIME ZONE GMT +1
INTERNATIONAL DIALLING CODE 376

ALBANIA

GOVERNMENT Multiparty republic
LANGUAGES Albanian (official)
CURRENCY Lek = 100 qindars
MEDICAL Water is untreated and not safe to drink. Medical facilities in the country are poor
TRAVEL Crime is high throughout parts of the country and visitors should remain vigilant at all times. It is advisable to dress down and avoid carrying expensive items. Street demonstrations against the government are common
WEATHER Jun to Sep warm and dry; Oct to May cool and wet
BANKING 0700–1500 Mon to Fri
EMERGENCY Police 24445; Fire 23333; Ambulance 22235
TIME ZONE GMT +1
INTERNATIONAL DIALLING CODE 355

AMERICAN SAMOA

GOVERNMENT US overseas territory
LANGUAGES Samoan, English
CURRENCY US dollar = 100 cents
MEDICAL Water is untreated and is unsafe to drink. Vaccination against polio and typhoid is recommended
TRAVEL Most visits to American Samoa are trouble-free and crime is low. Tourists should respect local culture and take usual precautions, especially in the towns
WEATHER Hot, tropical climate with heavy rainfall from Dec to Apr. The most comfortable time to visit is May to Sep
BANKING 0900–1500 Mon to Fri
EMERGENCY All services 911
TIME ZONE GMT –11
INTERNATIONAL DIALLING CODE 1 684

ANGOLA

GOVERNMENT Multiparty republic
LANGUAGES Portuguese (official), many others
CURRENCY Kwanza = 100 lwei
MEDICAL There is a risk of yellow fever, hepatitis A, polio, typhoid and malaria
TRAVEL Most governments currently advise against tourist and non-essential travel to Angola due to the aftermath of civil war. Visitors should remain vigilant, particularly after dark. Crime levels are high and land mines are widely distributed and unmarked
WEATHER Warm to hot all year; Nov to Apr wet; cooler and wetter climate in the south
BANKING 0845–1600 Mon to Fri
EMERGENCY Unavailable
TIME ZONE GMT +1
INTERNATIONAL DIALLING CODE 244

ANGUILLA

GOVERNMENT UK overseas territory
LANGUAGES English (official)
CURRENCY East Caribbean dollar = 100 cents
MEDICAL There are no specific health risks, but medical facilities are limited on the island
TRAVEL Most visits are trouble-free, but beachwear should be confined to resort areas. Travellers should take normal precautions, such as locking doors and securing valuables
WEATHER Tropical climate. Hurricane risk from Jun to Nov; Oct to Dec is the rainy season. Optimum diving conditions in summer months
BANKING 0800–1500 Mon to Thu; 0800–1700 Fri
EMERGENCY All services 911
TIME ZONE GMT –4
INTERNATIONAL DIALLING CODE 1 264

ANTIGUA & BARBUDA

GOVERNMENT Constitutional monarchy
LANGUAGES English (official), English patois
CURRENCY East Caribbean dollar = 100 cents
MEDICAL Visitors should take normal precautions against mosquito bites. Vaccinations recommended against polio and typhoid
TRAVEL Generally trouble-free, but visitors should avoid isolated areas, including beaches, after dark
WEATHER Tropical with little variation between the seasons; rainfall is minimal. The islands are at risk from hurricanes from Jun to Nov
BANKING 0800–1400 Mon to Thu; 0800–1700 Fri
EMERGENCY All services 999/911
TIME ZONE GMT –4
INTERNATIONAL DIALLING CODE 1 268

ARGENTINA

GOVERNMENT Federal republic
LANGUAGES Spanish (official)
CURRENCY Argentine peso = 10,000 australs
MEDICAL Cholera is a risk in the subtropical northern region
TRAVEL Occasional outbreaks of social unrest. It is inadvisable to walk in isolated, poorly-lit areas. Visitors should avoid carrying too much cash or wearing jewellery. Avoid military areas, which usually allow no stopping
WEATHER Jun to Aug cool in Buenos Aires area; Dec to Feb hot and humid; rain falls all year round
BANKING 1000–1500 Mon to Fri
EMERGENCY Police 101/107
TIME ZONE GMT –3
INTERNATIONAL DIALLING CODE 54

ARMENIA

GOVERNMENT Multiparty republic
LANGUAGES Armenian (official)
CURRENCY Dram = 100 couma
MEDICAL Visitors should protect against hepatitis and bacterial infection
TRAVEL The border areas with Azerbaijan should be avoided at all times. Crime remains relatively low in Armenia, but occasional thefts from cars and pickpocketing may occur. The local standard of driving is poor, but most visits are generally trouble-free
WEATHER Apr to Oct hot and sunny; Jul to Sep little rainfall; Dec to Feb cold with heavy snow
BANKING 0930–1730 Mon to Fri
EMERGENCY Unavailable
TIME ZONE GMT +4
INTERNATIONAL DIALLING CODE 374

ARUBA

GOVERNMENT Parliamentary democracy
LANGUAGES Dutch, English, Spanish, Papiamento
CURRENCY Aruba florin = 100 cents
MEDICAL Water is purified and should be safe; normal precautions should be taken with food
TRAVEL Beachwear should be confined to the beach. Travellers should take normal precautions, such as avoiding isolated areas after dark
WEATHER Tropical marine climate, warm and dry with average temperatures of 28°C [82°F]. Nov and Dec experience short showers
BANKING 0800–1200 and 1300–1600 Mon to Fri
EMERGENCY Police 11 000; Ambulance 74 300; Fire 115
TIME ZONE GMT –4
INTERNATIONAL DIALLING CODE 297

AUSTRALIA

GOVERNMENT Federal constitutional monarchy
LANGUAGES English (official)
CURRENCY Australian dollar = 100 cents
MEDICAL No vaccinations required. There are few health hazards, but visitors should protect against sunburn, spider and snake bites
TRAVEL Visitors should exercise caution in major urban areas, particularly after dark
WEATHER Tropical to temperate; Nov to Mar warm or hot in all areas; Jun to Aug mild in south-eastern region; Sep to May warm to hot; rain falls all year round and is heaviest Mar to Jul
BANKING 0930–1600 Mon to Thu; 0930–1700 Fri, but hours vary throughout the country
EMERGENCY Emergency Services 000
TIME ZONE East GMT +10; Cen. +9.30; West +8
INTERNATIONAL DIALLING CODE 61

AUSTRIA

Government Federal republic
Languages German (official)
Currency Euro = 100 cents
Medical There are no specific health risks in Austria
Travel Visitors to the Alps should contact the Austrian Tourist Agency for advice on safety. Austria benefits all year round by providing summer sightseeing and winter sports
Weather Jun to Aug warm and pleasant; Oct to Apr cold; Mar to Aug higher rainfall
Banking 0800–1230 and 1330–1500 Mon, Tue, Wed and Fri; Thu 0800–1230 and 1330–1730
Emergency Emergency Services 112; Police 133; Ambulance 144
Time zone GMT +1
International dialling code 43

AZERBAIJAN

Government Federal multiparty republic
Languages Azerbaijani (official), Russian
Currency Azerbaijani manat = 100 gopik
Medical Visitors should protect against malaria, yellow fever, diptheria, tick-borne encephalitis, hepatitis, rabies and typhoid fever
Travel Travel to the western region of Nagorno-Karabakh and surrounding occupied area should be avoided. Passport photocopies should be carried at all times. Do not enter or leave the country via the land borders with Russia
Weather May to Sep sunny, warm and dry; Oct to Apr mild with some rain
Banking 0930–1730 Mon to Fri
Emergency Unavailable
Time zone GMT +4
International dialling code 994

AZORES

Government Portuguese autonomous region
Languages Portuguese
Currency Euro = 100 cents
Medical There are no specific health risks in the Azores
Travel Most visits to the Azores are trouble-free. The nine large islands and numerous small ones are situated in the middle of the Atlantic Ocean and offer the traveller a wealth of stunning scenery
Weather Mild throughout the year; Jun to Sep sunny and warm; Jan to Apr changeable; Oct to Mar wet
Banking Visitors should check at their hotel
Emergency Unavailable
Time zone GMT −1
International dialling code Unavailable

BAHAMAS

Government Constitutional parliamentary democracy
Languages English (official), Creole
Currency Bahamian dollar = 100 cents
Medical Visitors should protect against dehydration, sunburn, tetanus and jellyfish
Travel Most visits are trouble-free, but crime exists in the cities of Nassau and Freeport. Keep valuables hidden and avoid walking alone
Weather Mild throughout the year; May to Oct warm and wet; Dec to Mar cooler and drier; Jun to Nov hurricanes occur
Banking 0930–1500 Mon to Thu; 0930–1700 Fri, but hours on each island vary
Emergency All Services 911
Time zone GMT −5
International dialling code 1 242

BAHRAIN

Government Monarchy (emirate) with a cabinet appointed by the Emir
Languages Arabic (official), English, Farsi, Urdu
Currency Bahrain dinar = 1,000 fils
Medical There are no specific health risks
Travel Generally calm, but any increase in regional tension may affect travel advice. Visitors should avoid village areas, particularly after dark. Keep cash and valuables out of sight at all times
Weather Jun to Sep very hot; Nov to Mar milder and pleasant
Banking 0800–1200 and 1600–1800 Sat to Wed; 0800–1100 Thu
Emergency All Services 999
Time zone GMT +3
International dialling code 973

BANGLADESH

Government Multiparty republic
Languages Bengali (official), English
Currency Taka = 100 paisas
Medical Visitors should protect against cholera, dysentery, hepatitis, malaria and meningitis
Travel Avoid political gatherings. Driving conditions are very poor. Visitors should keep valuables hidden and avoid travel after dark
Weather Jun to Sep monsoon with heavy rain and very high humidity; Nov to Feb sunny and cool; Mar to Jun hot with thunderstorms
Banking 0830–1430 Sun to Wed; 0830–1300 Thu. Closed Fri and Sat
Emergency Police Dhaka 866 551–3; Fire and Ambulance Service Dhaka 9 555 555
Time zone GMT +6
International dialling code 880

BARBADOS

GOVERNMENT Parliamentary democracy
LANGUAGES English (local Bajan dialect also spoken)
CURRENCY Barbados dollar = 100 cents
MEDICAL The sun is intense and visitors should wear strong sunscreen at all times. Other health risks include dengue fever
TRAVEL Travel is generally risk-free, but visitors should avoid deserted beaches at night
WEATHER Warm all year round; Jun to Dec wet season; Feb to May cooler and drier
BANKING 0800–1500 Mon to Thu; 0800–1300 and 1500–1700 Fri
EMERGENCY Police 112; Ambulance 115; All Services 119
TIME ZONE GMT –4
INTERNATIONAL DIALLING CODE 1 246

BELARUS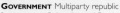

GOVERNMENT Multiparty republic
LANGUAGES Belarusian and Russian (both official)
CURRENCY Belarusian rouble = 100 kopecks
MEDICAL Visitors should avoid eating dairy produce, mushrooms and fruits of the forests which can carry high levels of radiation. Other health risks include hepatitis A and B, and typhoid
TRAVEL Pickpocketing and theft from vehicles or hotel rooms is common. Visitors should avoid demonstrations and rallies, and remain vigilant at all times
WEATHER May to Aug mild; Oct to Apr cold; Jan to Mar snow cover; rain falls all year round
BANKING 0900–1730 Mon to Fri
EMERGENCY Police 02; Ambulance 03
TIME ZONE GMT +2
INTERNATIONAL DIALLING CODE 375

BELGIUM

GOVERNMENT Federal constitutional monarchy
LANGUAGES Dutch, French, German (all official)
CURRENCY Euro = 100 cents
MEDICAL There are no specific health risks, but medical care is expensive
TRAVEL Most visits are trouble-free, but visitors should take sensible precautions to avoid the increasing threat of mugging, bag-snatching and pickpocketing, particularly in Brussels
WEATHER May to Sep mild; Nov to Mar cold; rain falls all year round, often as snow in winter
BANKING 0900–1200 and 1400–1600 Mon to Fri. Some banks open 0900–1200 Sat
EMERGENCY Police 101; Emergency Services 112 Fire/Ambulance 100 (112 from a mobile phone)
TIME ZONE GMT +1
INTERNATIONAL DIALLING CODE 32

BELIZE

GOVERNMENT Constitutional monarchy
LANGUAGES English (official), Spanish, Creole
CURRENCY Belizean dollar = 100 cents
MEDICAL Precautions should be taken against polio, typhoid and cholera. Malaria is present throughout the year, excluding urban areas
TRAVEL Nov to May is the best time to visit, but this is the busy tourist season when prices rise and hotels fill up. Belize has one of the longest barrier reefs in the world
WEATHER Hot and humid climate. Monsoon and hurricane season runs from Jun to Sep
BANKING 0800–1300 Mon to Thu; 0800–1200 and 1500–1800 Fri
EMERGENCY All services 911
TIME ZONE GMT –6
INTERNATIONAL DIALLING CODE 501

BENIN

GOVERNMENT Multiparty republic
LANGUAGES French (official), Fon, Adja, Yoruba
CURRENCY CFA franc = 100 centimes
MEDICAL Visitors should protect against cholera and malaria. Yellow fever vaccination certificates are required for entry. Water is unsafe to drink
TRAVEL Travel is generally safe, but driving out of towns at night should be avoided due to poor street lighting. Occasional incidents of mugging and armed robberies occur in Cotonou
WEATHER Warm to hot all year round; Mar to Jul and Sep to Oct are rainy seasons in the south
BANKING 0800–1100 and 1500–1600 Mon to Fri
EMERGENCY Consult foreign embassy
TIME ZONE GMT +1
INTERNATIONAL DIALLING CODE 229

BERMUDA

GOVERNMENT Self-governing British dependency
LANGUAGES English (some Portuguese is also spoken)
CURRENCY Bermuda dollar = 100 cents
MEDICAL There are no specific health risks
TRAVEL Most visits to Bermuda are trouble-free. Accommodation can be up to 40% cheaper between Nov and Mar, but events and entertainment are less plentiful at this time
WEATHER Jun to Sep very warm; Nov to Apr mild; rainfall is abundant and evenly distributed all year round
BANKING 0930–1500 Mon to Thu; 0930–1500 and 1630–1730 Fri
EMERGENCY All Services 911
TIME ZONE GMT –4
INTERNATIONAL DIALLING CODE 1 441

BOLIVIA

GOVERNMENT Multiparty republic
LANGUAGES Spanish, Aymara, Quechua (official)
CURRENCY Boliviano = 100 centavos
MEDICAL Altitude sickness is common. Visitors
should drink plenty of water and protect against
cholera, hepatitis, malaria, polio and tetanus
TRAVEL Pickpocketing is common and visitors
are advised to remain vigilant at all times. The
country is going through a period of unrest
WEATHER Average max. daily temperature
of 17–19°C [62–66°F] all year round; low annual
rainfall, most falling Dec to Mar
BANKING 0930–1500 Mon to Thu; 0930–1500
and 1630–1730 Fri
EMERGENCY All Services 911
TIME ZONE GMT −4
INTERNATIONAL DIALLING CODE 591

BOSNIA-HERZEGOVINA

GOVERNMENT Federal republic
LANGUAGES Bosnian, Serbian, Croatian
CURRENCY Convertible marka =
100 convertible pfenniga
MEDICAL Medical facilities are limited. There is
a risk of hepatitis and typhoid fever
TRAVEL Crime level is generally low, but isolated
incidents of violence can flare up. Unexploded
land mines and other ordnance still remain in
certain areas
WEATHER Jun to Sep warm; Dec to Feb cold;
spring and autumn mild; rain falls all year round
BANKING 0730–1530 Mon to Fri
EMERGENCY Consult foreign office in country
of residence before departure
TIME ZONE GMT +1
INTERNATIONAL DIALLING CODE 387

BOTSWANA

GOVERNMENT Multiparty republic
LANGUAGES English (official), Setswana
CURRENCY Pula = 100 thebe
MEDICAL There are no specific health risks, but
visitors should protect against malaria
TRAVEL Most visits are trouble-free, but there
is an increasing incidence of crime. Prolonged
rainfall may cause flooding and block roads
from Dec to Apr
WEATHER In the east, May to Sep mild with
little rainfall; Nov to Mar warm, rainy season but
nights can be cold
BANKING 0900–1430 Mon, Tue, Thu and Fri;
0815–1200 Wed; 0815–1045 Sat
EMERGENCY Police 351161
TIME ZONE GMT +2
INTERNATIONAL DIALLING CODE 267

BRAZIL

GOVERNMENT Federal republic
LANGUAGES Portuguese (official)
CURRENCY Real = 100 centavos
MEDICAL Visitors should take precautions
against AIDS, malaria, meningitis and yellow fever
TRAVEL High crime rate in major cities of Rio
de Janeiro and São Paulo. Dress down and avoid
wearing jewellery
WEATHER Jun to Sep pleasant in south-east;
Dec to Mar hot and humid with high rainfall
BANKING 1000–1630 Mon to Fri
EMERGENCY All Services 0
TIME ZONE Eastern GMT −3; North East
and East Pará −3; Western −4; Amapa and
West Pará −4; Acre State −5; Fernando de
Noronha Archipelago −2
INTERNATIONAL DIALLING CODE 55

BULGARIA

GOVERNMENT Multiparty republic
LANGUAGES Bulgarian (official), Turkish
CURRENCY Lev = 100 stotinki
MEDICAL There are no specific health risks
TRAVEL Most visits to Bulgaria are trouble-free,
but there is a risk of robbery. Pickpockets
operate in downtown Sofia and in the Black Sea
resorts. Car theft is commonplace
WEATHER May to Sep warm with some
rainfall; Nov to Mar cold with snow; rain falls
frequently during spring and autumn
BANKING 0800–1130 and 1400–1800 Mon to
Fri; 0830–1130 Sat
EMERGENCY Police 166; Fire 160;
Ambulance 150
TIME ZONE GMT +2
INTERNATIONAL DIALLING CODE 359

BURMA (= MYANMAR)

GOVERNMENT Military regime
LANGUAGES Burmese (official); minority ethnic
groups have their own languages
CURRENCY Kyat = 100 pyas
MEDICAL Visitors should protect against cholera,
dysentery, hepatitis, malaria, rabies and typhoid
TRAVEL Politically unsettled. Visitors should avoid
large crowds and should not visit Aung San Suu
Kyi without prior arrangement. Terrorist attacks
have been reported in some areas
WEATHER Monsoon climate; Feb to May hot
with very little rain; May to Oct wet; Nov to Feb
cooler and drier
BANKING 1000–1400 Mon to Fri
EMERGENCY Unavailable
TIME ZONE GMT +6.30
INTERNATIONAL DIALLING CODE 95

CAMBODIA

GOVERNMENT Constitutional monarchy
LANGUAGES Khmer (official), French, English
CURRENCY Riel = 100 sen
MEDICAL Visitors should protect against cholera, hepatitis, malaria, typhoid and rabies
TRAVEL Visitors should seek advice before travelling. The greatest risks are from traffic accidents and armed robbery after dark. Land mines exist in certain rural areas
WEATHER Tropical monsoon climate; May to Oct monsoon; Dec to Jan lower humidity and little rainfall; Feb to Apr hot; temperatures are constant throughout the country
BANKING 0800–1500 Mon to Fri
EMERGENCY Unavailable
TIME ZONE GMT +7
INTERNATIONAL DIALLING CODE 855

CANADA

GOVERNMENT Federal multiparty constitutional monarchy
LANGUAGES English and French (both official)
CURRENCY Canadian dollar = 100 cents
MEDICAL Medical treatment is expensive and it is essential that visitors have travel insurance. Blackfly and mosquitoes can cause problems in areas near water
TRAVEL Most visits to Canada are trouble-free
WEATHER Varies considerably; Jul to Aug tend to be warm all round the country; Nov to Mar very cold everywhere except west coast
BANKING 1000–1500 Mon to Fri
EMERGENCY Emergency Services 911 or 0
TIME ZONE Six zones exist from GMT –3.30 in Newfoundland to –8 on the Pacific coast
INTERNATIONAL DIALLING CODE 1

CANARY ISLANDS

GOVERNMENT Spanish autonomous region
LANGUAGES Spanish
CURRENCY Euro = 100 cents
MEDICAL The Canary Islands are part of Spain and there are no specific health risks
TRAVEL The islands are volcanic and the landscape is varied. Many resorts suffer the effects of mass tourism, but beyond these areas there are stunning, peaceful regions to be enjoyed
WEATHER Subtropical climate; generally hot and sunny all year round, but Dec to Feb slightly cooler than rest of year
BANKING Visitors should enquire at hotel
EMERGENCY Unavailable
TIME ZONE GMT
INTERNATIONAL DIALLING CODE 34

CAPE VERDE

GOVERNMENT Multiparty republic
LANGUAGES Portuguese, Creole
CURRENCY Cape Verde escudo = 100 centavos
MEDICAL Water is untreated and unsafe to drink. Avoid dairy products as they are unpasteurized. Polio and typhoid vaccinations are recommended; there is a risk of cholera and malaria
TRAVEL Most visits to Cape Verde are trouble-free. Visitors should avoid carrying valuables in pubilc and remain vigilant at all times
WEATHER Warm and temperate climate with a dry summer. The islands suffer periodically from drought
BANKING 0800–1400 Mon to Fri
EMERGENCY All services 87
TIME ZONE GMT –1
INTERNATIONAL DIALLING CODE 238

CAYMAN ISLANDS

GOVERNMENT British crown colony
LANGUAGES English (local dialects also spoken)
CURRENCY Cayman Islands dollar = 100 cents
MEDICAL There is a risk of sunburn and poisonous plants are present
TRAVEL Most visits to the Cayman Islands are trouble-free. Car hire is a good way to move around the islands
WEATHER Warm tropical climate all year round; May to Oct wet season with usually brief showers
BANKING 0900–1600 Mon to Thu; 0900–1630 Fri
EMERGENCY Police 911; Ambulance 555; All Services 911
TIME ZONE GMT –5
INTERNATIONAL DIALLING CODE 1 345

CHAD

GOVERNMENT Multiparty republic
LANGUAGES French and Arabic (both official)
CURRENCY CFA franc = 100 centimes
MEDICAL Visitors should be vaccinated against yellow fever, tetanus, cholera and hepatitis A
TRAVEL Visitors to Chad should remain vigilant at all times especially in the south-west region along the border with Cameroon. Areas to avoid include the Aozou Strip and the Tibesti area on the border with Libya, where minefields exist
WEATHER Hot tropical climate; Mar to May very hot; May to Oct wet in south; Jun to Sep wet in central areas; little rain in northern regions
BANKING 0900–1400 Mon to Fri
EMERGENCY Unavailable
TIME ZONE GMT +1
INTERNATIONAL DIALLING CODE 235

CHILE

GOVERNMENT Multiparty republic
LANGUAGES Spanish (official)
CURRENCY Chilean peso = 100 centavos
MEDICAL Visitors should protect themselves against cholera
TRAVEL Most visits are trouble-free, but visitors are advised to keep in groups and avoid walking alone, particularly after dark. Pickpockets and muggers are active in cities. Passport photocopies should be carried at all times
WEATHER Variable climate; Sep to Nov and Feb to Apr pleasant temperatures; Dec to Mar hotter; skiing is popular from Jun to Aug
BANKING 0900–1400 Mon to Fri
EMERGENCY Police 133; Fire 132
TIME ZONE GMT –4; Easter Island –6
INTERNATIONAL DIALLING CODE 56

CHINA

GOVERNMENT Single-party Communist republic
LANGUAGES Mandarin Chinese (official)
CURRENCY Renminbi yuan = 10 jiao = 100 fen
MEDICAL Rabies is widespread. A virulent strain of viral pneumonia has emerged in the south-east and malaria is common in southern areas
TRAVEL Violent crimes are rare. Crime occurs in cities, and extra care should be taken around street markets and popular bar areas at night
WEATHER Climate varies; Apr to Sep humid and hot; Jan to Mar very cold; rainfall high in central areas; Jul to Sep typhoon season in the south
BANKING 0930–1200 and 1400–1700 Mon to Fri; 0900–1700 Sat
EMERGENCY Police 110; Fire 119
TIME ZONE GMT +8
INTERNATIONAL DIALLING CODE 86

COLOMBIA

GOVERNMENT Multiparty republic
LANGUAGES Spanish (official)
CURRENCY Colombian peso = 100 centavos
MEDICAL Visitors should protect against altitude sickness, cholera, hepatitis A, B and D, and malaria
TRAVEL Guerrilla and criminal attacks close to Bogota are increasing. Violence and kidnapping are serious problems in Colombia. The border area with Panama and the Uraba region of Antioquia are particularly dangerous
WEATHER Hot and humid; May to Nov rainy season; cooler in upland areas
BANKING 0900–1500 Mon to Fri
EMERGENCY All Services 112 (01 in smaller towns and rural areas)
TIME ZONE GMT –5
INTERNATIONAL DIALLING CODE 57

COMOROS

GOVERNMENT Multiparty republic
LANGUAGES Arabic and French (both official)
CURRENCY CFA franc = 100 centimes
MEDICAL Strict food hygiene precautions are essential. Cholera and malaria are prevanlat and medical facilities are basic and limited
TRAVEL Generally crime-free, but be aware of pickpockets. Visitors should not walk around town centres unaccompanied at night
WEATHER Tropical climate with average temperatures of 25°C [77°F]. Cyclone risk between Jan and Apr
BANKING 0730–1300 Mon to Thu; 0730–1100 Fri
EMERGENCY Unavailable
TIME ZONE GMT +3
INTERNATIONAL DIALLING CODE 269

COSTA RICA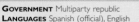

GOVERNMENT Multiparty republic
LANGUAGES Spanish (official), English
CURRENCY Costa Rican colón = 100 céntimos
MEDICAL Cases of dengue fever have been confirmed. Visitors should protect themselves against malaria, cholera and hepatitis
TRAVEL Daylight muggings can occur. Do not wear jewellery or carry large amounts of cash. Riptides are very common on all beaches
WEATHER Coastal areas warmer than inland low-lying regions; Dec to Apr warm and dry; May to Nov rainy season; landslides can occur
BANKING 0900–1500 Mon to Fri
EMERGENCY Police 104; Fire 103; Ambulance 225/1436 and 228/2187
TIME ZONE GMT –7
INTERNATIONAL DIALLING CODE 506

CROATIA

GOVERNMENT Multiparty republic
LANGUAGES Croatian
CURRENCY Kuna = 100 lipas
MEDICAL No specific health risks, although the health system is severely stretched at present
TRAVEL Exercise caution in the areas bordering Bosnia-Herzegovina and Serbia and Montenegro. There continue to be incidents of violence and many unexploded land mines remain undetected. It is inadvisable to use the Debelli Brijeg crossing-points into Montenegro
WEATHER Continental climate in the north and Mediterranean on the Adriatic Coast
BANKING 0700–1500 Mon to Fri
EMERGENCY Police 92; Fire 93; Ambulance 94
TIME ZONE GMT +1
INTERNATIONAL DIALLING CODE 385

CUBA

GOVERNMENT Socialist republic
LANGUAGES Spanish (official)
CURRENCY Cuban peso = 100 centavos
MEDICAL Tap water is unsafe to drink, with a risk of contracting hepatitis A
TRAVEL Street theft occurs, especially in Old Havana and major tourist sites. Do not carry large amounts of cash or jewellery. Do not travel with anyone other than your recognized tour operator. Avoid military zones
WEATHER May to Oct hot rainy season; Aug to Nov hurricane season; Dec to Apr cooler
BANKING 0830–1200 and 1330–1500 Mon to Fri; 0830–1030 Sat
EMERGENCY All Services 26811
TIME ZONE GMT −4
INTERNATIONAL DIALLING CODE 53

CYPRUS

GOVERNMENT Multiparty republic
LANGUAGES Greek and Turkish (both official)
CURRENCY Cypriot pound = 100 cents
MEDICAL There are no specific health risks, but visitors should be protected against hepatitis
TRAVEL Travel is generally trouble-free, but attempts to pass overland from the northern Turkish sector into the southern Greek region are not recommended
WEATHER Apr to May and Sep to Oct cool and pleasant; Jun to Aug hot and dry; Nov to Mar rainfall is heavier, but temperatures remain warm
BANKING 0815–1230 in tourist areas; 1530–1730 in winter; 1630–1830 in summer
EMERGENCY All Services 199
TIME ZONE GMT +2
INTERNATIONAL DIALLING CODE 357

CZECH REPUBLIC

GOVERNMENT Multiparty republic
LANGUAGES Czech (official)
CURRENCY Czech koruna = 100 haler
MEDICAL Visitors to forested areas should seek advice about immunization against tick-borne encephalitis and lyme disease
TRAVEL Most visits are trouble-free, but petty theft is a growing problem, particularly in Prague. Pickpocketing is very common at tourist attractions
WEATHER May to Sep mild; Apr and Oct much cooler
BANKING 0800–1800 Mon to Fri
EMERGENCY Police 158; Fire 150; Ambulance 155
TIME ZONE GMT +1
INTERNATIONAL DIALLING CODE 42

DENMARK

GOVERNMENT Parliamentary monarchy
LANGUAGES Danish (official), English
CURRENCY Danish krone = 100 øre
MEDICAL There are no specific health risks in Denmark
TRAVEL Visits to Denmark are generally trouble-free. Visitors will enjoy relatively low prices compared to other European countries
WEATHER Jun to Aug warm summer season; Oct to Mar cold and wet with chance of frost; spring and autumn are usually mild and pleasant
BANKING 0930–1700 Mon, Tue, Wed and Fri; 0930–1800 Thu. Some foreign exchange bureaux remain open until midnight
EMERGENCY Emergency Services 112
TIME ZONE GMT +1
INTERNATIONAL DIALLING CODE 45

DOMINICA

GOVERNMENT Parliamentary democracy
LANGUAGES English (official), Creole, French
CURRENCY East Caribbean dollar = 100 cents
MEDICAL Dengue fever is prevalent and visitors should guard against mosquito bites
TRAVEL Most visits are trouble-free. Visitors are advised to take sensible precautions and be vigilant at all times
WEATHER Tropical climate with heavy rainfall, particularly in Jun to Oct, which is also the hottest period. Tropical storms and hurricanes can occur between Jun and Nov
BANKING 0800–1500 Mon to Thu; 0800–1700 Fri
EMERGENCY All services 999
TIME ZONE GMT −4
INTERNATIONAL DIALLING CODE 1 767

DOMINICAN REPUBLIC

GOVERNMENT Multiparty republic
LANGUAGES Spanish (official)
CURRENCY Dominican peso = 100 centavos
MEDICAL Tourists should protect against polio and typhoid. There are occasional outbreaks of malaria and dengue fever; anti-mosquito skin repellants are recommended
TRAVEL Border areas should be avoided while the political unrest in neighbouring Haiti continues. Avoid any excursions that are not recommended by tour operators
WEATHER Hot tropical climate; Jun to Nov rainy season with the risk of hurricanes
BANKING 0800–1600 Mon to Fri
EMERGENCY Emergency Services 711
TIME ZONE GMT −4
INTERNATIONAL DIALLING CODE 1 809

ECUADOR

GOVERNMENT Multiparty republic
LANGUAGES Spanish (official), Quechua
CURRENCY US dollar = 100 cents
MEDICAL There is a risk of dengue fever, hepatitis, malaria, typhoid, diptheria and rabies
TRAVEL Street crimes such as muggings and pickpocketing are common in the cities. Visitors should avoid travel to the provinces bordering Colombia due to incidents of kidnapping
WEATHER Jan to Apr warm and rainy on mainland and Galapagos; Jun to Aug cold; Jun to Aug dry in Highlands; Aug to Feb dry in Oriente
BANKING 0900–1330 and 1430–1830 Mon to Fri
EMERGENCY Police 101; Ambulance 131
TIME ZONE GMT –5; Galapagos Islands –6
INTERNATIONAL DIALLING CODE 593

EL SALVADOR

GOVERNMENT Republic
LANGUAGES Spanish (official)
CURRENCY US dollar = 100 cents
MEDICAL Tourists should protect against cholera, hepatitis, malaria, rabies and typhoid
TRAVEL El Salvador is more politically stable than ever, but has high levels of violent crime. Visitors travelling alone should be vigilant at all times
WEATHER Hot subtropical climate; Nov to Apr dry season; May to Oct rainy season with cooler evenings
BANKING 0900–1300 and 1345–1600 Mon to Fri
EMERGENCY All Services 123/121
TIME ZONE GMT –6
INTERNATIONAL DIALLING CODE 503

ETHIOPIA

GOVERNMENT Federation of nine provinces
LANGUAGES Amharic (official), many others
CURRENCY Birr = 100 cents
MEDICAL Water-borne diseases and malaria are prevalent. Medical facilities outside the capital are extremely poor
TRAVEL Most governments advise against travel to the Gambella region and the Eritrean border. There is currently a high risk of terrorism throughout the country
WEATHER Lowlands are hot and humid, it is warm in the hills and cool in the upland areas
BANKING 0800–1200 and 1300–1700 Mon to Thu; 0830–1100 and 1300–1700 Fri
EMERGENCY Not available
TIME ZONE GMT +3
INTERNATIONAL DIALLING CODE 251

EGYPT

GOVERNMENT Republic
LANGUAGES Arabic (official), French, English
CURRENCY Egyptian pound = 100 piastres
MEDICAL There are no specific health risks in Egypt
TRAVEL Due to continuing tensions, visitors should keep in touch with developments in the Middle East and remain vigilant at all times. Particular care should be taken when travelling in Luxor and beyond in the Nile Valley
WEATHER Jun to Aug very hot and dry; Sep to May dry and cooler; spring and autumn months are pleasant; dusty Saharan winds during Apr
BANKING 0830–1400 Sun to Thu
EMERGENCY Unavailable
TIME ZONE GMT +2
INTERNATIONAL DIALLING CODE 20

ESTONIA

GOVERNMENT Multiparty republic
LANGUAGES Estonian (official), Russian
CURRENCY Estonian kroon = 100 senti
MEDICAL There are no specific health risks
TRAVEL Most visits are trouble-free. Despite independence in 1991, much tradition exists in Estonia. Skiing, skating and ice fishing are popular during the winter months
WEATHER Large temperature variations; Apr to May warm and pleasant; Jun to Sep hot.; Dec to Mar very cold with heavy snowfall; rain falls all year round
BANKING 0930–1630 Mon to Fri
EMERGENCY Police 02; Fire 01; Ambulance 03 (dial an extra 0 first if in Tallinn)
TIME ZONE GMT +2
INTERNATIONAL DIALLING CODE 372

FIJI ISLANDS

GOVERNMENT Transitional
LANGUAGES English (official), various Fijian dialects
CURRENCY Fijian dollar = 100 cents
MEDICAL Visitors should protect against dengue fever and should avoid mosquito bites
TRAVEL There has been an increase in petty crime due to the unsettled economic and political situations
WEATHER Tropical climate; Dec to Apr humid, rainy season with a risk of tropical cyclones; May to Oct cooler, dry season
BANKING 0930–1500 Mon to Thu; 0930–1600 Fri
EMERGENCY All Services 000
TIME ZONE GMT +12
INTERNATIONAL DIALLING CODE 679

FINLAND

GOVERNMENT Multiparty republic
LANGUAGES Finnish and Swedish (both official)
CURRENCY Euro = 100 cents
MEDICAL There are no specific health risks, but if mushroom-picking/eating, seek advice on safety
TRAVEL Visits to Finland are generally trouble-free
WEATHER Temperate climate; May to Sep warm with midnight sun; Oct to Mar very cold; Nov to May snow cover in the north; skiing starts in Feb, the coldest month, and continues until Jun in Lapland
BANKING 0915–1615 Mon to Fri
EMERGENCY Police 002; Fire/Ambulance 000; Emergency Services 112; Doctor 008
TIME ZONE GMT +2
INTERNATIONAL DIALLING CODE 358

FRANCE

GOVERNMENT Multiparty republic
LANGUAGES French (official)
CURRENCY Euro = 100 cents
MEDICAL There are no specific health risks
TRAVEL Most visits to France are trouble-free. There have been sporadic bomb attacks on the island of Corsica and care should be exercised
WEATHER Temperate climate in the north; rain falls all year round; Mediterranean climate in the south; mild in the west; May to Sep hot and sunny; Oct to Nov pleasant temperatures
BANKING 0900–1200 and 1400–1600 Mon to Fri. Some banks close on Mondays
EMERGENCY Police 17; Fire 18; Ambulance 15; Emergency Services 112
TIME ZONE GMT +1
INTERNATIONAL DIALLING CODE 33

FRENCH POLYNESIA

GOVERNMENT French overseas territory
LANGUAGES French and Polynesian (both official)
CURRENCY French Pacific franc = 100 cents
MEDICAL Water is untreated and dairy foods are unpasteurized. Vaccinations against polio and typhoid are recommended
TRAVEL Most visits are trouble-free, but visitors should remain vigilant at al times. French Polynesia is made up of 130 islands, Tahiti being the most popular
WEATHER Tropical but moderate climate with occasional cyclonic storms in Jan. Cool and dry Mar to Nov
BANKING 0745–1530 Mon to Fri
EMERGENCY Dial operator
TIME ZONE GMT –9 to GMT –10
INTERNATIONAL DIALLING CODE 689

GAMBIA, THE

GOVERNMENT Military regime
LANGUAGES English (official), Mandinka, Wolof
CURRENCY Dalasi = 100 butut
MEDICAL Water-borne diseases and malaria are common. Other health risks include yellow fever, hepatitis, rabies and typhoid
TRAVEL Exercise caution when walking at night. Do not travel with valuables and dress modestly
WEATHER Nov to Mar dry and cool with winds from the Sahara; Jun to Oct rainy season; inland the cool season is shorter and temperatures are hot from Mar to Jun
BANKING 0800–1330 Mon to Thu; 0800–1100 Fri
EMERGENCY Consult foreign embassy
TIME ZONE GMT
INTERNATIONAL DIALLING CODE 220

GEORGIA

GOVERNMENT Multiparty republic
LANGUAGES Georgian (official), Russian
CURRENCY Lari = 100 tetri
MEDICAL Diptheria and rabies cases have been reported. Tap water is unsafe to drink. Anthrax has been reported in the east. Medical care is poor and visitors should carry their own syringes
TRAVEL The regions of Abkhazia and South Ossetia should be avoided. Do not attempt access across the land borders with Russia
WEATHER Jul to Sep hot; Dec to Mar mild, especially in the south-west; low temperatures in alpine areas; rainfall heavy in south-west
BANKING 0930–1730 Mon to Fri
EMERGENCY Police 02; Fire 01; Ambulance 03
TIME ZONE GMT +4
INTERNATIONAL DIALLING CODE 995

GERMANY

GOVERNMENT Federal multiparty republic
LANGUAGES German (official)
CURRENCY Euro = 100 cents
MEDICAL There are no specific health risks, but medical care is expensive
TRAVEL Visits to Germany are generally trouble-free. Travellers are able to enjoy a wealth of arts and culture, plus stunning natural scenery
WEATHER Very variable, temperate climate throughout the country; May to Oct warm; Nov to Apr cold; rain falls all year round
BANKING 0830–1300 and 1400/30–1600 Mon to Fri
EMERGENCY Police 110; Fire 112; Emergency Services 112
TIME ZONE GMT +1
INTERNATIONAL DIALLING CODE 49

GIBRALTAR

GOVERNMENT UK overseas territory
LANGUAGES English and Spanish
CURRENCY Gibraltar pound = 100 pence
MEDICAL There are no specific health risks in Gibraltar
TRAVEL Most visits to Gibraltar are trouble-free. The country was recognized as a British possession in 1713, and despite Spanish claims, its population has consistently voted to retain its contacts with Britain
WEATHER Warm all year round; Jun to Sep hot and can be humid; Nov to Mar mild
BANKING 0900–1530 and 1630–1800 Mon to Fri
EMERGENCY All Services 999
TIME ZONE GMT +1
INTERNATIONAL DIALLING CODE 350

GREECE

GOVERNMENT Multiparty republic
LANGUAGES Greek (official)
CURRENCY Euro = 100 cents
MEDICAL There is a risk of sunburn
TRAVEL Visitors should exercise normal precautions regarding safety and security. Tourists are strongly advised not to hire motorcycles, scooters or mopeds
WEATHER Mediterranean climate; Aug to Nov pleasant temperatures; Nov to Mar heavy rainfall; Apr to Jun hot
BANKING 0800–1400 Mon to Fri
EMERGENCY Police 100; Fire 199; Ambulance 166; Emergency Services 112
TIME ZONE GMT +2
INTERNATIONAL DIALLING CODE 30 + 1 for Athens; 31 Thessaloniki; 81 Heraklion; 661 Corfu

GRENADA

GOVERNMENT Constitutional monarchy
LANGUAGES English (official)
CURRENCY East Caribbean dollar = 100 cents
MEDICAL Tourists should protect against polio and typhoid. Anti-mosquito repellants are recommended
TRAVEL Trips are mostly trouble-free; however, tourists should remain vigilant at all times
WEATHER Tropical climate, rainy season is Jun to Sep when tropical storms and hurricanes occur. Jan to May is drier and less humid
BANKING 0800–1400 Mon to Thu; 0800–1300 and 1400–1700 Fri
EMERGENCY Police 112; Ambulance 434; Emergency services 911
TIME ZONE GMT –4
INTERNATIONAL DIALLING CODE 1 473

GUADELOUPE

GOVERNMENT French overseas territory
LANGUAGES French (official), Creole
CURRENCY Euro = 100 cents
MEDICAL Polio and typhoid vaccinations are recommended. Water is untreated and unsafe to drink
TRAVEL Visits to Guadeloupe are generally trouble-free, and the French culture and influence is clearly evident. Soufriere de Guadeloupe is an active volcano
WEATHER Warm, humid weather all year round. Rainy season from Jun to Oct, when there is a risk of hurricanes
BANKING 0800–1600 Mon to Fri
EMERGENCY Police 17; Fire and Ambulance 18
TIME ZONE GMT –4
INTERNATIONAL DIALLING CODE 590

HONG KONG

GOVERNMENT Special administrative region of China
LANGUAGES Chinese and English; Cantonese is most widely spoken
CURRENCY Hong Kong dollar = 100 cents
MEDICAL Visitors should protect against polio and typhoid. Slight risk of malaria in rural areas
TRAVEL Most visits are trouble-free
WEATHER Nov to Dec warm with pleasant breeze; Jan to Feb much cooler; Mar to Apr warmer; May to Sep very humid and uncomfortable, with a risk of cyclones in Sep
BANKING 0900–1630 Mon to Fri; 0900–1330 Sat
EMERGENCY All Services 999
TIME ZONE GMT +8
INTERNATIONAL DIALLING CODE 852

HUNGARY

GOVERNMENT Multiparty republic
LANGUAGES Hungarian (official)
CURRENCY Forint = 100 fillér
MEDICAL There are no specific health risks in Hungary
TRAVEL Street theft is common in tourist areas, particularly in Budapest. It is illegal to drive having consumed alcohol. Passports to be carried at all times. Do not take photographs of anything connected with the military
WEATHER Jun to Aug very warm and sunny; spring and autumn mild and pleasant; Jan to March very cold
BANKING 0900–1400 Mon to Fri
EMERGENCY Police 107; Fire/Ambulance 104
TIME ZONE GMT +1
INTERNATIONAL DIALLING CODE 36

ICELAND

GOVERNMENT Multiparty republic
LANGUAGES Icelandic (official)
CURRENCY Icelandic króna = 100 aurar
MEDICAL There is a risk of hypothermia if trekking during the winter months
TRAVEL Visitors planning to travel off-road do so at their own risk and must contact the local authorities (Vegagerdin) prior to departure. Interior roads are closed in winter
WEATHER Weather is highly changeable all year round; May to Aug is mild with nearly 24 hours of daylight in Reykjavik; Sep to Apr is cold
BANKING 0915–1600 Mon to Fri
EMERGENCY Unavailable
TIME ZONE GMT
INTERNATIONAL DIALLING CODE 354

INDIA

GOVERNMENT Multiparty federal republic
LANGUAGES Hindi, English, Telugu, Bengali, Marathi, Tamil, Urdu, Gujarati, Malayalam, Kannada, Oriya, Punjabi, Assamese, Kashmiri, Sindhi and Sanskrit (all official)
CURRENCY Indian rupee = 100 paisa
MEDICAL There is a risk of malaria, AIDS and intestinal problems. Precautions should be taken
TRAVEL Visitors are advised to avoid the Pakistan border areas, as well as Jammu and Kashmir
WEATHER Hot tropical climate that varies from region to region; Apr to Sep very hot with monsoon rains
BANKING 1000–1400 Mon to Fri
EMERGENCY Unavailable
TIME ZONE GMT +5.30
INTERNATIONAL DIALLING CODE 91

INDONESIA

GOVERNMENT Multiparty republic
LANGUAGES Bahasa Indonesian (official)
CURRENCY Indonesian rupiah = 100 sen
MEDICAL There is a risk of polio, typhoid, hepatitis B, yellow fever and TB. Unpasteurized dairy produce should be avoided
TRAVEL Non-essential travel to Indonesia is not recommended due to the risk of terrorism against Western interests
WEATHER Tropical, varying climate; May to Oct dry weather from eastern monsoon; Nov to Apr rains from western monsoon. In northern Sumatra this pattern is reversed
BANKING 0800–1500 Mon to Fri
EMERGENCY Police 110; Ambulance 118
TIME ZONE West GMT +7; Central +8; East +9
INTERNATIONAL DIALLING CODE 62

IRAN

GOVERNMENT Islamic republic
LANGUAGES Persian, Turkic, Kurdish
CURRENCY Iranian rial = 100 dinars
MEDICAL There is a risk of polio, typhoid, malaria and cholera
TRAVEL Visitors should monitor media reports before travelling. Any increase in regional tension will affect travel advice. Visitors should exercise caution and avoid carrying large sums of money since robbery and bag-snatching are common
WEATHER Dec to Mar very cold; Apr to Jun and Sep to Nov warm; Jun to Sep extremely hot
BANKING 0900–1600 Sat to Wed; 0900–1200 Thu. Closed on Fri
EMERGENCY Unavailable
TIME ZONE GMT +3.30
INTERNATIONAL DIALLING CODE 98

IRELAND

GOVERNMENT Multiparty republic
LANGUAGES Irish (Gaelic) and English (both official)
CURRENCY Euro = 100 cents
MEDICAL There are no specific health risks
TRAVEL The Irish usually have close community bonds. Visitors should find people very friendly. Strong economic growth continues
WEATHER Rain falls all year round; Jul to Sep warm; Nov to Mar wet and cold; spring and autumn mild
BANKING 1000–1600 Mon to Fri. Banks may open later in Dublin
EMERGENCY Emergency Services 112; All Services 999
TIME ZONE GMT
INTERNATIONAL DIALLING CODE 353

ISRAEL

GOVERNMENT Multiparty republic
LANGUAGES Hebrew and Arabic (both official)
CURRENCY New Israeli shekel = 100 agorat
MEDICAL There are no specific health risks
TRAVEL Most governments currently strongly advise against travel to the West Bank, Gaza and Jerusalem, or near their border areas with Israel. Visitors should keep car doors locked when travelling and avoid carrying large sums of cash
WEATHER Jul to Sep hot and windy; Dec to Mar cool in the north; spring and autumn are warm and pleasant
BANKING 0830–1230 and 1600–1730 Mon, Tue and Thu; 0830–1230 Wed; 0830–1200 Fri
EMERGENCY Police/Fire 100; Ambulance 101
TIME ZONE GMT +2
INTERNATIONAL DIALLING CODE 972

ITALY

GOVERNMENT Multiparty republic
LANGUAGES Italian (official), German, French, Slovene
CURRENCY Euro = 100 cents
MEDICAL There are no specific health risks
TRAVEL Crime is rare, but visitors in tourist areas and city centres should remain vigilant after dark
WEATHER Apr to May and Oct to Nov warm and pleasant; Jun to Sep hot; Dec to Mar colder temperatures with heavy snow in mountain areas; warmer in the south
BANKING Generally 0830–1330 and 1530–1930 Mon to Fri
EMERGENCY Police 112; Fire 115; Ambulance 113; Emergency Services 112
TIME ZONE GMT +1
INTERNATIONAL DIALLING CODE 39

JAMAICA

GOVERNMENT Constitutional monarchy
LANGUAGES English (official), patois English
CURRENCY Jamaican dollar = 100 cents
MEDICAL There are no specific health risks
TRAVEL Most visits are trouble-free, but violent crime does exist, mainly in Kingston. Visitors should avoid walking alone in isolated areas, and be particularly alert after dark and using public transport
WEATHER Tropical climate; temperatures remain high all year round; May to Oct rainy season, but showers can occur at any time
BANKING 0900–1400 Mon to Thu; 0900–1500 Fri
EMERGENCY Police 119; Fire/Ambulance 110
TIME ZONE GMT –5
INTERNATIONAL DIALLING CODE 1 876

JAPAN

GOVERNMENT Constitutional monarchy
LANGUAGES Japanese (official)
CURRENCY Yen = 100 sen
MEDICAL Health and hygiene standards are high and visitors are not required to have vaccinations
TRAVEL Most visits remain trouble-free. There is a high risk of earthquakes and typhoons which often hit the country
WEATHER Sep to Nov typhoons and rain; Jun to Sep warm/very hot with rain in Jun; Mar to May pleasant; Dec to Feb cold winds and snow in western areas, but dry and clear on Pacific coast
BANKING 0900–1500 Mon to Fri
EMERGENCY Tokyo English Life Line 3403 7106; Japan Helpline 0120 461 997
TIME ZONE GMT +9
INTERNATIONAL DIALLING CODE 81

JORDAN

GOVERNMENT Constitutional monarchy
LANGUAGES Arabic (official)
CURRENCY Jordan dinar = 1,000 fils
MEDICAL There are no specific health risks, but visitors should consider vaccination against hepatitis, polio, tetanus, typhoid and diptheria
TRAVEL Before travelling, visitors should monitor media reports for any increase in regional tension. Crime is low, but visitors should dress modestly and respect local customs
WEATHER Jun to Sep hot and dry with cool evenings; Nov to Mar cooler with rainfall
BANKING 0830–1230 and 1530–1730 Sat to Thu; 0830–1000 during Ramadan
EMERGENCY Police 192; Fire/Ambulance 193
TIME ZONE GMT +2
INTERNATIONAL DIALLING CODE 962

KENYA

GOVERNMENT Multiparty republic
LANGUAGES Kiswahili and English (both official)
CURRENCY Kenyan shilling = 100 cents
MEDICAL Malaria is endemic and AIDS is widespread. Water is unsafe to drink
TRAVEL Be alert at all times, particularly in Nairobi and Mombasa. Avoid travelling after dark and in isolated areas
WEATHER Complex and changeable; Jan to Feb hot and dry; Mar to May hot and wet; Jun to Oct warm and dry; Nov to Dec warm and wet; Cooler with rain at any time at higher altitudes
BANKING 0900–1500 Mon to Fri; 0900–1100 on first and last Sat of each month
EMERGENCY All Services 336886/501280
TIME ZONE GMT +3
INTERNATIONAL DIALLING CODE 254

KOREA, SOUTH

GOVERNMENT Multiparty republic
LANGUAGES Korean (official)
CURRENCY South Korean won = 100 chon
MEDICAL There are no specific health risks, but medical and dental treatment can be expensive
TRAVEL Travel to South Korea is generally trouble-free, but some form of identification should be carried at all times
WEATHER Jul to Aug hot with heavy rainfall and a chance of typhoons; Sep to Nov and Apr to May mild and dry; Dec to Mar cold but dry, with good skiing
BANKING 0930–1630 Mon to Fri; 0930–1330 Sat
EMERGENCY Unavailable
TIME ZONE GMT +9
INTERNATIONAL DIALLING CODE 82

KUWAIT

GOVERNMENT Constitutional monarchy
LANGUAGES Arabic (official), English
CURRENCY Kuwaiti dinar = 1,000 fils
MEDICAL Vaccinations against polio, typhoid and cholera are recommended
TRAVEL Visitors should monitor media reports before travelling. Any increase in regional tension will affect travel advice. There is a danger from unexploded bombs and land mines on beaches and in rural areas. All Islamic laws should be respected. Photography permits are required
WEATHER Apr to Oct hot, humid with little rain; Nov to Mar cool and dry
BANKING 0800–1200 Sun to Thu
EMERGENCY Unavailable
TIME ZONE GMT +3
INTERNATIONAL DIALLING CODE 965

LATVIA

GOVERNMENT Multiparty republic
LANGUAGES Latvian (official), Lithuanian, Russian
CURRENCY Latvian lat = 10 santimi
MEDICAL Visitors should protect themselves against tick-borne encephalitis, particularly if visiting forested areas
TRAVEL Most visits are trouble-free, but tourists should exercise caution since muggings and pickpocketing have increased recently. Use guarded car parks and keep valuables hidden
WEATHER Temperate climate; Apr to Sep warm and clear; Nov to Mar extremely cold; spring and autumn mild
BANKING 1000–1800 Mon to Fri
EMERGENCY Police 02; Fire 01; Ambulance 03
TIME ZONE GMT +2
INTERNATIONAL DIALLING CODE 371

LEBANON

GOVERNMENT Multiparty republic
LANGUAGES Arabic (official), French, English
CURRENCY Lebanese pound = 100 piastres
MEDICAL Protection against polio and typhoid is recommended
TRAVEL Visitors should remain alert to international developments in the Middle East. Most governments currently advise against travel to areas within the Israeli Occupied Zone
WEATHER Jun to Sep hot and dry, but humid along the coast; Dec to May high rainfall with snow in mountains; spring and autumn pleasant
BANKING 0830–1200 Mon to Sat
EMERGENCY Police 386 440 425; Fire 310 105; Ambulance 386 675
TIME ZONE GMT +2
INTERNATIONAL DIALLING CODE 961

LIBYA

GOVERNMENT Single-party socialist state
LANGUAGES Arabic (official), Berber
CURRENCY Libyan dinar = 1,000 dirhams
MEDICAL There is a slight risk of malaria, cholera and hepatitis
TRAVEL Most visits to Libya are trouble-free, but any increase in regional tension will affect travel advice
WEATHER Warm all year round; Nov to Mar occasional rainfall; Apr to Sep can be very hot; May to Jun severe sandstorms from the south
BANKING 0800–1200 Sat to Wed (during winter); 0800–1200 Sat to Thu; 1600–1700 Sat and Wed (during summer)
EMERGENCY Unavailable
TIME ZONE GMT +1
INTERNATIONAL DIALLING CODE 218

LIECHTENSTEIN

GOVERNMENT Hereditary constitutional monarchy
LANGUAGES German (official)
CURRENCY Swiss franc = 100 centimes
MEDICAL There is a risk of altitude sickness, sunburn and hypothermia in the Alps
TRAVEL Most visits to Liechtenstein are trouble-free. The country is culturally and economically extremely similar to Switzerland. Winter sports are very popular in the Alps from Nov to Apr
WEATHER Temperate climate; Nov to Apr cool or cold; Jun to Sep warm with high rainfall
BANKING 0800–1630 Mon to Fri
EMERGENCY Police 117; Ambulance 144
TIME ZONE GMT +1
INTERNATIONAL DIALLING CODE 41 75

LITHUANIA

GOVERNMENT Multiparty republic
LANGUAGES Lithuanian (official), Russian, Polish
CURRENCY Litas = 100 centai
MEDICAL Travellers to forested areas should seek advice about protection against rabies and tick-borne encephalitis
TRAVEL There is a risk of pickpocketing, mugging and bag-snatching, particularly on public transport. Be alert at all times and avoid quiet areas after dark
WEATHER Temperate climate; May to Sep warm; Oct to Nov mild; Nov to Mar can be very cold with snowfall common
BANKING 0900–1700 Mon to Fri
EMERGENCY Police 02; Fire 01; Ambulance 03
TIME ZONE GMT +2
INTERNATIONAL DIALLING CODE 370

LUXEMBOURG

GOVERNMENT Constitutional monarchy (Grand Duchy)
LANGUAGES Luxembourgish (official), French, German
CURRENCY Euro = 100 cents
MEDICAL There are no specific health risks
TRAVEL Most travel to Luxembourg is trouble-free. The country is prosperous with a very high quality of life. Visitors may find it expensive compared to other European countries
WEATHER May to Sep warm with rainfall; Oct to Apr cold with snow
BANKING Varies greatly but generally 0900–1200 and 1330–1630 Mon to Fri
EMERGENCY Police 113; Fire/Ambulance 112
TIME ZONE GMT +1
INTERNATIONAL DIALLING CODE 352

MADAGASCAR

GOVERNMENT Republic
LANGUAGES Malagasy and French (both official)
CURRENCY Malagasy franc = 100 centimes
MEDICAL There is a risk of polio, typhoid, bilharzia, cholera, rabies and hepatitis. Precautions should be taken. Water is unsafe to drink and unpasteurized dairy products should be avoided
TRAVEL Locals are very welcoming and have a relaxed attitude towards time. Local culture should be respected
WEATHER Generally hot and subtropical with varying temperatures. Inland is more temperate, and the south is dry and arid
BANKING 0800–1300 Mon to Fri
EMERGENCY Unavailable
TIME ZONE GMT +3
INTERNATIONAL DIALLING CODE 261

MALAWI

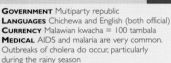

GOVERNMENT Multiparty republic
LANGUAGES Chichewa and English (both official)
CURRENCY Malawian kwacha = 100 tambala
MEDICAL AIDS and malaria are very common. Outbreaks of cholera do occur, particularly during the rainy season
TRAVEL Be alert at all times, particularly after dark. Avoid travel out of town at night since the condition of roads is poor. Cases of muggings and bag-snatching are increasing. Do not resist demands since attacks can be very violent
WEATHER Apr to Oct hot and dry; May to Jul cool and cold at night; Nov to Apr rainy season
BANKING 0800–1300 Mon to Fri
EMERGENCY Unavailable
TIME ZONE GMT +2
INTERNATIONAL DIALLING CODE 265

MALAYSIA

GOVERNMENT Federal constitutional monarchy
LANGUAGES Malay (official), Chinese, English
CURRENCY Ringgit (Malaysian dollar) = 100 cents
MEDICAL No vaccinations required, but visitors should be up-to-date with typhoid, tetanus and hepatitis B. Also check malarial status of region
TRAVEL The penalty for all drug offences is harsh. There has been a recent increase in street crime in Kuala Lumpur
WEATHER Nov to Feb heavy rains in eastern areas; Apr to May and Oct thunderstorms in western areas; showers can occur all year round
BANKING 1000–1500 Mon to Fri
EMERGENCY All Services 999
TIME ZONE GMT +8
INTERNATIONAL DIALLING CODE 60

MALDIVES

GOVERNMENT Republic
LANGUAGES Maldivian Dhivehi, English
CURRENCY Rufiyaa = 100 laari
MEDICAL There is a high risk of sunburn all year round
TRAVEL Travel to the Maldives is generally trouble-free, but visitors should be aware that there are very harsh penalties for drug offences. Visitors should respect the Islamic religion and act accordingly
WEATHER Hot, tropical climate; May to Oct warm, but humid and wet from the south-west monsoon; Nov to Apr hot and dry
EMERGENCY Police 119; Fire 118; Ambulance 102
TIME ZONE GMT +5
INTERNATIONAL DIALLING CODE 960

MALTA

GOVERNMENT Multiparty republic
LANGUAGES Maltese and English (both official)
CURRENCY Maltese lira = 100 cents
MEDICAL There are no specific health risks
TRAVEL Most visits are trouble-free and crime is rare. However, bag-snatching and pickpocketing can occur. Caution should be exercised when travelling by car since many roads are poorly maintained. Visitors should dress modestly when visiting churches
WEATHER Jul to Sep hot with cool breezes; Feb to Jun mild; occasional sudden bursts of rain
BANKING 0800–1200 Mon to Thu; 0800–1200 and 1430–1600 Fri; 0800–1130 Sat
EMERGENCY Police 191; Ambulance 196
TIME ZONE GMT +1
INTERNATIONAL DIALLING CODE 356

MARTINIQUE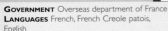

GOVERNMENT Overseas department of France
LANGUAGES French, French Creole patois, English
CURRENCY Euro = 100 cents
MEDICAL There is a risk of sunburn and intestinal parasites. Bilharzia (schistosomiasis) may be present in fresh water
TRAVEL Travel to Martinique is generally trouble-free
WEATHER Warm all year round; Sep can be very humid; Feb to May cooler and dry; Oct to Dec higher rainfall; upland areas are cooler than lowlands
BANKING 0800–1600 Mon to Fri
EMERGENCY Police 17; Fire/Ambulance 18
TIME ZONE GMT −4
INTERNATIONAL DIALLING CODE 596

MAURITIUS

GOVERNMENT Multiparty democracy
LANGUAGES French (official), Creole, English
CURRENCY Mauritian rupee = 100 cents
MEDICAL Malaria exists in the northern rural areas and there is a risk of bilharzia
TRAVEL Visitors should always respect local customs and traditions. Most visits are trouble-free, crime levels are low, but sensible precautions should be taken
WEATHER The weather is warm with a year-round sea breeze. Jan to May are the best months to visit. Tropical storms are likely to occur from Dec to Mar
BANKING 0930–1430 Mon to Fri; 0930–1130 Sat
EMERGENCY Unavailable
TIME ZONE GMT +4
INTERNATIONAL DIALLING CODE 230

MEXICO

GOVERNMENT Federal republic
LANGUAGES Spanish (official)
CURRENCY Mexican peso = 100 centavos
MEDICAL Visitors should protect themselves against polio, tetanus, typhoid and hepatitis A
TRAVEL Most visits are trouble-free, but visitors should remain aware of incidents of armed robbery in urban areas, particularly Mexico City, and should dress down accordingly
WEATHER May to Oct humid, rainy season; Oct to May warm and dry; lowland areas are warmer and upland areas are cooler all year round
BANKING 0900–1330 Mon to Fri
EMERGENCY All Services 08
TIME ZONE Spans three time zones from GMT −6 to −8
INTERNATIONAL DIALLING CODE 52

MONACO

GOVERNMENT Constitutional monarchy
LANGUAGES French, English, Italian, Monegasque
CURRENCY Euro = 100 cents
MEDICAL There are no specific health risks, but visitors should protect against hepatitis
TRAVEL Most visits to Monaco are trouble-free. This is the country where Europe's wealthiest are to be found living a rich, glamorous lifestyle
WEATHER Mild climate throughout the country; Jun to Aug can be very hot; Jan to Feb cool with low rainfall; Apr to May and Sep to Oct warm and dry
BANKING 0900–1200 and 1400–1630 Mon to Fri
EMERGENCY Police 17; Fire/Ambulance 18
TIME ZONE GMT +1
INTERNATIONAL DIALLING CODE 377

MONGOLIA

GOVERNMENT Multiparty republic
LANGUAGES Khalkha Mongolian (official), Turkic, Russian
CURRENCY Tugrik = 100 möngös
MEDICAL Visitors should protect against brucellosis, cholera and meningitis
TRAVEL Petty street crime is increasing. Visitors should avoid travelling alone after dark. In rural areas always carry a GPS and satellite phone
WEATHER May to Oct dry and mild; Nov to Apr bitterly cold. Note that between Oct and May sudden snowstorms can block roads and bring transport systems to a standstill
BANKING 1000–1500 Mon to Fri
EMERGENCY Unavailable
TIME ZONE GMT +9
INTERNATIONAL DIALLING CODE 976

MOROCCO

GOVERNMENT Constitutional monarchy
LANGUAGES Arabic (official), Berber, French
CURRENCY Moroccan dirham = 100 centimes
MEDICAL There are no specific health risks, but malaria is present in northern coastal areas
TRAVEL Visits are usually trouble-free, but visitors should only use authorized guides. Theft is increasing in major cities and valuables should be hidden at all times
WEATHER Winter cool and wet in north; Oct to Apr warm to hot in lowlands; Dec to Mar very cold in upland areas
BANKING 0830–1130 and 1430–1700 Mon to Fri (winter); 0800–1530 Mon to Fri (summer)
EMERGENCY Police 19; Fire/Ambulance 15
TIME ZONE GMT
INTERNATIONAL DIALLING CODE 212

NAMIBIA

GOVERNMENT Multiparty republic
LANGUAGES English (official), Afrikaans, German
CURRENCY Namibian dollar = 100 cents
MEDICAL Malaria and bilharzia are endemic in the north and east respectively
TRAVEL Most visits are trouble-free. The Angola border should be avoided because of land mines left undetected after the civil war. Visitors should seek advice before travelling to townships
WEATHER Oct to Apr rain inland; May to Oct hot and dry; the coast is cool and relatively free of rain all year round
BANKING 0900–1530 Mon to Fri
EMERGENCY Police 1011; Fire 2032270; Ambulance 2032276
TIME ZONE GMT +2
INTERNATIONAL DIALLING CODE 264

NEPAL

GOVERNMENT Constitutional monarchy
LANGUAGES Nepali (official), local languages
CURRENCY Nepalese rupee = 100 paisa
MEDICAL There is a risk of altitude sickness, hepatitis A, malaria (in lowland areas) and typhoid
TRAVEL There is now a cease-fire between the government and the Communist party. Trekkers should not venture out without a professional guide and should obtain up-to-date advice regarding the safety of their chosen route
WEATHER Oct to Nov clear and dry, and not too cold at higher altitudes; Dec to Jan cool; Feb to Apr warm; Jun to Sep monsoon season
BANKING 1000–1450 Sun to Thu; 1000–1230 Fri
EMERGENCY Unavailable
TIME ZONE GMT +5.45
INTERNATIONAL DIALLING CODE 977

NETHERLANDS

GOVERNMENT Constitutional monarchy
LANGUAGES Dutch (official), Frisian
CURRENCY Euro = 100 cents
MEDICAL There are no specific health risks in the Netherlands
TRAVEL Most visits to the Netherlands are trouble-free. Attitudes here are very liberal. Locals are extremely welcoming and speak very good English
WEATHER Jun to Sep usually warm but changeable; Nov to Mar can be bitterly cold with some snow; rain falls all year round; Apr is best for daffodils and May is best for tulips
BANKING 0900–1600 Mon to Fri
EMERGENCY Emergency Services 112
TIME ZONE GMT +1
INTERNATIONAL DIALLING CODE 31

NETHERLANDS ANTILLES

GOVERNMENT Parliamentary democracy
LANGUAGES Dutch (official), French, English, Spanish, many others
CURRENCY Netherlands Antillean gilder = 100 cents
MEDICAL Polio and typhoid vaccinations are recommended. Water is considered drinkable and normal precautions should be taken with food
TRAVEL Most visits to the Netherlands Antilles are trouble-free
WEATHER Hot and tropical climate with cool sea breezes
BANKING 0830–1530 Mon to Fri
EMERGENCY Police 599/5/22222; Ambulance 599/5/22111
TIME ZONE GMT –4
INTERNATIONAL DIALLING CODE 599

NEW ZEALAND

GOVERNMENT Constitutional monarchy
LANGUAGES English and Maori (both official)
CURRENCY New Zealand dollar = 100 cents
MEDICAL There are no specific health risks
TRAVEL Most visits are trouble-free, but visitors should take precautions against street crime in urban areas after dark. Travel within the country is relatively cheap and efficient, and accommodation is varied and affordable
WEATHER Subtropical climate in North Island; no extremes of heat or cold, but Nov to Apr warmer; temperate in South Island with cool temperatures; rainfall occurs all year round
BANKING 0900–1630 Mon to Fri
EMERGENCY All Services 111
TIME ZONE GMT +12
INTERNATIONAL DIALLING CODE 64

NIGERIA

GOVERNMENT Federal multiparty republic
LANGUAGES English (official), Hausa, Yoruba, Ibo
CURRENCY Naira = 100 kobo
MEDICAL Visitors must have a yellow fever vaccination and protect against cerebral malaria
TRAVEL Incidences of kidnapping are increasing. Violent street crime, armed robberies and car theft are common throughout the country. Visitors should avoid using public transport and travelling after dark outside tourist areas
WEATHER Mar to Nov hot, humid and wet; Apr to Sep wet; Dec to Mar dusty winds, but cooler
BANKING 0800–1500 Mon; 0800–1330 Tue to Fri
EMERGENCY Unavailable
TIME ZONE GMT +1
INTERNATIONAL DIALLING CODE 234

NORWAY

GOVERNMENT Constitutional monarchy
LANGUAGES Norwegian (official)
CURRENCY Norwegian krone = 100 ore
MEDICAL There are no specific health risks in Norway
TRAVEL Most visits to Norway remain trouble-free. The country offers beautiful mountain scenery and year-round skiing
WEATHER May to Sep sunny and warm with long daylight hours; Dec to Mar very cold and dark; midnight sun occurs from 13 May to 29 Jul, and from 28 May to 14 Jul in the Lofoten Islands
BANKING 0900–1700 Mon to Thu; 0900–1530 Fri
EMERGENCY Police (Oslo) 002; Ambulance 003
TIME ZONE GMT +1
INTERNATIONAL DIALLING CODE 47

OMAN

GOVERNMENT Monarchy with consultative council
LANGUAGES Arabic (official), Baluchi, English
CURRENCY Omani rial = 100 baizas
MEDICAL Visitors should protect against malaria
TRAVEL Most visits to Oman are trouble-free, but visitors should remain informed of developments in the Middle East. There are harsh penalties, including the death penalty, for drug offences. Driving conditions are hazardous
WEATHER Jun to Sep very hot; Oct to Mar pleasant; the rest of the year is cooler
BANKING 0800–1200 Sat to Wed; 0800–1130 Thu
EMERGENCY All Services 999
TIME ZONE GMT +4
INTERNATIONAL DIALLING CODE 698

PAKISTAN

GOVERNMENT Military regime
LANGUAGES Urdu (official), many others
CURRENCY Pakistan rupee = 100 paisa
MEDICAL Visitors should protect against dengue fever, hepatitis A and malaria. There is also a risk of encephalitis in rural regions
TRAVEL Due to the threat from terrorism, most Western governments advise against all travel to Pakistan, except for their nationals of Pakistan origin
WEATHER Nov to Apr warm; Apr to Jul hot; Jul to Sep monsoon with high rainfall in upland areas
BANKING 0900–1300 and 1500–2000 Sun to Thu; closed on Fri. Some banks open on Sat
EMERGENCY Unavailable
TIME ZONE GMT +5
INTERNATIONAL DIALLING CODE 92

PARAGUAY

GOVERNMENT Multiparty republic
LANGUAGES Spanish and Guaraní (both official)
CURRENCY Guaraní = 100 céntimos
MEDICAL There is a risk of cholera, hepatitis, hookworm, typhoid, malaria and tuberculosis
TRAVEL Most visits to Paraguay are trouble-free, but there is economic recession and some political instability. Attractions include several national parks, including the Chaco – South America's great wilderness
WEATHER Subtropical climate; Dec to Mar is the hottest and wettest season, but rain falls all year round
BANKING 0845–1215 Mon to Fri
EMERGENCY All Services 00
TIME ZONE GMT +5
INTERNATIONAL DIALLING CODE 595

PERU

GOVERNMENT Transitional republic
LANGUAGES Spanish and Quechua (both official), Aymara
CURRENCY New sol = 100 centavos
MEDICAL Visitors should protect against altitude sickness, cholera, typhoid, hepatitis and malaria
TRAVEL Tourist areas are generally safe, but visitors should exercise caution, particularly in Lima and Cuzco, where crime has become a serious problem for foreign visitors
WEATHER Oct to Apr hot and dry in coastal areas, and much rainfall in highlands; May to Sep is dry and the best time to visit the highlands
BANKING 0930–1600 Mon to Fri
EMERGENCY All Services 011/5114
TIME ZONE GMT –5
INTERNATIONAL DIALLING CODE 51

PHILIPPINES

GOVERNMENT Multiparty republic
LANGUAGES Filipino (Tagalog) and English (both official), Spanish, many others
CURRENCY Philippine peso = 100 centavos
MEDICAL Visitors should protect against cholera, malaria, rabies and hepatitis
TRAVEL Visitors should check developments before travelling. Bomb explosions and kidnapping by organized gangs or terrorists have occurred in Manila and Mindanao
WEATHER Tropical climate with sea breeze; Jun to Sep wet; Oct to Feb cool and dry; Mar to May hot and dry; Jun to Sep typhoons occur
BANKING 0900–1600 Mon to Fri
EMERGENCY Unavailable
TIME ZONE GMT +8
INTERNATIONAL DIALLING CODE 63

POLAND

GOVERNMENT Multiparty republic
LANGUAGES Polish (official)
CURRENCY Zloty = 100 groszy
MEDICAL Medical care is generally poor, particularly in rural regions
TRAVEL Most visits to Poland are trouble-free, but there is a serious risk of robbery when using public transport. Locals are very hospitable and welcoming
WEATHER Temperate climate; May to Sep warm; Nov to Mar cold and dark; spring and autumn are warm and pleasant; rain falls all year round
BANKING 0800–1800 Mon to Fri
EMERGENCY Police 997; Ambulance 999
TIME ZONE GMT +1
INTERNATIONAL DIALLING CODE 48

PORTUGAL

GOVERNMENT Multiparty republic
LANGUAGES Portuguese (official)
CURRENCY Euro = 100 cents
MEDICAL Sunburn is a risk during summer
TRAVEL Most visits are trouble-free. Children under 18 years travelling to Portugal should be accompanied by parents/guardians, or someone in the country should be authorized to have responsibility for them
WEATHER Apr to Oct hot and sunny; Nov to Mar wetter, particularly in the north; summers are hotter and winters are longer in the north
BANKING 0830–1500 Mon to Fri
EMERGENCY Emergency Services 112; All Services 115
TIME ZONE GMT
INTERNATIONAL DIALLING CODE 351

PUERTO RICO

GOVERNMENT Commonwealth of the United States
LANGUAGES Spanish and English (both official)
CURRENCY US dollar = 100 cents
MEDICAL There is a risk of sunburn and a slight risk of hepatitis and bilharzia
TRAVEL Most visits to Puerto Rico are trouble-free
WEATHER Tropical climate with little variation in temperature all year round; May to Nov hurricane season; cooler in upland regions
BANKING 0900–1430 Mon to Thu; 0900–1430 and 1530–1700 Fri
EMERGENCY Police 787 343 2020; Fire 787 343 2330; All Services 911
TIME ZONE GMT –4
INTERNATIONAL DIALLING CODE 1 787

QATAR

GOVERNMENT Constitutional absolute monarchy
LANGUAGES Arabic (official), English,
CURRENCY Qatari riyal = 100 dirhams
MEDICAL There are no specific health risks
TRAVEL Visitors should keep informed of international developments before travelling. It is prohibited to bring drugs, alcohol, religious material or pork products into the country; videos may be censored. Visitors should dress modestly and respect local customs
WEATHER Jun to Sep very hot and dry; Apr to May and Dec to Feb frequent sandstorms; Nov and Feb to Mar warm with little wind
BANKING 0730–1130 Sat to Thu
EMERGENCY All Services 999
TIME ZONE GMT +3
INTERNATIONAL DIALLING CODE 974

RÉUNION

GOVERNMENT Overseas department of France
LANGUAGES French (official), Creole
CURRENCY Euro = 100 cents
MEDICAL Precautions should be taken against typhoid and rabies. Water is unsafe to drink and dairy products should be avoided as they are unpasteurized
TRAVEL Most trips to Réunion are trouble-free. Its society and culture are similar to Western Europe. Usual precautions should be taken
WEATHER Hot and tropical with cooler temperatures in the hills. Cool and dry from May to Nov; hot and wet from Dec to Apr
BANKING 0800–1600 Mon to Fri
EMERGENCY Police 17; Fire 18; Ambulance 15
TIME ZONE GMT +4
INTERNATIONAL DIALLING CODE 262

ROMANIA

GOVERNMENT Multiparty republic
LANGUAGES Romanian (official), Hungarian
CURRENCY Leu = 100 bani
MEDICAL Visitors should protect against rabies, typhoid and encephalitis
TRAVEL Petty theft is common in urban areas. It is illegal to exchange money on the street. Corruption is widespread. Roads are poorly maintained
WEATHER May to Oct warm, but coastal areas are cooled by sea breezes; Nov to Apr harsh winter with snow, but milder along the coast
BANKING 0900–1200 Mon to Fri; 1300–1500 Mon to Fri (currency exchange only)
EMERGENCY Police 955; Fire 981; Ambulance 961
TIME ZONE GMT +2
INTERNATIONAL DIALLING CODE 40

RUSSIA

GOVERNMENT Federal multiparty republic
LANGUAGES Russian (official), many others
CURRENCY Russian ruble = 100 kopeks
MEDICAL Visitors should protect against diptheria, hepatitis A, typhoid and encephalitis
TRAVEL Travel to the Chechen Republic and northern Caucasus is inadvisable. Visitors should keep all valuables out of sight
WEATHER Variable climate in north and central regions; Jul to Aug warm and wet; May to Jun and Sep to Oct dry; Nov to Apr very cold with snow
BANKING 0930–1730 Mon to Fri
EMERGENCY Police 02; Fire 01; Ambulance 03
TIME ZONE GMT +3 in Moscow and St Petersburg. Other areas vary
INTERNATIONAL DIALLING CODE 7

ST KITTS & NEVIS

GOVERNMENT Constitutional monarchy
LANGUAGES English
CURRENCY East Caribbean dollar = 100 cents
MEDICAL Visitors should protect against mosquito bites as dengue fever is present. Water is untreated and is unsafe to drink
TRAVEL Most visits are trouble-free. The islands are now commercialized and tourists are welcomed. Usual precautions should be taken
WEATHER Hot and tropical with cooling sea breezes. There is little seasonal temperature variation. Hurricane season is Aug to Oct
BANKING 0800–1500 Mon to Thu; 0800-1500/1700 Fri; 0830-1100 Sat
EMERGENCY All Services 911
TIME ZONE GMT –4
INTERNATIONAL DIALLING CODE 1 869

ST LUCIA

GOVERNMENT Parliamentary democracy
LANGUAGES English (official), French patois
CURRENCY East Caribbean dollar = 100 cents
MEDICAL Dengue fever is present; precautions should be taken against mosquito bites. Polio and typhoid vaccinations are recommended
TRAVEL Most trips to St Lucia are trouble-free, but sensible precautions should be taken. Beachwear should not be worn in towns
WEATHER Tropical climate moderated by trade winds. Temperatures are uniform at about 26°C [79°F]. St Lucia lies in the hurricane belt
BANKING 0800–1500 Mon to Thu; 0800–1700 Fri; 0800–1200 Sat
EMERGENCY All Services 999
TIME ZONE GMT –4
INTERNATIONAL DIALLING CODE 1 758

ST VINCENT & THE GRENADINES

GOVERNMENT Parliamentary democracy
LANGUAGES English
CURRENCY East Caribbean dollar = 100 cents
MEDICAL Protection from polio, typhoid and mosquito bites are recommended
TRAVEL Sensible precautions should be taken. There is a relaxed society and most visits are trouble-free. Excellent West Indian cuisine can be found on St Vincent
WEATHER Tropical climate with cooling trade winds. Hottest months are Jun and Jul. Tropical storms may occur from Jun to Nov
BANKING 0800–1500 Mon to Thu; 0800–1700 Fri
EMERGENCY All Services 999
TIME ZONE GMT –4
INTERNATIONAL DIALLING CODE 1 809

SAMOA

GOVERNMENT Mix of parliamentary democracy and constitutional monarchy
LANGUAGES Samoan (Polynesian), English
CURRENCY Samoan dollar = 100 sene
MEDICAL Vaccination against polio and typhoid are recommended. Water is untreated and is unsafe to drink
TRAVEL Most visits are trouble-free, but traditional moral and religious codes are very important. Beachwear should not be worn outside resorts
WEATHER Tropical climate with cooler temperatures in the evenings. The rainy season is from Dec to Apr
BANKING 0900–1500 Mon to Fri; 0830–1130 Sat
EMERGENCY All services 999
TIME ZONE GMT –11
INTERNATIONAL DIALLING CODE 685

SAUDI ARABIA

GOVERNMENT Absolute monarchy with consultative assembly
LANGUAGES Arabic (official)
CURRENCY Saudi riyal = 100 halalas
MEDICAL Cases of cerebral malaria have been reported in Jizan, south-west Saudi Arabia
TRAVEL Visitors should seek advice on recent developments. Islamic customs must be followed. Bombings have occurred in Riyadh and visitors should remain extremely vigilant
WEATHER Desert climate; extremely dry; May to Oct very hot; Nov to Feb mild
BANKING 0830–1200 and 1700–1900 Sat to Wed; 0830–1200 Thu
EMERGENCY Unavailable
TIME ZONE GMT +3
INTERNATIONAL DIALLING CODE 966

SERBIA & MONTENEGRO

GOVERNMENT Federal republic
LANGUAGES Serbian (official), Albanian
CURRENCY New dinar = 100 paras
MEDICAL Visitors should protect themselves against hepatitis
TRAVEL The situation in Serbia and Montenegro is calm at present, though visitors should seek advice on developments before travelling. Travel to Kosovo is still inadvisable
WEATHER Serbia has a continental climate; Nov to Mar very cold; Jun to Sep warm; Montenegro is similar with colder conditions in mountain regions
BANKING 0900–1400 Mon to Fri
EMERGENCY Police 107; Fire/Ambulance 104
TIME ZONE GMT +1
INTERNATIONAL DIALLING CODE 36

SEYCHELLES

GOVERNMENT Democratic republic
LANGUAGES English, French, French Creole
CURRENCY Seychelles rupee = 100 cents
MEDICAL There are no specific health risks
TRAVEL Crime is relatively rare, but incidents of theft do occur in tourist areas. Visitors, particularly women, should remain vigilant and avoid walking in quiet areas after dark. Roads often have sheer drops and no barriers
WEATHER Nov to Feb hot, humid monsoon; very warm temperatures all year round; May and Oct breezy at the start and finish of the trade winds
BANKING 0830–1430 Mon to Fri
EMERGENCY Unavailable
TIME ZONE GMT +4
INTERNATIONAL DIALLING CODE 248

SINGAPORE

GOVERNMENT Multiparty republic
LANGUAGES Chinese, Malay, Tamil and English (all official)
CURRENCY Singapore dollar = 100 cents
MEDICAL There are no specific health risks
TRAVEL The crime rate is very low in Singapore and most visits remain trouble-free. There are harsh penalties, including the death penalty, for all drug offences. Smoking is illegal in public places
WEATHER Hot and humid all year round; Nov to Jan cool with most rainfall
BANKING 1000–1500 Mon to Fri; 1100–1600 Sat
EMERGENCY All Services 999
TIME ZONE GMT +8
INTERNATIONAL DIALLING CODE 65

SLOVAK REPUBLIC

GOVERNMENT Multiparty republic
LANGUAGES Slovak (official), Hungarian
CURRENCY Slovak koruna = 100 halierov
MEDICAL There is risk from rabies and tick-borne encephalitis in forested areas during summer months
TRAVEL Pickpockets operate around the main tourist areas, and foreigners are easily identified and targeted. Sensible precautions should be taken
WEATHER A temperate climate with cold winters and mild summers
BANKING 0800–1700 Mon to Fri
EMERGENCY Fire 150; Ambulance 155; Police 158
TIME ZONE GMT +1 in winter; GMT +2 in summer
INTERNATIONAL DIALLING CODE 42

SLOVENIA

GOVERNMENT Multiparty republic
LANGUAGES Slovene (official), Serbo-Croatian
CURRENCY Tolar = 100 stotin
MEDICAL Summer visitors to forested areas should seek advice about protection against tick-borne encephalitis
TRAVEL Harsh fines are given for traffic offences and jaywalking. Passports and international driving licences should be carried at all times
WEATHER Continental climate inland; Jun to Sep warm; Nov to Mar cold; Mediterranean climate in coastal areas; Sep is the best time for hiking and climbing
BANKING 0800–1800 Mon to Fri
EMERGENCY Police 92; Fire 93; Ambulance 94
TIME ZONE GMT +1
INTERNATIONAL DIALLING CODE 386

SOUTH AFRICA

GOVERNMENT Multiparty republic
LANGUAGES Afrikaans, English, Ndebele, Pedi, Sotho, Swazi, Tsonga, Tswana, Venda, Xhosa and Zulu (all official)
CURRENCY Rand = 100 cents
MEDICAL There is a high incidence of HIV/AIDS. Malaria is a risk in certain areas. Hygiene and water standards are high in tourist areas
TRAVEL Violent crime is high in the townships. There is a risk of car-jacking and armed robbery. Visitors should hide valuables and seek advice about which areas to avoid
WEATHER Generally warm and sunny all year
BANKING 0830–1530 Mon to Fri
EMERGENCY Police 1011; Ambulance 10222
TIME ZONE GMT +2
INTERNATIONAL DIALLING CODE 27

SPAIN

GOVERNMENT Constitutional monarchy
LANGUAGES Castilian Spanish (official), Catalan, Galician, Basque
CURRENCY Euro = 100 cents
MEDICAL There are no specific health risks in Spain
TRAVEL Most visits to Spain are trouble-free. The country is rich in arts and culture
WEATHER Temperate in north; Apr to Oct hot and dry, particularly in the south; central plateau can be very cold during winter
BANKING 0900–1400 Mon to Fri; 0900–1300 Sat (but not during summer)
EMERGENCY Police 091; Fire/Ambulance 085; Emergency Services 112
TIME ZONE GMT +1
INTERNATIONAL DIALLING CODE 34

SRI LANKA

GOVERNMENT Multiparty republic
LANGUAGES Sinhala and Tamil (both official)
CURRENCY Sri Lankan rupee = 100 cents
MEDICAL There is a risk of cholera and malaria. Rabies is widespread
TRAVEL The northern region and the eastern coast remain heavily mined. A cease-fire between the Tamil Tigers and the government was signed in February 2002
WEATHER Tropical climate; May to Jul and Dec to Jan monsoon seasons; coastal regions are cool due to sea breezes
BANKING 0900–1300 Mon to Sat; 0900–1500 Tue to Fri
EMERGENCY All Services 1 691095/699935
TIME ZONE GMT +5.30
INTERNATIONAL DIALLING CODE 94

SWEDEN

GOVERNMENT Constitutional monarchy
LANGUAGES Swedish (official), Finnish, Sami
CURRENCY Swedish krona = 100 öre
MEDICAL There are no specific health risks
TRAVEL Most visits to Sweden are generally trouble-free. Since devaluation of the Swedish currency, the country has become considerably more affordable
WEATHER May to Jul hot and dry, but Aug can be wet; the midnight sun can be seen from May to Jun above the Arctic Circle; Nov to Apr extremely cold, particularly in the north
BANKING 0930–1500 Mon to Fri
EMERGENCY Emergency Services 112; All Services 90 000/112
TIME ZONE GMT +1
INTERNATIONAL DIALLING CODE 46

SWITZERLAND

GOVERNMENT Federal republic
LANGUAGES French, German, Italian and Romansch (all official)
CURRENCY Swiss franc = 100 centimes
MEDICAL There is a risk of altitude sickness, sunburn and hypothermia in the Alps
TRAVEL Most visits to Switzerland remain trouble-free
WEATHER Climate varies from region to region; Alpine regions have lower temperatures; Jun to Sep warm and sunny; Nov to Apr cold with snow which starts to melt in Apr
BANKING 0830–1630 Mon to Fri
EMERGENCY Police 117; Fire 118; Ambulance 144
TIME ZONE GMT +1
INTERNATIONAL DIALLING CODE 41

SYRIA

GOVERNMENT Multiparty republic
LANGUAGES Arabic (official), Kurdish, Armenian
CURRENCY Syrian pound = 100 piastres
MEDICAL Visitors should vaccinate against polio, hepatitis A and B, and tetanus
TRAVEL Visitors should keep informed of developments in the Middle East. They should dress modestly and avoid driving out of main cities at night. Harsh penalties exist for drug offences
WEATHER Apr to Jun mild and dry; Jun to Sep hot; Dec to Mar very cold, particularly in coastal and upland regions
BANKING 0800–1400 Sat and Thu
EMERGENCY Contact hotel operator
TIME ZONE GMT +2
INTERNATIONAL DIALLING CODE 963

TAIWAN

GOVERNMENT Unitary multiparty republic
LANGUAGES Mandarin Chinese (official)
CURRENCY New Taiwan dollar = 100 cents
MEDICAL There are no specific health risks, but visitors should be vaccinated against hepatitis
TRAVEL Most visits to Taiwan are trouble-free. Petty crime exists, but is not common. Some roads in central and southern areas may still be blocked by landslides following the 1999 earthquake
WEATHER Subtropical climate with moderate temperatures in the north; Jun to Sep very hot and humid; Jun to Oct typhoon season
BANKING 0900–1530 Mon to Fri; 0900–1230 Sat
EMERGENCY Police 110
TIME ZONE GMT +8
INTERNATIONAL DIALLING CODE 886

TANZANIA

GOVERNMENT Multiparty republic
LANGUAGES Swahili and English (both official)
CURRENCY Tanzanian shilling = 100 cents
MEDICAL There is a risk of yellow fever, malaria, cholera and hepatitis. AIDS is widespread
TRAVEL Most visits are trouble-free, but crime does occur, particularly on public transport and in tourist areas. There are increased risks in Zanzibar where bomb explosions have occurred
WEATHER Tropical climate; Mar to May rainy season in coastal areas; Jan to Feb hot and dry; Nov to Dec and Feb to May rainy season in highland areas
BANKING 0830–1600 Mon to Fri
EMERGENCY Unavailable
TIME ZONE GMT +3
INTERNATIONAL DIALLING CODE 255

THAILAND

GOVERNMENT Constitutional monarchy
LANGUAGES Thai (official), English, local dialects
CURRENCY Baht = 100 satang
MEDICAL Visitors should protect against malaria, dengue fever, AIDS and cholera
TRAVEL Harsh penalties exist for drug offences. Tourists should use licensed taxis with yellow number plates. Visitors should seek advice before travelling to border areas with Burma or Cambodia. Riptides occur off the coast of Phuket
WEATHER Jun to Oct hot and rainy monsoon; Nov to Feb dry and pleasant; Mar to May hot; temperatures are more consistent in the south
BANKING 0830–1530 Mon to Fri
EMERGENCY Unavailable
TIME ZONE GMT +7
INTERNATIONAL DIALLING CODE 66

TRINIDAD & TOBAGO

GOVERNMENT Parliamentary democracy
LANGUAGES English (official), Spanish
CURRENCY Trinidad & Tobago dollar = 100 cents
MEDICAL Dengue fever has become a problem in recent years. Medical facilities are basic and limited
TRAVEL While most visits are trouble-free, attacks on travellers are on the increase. Visitors should remain vigilant and alert at all times, and take sensible precautions
WEATHER Tropical climate with cooling trade winds. Hottest and wettest time is Jun to Nov
BANKING 0900–1400 Mon to Thu; 0900–1200 and 1500–1700 Fri
EMERGENCY Police 999; Ambulance/Fire 990
TIME ZONE GMT –4
INTERNATIONAL DIALLING CODE 1 868

TUNISIA

GOVERNMENT Multiparty republic
LANGUAGES Arabic (official), French
CURRENCY Tunisian dinar = 1,000 millimes
MEDICAL There is a risk of yellow fever and malaria
TRAVEL Travel to Tunisia is generally trouble-free, but visitors to southern desert areas and to areas close to the Algerian border should exercise caution. Tunisian laws and customs should be respected. Drug offences carry harsh penalties
WEATHER Jun to Aug hot and humid; Jan to Feb. cooler; hotter inland; higher rainfall in winter
BANKING 0830–1200 and 1300–1700 Mon to Fri
EMERGENCY Unavailable
TIME ZONE GMT +1
INTERNATIONAL DIALLING CODE 216

TURKEY

GOVERNMENT Multiparty republic
LANGUAGES Turkish (official), Kurdish, Arabic
CURRENCY New Turkish lira = 100 kurus
MEDICAL Contagious diseases are increasing and visitors should keep inoculations up-to-date
TRAVEL Most visits are trouble-free, but visitors should exercise caution, particularly in the tourist areas of Istanbul where street robbery is common, and seek recent advice before travelling
WEATHER Mediterranean climate; summers are hot and winters are mild
BANKING 0830–1200 and 1300–1700 Mon to Fri
EMERGENCY Police 155; Fire 111; Ambulance 112
TIME ZONE GMT +2
INTERNATIONAL DIALLING CODE 90

UGANDA

GOVERNMENT Republic in transition
LANGUAGES English and Swahili (both official)
CURRENCY Ugandan shilling = 100 cents
MEDICAL There is a risk of AIDS, yellow fever and malaria
TRAVEL Most visits to Uganda are trouble-free, but visitors should seek recent advice before travelling. It is inadvisable to travel to areas bordering the Democratic Republic of the Congo or Sudan, and visitors should remain cautious if travelling to areas bordering Rwanda
WEATHER Dec to Feb and Jun to Aug hot and dry; Mar to May and Oct to Nov heavy rain
BANKING 0830–1400 Mon to Fri
EMERGENCY Unavailable
TIME ZONE GMT +3
INTERNATIONAL DIALLING CODE 256

UKRAINE

GOVERNMENT Multiparty republic
LANGUAGES Ukrainian (official), Russian
CURRENCY Hryvnia = 100 kopiykas
MEDICAL There is a risk of diptheria in western Ukraine. Tick-borne encephalitis is common in forested areas. Do not drink tap water without first boiling it
TRAVEL Crime in the Ukraine remains low, but visitors should remain vigilant and keep valuables out of sight, particularly in crowded areas where pickpocketing and bag-snatching can occur
WEATHER Jun to Aug warm; Oct to Nov sunny but cold; Dec to Mar cold with snowfall
BANKING 0900–1600 Mon to Fri
EMERGENCY Unavailable
TIME ZONE GMT +2
INTERNATIONAL DIALLING CODE 380

UNITED ARAB EMIRATES

GOVERNMENT Federation of seven emirates, each with its own government
LANGUAGES Arabic (official), English
CURRENCY Dirham = 100 fils
MEDICAL There is a risk of hepatitis A and B
TRAVEL Visitors should remain informed of recent international developments before travelling. They should dress modestly and respect local customs. Penalties for all drug offences are harsh and can include the death penalty
WEATHER Jun to Sep very hot and dry; Oct to May cooler and is the best time to visit
BANKING 0800–1200 Sat to Wed and 0800–1100 Thu
EMERGENCY All Services 344 663
TIME ZONE GMT +4
INTERNATIONAL DIALLING CODE 971

UNITED KINGDOM

GOVERNMENT Constitutional monarchy
LANGUAGES English (official), Welsh, Gaelic
CURRENCY Pound sterling = 100 pence
MEDICAL No vaccinations are required in the UK and citizens of all EU countries are entitled to free medical treatment at National Health Service hospitals
TRAVEL Most visits are trouble-free, but visitors should exercise caution in urban areas after dark
WEATHER May to Aug warm and wet; Sep to Apr mild and wet
BANKING 0900–1730 Mon to Fri. Some bank branches open on Saturday mornings
EMERGENCY Police/Fire/Ambulance 999; Emergency Services 112
TIME ZONE GMT
INTERNATIONAL DIALLING CODE 44

UNITED STATES OF AMERICA

GOVERNMENT Federal republic
LANGUAGES English (official), Spanish, more than 30 others
CURRENCY US dollar = 100 cents
MEDICAL There are no specific health risks, but medical treatment is expensive
TRAVEL Most visits to the USA are trouble-free, but visitors should remain vigilant and avoid wearing valuable jewellery or walking through isolated urban areas after dark
WEATHER Varies considerably; check climate before travelling
BANKING 0900–1500 Mon to Fri
EMERGENCY Emergency Services 911
TIME ZONE USA has six time zones from GMT −5 on East coast to −10 in Hawai'i
INTERNATIONAL DIALLING CODE 1

URUGUAY

GOVERNMENT Multiparty republic
LANGUAGES Spanish (official)
CURRENCY Uruguayan peso = 100 centésimos
MEDICAL There are no specific health risks, but medical treatment can be expensive
TRAVEL Most visits to Uruguay are trouble-free, but street crime exists in urban areas, including Montevideo. It is, however, less common than in other Latin American countries
WEATHER Dec to Mar hot, but nights can be cool; Apr to Nov mild
BANKING 1330–1730 Mon to Fri (summer); 1300–1700 Mon to Fri (winter)
EMERGENCY Police 109; Fire 104; Ambulance 105; All Services 999
TIME ZONE GMT −3
INTERNATIONAL DIALLING CODE 598

VENEZUELA

GOVERNMENT Federal republic
LANGUAGES Spanish (official), local dialects
CURRENCY Bolívar = 100 céntimos
MEDICAL There is a risk of yellow fever, cholera, dengue fever and hepatitis
TRAVEL The incidence of violent crime is high and the political situation is volatile. Visitors should take precautions. Terrorist and narcotic gangs are active in areas bordering Colombia, where there is the risk of kidnapping
WEATHER May to Dec rainy season; Jan to Apr pleasant temperatures
BANKING 0830–1130 and 1400–1630 Mon to Fri
EMERGENCY Doctor 02 483 7021; Ambulance 02 545 4545
TIME ZONE GMT −4
INTERNATIONAL DIALLING CODE 58

VIETNAM

GOVERNMENT Socialist republic
LANGUAGES Vietnamese (official), English, Chinese
CURRENCY Dong = 10 hao = 100 xu
MEDICAL Malaria, dengue fever and encephalitis are common throughout the country. Visitors should avoid mosquito bites. Typhoid is common in the Mekong Delta
TRAVEL Take care if travelling in border areas. Unexploded mines and bombs still exist in certain areas. Drug smuggling carries the death penalty. Serious flooding can occur in central areas
WEATHER May to Oct tropical monsoons; Nov to Apr hot and dry
BANKING 0800–1630 Mon to Fri
EMERGENCY Police 13; Fire 14; Ambulance 15
TIME ZONE GMT +7
INTERNATIONAL DIALLING CODE 84

VIRGIN ISLANDS, BRITISH

GOVERNMENT UK overseas territory
LANGUAGES English (official)
CURRENCY US dollar = 100 cents
MEDICAL Medical facilities are limited. Precautions should be taken against polio, typhoid and dengue fever
TRAVEL There is a low crime rate, but sensible precautions should be taken. Backpacking is discouraged throughout the 60 islands
WEATHER Subtropical and humid climate moderated by trade winds. Hurricanes are a risk from Jul to Oct
BANKING 0900–1500 Mon to Thu; 0900–1700 Fri
EMERGENCY Police 114; Ambulance 112
TIME ZONE GMT –4
INTERNATIONAL DIALLING CODE 1 284

VIRGIN ISLANDS, US

GOVERNMENT US overseas territory
LANGUAGES English, Spanish, French, Creole
CURRENCY US dollar = 100 cents
MEDICAL Visitors should protect against typhoid and polio. Water is generally considered drinkable
TRAVEL Most visit are trouble-free and normal precautions should be taken. There is a large selection of hotel accommodation available
WEATHER Hot climate with cool winds. Low humidity with little seasonal temperature variation. The rainy season is Sep to Nov
BANKING 0900–1430 Mon to Thu; 0900–1400 and 1530–1700 Fri
EMERGENCY All services 911
TIME ZONE GMT –4
INTERNATIONAL DIALLING CODE 1 340

YEMEN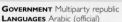

GOVERNMENT Multiparty republic
LANGUAGES Arabic (official)
CURRENCY Yemeni rial = 100 fils
MEDICAL Visitors should protect against hepatitis A and B
TRAVEL Most governments currently strongly advise against travel to Yemen. Random armed kidnapping is common, and foreigners are targets for crime and terrorism
WEATHER Varies with altitude; Oct to Mar nights can be very cold in upland regions; Apr to Sep very hot; Oct to Apr cool, dry and dusty
BANKING 0800–1200 Sat to Wed; 0800–1100 Thu. Closed on Fridays
EMERGENCY Unavailable
TIME ZONE GMT +3
INTERNATIONAL DIALLING CODE 967

ZAMBIA

GOVERNMENT Multiparty republic
LANGUAGES English (official), Bemba, Nyanja
CURRENCY Zambian kwacha = 100 ngwee
MEDICAL Outbreaks of cholera and dysentery are common. Malaria is endemic, and cases of AIDS and tuberculosis are very high
TRAVEL Visitors should avoid travelling to areas bordering Angola and the Democratic Republic of the Congo. Armed robbery, bag-snatching and mugging are increasing, particularly in downtown areas. Keep valuables out of sight
WEATHER May to Sep very cool and dry; Oct to Nov hot and dry; Dec to Apr hot and wet
BANKING 0815–1430 Mon to Fri
EMERGENCY All Services 1 2 25067/254798
TIME ZONE GMT +2
INTERNATIONAL DIALLING CODE 260

ZIMBABWE

GOVERNMENT Multiparty republic
LANGUAGES English (official), Shona, Ndebele
CURRENCY Zimbabwean dollar = 100 cents
MEDICAL There is a risk of bilharzia, cholera, malaria, yellow fever and rabies. Incidences of HIV/AIDS are very high
TRAVEL There is currently political and social unrest throughout the country, in both rural and urban areas. Visitors should exercise caution and avoid large crowds and demonstrations
WEATHER May to Oct warm and dry, but cold at night; Nov to Apr wet and hot
BANKING 0800–1500 Mon, Tue, Thu and Fri. 0800–1300 Wed and 0800–1130 Sat
EMERGENCY Police 995; Ambulance 994
TIME ZONE GMT +2
INTERNATIONAL DIALLING CODE 263

WORLD MAPS — GENERAL REFERENCE

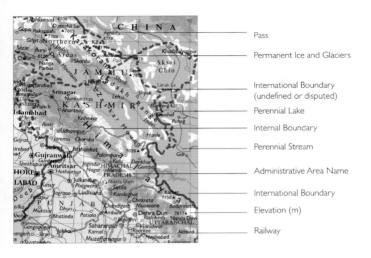

- Pass
- Permanent Ice and Glaciers
- International Boundary (undefined or disputed)
- Perennial Lake
- Internal Boundary
- Perennial Stream
- Administrative Area Name
- International Boundary
- Elevation (m)
- Railway

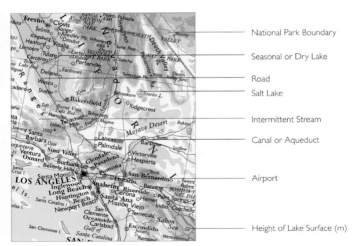

- National Park Boundary
- Seasonal or Dry Lake
- Road
- Salt Lake
- Intermittent Stream
- Canal or Aqueduct
- Airport
- Height of Lake Surface (m)

Settlements

Settlement symbols and type styles vary according to the scale of each map and indicate the importance of towns rather than speciific population figures.

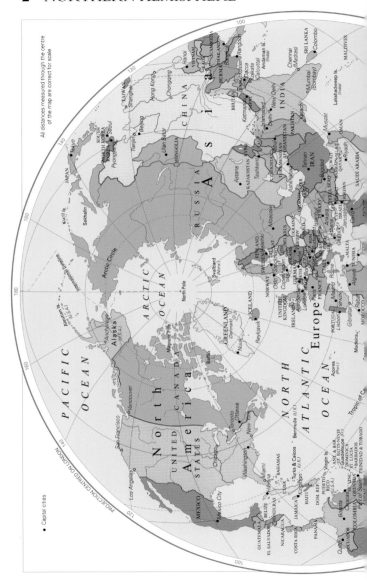

All distances measured through the centre of the map are correct for scale

PROJECTION CENTRED ON LONDON

• Capital cities

3

PROJECTION CENTRED ON CAPE TOWN

PROJECTION CENTRED ON SAN FRANCISCO

TIME ZONES

Zones using Greenwich Mean Time

Zones fast of Greenwich Mean Time

Zones slow of Greenwich Mean Time

Standard Time not the Zone hour

No Official Time

Projection: Oblique Azimuthal Equidistant

COPYRIGHT PHILIP'S

PROJECTION CENTRED ON THE ANTIPODES OF LONDON

All distances measured through the centre
of the map are correct for scale

West from Greenwich

East from Greenwich

International Dateline

• Capital cities

PACIFIC OCEAN

INDIAN OCEAN

Tropic of Cancer

Tropic of Capricorn

Equator

Antarctic Circle

Galapagos Is.
(Ecuador)

Easter I.
(Chile)

Marquesas Is.
(Fr.)

Tuamotu Arch.
(Fr.)

Tahiti (Fr.)

FRENCH POLYNESIA

Pitcairn I.
(U.K.)

Hawaiian Is.
(U.S.A.)

Midway I.
(U.S.A.)

Cook Is.
(N.Z.)

SAMOA

KIRIBATI

TONGA

Kermadec Is.
(N.Z.)

Chatham Is.
(N.Z.)

Antipodes Is.
(N.Z.)

Wake I.
(U.S.A.)

MARSHALL IS.

TUVALU

FIJI

Auckland

Wellington

NEW ZEALAND

Auckland Is. (N.Z.)

Macquarie I. (Austral.)

Magnetic Pole

Victoria Land

Bonin Is.
(Japan)

Northern
Marianas
(U.S.A.)

Guam
(U.S.A.)

FED. STATES OF
MICRONESIA

SOLOMON IS.

VANUATU

New Caledonia
(Fr.)

Oceania

PAPUA
NEW GUINEA

Port Moresby

Brisbane

Sydney

Canberra

AUSTRALIA

Adelaide

Perth

Tasmania

PHILIPPINES

PALAU

VIETNAM

Ho Chi
Minh City

BRUNEI

Borneo

Ujung
Pandang

MALAYSIA INDONESIA

EAST
TIMOR

SINGAPORE

Kuala Lumpur

Jakarta

Manila

Cocos Is.
(Austral.)

100

120

140

160

180

160

140

120

100

80

08

80

5

Projection: Bonne   West from Greenwich   0   East from Greenwich   5   7   10   15   9   ■ LONDON Capital Cities

Labels on the map:

Arctic Circle

ICELAND
Reykjavik

Norwegian Sea

Faroe Is. (Den)

SWEDEN
Tromsø
Trondheim
NORWAY
Bergen   Oslo
Stavanger
Gövle
Uppsala
Örebro   Stockholm
Skagerrak   Tärnen   Jönköping
Älborg   Kattegat
DENMARK   Gothenburg
Ärhus
Copenhagen   Malmö   Gotland
Kiel
Hamburg   Baltic

Shetland Is.

UNITED KINGDOM

ATLANTIC
Hebrides
Orkney Is.
SCOTLAND
Aberdeen
Glasgow   Dundee
IRELAND   Edinburgh
Belfast
North Sea
IRELAND   Newcastle-upon-Tyne
Dublin   Manchester   Leeds
Cork   Liverpool   Sheffield
WALES   Birmingham
Cardiff   ENGLAND
Bristol   LONDON   Amsterdam   The Hague   NETHER-LANDS
Plymouth   Southampton   Rotterdam   GERMANY
Channel Is. (U.K.)   BELGIUM   Antwerp   Essen   Bremen   Elbe   Berlin
English Channel   Brussels   Dortmund   Hannover   Magdeburg
Le Havre   Lille   Bonn   Cologne   Halle   POL
Brest   Rouen   Frankfurt   Leipzig
PARIS   am Main   Chemnitz   Dresden
Wiesbaden   Poznań
Łódź
Katowice
Wrocław

OCEAN

Bay of Biscay

Nantes   Loire   FRANCE   Dijon   Strasbourg   Stuttgart   Nuremberg   Prague   Ostrava
Limoges   Rhine   Munich   CZECH REP.
Luxembourg   LIECH.   Zürich   AUSTRIA   Vienna   SLO
Bordeaux   St-Étienne   SWITZERLAND   Innsbruck   Linz   Salzburg   Bratislava
Lyons   Geneva   Graz   Budapest   HUNG
Grenoble   Milan   SLOVENIA   Ljubljana
Toulouse   Nice   Turin   Venice   Zagreb
ANDORRA   Andorra-la-Vella   MONACO   Genoa   CROATIA
Marseilles   Bologna   Florence   BOSNIA-HERZ.
Toulon   Adriatic Sea   Split   Sarajevo

Vigo   La Coruña
Porto   Douro
PORTUGAL   Bilbao
Lisbon   Tagus   Valladolid   Ebro   Zaragoza
SPAIN   Madrid   Barcelona   Corsica   Ajaccio   ITALY   SAN MARINO   Rome   Tira
Guadiana   Valencia   Balearic Is.   Palma
Cádiz   Córdoba   Guadalquivir   Murcia   Alicante   Minorca   Sardinia   Naples   Bari
Seville   Granada   Ibiza   Majorca   Tyrrhenian Sea   Taranto   ALI
Málaga   Cagliari
Str. of Gibraltar   Gibraltar (U.K.)   Ceuta (Sp.)
Tangier   Melilla (Sp.)   Algiers   Palermo   Messina
MOROCCO   Africa   ALGERIA   Annaba   Pantelleria (Italy)   Catánia   Ionia Sea
Constantine   Tunis   MALTA   Valletta
TUNISIA

Mediterranean Sea

100 0 100 200 300 400 500 600 700 800 km
100 0 100 200 300 400 500 miles

C

10 11 12 13 14 15 16 17 18 19

Hammerfest

Murmansk

White Sea

Arkhangelsk

Ob

60

uma

D

Luleå

L. Onega

N. Dvina

Kotlas

Nizhniy Tagil

Perm

Vaasa

FINLAND

Yekaterinburg

55

Vyborg L.

mpere

Turku

Ladoga

Kirov

Chelyabinsk

Helsinki

ST. PETERSBURG

Rybinsk Res.

Vologda

Ufa

E

Tallinn

ESTONIA

L. Chudskoye

Yaroslavl

Kostroma

Nizhniy Novgorod

Kazan

Magnitogorsk

a

LATVIA

Riga

R U S S I A

Ivanovo

Sea

MOSCOW

Simbirsk

Samara

Orenburg

LITHUANIA

W. Dvina

Kaliningrad (Russia)

Vilnius

Vitebsk

Smolensk

Tula

Penza

50

Uralsk

Kaunas

Mogilev

Volga

N D

Białystok

Minsk

BELARUS

Orel

Tambov

Saratov

KAZAKHSTAN

F

Warsaw

Brest

Gomel

Pripet

Kursk

Voronezh

Ural

Atyraü

Lublin

Chernigov

Kharkov

Volgograd

raków

Zhitomir

Kiev

Dnieper

Don

Astrakhan

45

K REB

Lvov

UKRAINE

Dnepropetrovsk

Donetsk

Rostov

Caspian

Y

Miskolc

Dniester

Krivoy Rog

Zaporozhye

Taganrog

Sea

Debrecen

MOLDOVA

Nikolayevid

Kherson

Makhachkala

Cluj-Napoca

Kishinev

Stavropol

R O M A N I A

Odessa

Krasnodar

G

Timișoara

Galați

Crimea

GEORGIA

Tbilisi

Belgrade

Brașov

Sevastopol

AZERBAIJAN

Baku

40

ERBIA &

Bucharest

Ploiesti

ARMENIA

ONTENEGRO

Danube

Constanța

B l a c k   S e a

Yerevan

Araks

Niš

Sofia

Varna

Samsun

Erzurum

Tabriz

IRAN

Skopje

BULGARIA

Bosporus

MACEDONIA

Plovdiv

ISTANBUL

a

IA

Thessaloníki

Bursa

Ankara

T U R K E Y

Diyarbakir

35

GREECE

Aegean Sea

Izmir

Kayseri

Euphrates

IRAQ

Patrai

Athens

Konya

Adana

Aleppo

Tigris

Antalya

SYRIA

Baghdad

Rhodes

CYPRUS

Nicosia

Crete

10 11 12 13 14 15

30 35

COPYRIGHT PHILIP'S

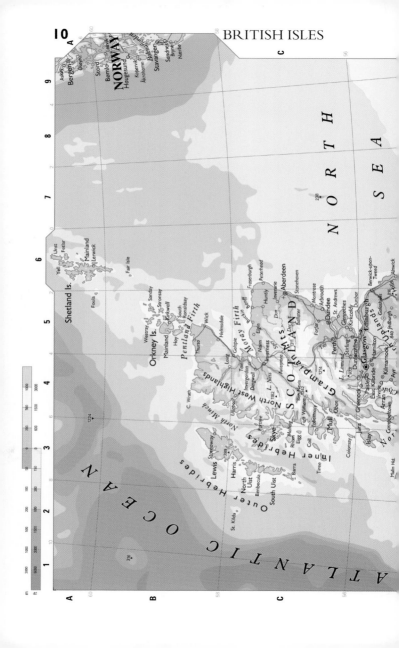

NORWAY
Bergen
Stord
Bømlo
Haugesund
Stavanger
Kopervik
Åkrehamn
Sandnes
Bryne
Narbø

Shetland Is.
Unst
Fetlar
Yell
Mainland
Lerwick
Fair Isle
Foula

Orkney Is.
Westray
Sanday
Stronsay
Kirkwall
Mainland
South Ronaldsay
Hoy
Pentland Firth
Thurso
Wick
Helmsdale
C. Wrath
Golspie
Loth
Inverness
Dingwall
Ullapool
L. Ness
North West Highlands
Ben Nevis
Fort William
Loch
Skye
Mallaig
Portree
Raasay
Rhum
Eigg
Muck
Coll
Tiree
Mull
Tobermory
Oban
Colonsay
Jura
Islay
Campbeltown
Malin Hd.

North Minch
Lewis
Stornoway
Harris
North Uist
Benbecula
South Uist
Barra
Outer Hebrides
Inner Hebrides
St. Kilda

SCOTLAND
Grampian Mts.
Moray Firth
Nairn
Elgin
Fraserburgh
Peterhead
Huntly
Banff
Inverurie
Aberdeen
Stonehaven
Montrose
Arbroath
Forfar
Brechin
Dundee
St. Andrews
Perth
Stirling
Dunfermline
Dunbar
Crieff
Gleneagles
Kirkcaldy
Edinburgh
Berwick-upon-Tweed
Glasgow
Hamilton
East Kilbride
Kilmarnock
Ayr
Arran
Paisley
Greenock
L. Lomond
Galashiels
Jedburgh
Southern Uplands
Hawick
Alnwick

NORTH SEA

ATLANTIC OCEAN

m   ft
2000 6000
1000 3000
500   1500
250   600
100   300
50   150
0   0

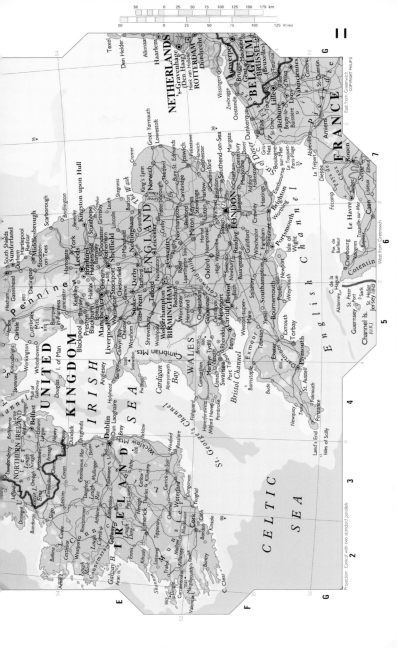

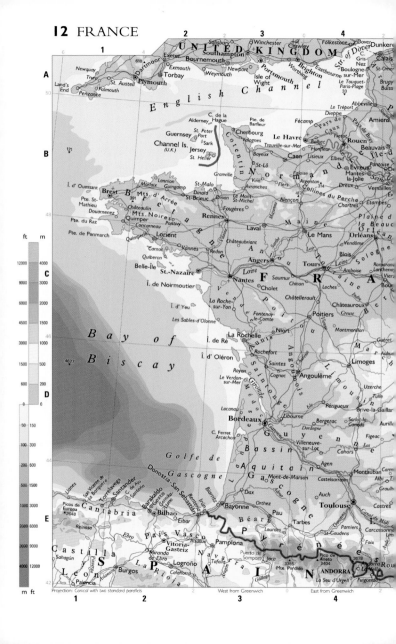

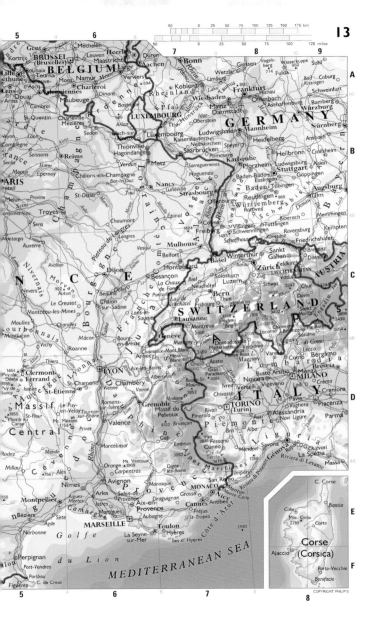

50   0   25   50   75   100   125   150   175 km
50   0   25   50   75   100   125 miles

5   **6**   **7**   **8**   **9**

A

Gent Mechelen Heerlen Düren Bonn
Kortrijk BRUSSEL Leuven Maastricht Aachen Köln
(Bruxelles) Liège Verviers Limburg Giessen Vogels- Wasserkuppe Suhl
Roubaix BELGIUM Namur Meuse Rheinland 804 890 Fulda berg 950
Béthune Tournai Mons Charleroi Dinant Koblenz Wetzlar Bad- Coburg
Valenciennes Bastogne Pfalz Wiesbaden Frankfurt Hanau Offenbach Schweinfurt Kissingen
Douai Maubeuge Idar- Mainz Aschaffenburg Bamberg Würzburg
Arras Cambrai LUXEMBOURG Trier Oberstein Darmstadt GERMANY Nürnberg
St-Quentin Charleville- Arlon Luxembourg Kaiserslautern Mannheim Ansbach
Noyon Mézières Esch-sur- Ludwigshafen Heidelberg Crailsheim
Laon Sedan Thionville Saarbrücken Neunkirchen Speyer Heilbronn Aalen
Compiègne Hagondange Pirmasens Karlsruhe Ludwigsburg Stuttgart Göppingen

B

Reims Verdun Metz Sarreguemines Pforzheim Esslingen
Meaux Épernay Châlons-en-Champagne Baden-Baden Tübingen Augsburg
Bar-le-Duc Nancy Haguenau Baden Reutlingen Donau Ulm
Melun Provins St-Dizier Lunéville Strasbourg Offenburg Württemberg Rottweil Memmingen
Fontainebleau Seine Toul Épinal Colmar Freiburg Schwenningen Ravensburg Friedrichshafen Kempten

C

Montargis Troyes Chaumont Vesoul Mulhouse Schaffhausen Konstanz Bregenz Dornbirn
Auxerre Avallon Langres Belfort Basel Winterthur Sankt AUSTRIA
Nevers Dijon Besançon Montbéliard Biel Aarau Zürich Gallen Feldkirch
Le Creusot Beaune Dole Neuchâtel Solothurn LIECHTENSTEIN Vaduz Chur
Montceau-les-Mines Chalon-sur-Saône Bern Thun Schwyz 3247
Charolles Lons-le-Saunier Fribourg Interlaken SWITZERLAND

D

Moulins Mâcon Bourg- Lausanne Montreux Sion Locarno Bellinzona Sondrio
Vichy Roanne en-Bresse Genève Martigny Domodossola Verbania Lugano di Como Lecco
Thiers Chamonix-Mont Blanc Matterhorn Lago Bérgamo
Clermont- St-Chamond Annecy Mont Aosta Maggiore Como
Ferrand St-Étienne Aix-les-Bains Blanc 4807 Gran Busto Arsizio MILANO
Puy de Albertville Paradiso Ivrea Vigevano Novara Vercelli (Milan) Cremona
Dôme Issoire LYON Chambéry Voiron Bourg-St- 4061 Monza
Vienne Romans- Maurice Rivoli TORINO Alessandria Piacenza
Grenoble sur-Isère Modane (Turin) Novi Ligure Parma

E

Massif Le Puy- Tournon- Pinerolo Po Asti Voghera
St-Flour en-Velay sur-Rhône Massif du Briançon Piemonte Alba
Central Mézence Valence Pelvoux Gap Cuneo Savona Génova Chiavari La Spézia
Privas 4102 3841 Fossano Rapallo Massa
Mende Montélimar Embrun 3052 1770 Mondovì Riviera di Levante
Rodez Orange Mt Ventoux Digne- Alpes Imperia
Millau 1909 Carpentras les-Bains Maritimes 1389 San Remo C. Corse Calvi Bastia
Nîmes Avignon Manosque Riviera di Ponente Menton Mte Cinto Corte
Alès Arles Salon- Draguignan Grasse Monte-Carlo 2710
Montpellier Aigues- Provence Aix-en- Cannes Antibes MONACO Corse
Béziers Mortes Istres Provence Fréjus Nice (Corsica)

F

Narbonne Sète Martigues Aubagne St-Tropez Côte d'Azur Ajaccio
Agde MARSEILLE Toulon Hyères 2580
Perpignan Golfe La Seyne- Îles d'Hyères Porto-Vecchio
Port-Vendres sur-Mer Bonifacio
Figueres C. de Creus du Lion MEDITERRANEAN SEA

5   **6**   **7**   **8**

NORTH SEA

UNITED KINGDOM

NETHERLANDS

BELGIUM

LUXEMBOURG

SWITZERLAND

FRANCE

GERMANY

DENMARK

Norwich
Great Yarmouth
Lowestoft
Ipswich
Felixstowe
Harwich
Margate
Dover
Calais
Boulogne-sur-Mer
Abbeville
Amiens
Beauvais
St-Denis
PARIS
Créteil
Melun
Fontainebleau
Sens
Troyes
Auxerre
Avallon
Nevers
Moulins
Montceau-les-Mines
Charolles
Mâcon
Vichy
Roanne
Thiers
St-Étienne

Sylt
Westerland
Föhr
Nordfriesische Inseln
Helgoland
Deutsche Bucht
Ost-friesische Inseln
Norderney
Borkum
Cuxhaven
Wilhelmshaven
Emden
Aurich
Leer
Bremerhaven
Stade
Oldenburg
Bremen
Delmenhorst
Cloppenburg
Verden
Nienburg
Niedersachsen
Celle
Hannover
Hildesheim
Hameln
Detmold
Höxter
Goslar
Göttingen
Nordhausen
Kassel
Münden
Eisenach
Erfurt
Marburg
Giessen
Fulda
Wasserkuppe
Suhl
Hessen
Wetzlar
Limburg
Frankfurt
Wiesbaden
Mainz
Offenbach
Hanau
Aschaffenburg
Schweinfurt
Bad Kissingen
Würzburg
Bamberg
Darmstadt
Worms
Mannheim
Heidelberg
Speyer
Ludwigshafen
Kaiserslautern
Neunkirchen
Saarbrücken
Pirmasens
Karlsruhe
Baden-Baden
Stuttgart
Esslingen
Pforzheim
Heilbronn
Erlangen
Fürth
Nürnberg
Ansbach
Crailsheim
Göppingen
Reutlingen
Tübingen
Ulm
Augsburg
Württemberg
Schwäbische
Rottweil
Schwenningen
Villingen
Tuttlingen
Ravensburg
Biberach
Memmingen
Kempten
Friedrichshafen
Bregenz
Dornbirn
Feldkirch
Landeck
Wildspitze
LIECHTENSTEIN
Vaduz
Chur
Davos
Sankt Moritz
Merano
Lago di Garda
Bergamo
Lecco
Como
Varese
Busto Arsizio
Aosta
Gran Paradiso
Verbania
Lugano
Bellinzona
Locarno
Domodossola
Monte Rosa
Matterhorn
Brig
Sion
Montreux
Genève
Lausanne
Thun
Bern
Fribourg
Neuchâtel
Biel
Solothurn
Luzern
Zug
Schwyz
Zürich
Aarau
Sankt Gallen
Winterthur
Schaffhausen
Konstanz
Basel
Mulhouse
Belfort
Montbéliard
Besançon
La Chaux-de-Fonds
Pontarlier
Dijon
Beaune
Chalon-sur-Saône
Bourg-en-Bresse
LYON
St-Chamond
Vienne
Annecy
Aix-les-Bains
Chambéry
Albertville
Voiron
Grenoble

Cromer

's-Gravenhage (Den Haag)
AMSTERDAM
Haarlem
Alkmaar
Hoorn
Den Helder
Leiden
Hoek van Holland
Gouda
Utrecht
ROTTERDAM
Dordrecht
Breda
Tilburg
's-Hertogenbosch
Eindhoven
Turnhout
ANTWERPEN
Gent
Brugge
Oostende
Zeebrugge
Vlissingen
Mechelen
BRUSSEL (Bruxelles)
Leuven
Aalst
Roubaix
Lille
Tournai
Mons
Namur
Charleroi
Maubeuge
Valenciennes
Dinant
Cambrai
St-Quentin
Charleville-Mézières
Sedan
Bastogne
Arlon
Esch-sur-Alzette
LUXEMBOURG
Luxembourg
Thionville
Hagondange
Metz
Nancy
Lunéville
Épinal
Colmar
Freiburg
Strasbourg
Hagenau
Sarreguemines
Saarlouis
Verdun
Bar-le-Duc
Toul
Châlons-en-Champagne
Épernay
Reims
Laon
Soissons
Compiègne
Noyon

Groningen
Assen
Emmen
Meppel
Zwolle
Kampen
Almelo
Deventer
Apeldoorn
Arnhem
Nijmegen
Enschede
Münster
Osnabrück
Minden
Herford
Bielefeld
Gütersloh
Paderborn
Dortmund
Hamm
Hagen
Bochum
Essen
Duisburg
Krefeld
Mönchengladbach
Wuppertal
Solingen
Düsseldorf
Köln (Cologne)
Bonn
Aachen
Düren
Liège
Verviers
Siegen
Koblenz
Westerwald
Eifel
Trier
Idar-Oberstein

Leeuwarden
Sneek
Texel
Terschelling
Ameland
Schiermonnikoog
Vlieland

Flensburg
Abenrå
Schleswig
Rendsburg
Kiel
Neumünster
Itzehoe
Lübeck
Elmshorn
HAMBURG
Lüneburger Heide
Lüneburg

Projection: Conical with two standard parallels

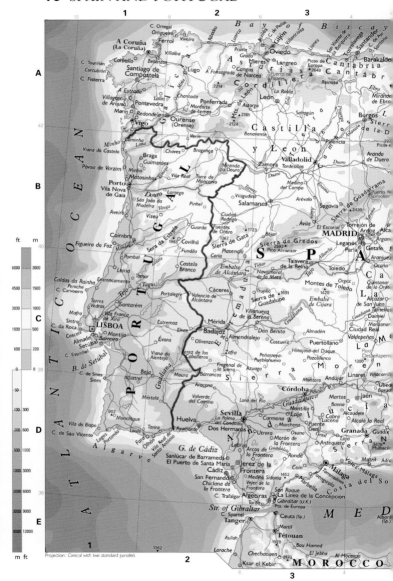

Projection: Conical with two standard parallels

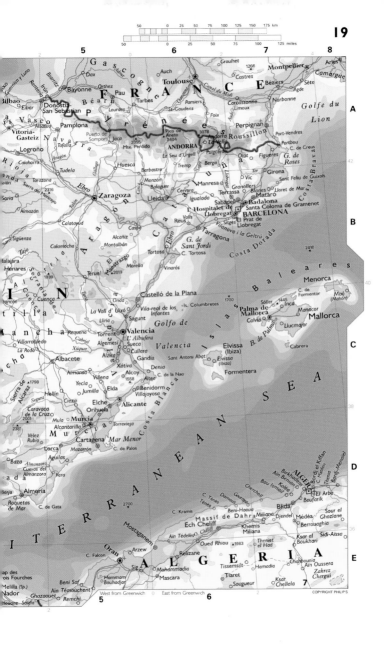

50   0   25   50   75   100 125 150 175 km

50   0   25   50   75   100 125 miles

5   6   7   8

France

Graulhet · 1266   Montpellier · Arles

G a s c o g n e   Auch   Camargue
Dax · Orthez   Toulouse · Canal du Midi   Castres · Béziers · Sète
Bayonne · Pau   Narbonne   Golfe du
Bilbao · Eibar · Oloron   B é a r n   Tarbes · St-Gaudens · Pamiers   Carcassonne   Limoux   **A**   Lion
Donostia · San Sebastián   Lourdes   P y r é n é e s   Foix   Perpignan
Vitoria-   Pamplona   Puerto de   Jaca · 3556   Pico de   3078   **Andorra**   R o u s s i l l o n   Port-Vendres
Gasteiz   N a v a r r a   Somport   Mte. Perdido   Aneto   La Vella   Olot   Figueres   C. de Creus
Logroño   Tafalla   Aragón   3404   **ANDORRA**   Puigcerdà   C. de Roses   Portbou
Rioja   Calahorra   Huesca   La Seu d'Urgell   Tremp · Berga   Ter   G. de Roses
Soria · Tudela   Barbastre   Balaguer   Vic   Girona   Sant Feliu de Guíxols
Almazán   Sierra del Moncayo   Ebro   Monzón   Cervera   Igualada   Terrassa   Blanes   Lloret de Mar   Costa Brava   42
Tarazona   2316   Zaragoza   Lleida · Manresa   Sabadell   Mataró
Calatayud   Caspe   Reus   L'Hospitalet de   Santa Coloma de Gramenet
Sigüenza   Alcañiz   Valls   Llobregat   **BARCELONA**   **B**
Molina de Aragón   Montalbán   Tortosa   Tarragona   El Prat de Llobregat   Sitges   Vilanova i la Geltrú
Henares   Serranía de   Teruel   2019   Morella   G. de Sant Jordi   C. Tortosa   Costa Dorada   2410
Cuenca   1839   El Maestrazgo   Vinaròs
Tarancón   I s l a s   B a l e a r e s   40
Requena   Onda   Castelló de la Plana   Menorca
Castilla   La Vall d'Uixó   Is. Columbretes   1700   C. de Formentor   Maó (Mahón)
Villarrobledo   La Reda   Llíria · Sagunt   Sóller · 1445 · Inca   Manacor
Albacete   Cabriel   Torrent   **Valencia**   Palma de   Mallorca   Llucmajor   Mallorca   **C**
Alzira   L'Albufera   Colvià   B. de Palma
Almansa   Xàtiva   Sueca   V a l e n c i a   Cabrera
Sierra de   Villena   Alcoy   Cullera   Eivissa (Ibiza)
Alcaraz   1798   Benidorm   Gandia   Sant Antoni Abat   Eivissa (Ibiza)
Hellín   Yecla   Jumilla · Elda · Villajoyosa   Denia   C. de la Nao   Formentera
Cieza   Elche   **Alicante**   38
Caravaca de la Cruz   Mula · Orihuela
2001   **Murcia**   Torrevieja   M e d i t e r r a n e a n   S e a
2381   Alcantarilla   Mar Menor
Vélez Rubio   M u r c i a   Cartagena   C. de Palos
Baza   Lorca   Mazarrón
Almanzora   Aguilas
Cuevas del   Vera   **ALG**   Bordj el Kiffan
Serja   Almería   Almanzora   Burkhadem   Bordj Menaiel
Roquetas   C. de Gata   2700   Cherchell   Ain Benaid   El Arba   **D**
de Mar   C. Ténès   Domaous   Bou Ismail   Boufarik
M e d i t e r r a n e a n   Ténès   Gouraya   **Blida**   Sour el
Cap des   C. Falcon   C. Kramis   Beni-Haoua   Djendel · Miliana   Médéa   Ghozlane
Trois Fourches   I T E R R A N E A N   Massif de Dahra   Khemis   Berrouaghia   36
Melilla (Sp.)   Mostaganem   Ech Cheliff   Miliana   Ksar el   Sidi-Aissa
Nador   Oran   Arzew   Ain Tédelès · 1983   Theniet   Boukhari
Houghe   Saïdia   Sig · Relizane   Oued Rhiou   el Had   Chahbounia   Ain Oussera
 2   West from Greenwich   East from Greenwich   Zahrez Chergui
Beni Saf   Hammam   Mohammadia   Tissemsilt   Hamadia   Sougueur   Ksar   7
Ghazaouet   Bouhadjar   Mascara   Tiaret   Chellala   **E**
Ain Témouchent   **A L G E R I A**
Remchi   COPYRIGHT PHILIP'S

5   6   7

50   0   25   50   75   100   125   150   175 km

50   0   25   50   75   100   125 miles

COPYRIGHT PHILIP'S

IONIAN SEA

MEDITERRANEAN SEA

TYRRHENIAN SEA

Golfo di Taranto

Str. di Messina

NAPOLI

Sardegna (Sardinia)

Isole Eólie

Monti Nébrodi

Sicilia

MALTA

Valletta

Gozo

Pantelleria (Italy)

Isole Pelagie (Italy)

Lampedusa

Linosa

Ustica (Italy)

Golfe de Hammamet

Golfe de Tunis

Tunis

TUNISIA

ALGERIA

Etna

Lecce

Brindisi

Otranto

Gallipoli

Tàranto

Altamura

Matera

Potenza

Cosenza

Catanzaro

Crotone

Reggio di Calabria

Messina

Catània

Siracusa

Ragusa

Palermo

Marsala

Trápani

Caltanissetta

Cágliari

Oristano

Alghero

East from Greenwich

Projection: Conical with two standard parallels

m   4000   3000   2000   1000   500   200   0

ft   12000   9000   6000   3000   1500   600   0

4000   3000   2000   1000   500   200   150   100

12000   9000   6000   3000   1500   600   380   200

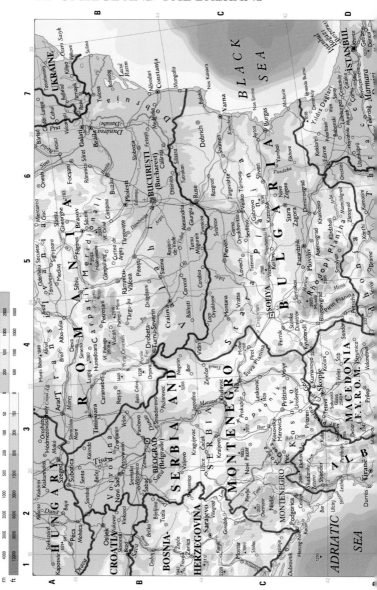

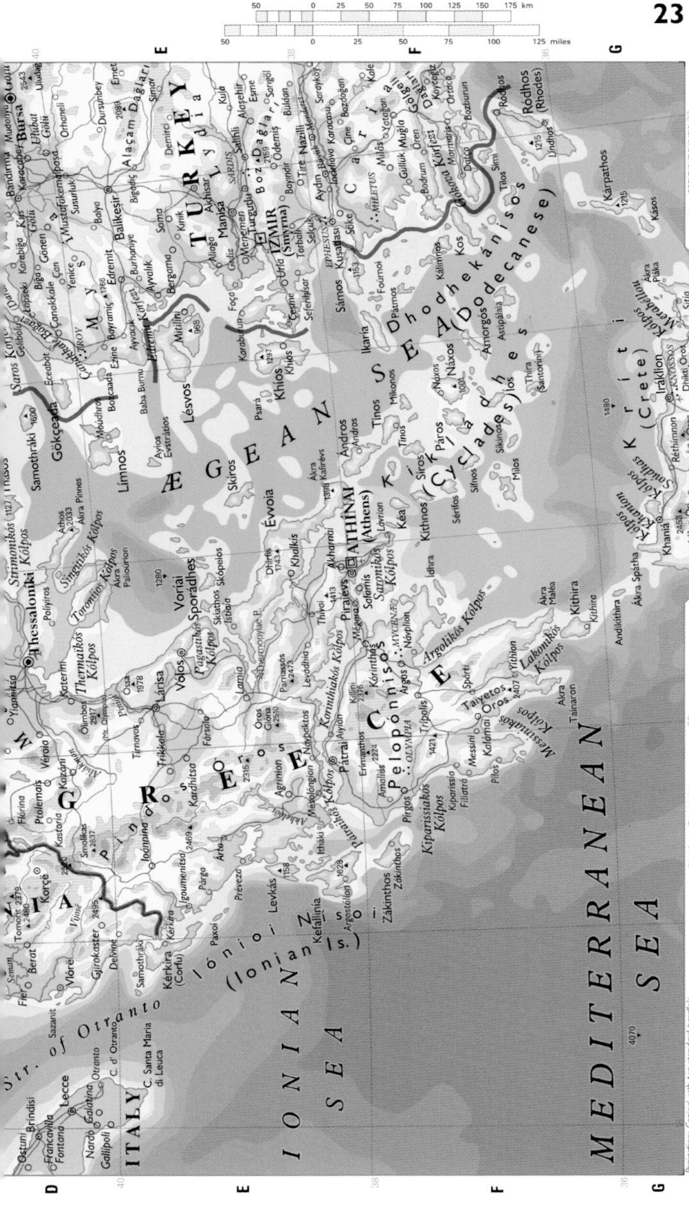

50 0 25 50 75 100 125 150 175 km

50 0 25 50 75 100 125 miles

TURKEY

İZMIR (Smyrna)

Bursa

Bandırma

Manisa

Balıkesir

Bergama

Aydın

Denizli

Muğla

Bodrum

Rodhos (Rhodes)

Lindhos

Karpathos

Kasos

Æ G E A N   S E A

Lésvos

Limnos

Samothráki

Gökçeada

Thessaloníki

Skíros

Évvoia

ATHÍNAI (Athens)

Piraiévs

Khíos

Sámos

Ikaría

Dhodhekánisos (Dodecanese)

Náxos

Páros

Andros

Tínos

Mýkonos

Íos

Thíra (Santoríni)

Kykládhes (Cyclades)

Sífnos

Sérifos

Kíthnos

Kéa

Mílos

Kríti (Crete)

Iráklion

Réthimnon

Khaniá

Soúdhas Kólpos

Kíthira

Andikíthira

Akra Spátha

G R E E C E

Vólos

Lárisa

Tríkkala

Kardítsa

Pínos

Agrínion

Pátrai

Pelópónnisos

Kórinthos

Trípolis

Kalámai

Pírgos

Spárti

Taíyetos Óros

Korinthiakós Kólpos

Argolikós Kólpos

Messiniakós Kólpos

Lakonikós Kólpos

Náfplion

MYCENAE

OLYMPIA

Ioánnina

Kérkira (Corfu)

Iónioi (Ionian Is.)

Zákinthos

Kefallinía

Paxoí

Levkás

I O N I A N   S E A

Str. of Otranto

ITALY

Brindisi

Lecce

Gallipoli

Otranto

C. Santa Maria di Leuca

M E D I T E R R A N E A N   S E A

ALBANIA

Berat

Vlorë

Gjirokastër

Korçë

East from Greenwich

Projection: Conical with two standard parallels

COPYRIGHT PHILIP'S

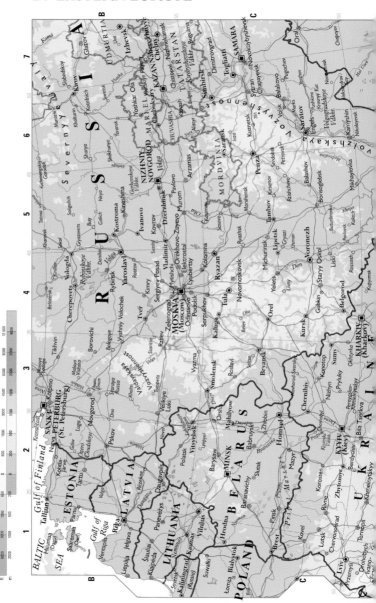

50 0   100   200   300   400 km
50 0   50   100   150   200   250 miles

F

E

D

C A S P I A N S E A

KAZAKHSTAN

Depression

Caspian

VOLGOGRAD

Volga

KALMYKIA

Vozyyshennost

Ergeni

Don

ROSTOV

DONETSK

DNIPROPETROVSK

Kremenchuk

Kirovohrad

ODESA

MOLDOVA

Chişinău

ROMANIA

BUCUREŞTI
(Bucharest)

BULGARIA

Varna

Burgas

B L A C K   S E A

Sea of Azov

CRIMEA

Sevastopol

Yalta

Simferopol

Kherson

Mykolayiv

Krasnodar

Novorossiysk

Tuapse

Sochi

Sokhumi

ABKHAZIA

Batumi

C a u c a s u s

M o u n t a i n s

Stavropol

Elista

Astrakhan

Derbent

Makhachkala

DAGESTAN

CHECHENIA

Grozny

Vladikavkaz

GEORGIA

TBILISI

ARMENIA

YEREVAN

AZERBAIJAN

BAKU
Bakı

Sumqayıt

Gäncä

Rustavi

Kutaisi

Poti

Trabzon

Kuzey Anadolu Dağları

Rize

Artvin

Kars

Gyumri

Erzurum

Van

I R A N

TABRİZ

T U R K E Y

Anatolia

ANKARA

İSTANBUL

İZMIR
(Smyrna)

BURSA

Sivas

Kayseri

Samsun

Giresun

Sinop

Zonguldak

Sakarya

Eskişehir

Konya

Erzincan

Malatya

Amasya

Tokat

Çorum

Kastamonu

Projection: Conical with two standard parallels

East from Greenwich

COPYRIGHT PHILIP'S

6

5

4

3

2

Capital Cities

Projection: Bonne 30

500   0 250 500 750 1000 1250 1500 1750 km
500   0   250   500   750   1000   1250 miles

B   C   D

evernaya
Zemlya
OCEAN   New
              Siberian
Laptev Sea   Is.   Wrangel I.   ALASKA
                                                       (USA)
Khatanga   Bering
        Verkhoyansk   Sea
                                                 Gizhiga   Aleutian Is.
iorsk   (USA)
        Yakutsk
                                      Okhotsk Magadan
        Lena   Petropavlovsk-
                        Sea   Kamchatskiy
Angara   of Okhotsk
Krasnoyarsk Bratsk L. Baikal   Komsomolsk   Sakhalin
                         Blagoveshchensk   Yuzhno-
Novokuznetsk Irkutsk Chita Amur   Khabarovsk Sakhalinsk Hokkaidō
        Ulan Ude   Sapporo
                                    Hailar Qiqihar
        Ulan Bator   Harbin   Vladivostok   Honshū
Ürümqi   Changchun   TŌKYŌ
Harni   MONGOLIA   Jilin   Sea of   Yokohama
                                 SHENYANG Anshan   Japan   Kyōto Nagoya JAPAN
ANG   Baotou Jinzhou Dalian NORTH   Ōsaka
rim   Yumen   BEIJING TIANJIN Pyongyang KOREA Hiroshima Kitakyūshū
UR   Lanzhou Taiyuan   Jinan   SEOUL SOUTH
                                       Pusan KOREA
BET   Xi'an Hwang-ho Yellow Sea   Ryukyu Is.
     Lhasa C H I N A   Nanjing SHANGHAI   Bonin Is.
Thimphu   Chengdu Wuhan   East   (Japan)
BHUTAN   CHONGQING   Nanchang China   Volcano Is.
Kathmandu Brahmaputra HANGZHOU Fuzhou Sea   (Japan)
Patna BANGLADESH Changsha   Taipei   Tropic of Cancer
Ganges   Kunming GUANGZHOU TAIWAN
OLKATA DACCA BURMA Si Kiang HONG KONG
(Calcutta) Chittagong (MYANMAR) Macau
                 LAOS Hanoi Haiphong Hainan Luzon
Bay of   Rangoon Vientiane VIETNAM   MANILA PHILIPPINES FED. STATES
Bengal THAILAND Mekong   Cebu OF MICRONESIA
Andaman Is. BANGKOK   Palawan Mindanao PALAU
(India)   CAMBODIA Phnom Penh   Sulu Dāvao
          Ho Chi Minh   Sea   Zamboanga
ANKA Nicobar Is. G. of City   Halmahera
      (India) Thailand South China Sea BRUNEI SABAH Manado
                         PEN.   Bandar Seri Begawan Celebes
EAN   MALAYSIA Kuala Lumpur SARAWAK   Sea   Papua
       Medan MALAYSIA   Borneo Celebes Ceram
       SINGAPORE   Ambon Banda
       Sumatra   Banjarmasin I N D O N E S I A EAST Sea Arafura Sea
       Palembang   Ujung Pandang Flores TIMOR
              JAKARTA Semarang Java Sea Dili Timor
                     Bandung Surabaya Java Sumba Timor Sea AUSTRALIA

12   90   13   100   14   110   15   120   16   130   17

COPYRIGHT PHILIP'S

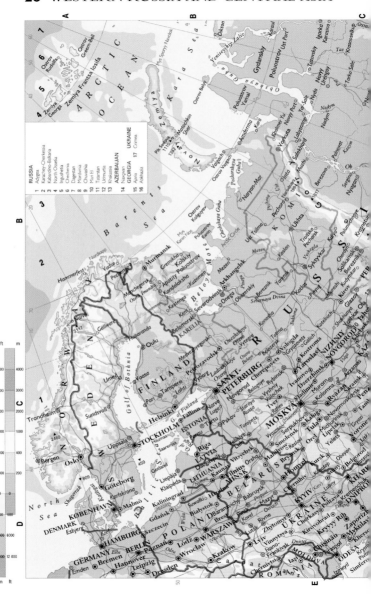

RUSSIA
1 Adygea
2 Karachay-Cherkessia
3 Kabardino-Balkaria
4 North Ossetia
5 Ingushetia
6 Chechenia
7 Dagestan
8 Mordovia
9 Chuvashia
10 Mari El
11 Tatarstan
12 Udmurtia
13 Khakassia

AZERBAIJAN
14 Naxçivan

GEORGIA
15 Ajaria
16 Abkhazia

UKRAINE
17 Crimea

29

100 0 100 200 300 400 500 600 700 800 km
100 0 100 200 300 400 500 miles

COPYRIGHT PHILIP'S

East from Greenwich

Projection: Conical Orthomorphic with two standard parallels

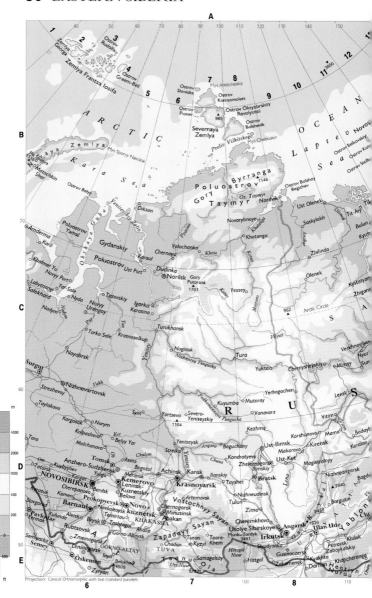

A

1 2 3
Zemlya Ostrov
Georga Rudolfa
Zemlya Frantsa Iosifa 4
Ostrov
Green-Bell 5 6 7 8
Ostrov Mys Arkticheskiy
Ostrov Shmidta Ostrov
Ostrov Komsomolets 9
Ostrov Oktyabrskoy
Pioner 965 Revolyutsii 10 11 2800 12
Severnaya Ostrov
Zemlya Bolshevik

ARCTIC OCEAN

B Zemlya Prolic Vilkitskoy Laptev Novos
Mys Sporyy Navolok Mys Chelyuskin Sea
Karskaya Kara Sea Ostrov Belkovskiy
Malochkin Shar Ostrov Belyy Gory Byrranga 1146 Ostrov Stolb
Amderma Poluostrov Poluostrov Gory Ostrov Bolshoy
Kara Yamal Yeniseyskiy Zaliv Dikson Taymyr Oz. Taymyr Begichev
Khalmer Yu Gydanskiy Nordvik Ust Olenek Tit-Ary
Novyy Port Karaul Novoryrbnoye Saskylakh Bulun
70 Ta-Sale Chernaya Dudinka Norilsk Khatanga Zhilinda Kys
Labytnangi Nyda Gory Olenek Kystatyan
Salekhard Tazovskiy Igarka Putorana Yessey Zhigans
Nadym Novyy Karasino 1701 Ust Port Volochanka Kheta 962 Arctic Circle SA
Noyabrsk Urengoy Turukhansk Noginsk Tura Verkhneviyu
Tarko Sale Krasnoselkup Nizhnyaya Tunguska Vilyuy Nyur
Surgut Vakh Yukta Yerbogachen Mirnyy
Nizhnevartovsk Sym Podkamennaya Tunguska Kuyumba Mutoray Vanavara Vitim S
Strezhevoy Yartsevo Severo- Angara Lensk
Taylakova Yeniseyskiy 1104 Korshunovo Mama
Kargasok Narym Boguchany Ust-Ilimsk Kirensk Boday
Tara Kolpashevo Belyy Yar Yeniseysk Makarovo Karalon
Molchanovo Strelka Ust-Kut Magistralnyy
Omsk Chulym Kezhma Kondratyevo Zheleznogorsk
D Tomsk Asino Bogotol Ilanskiy Nizhneangarsk Bogd
Anzhero-Sudzhensk Achinsk Kansk Tayshet Bratsk 2840
NOVOSIBIRSK Yurga Mariinsk Krasnoyarsk Nizhneudinsk
Kargat Kemerovo Leninsk- Artemovsk Tulun Barguzin
Cherepanovo Kuznetsk Vostochnyy Zima
Barnaul Belovo Novo- Chernogorsk Sayan Cheremkhovo Angarsk
Biysk Prokopyevsk kuznetsk Minusinsk 1620
Rubtsovsk Temirtau KHAKASSIA Abakan Usolye Sibirskoye Ulan Ude
Zmeinogorsk Gorno-Altaysk Abaza Munku-Sardyk Irkutsk Khilok
Semey Leningorsk GORNO-ALTAY Zapadnyy Sayan 3491 Slyudyanka Zakamensk
Inya TUVA Turan Toora- Munku Gusinoozersk
Pavlik Semiyarka Belukha Kyzyl Khem Darkhan Khapcheranga
Oskemen 4506 Chadan Hovsgol Hatgal Kyakhta
Zyryan Samagaltay Nuur
Tannu Ola Us Erzin

Projection: Conical Orthomorphic with two standard parallels

6 7 100 8 110

ft m
12 000 4000
6000 2000
3000 1000
1200 400
800 200
0 0
-200 -600
m ft

100 0 100 200 300 400 500 600 700 800 km
100 0 100 200 300 400 500 miles

14   **B**   **15**   **16**   **C**

Mys Dezhneva
(East C.)
Uelen

Ostrov
Genriyetty Ostrova
Zhannetty

Chukchi
Sea

Ostrov Vrangelya

60

Vilkitskiy

Providenya
Anadyrskiy Zaliv
St. Lawrence I.
(U.S.A.)

Ostrov
Bennetta Ostrova Delonga

ye Ostrova
Ostrov Faddeyevskiy

Ostrov Novaya Sibir

Pevek
Chukotskoye Nagorye

Ust Chaun

Egvekinot
Beringovskiy

Ostrov Malyy
Lyakhovskiy

Ostrov Bolshoy
Lyakhovskiy

Ambarchik
Chersky

Bilibino

Anadyr

D

Mkhovskoye
Ostrova

East Siberian Sea

Ostrov
Medvezhi

Iul'tin

Markovo

Pezhdino

Mayna

Mys Buorkhaya

Prolив Dmitriya Lapteva

Nizhne Kolymsk

Bolshoy Anyuy

Oloy

Yedabal

Koryakskoye Nagorye

Kamenskoye
Oklan

Ossora
Karaginskiy

Ostrova
Komandorskiye Ostrova

Bering
Sea

Kazachye

Srednekolymsk

Chokurdakh

Omolon

Omolon
Zyryanka

Gizhiga

Slautnoye

Tilichiki

Kayenda

Ust Kuyga

Druzhina

Fedorka

Kalyma

Taskan

Orotukan

Evensk

Gizhiginskaya

Polana

Ossora

Deputatsky

Khonuu

Gorn Chen
2087

Pobeda
3147

Omsukchan

Yagodnoye

Naykhan

Zaliv
Shelikhova

Gabyi

Palana

Sredinnyy

Verkhoyansk

Khrebet Cherskogo

Omyakon
2389

Sasuman

Ust-Omchug

Magadan

Tigil

Poluostrov

Batagay

Ozernovskiy

Yugorenok

Ulkan

Esso
1829

Kamchatka

Khandyga

Khrebet

K

h

r

e

b

e

t

Ust Nera
3147

Kirovskiy

Ust-Kamchatsk

Nikolskoye Ostrova

Sangar

Okhotsk
Perevoz

Ulye

Ust Khayuzovo

Khrebet
Zhugdzur

Sea

of

Okhotsk

Petropavlovsk-
Kamchatskiy

V

e

r

k

h

o

y

a

n

s

k

i

y

Vitim

Lena

Borgoontsy

Ytyk-Kyuyel

Khandyga

Amga

Nelkan

Aim

Ayan

50

Namtsy

Ust Maya

Ostrov Bolshoy
Shamtar

1790

Ostrova
Paramushir Kurilsk

Yakutsk
Pokrovsk

Maya

Chumikan

Sakhalinskiy
Zaliv

Okha

Sinsk

Ust-Mila

Tugur

Nikolayevsk-
na-Amure

S

Olekminsk

Tommot

Chagda

Uda

Sakhalin

Ostrov Iturup

Kurilskiye Ostrova

Yenyuka

Okhma

Aldan
2246

Nogorny

Chumikan

Aleksandrovsk-
Sakhalinskiy

Gora Lopatina
1609

Poronaysk

Ostrov Kunashir
Kurilsk

E

Chara
1999

Neryungri
2246

Stanovoy Khrebet

Ilyinskiy

Yuzhno-Sakhalinsk

Ostrov Iturup

Ust-Nyukzha

Tynda

Zeya

Shumun

Norsk

Uda

Udd

Uglegorsk

Korsakov

Kholmsk

Wakkanai

Kalakan

Megochu

Skovorodino

Dzhalinda

Shimanovsk

2640

Komsomolsk

2078

Yampol

Otaru

Kumora

Gulian

Svobodnyy

Belogorsk

Chegdomyn

Poyarkovo

Amursk

Birobidzhan

Smidovich

Khabarovsk

Rumoi

Abashiro

2290

Kushiro

Sapporo

Ust-Nyukzha

Nerchinsk

1054

Blagoveshchensk

Zavitinsk

Bryochikhinsk

Obluchye

Bikin

Khrebet Sikhote Alin

3669

Hokkaido

Hakodate

Chara

Shilka

Sretensk

Heihe

Jiayin

Lesozavodsk

Terney

Amgu

Amur

Ternej

Amuri

Tomori

Aginskoye
Oloyyannaya

Zabaykalsk

Nenjiang

Jiamusi

Dalnerechensk

Olga

Dalnegorsk

Hachinohe

Borzya

Manzhouli

Hailar

An'gangxi

Songhua Jiang

Hegang

Mudanjiang

Spassk
Dalniy

Arsenyev

Olga

Nakhodka

JAPAN

40

Hulun Nur

C H I N A

QIQIHAR

HARBIN

Usuri

Ussuriysk

Artem

Vladivostok

Nakhodka

Yanji

9   120   **10**   **11**

East from Greenwich

COPYRIGHT PHILIP'S

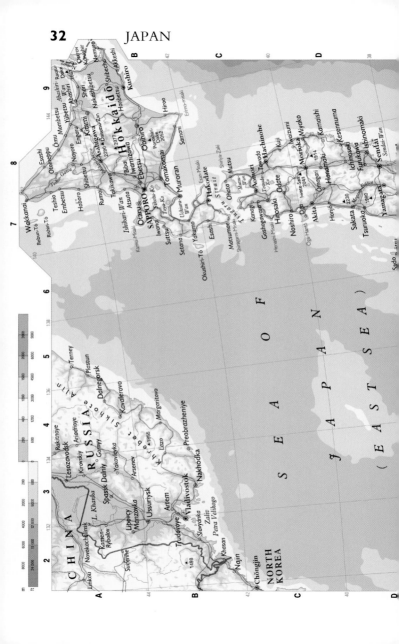

CHINA

RUSSIA

Sikhote Alin

Linkou
Novokachalinsk
Rakitnoye
Lesozavodsk
Ariadnoye
Kirovskiy
Spassk-Dalniy
Gornyy
Yakovlevka
Dalnegorsk
Plastun
Terney

Kamen-
Rybolov
L. Khanka
Lipovcy
Manzovka
Ussurysk
1855
Arsenev
Lazo
Kavalerovo
Margaritovo
Preobrazheniye

Suifenhe
Trudovoye
Slavyanka
Zarubino
Vladivostok
Artem
Patra Velikogo
Nakhodka

NORTH
KOREA
1498
Khasan
Najin
Chŏngjin

S E A   O F

J A P A N

(E A S T   S E A)

Sado

Wakkanai
Rebun-Tō
Rishiri-Tō
Esashi
Otoineppu
Omu
Teshio
Haboro
Embetsu
Shibetsu
Nayoro
Engaru
Mombetsu
Yūbetsu
Abashiri
Shari
Rausu
Dake
Nemuro
Shibecha
Akkeshi
Kushiro

HOKKAIDŌ

Kitami
Daisetsu-zan
2290
Asahikawa
Bibai
Iwamizawa
Ebetsu
Obihiro
Hontetsu
Nakashibetsu
Hiroo
Erimo-misaki

Tenryū Gawa
Runoi
Tokikawa-Wan
Ishikari-Wan
Atsuta
Otaru
SAPPORO
Iwanai
Kamui-Misaki
Suttsu
Setana
Toya-Ko
Shikotsu-Ko
Shiraoi
Tomakomai
Muroran
Uchiura-Wan
Yakumo
Okushiri-Tō
Esashi
Matsumae
Setana
Shiriuchi
Shirakami-Misaki
Tappi-Misaki

Tsugaru Strait

Esan-Misaki
Hakodate
Ōhata
Mutsu
Kanagi
Shiriya-Zaki
Mutsu-Wan
Ōma
Goshogawara
Aomori
Hirosaki
Noshiro
Oga-Hantō
Akita

Towada-
Ko
Iwate-San
2041
Hachinohe
Misawa
Ninohe
Morioka
Iwaizumi
Miyako
Kamaishi
Kesennuma
Ichinoseki
Ishinomaki
Sendai
Sendai-Wan

Honjō
Sakata
Tsuruoka
Yamagata
Gassan
1980
Zaō-San
2230

140
132
134
136
138
144

A
B
C
D

2
3
4
5
6
7
8
9

44
42
40

42
40
38

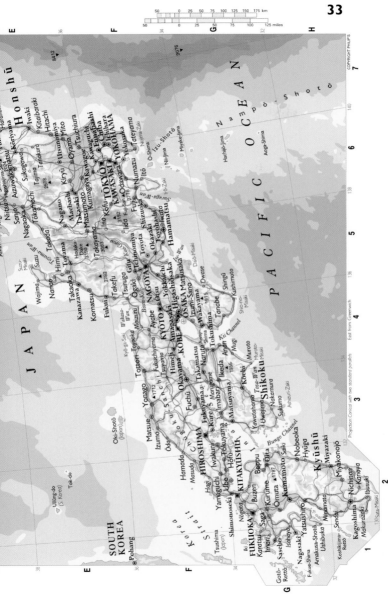

33

50 0 25 50 75 100 125 150 175 km
50 0 25 50 75 100 125 miles

E   F   G   H

36   34   32

7   6   5   4   3   2   1

Honshū

Harohiro
Iwaki
Koriyama
Hitachi
Kitaibaraki
Utsunomiya
Mito
Sukagawa
Azuwatehatsu
Nagaoka
Oyama
Sanjō
Tsuchiura
Niitsu
Nagata—Nagataimbari-Seki
Aikuru
Takamachi
Tajima
Tōkamachi
Kiryū
Maebashi
Noda
Tokada
Kashiwa
Chiba
Nagano
Takasaki
Kumagaya Kawagoe
Matsumoto
Saitama
Ino
Kōfu
TOKYO
Takada
Matsumoto
KAWASAKI
YOKOHAMA
Toyama
Suzu-Misaki
Takaoka
Hōdaka
3192
Fuji-San
3776
Yokosuka
Himi
Dake
3190
Ida
Shizuoka
Numazu
Itō
Izu-Shotō
Nanao
Kanazawa
Takefu
Tsuruga
Gifu
Ōgaki
Toyota
Okazaki
Hamamatsu
Ō-Shima
Noto-Hantō
Wajima
Komatsu
NAGOYA
Toyohashi
Iwato
Nii-Jima
Miyakejima
Fukui
Tsuruga
Biwa-Ko
Yokkaichi
Ōbama
Ayabe
Ōtsu
Daiō-Misaki
Miyake-Jima
Tottori
Toyooka
Fukuchiyama
KYŌTO
Ōsu
Amagasaki
Higashiōsaka
Owase
Aogo-Shima
Matsue
Yonago
Tsuyama
Himeji
OSAKA
Matsusaka
Wakayama
Shingū
Kii-Suidō
Izumo
Odai
Fuchū
Okayama
Kōbe
Nara
Ikeda
Shiono-Misaki
Hamada
HIROSHIMA
Kurashiki
Marugame
Takamatsu
Naruto
Tokushima
Kōchi
Muroto
Muroto-Misaki
Masuda
Iwakuni
Kure
Fukuyama
Matsuyama
Ashizuri-Zaki
Hagi
Tokuyama
Shikoku
Nakamura
Sukumo
Yamaguchi
Hōfu
KITAKYŪSHŪ
Ōita
Bungo Channel
Ube
Buzen
Nōgata
Beppu
Shimonoseki
Kurume
Saiki
Nobeoka
FUKUOKA
Karatsu
Saga
Ōmuta
Kumamoto
Hyūga
Iki
Imari
Arao
Isahaya
Mifunato
Kyūshū
Miyazaki
Tsushima
(Japan)
Sasebo
Nagasaki
Yatsushiro
Ushibuka
Miyakonojō
Fukue-Shima
Amakusa-Shotō
Nichinan
Gotō-
Rettō
Isohaya
Sendai
Kagoshima
Kanoya
Koshikijima-
Rettō
Mikurazaki
Ibusuki
Ō-Sata-Misaki

JAPAN

Oki-Shotō
(Japan)

Kyō-ga-Saki
Wakasa-Wan

Sanin

Kurayoshi-Wan

Chūgoku

Korea
Strait
(Japan)

**SOUTH
KOREA**

Pohang

Ullung-do
(S. Korea)

Tok-do

PACIFIC OCEAN

Nampō-Shotō

Hachijō-Jima

Izu-Shotō

8432

9076

2753

2785

2702

2782

4787

1915

1956

3192

3776

132   134   136   138   140

East from Greenwich

Projection: Conical with two standard parallels

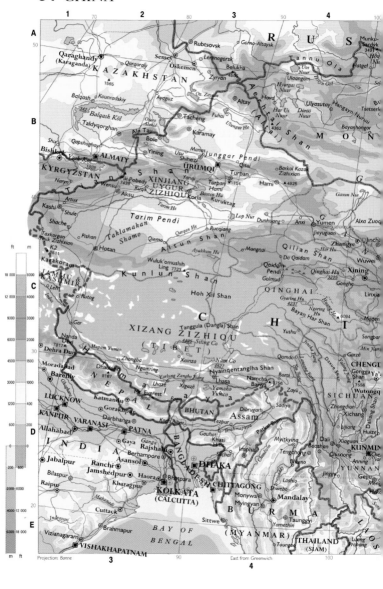

Projection: Bonne

East from Greenwich

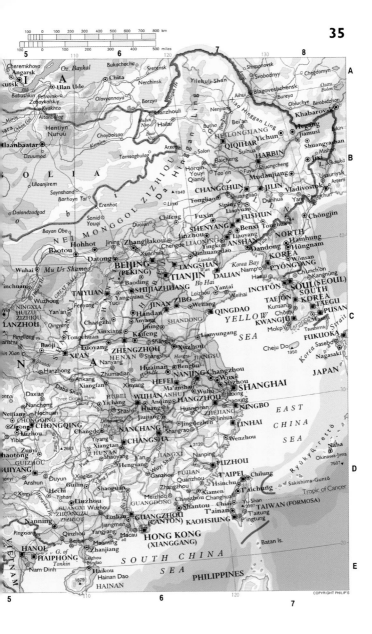

100 0 100 200 300 400 500 600 700 800 km
100 0 100 200 300 400 500 miles

A

Cheremkhovo
Angarsk
I A
Bukachacha
Sretensk
Shimanovsk
Chegdomyn
Oz. Baykal
455
Ulan Ude
Chita
Nerchinsk
Yilehuli Shan
Svobodnyy
Blagoveshchensk
Bureya
Obluche
Birobidzhan
Ozero
Bolon
Khabarovsk
Babushkin
Petrovsk-
Zabaykalskiy
Kyakhta
Manzhouli
Borzya
Olovyannaya
Nenjiang
Bei'an
Aihui
Hegang
Jiamusi
Bikin
Altanbulag
Hentiyn
Nuruu
Nara Chion Gol
Kerulen
Hailar
Butha Qi
HEILONGJIANG
Yichun
Suihua
Shuangyashan
Mishan
Ulaanbaatar
Dzuumod
Choybalsan
Solon
QIQIHAR
HARBIN
Shuangcheng
L. Khanka
Ussuriysk
MONGOLIA
Saynshand
Tamsagbulag
Arxan
Baicheng
Taon an
Fuyu
Mudanjiang
Artem

B

Ulaanjirem
Borhoyn Tal
Horqin
Youyi
Qianqi
CHANGCHUN
Shuangliao
JILIN
Vladivostok
Yanji
Chŏngjin
Dalandzadgad
Bayan Bar
Sonid
Youqi
Duolun
Linxi
Chifeng
Fuxin
Tongliao
Liaoyuan
Siping
SHENYANG
FUSHUN
Erenhot
Hohhot
Jining
Zhangjiakou
Jinzhou
Chengde
Benxi Tonghua
NORTH
KOREA
Baotou
Datong
Xuanhua
Yingkou
ANSHAN
LIAONING
Huanghua
Dandong
Hamhung
Hungnam
NEI MONGGOL ZIZHIQU

C

Wuhai
Mu Us Shamo
GREAT WALL
BEIJING
(PEKING)
TANGSHAN
TIANJIN
DALIAN
Korea Bay
Nampo
P'YONGYANG
Wŏnsan
Chunch'ŏn
Kangnŭng
inchuan
Yinchuan
Wuzhong
TAIYUAN
Baoding
Bo Hai
Laizhou
Yantai
Weihai
Haeju
INCH'ŎN
SŎUL(SEOUL)
SOUTH
NINGXIA
HUIZU
ZIZHIQU
Yan'an
Fenyang
Yuci
Yangquan
SHIJIAZHUANG
JINAN
ZIBO
Weifang
QINGDAO
TAEJŎN
KOREA
TAEGU
LANZHOU
Qingyang
Changzhi
Handan
Anyang
Jining
SHANDONG
YELLOW
KWANGJU
PUSAN
Tongchuan
Xinxiang
Kaifeng
Lianyungang
Mokp'o
Tsushima
FUKUOKA
Baoji
Luoyang
ZHENGZHOU
Xuzhou
JIANGSU
Cheju Do
Sasebo
XI'AN
HENAN
Shangshui
JIANGSU
Nagasaki
Hanzhong
Nanyang
Zhumadian
Huainan
Bengbu
NANJING
Changzhou
Wuxi
Suzhou
JAPAN
Daxian
Xiangfan
Xinyang
HEFEI
ANHUI
Ma'anshan
Wuhu
SHANGHAI
Three Gorges Dam
Yichang
Anqing
HANGZHOU
Jiaxing
Shaoxing
NINGBO

D

Neijiang
Nanchong
Hechuan
CHONGQING
Changde
Huangshi
Jiujiang
Jingdezhen
Jinhua
ZHEJIANG
LINHAI
EAST
CHINA
SEA
Luzhou
Zunyi
Yibin
Yiyang
NANCHANG
Shangrao
Wenzhou
Ryūkyū-rettō
Okinawa-Jima
zhaotong
GUIYANG
Xiangtan
CHANGSHA
JIANGXI
UIYANG
Duyun
HUNAN
Shaoyang
Ji'an
Jing Shan
Nanping
FUZHOU
Sakishima-Guntō
Naha
Anshun
Hechi
Guilin
Hengyang
Xing'an
FUJIAN
Quanzhou
Hsinchu
TAIPEI
Chilung
Tropic of Cancer
Ximgyi
Yishan
Liuzhou
Shaoguan
GUANGDONG
Zhangzhou
Xiamen
Changhua
T'aichung
Nanning
GUANGXI
ZHUANGZU
ZIZHIQU
Wuzhou
Foshan
GUANGZHOU
(CANTON)
Meizhou
Shantou
Chaozhou
T'ainan
Yü Shan
Chiai
KAOHSIUNG
P'ingtung
T'aitung
TAIWAN (FORMOSA)
Pingxiang
Qinzhou
Yangjiang
Jiangmen
Macau
HONG KONG
(XIANGGANG)
Batan Is.
HANOI
HAIPHONG
Beihai
Maoming
Zhanjiang
Leizhou
Bandao
SOUTH CHINA
SEA
Nam Dinh
Haikou
Hainan Dao
HAINAN
PHILIPPINES

E

VIETNAM
G. of
Tonkin

COPYRIGHT PHILIP'S

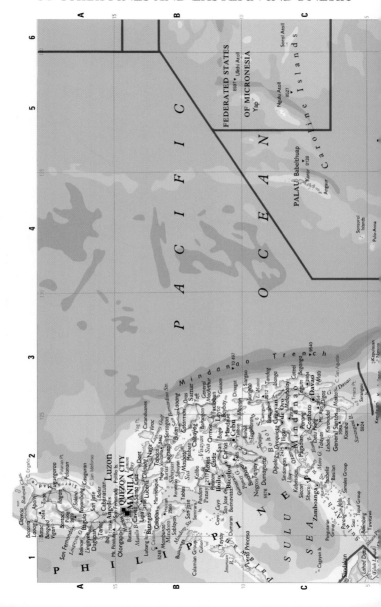

100   0   100   200   300   400   500 km
100   0   50   100   150   200   250   300   350 miles

COPYRIGHT PHILIP'S

PAPUA NEW GUINEA

Equator

Helen Atoll

Tobi

CELEBES

SEA

Sangkulirang

Tanjung Selatan

Teluk Sebuku

Sangihe

Tahuna

Pulau Sangihe

Siau

Kepulauan Sangihe

Salibabu

Talaud

Pulau Talaud

Karakitang

Kaburuang

Biaro

Manado

Bungka

Tahulandang

Tanjung Flesko

Tondano

Kema

Gorontalo

Amurang

Kwandang

Bolaang Mongondow

Kotamobagu

Paleleh

UTARA

Buol

Toli-Toli

Sumalata

Tanjung Tuang

Moutong

Morotai

Berebere

Tobelo

Galela

Akelamo

Sofi

MALUKU

HALMAHERA

Weda

Teluk Buli

Teluk Weda

Patani

Gebe

Gani

Dosi

Jailolo

Ternate

Tidore

Moti

Makian

4970

Kepulauan Bacan

Mandioli

Obi

Pulau Gag

Waigeo

Kepulauan Raja Ampat

Salawati

PAPUA

Jayapura

Sentani

Arso

Genyem

Tanah Merah

Merauke

INDONESIA

Pegunungan Maoke

4702 Puncak Mandala

Puncak Jaya 4884

Pegunungan Van Rees

Pegunungan Jayawijaya

Pegunungan Sudirman

Puncak Trikora 4750

CERAM SEA

BANDA SEA

SERAM

Kepulauan Aru

ARAFURA SEA

Pulau Dolak

Pulau Kimaam

Projection: Mercator

East from Greenwich

m   24 000   18 000   12 000   9000   6000   4000   3000   2000   1500   1200   900   600   300   0   200   400   600   800   1000   2000   3000   4000   5000   6000   9000   12 000

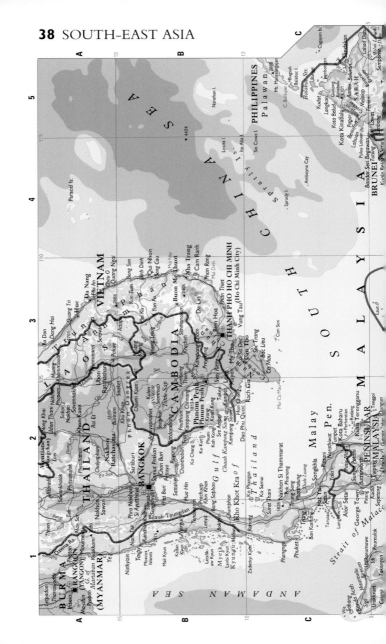

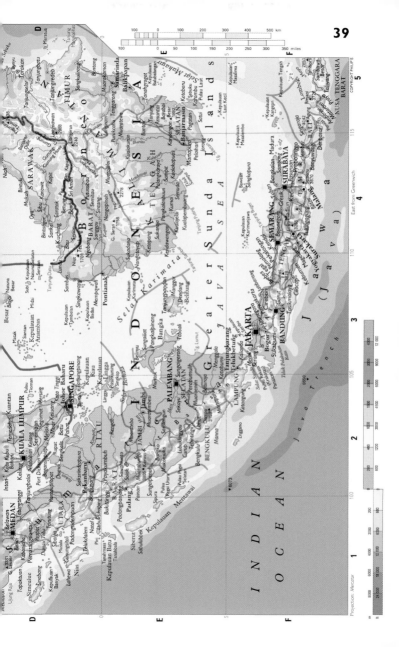

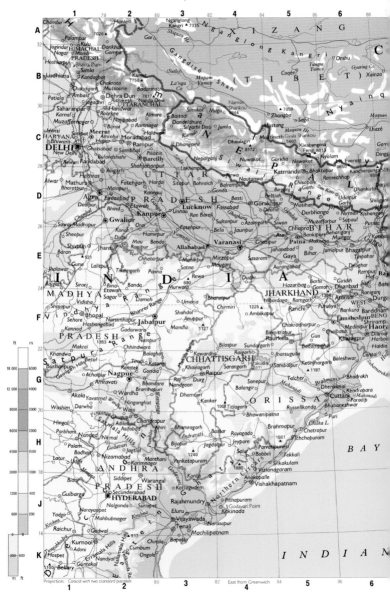

41

COPYRIGHT PHILIP'S

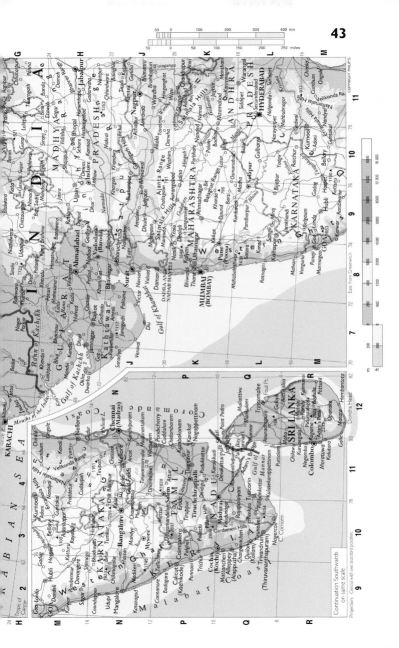

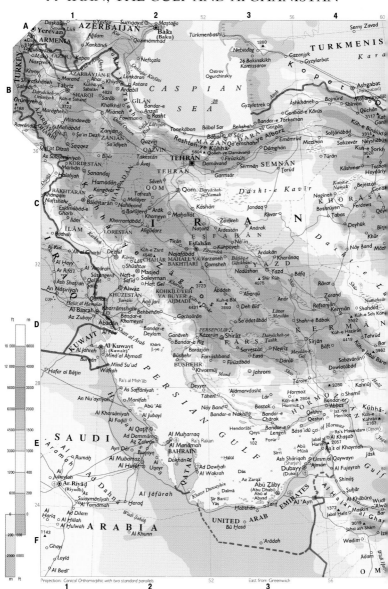

ft   m

18 000   6000
12 000   4000
9000   3000
6000   2000
4500   1500
3000   1000
1200   400
600   200
0   0
          200
2000   6000
m   ft

Projection: Conical Orthomorphic with two standard parallels

East from Greenwich

45

50 0 100 200 300 400 km
50 0 50 100 150 200 250 miles

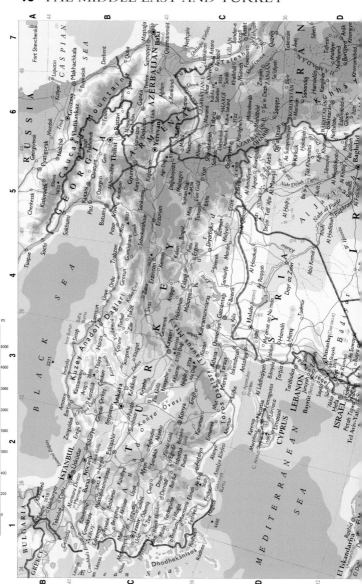

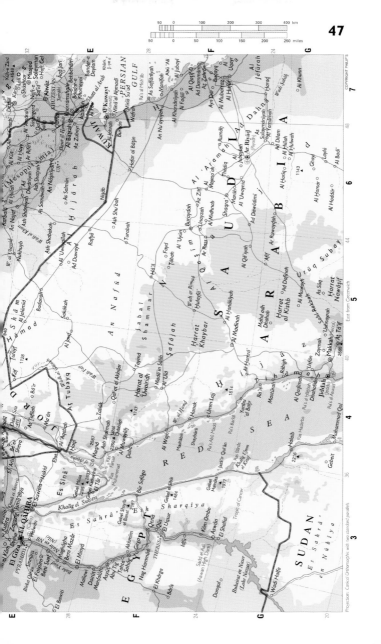

50 0   100   200   300   400 km

50 0   50   100   150   200   250 miles

East from Greenwich

Projection: Conical Orthomorphic with two standard parallels

PERSIAN GULF

Khārg I.
Bandar-e
Bebehūn

Bandare
Khomeyni

Rūd-e Zard
4548
Masjed-e
Soleymān
Hoft Gel
Ahwāz
Shūshtar

Neft-e
Safid

Jarrāhi

KHŪZESTĀN

Shatt al 'Arab
Bandar-e
Māh Shahr
Ābādān
Al Fāw
Khorramshahr

Al Kūt
Al Ḥayy
An Nāṣirīyah

Al Baṣrah
Az Zubayr

KUWAIT
Al Kuwayt
Mīnā al Aḥmadī

Al Wafrah
Mīnā Sa'ūd

As Sāmāwah

An Najaf

Karbalā'

Al Ḥillah
Ad Dīwānīyah
Ash Shaṭrah

Ash Shabakah

Nukhayb

As Salmān

Ḥafar al Bāṭin

Umm Qaṣr
Būbīyān

An Nu'ayrīyah

Al Khafjī
Aḅū 'Alī
As Saffānīyah
Al Manīfah

Al Jubayl
Ad Dammām

Al Qaṭīf
Al Hufūf

Al Fuḍayḥ

Al Mubarraz

Aḏ Ẕ̣ahrān
Buraydah

'Ayn Dar

Ar Rumaḥ

Dhahran

Al Jafūrah

Rā's al Mish'āb

Al Khunn

S A U D I   A R A B I A

Al Quṣūrīyah

Al 'Aramah

Manīḍ al 'Irḍ

Thādiq

Al Muḥtaraqah

Zilfī

Al Majma'ah

Sulaymānīyah

At Tamīmah

A D   D a h n a

Ḥarad

Nijāb

Nizwā

Ash Shu'bah

Turabah

Raḥḥā

Ḥā'il

Al Madnab

Az Zilfī

Ar Riyāḍ

Al Hilāl

Al Ḥulwah

Al Ḥamar

Al Ḥaddār

Loylā

Al Badī'

Ghayl

1143

Al Ḥāriq

Al Dawādimī

'Afīf

'Al Qay'īyah

Ad Dafīnah

Zamah

Ẓalm

As Sūq

Ḥarrat
Nawāṣif

'Urūq Subay'

Al Muwayh
Al Rawnghah

Mahd edh
Dhahab

'Ushayqir

Zaymah

Makkah (Mecca)
2566
Aṭ Ṭā'if

H e j a z

Ḥarrat
al Kishb

Al Madīnah

Ḥarrat Khaybar

Ḥarrat 'Uwayriḍ

Ḥarrat al Rahā'

Wādi al Ḥamḍ

Mahd
adh
Dhahab

Al Ḥamḍah

Al Madā'in Ṣāliḥ

Tabūk

Ḥaql

Al Jawf

Tayma'

Al 'Ula

1614

Rā's al Ḥamra

Umm Laj

Yanbu'
al Baḥr

Rābigh

'Uṣfān

Jiddah
(Jedda)

Al Qaḍīmah

Dhahran al Janūb

Maṣṭābah

Shaybārā

Wajh

Raḥs Abū Madd

Sharmah

An Nafūd

Baḍanah

Saḳākah

Al 'Uwayqīlah

Ar Rafḥā'

Ad Duwayd

Jabal Shammar

Ṣafājah

1128

Badanah

Al Jawf

Al Qaysūmah

Turayf

'Ar'ar

Tall 'Afar

H a m a d

Ḥ a ḏ ḏ

D E S E R T   S y r i a n

Bīr

Maqnā

Faṣīah

2357

Jabal
al Lawz

2580

Ash Sharmah

Ḍibā

Al Muwaylilḥ

Al Wajh

An Nafūd

El Kûntilla
Qala'at en Nakhl

Es Sīnā'

Gebel Mūsa
2637

Gebel Katherina
2642

Raḥs Muḥammad

Raḥs Abū Darag

Gebel Shā'ib
al Bant

Bûr Safâga

Gebel
Ḥamâta
1977

Gebel Ghārib
1464

Sharqiya

Es Sahrâ'

Quseir

El Qâhira (Cairo)
El Gîza
EL QÂHIRA

El Faiyûm
Beni Suef

El Maghra
El Faiyûm

Beni Mazâr

Mallawî

Deirût

Ayyût

Tahta

Naq Hammâdi

THEBES

Qena

Qûs

El Uqsur (Luxor)

E G Y P T

Dakhla

El Khârga

Būr Safâga

El Ḥurghada

Idfu

Kôm Ombo

Aswân

(Aswan High Dam)

El Shallâl

2216

Gebet

Ḥalaïb

Rā's Ḥadarba

Rā's Benâs

R E D   S E A

Es Sahrâ'   en Nûbiya

Birka Qârûn

El Kâb

Abu Tîg

Gebel Shandîb

Maḥamîd

Dungul

Bîr Mazâr

Baharîya

El Fayyûm

El Bawîti

Nakhl

El Kûfra

Ed Dakhla

SUDAN

Wâdi Ḥalfa

Buhairat en Nāṣir
(Lake Nasser)

Tropic of Cancer

TROPIC OF CANCER

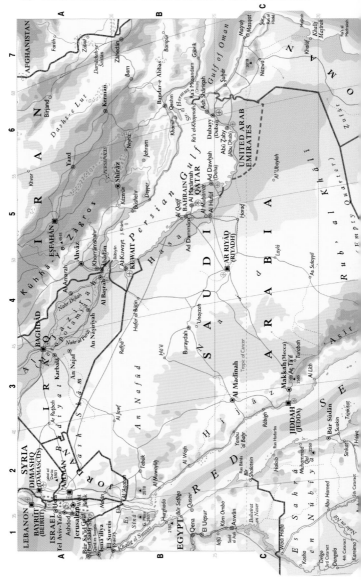

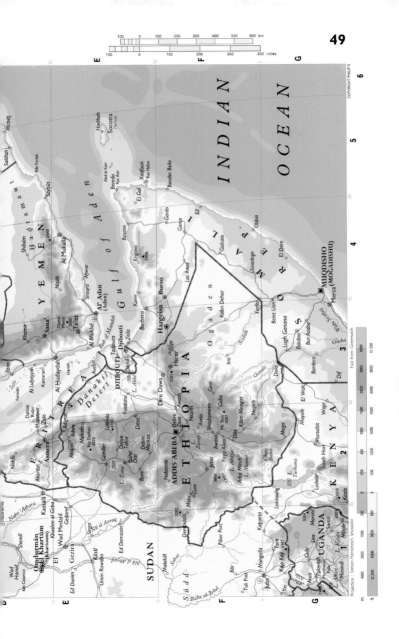

100 0 100 200 300 400 500 600 km
100 0 100 200 300 400 miles

E F G

6

COPYRIGHT PHILIP'S

5

I N D I A N

O C E A N

Mirbāt

Ra's Fartak

Hadiboh

Socotra (Yemen)

Abd al Kūri
Ra's Asir

Berbera
Xaafuun
Ras Hafun

Bender Beila

Şayḥūt

Sayḥūt

Shibām Al Mukallā 2469

H a d r a m a w t

Y E M E N

Ghayḍah

Nişāb Ajwar

Qarin

Eyl El Gal

Gardo

Bōsaso

Ergavo 2406

S O M A L I A

Galcaio

Dusa Mareb

El Dēre

MUQDISHO (MOGADISHU)

Merca Marca

Gijba

Bur Acaba

Boidoa S

Lugh Ganana

Giuba

Belet Uen

Baardheere

Bardera

Dif

El Wak

Wajir

Moyale

Marsabit

K E N Y A

South Horr

L. Turkana 5199

Lodwar

Lokitaung

Kapedo

3025

Maralal

Moroto 3084

Soroti

U G A N D A

L. Kyoga Mbale 4321

Tororo

Iganga

Bukwa

Busia

Jinja

L. Albert

Murchison Falls

Masindi

Gulu

Lira

Bél

Juba

Yei

Tali Post

S u d d

Bahr el Jebel

Mongalla

Pibor Post

Bōr

Malakāl

Sobat

Kapoeta

N. Omo

Lokichar

Dembi Dolo

Metu Gore

3696

Mēga

Arba Minch'

Chew Bahir

L. Shamo

L. Abaya

Dīla

Nazrēt

Negēlē

Mēga

Sh

Goba

Kibre Mengist

Bōra 4307

Mt. Batu

Dīla

Ginir

Dolo

Kebri Dehar

Genalē

El Woito

Gabredarre

Ferfer

O g a d e n

Shabelle

Irni

Goba

Asela

Mēga

Nekemte

A D D I S   A B E B A

Debre Zeyt

Awash

L. Zway

Jima

Awasa

Tirgo Alem

E T H I O P I A

Debre Markos

Bahir Dar

Debre Tabor

Gonder

3620

L. Tana

Bure

Ras Dashen 4620

Aksum

Adwa

Mek'elē

Lalibela 4190

Āsela

Desē

Tendaho

L. Abbe

D a n a k i l   D e s e r t

Dīre Dawa

Harer 3381

Āwash

Jijiga

Hargeisa

Burao

Las Anod

Garoe

G u l f   o f   A d e n

Berbera

Zeila

Djibouti

DJIBOUTI 153 Dikhil

Tadjoura

Āsēb

Dahlak Kebir

Zula L. Abbe

Karin

E R I T R E A

Massawa

Mits'iwa

Āk'ordat

Asmera

Keren

Nefasit

Farasan

Kamaran

Al Luḥayyah

Al Ḥudaydah

Ḥanīsh

Djebel Menal 3760

Taʿizz

Al Mukhā

Bab al Mandab

Al ʿAdan (Aden)

Sanaʿ

Khamir

Ta'izz

Yizān

Nahr ʿAṭbara

Kassalā

Gedaref

Khashm el Girba

Shendi

6th Cataract

Omdurmān
Umm Durmān
El Khartum (Khartoum)

Wad Ḥāmid

Ed Dueim

Umm Ruwāba

Kōsti

El Geili

Wad Medani

El Gezira

Sennar

Singa

Ed Damazin

Nil el Azraq

Kōsti

Malakāl

S U D A N

Nil el Abyad

Projection: Sanson-Flamsteed's Sinusoidal

East from Greenwich

m 0 200 400 600 1000 2000 3000 6000 12 000

ft 0 500 1000 2000 3000 4500 6000 9000 12 000

15 000

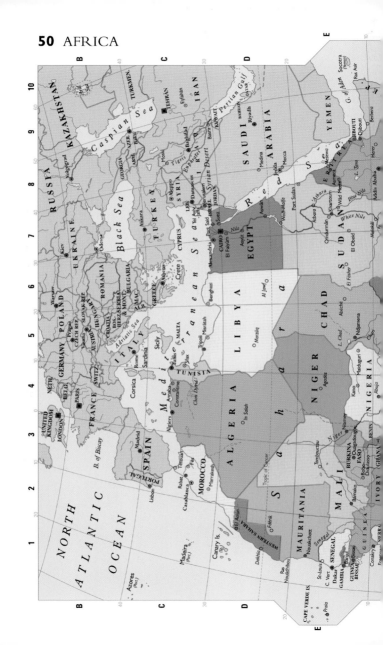

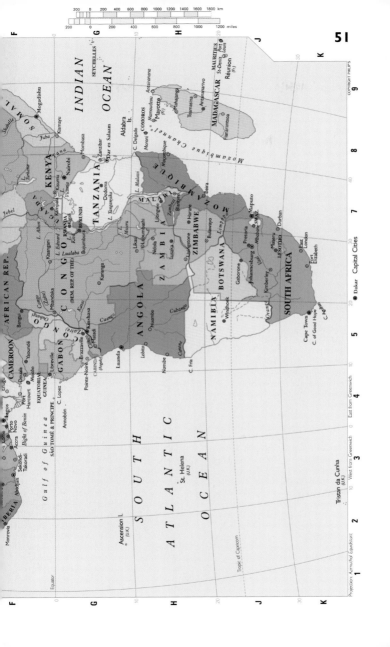

51

Projection: Azimuthal Equidistant

COPYRIGHT PHILIP'S

Scale bar

```
200   0   200   400   600   800  1000  1200  1400  1600  1800 km
200   0   200   400   600       800        1000       1200 miles
```

SOUTH ATLANTIC OCEAN

INDIAN OCEAN

SOMALIA

Mogadishu
Kismayu
Juba
Shebele

KENYA
Mombasa
Nairobi
Kisumu
L. Turkana
Tana
L. Victoria

UGANDA
Kampala
L. Albert
L. Edward
L. Kivu
Kigali
RWANDA
Kigali
BURUNDI
Bujumbura
L. Tanganyika

TANZANIA
Dodoma
Dar es Salaam
Zanzibar
Tabora
L. Malawi

ETHIOPIA
Jebel

CONGO (DEM. REP. OF THE) (ZAIRE)
Kisangani
Lualaba
Mbandaka
Kananga
Kananga
Lukasi
Lubumbashi
Kasai
Kwango
Kwilu

CENTRAL AFRICAN REP.
Bangui
Ubangi

CAMEROON
Douala
Yaoundé
Malabo

EQUATORIAL GUINEA
SÃO TOMÉ & PRÍNCIPE
Annobón
C. Lopez

GABON
Libreville
Port-Gentil
Ogooué

CONGO
Brazzaville
Pointe-Noire
CABINDA (Angola)
Matadi
Kinshasa
Congo (Zaïre)

ANGOLA
Luanda
Lobito
Benguela
Huambo
Cuango
Cuanza
Cuando
Cunene
Cubango
C. Frio
Namibe

ZAMBIA
Lusaka
Ndola
Kafue
Zambezi

MALAWI
Lilongwe
Blantyre

MOZAMBIQUE
C. Delgado
Mozambique
Beira
Zambezi

ZIMBABWE
Harare
Bulawayo
Limpopo

BOTSWANA
Gaborone
Okavango

NAMIBIA
Windhoek
Orange

SOUTH AFRICA
Cape Town
C. of Good Hope
Port Elizabeth
East London
Durban
Johannesburg
Pretoria
Kimberley
Vaal
Maseru
LESOTHO
SWAZILAND
Mbabane

Gulf of Guinea
Bight of Benin

NIGERIA
Lagos
Porto Novo
Accra
Sekondi-Takoradi
Abidjan
Monrovia
LIBERIA
Volta

Tropic of Capricorn

Equator

West from Greenwich
East from Greenwich

St. Helena (UK)
Ascension I. (UK)
Tristan da Cunha

COMOROS
Moroni
Mayotte (Fr.)
Aldabra Is.

SEYCHELLES

MADAGASCAR
Antsiranana
Mahajanga
Toamasina
Antananarivo
Fianarantsoa

Mozambique Channel

MAURITIUS
Réunion (Fr.)
St-Denis
Port Louis

● Dakar Capital Cities

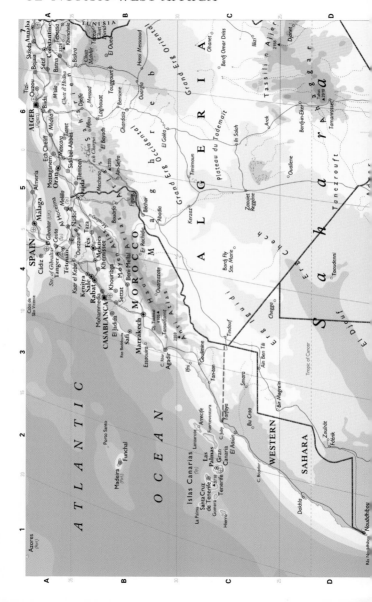

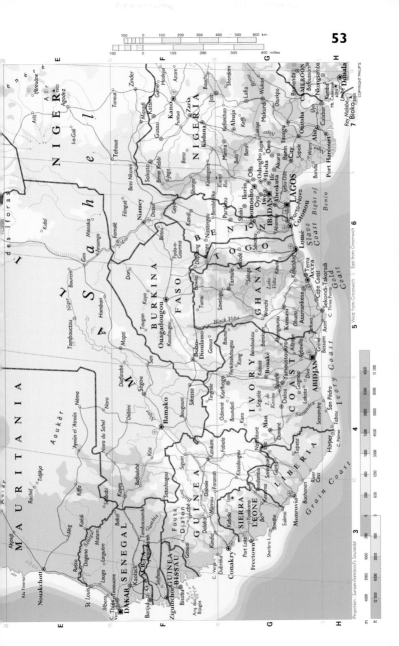

53

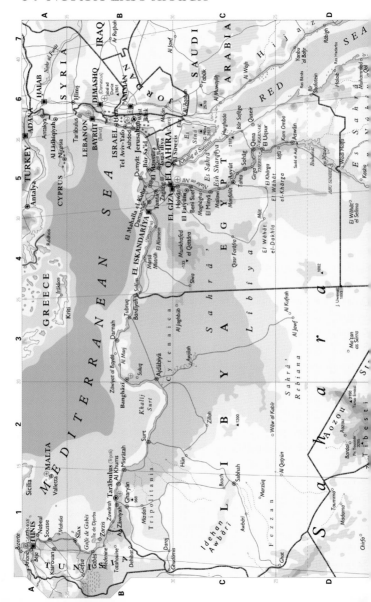

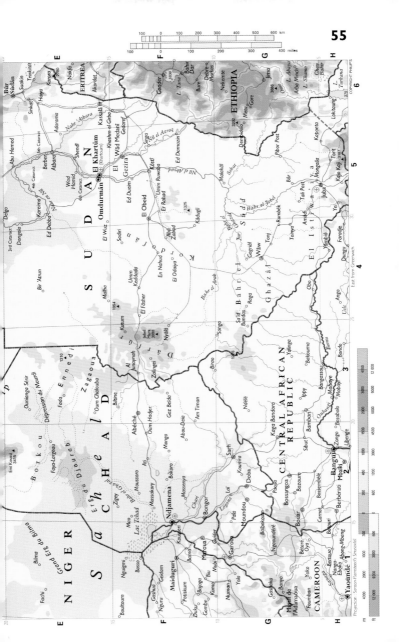

55

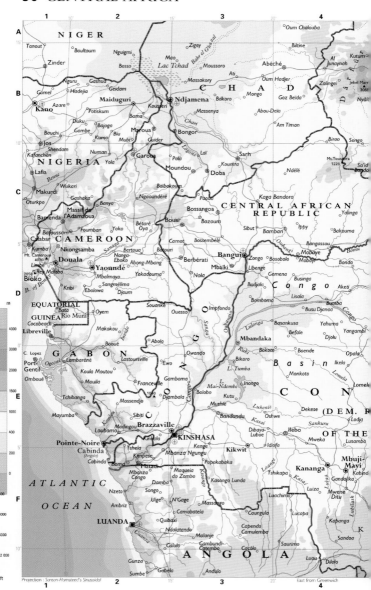

A
B
C
D
E
F

1   2   3   4

NIGER

Tanout
Zinder
Boultoum
Nguigmi
Bosso
Mao
Lac Tchad
Bahr el Ghazal
Zigey
Moussoro
Oum Chalouba
Biltine
Kutum
Al Junaynah
Jebel Marra
3088

Gumel
Azare
Hadeja
Geidam
Gashua
Potiskum
Kousséri
Ndjamena
Massakory
Massenya
Ati
Mongo
Oum Hadjer
Abéché
Goz Beïda
Zalingei
Nyala

Kano
Duku
Bama
Bajoga
Gombe
Biu
Mubi
Maroua
Bongor
Chari
Boko
Abou-Deïa
Am Timan

Bauchi
Shendam
Numan
Yola
Garoua
Guider
Palo
Laï
Sarh
Birao
Songo

Jos
Kafanchan
Lafia
Makurdi
NIGERIA
Wukari
Gashaka
Benue
Yoko
Ngaoundéré
Baïbokoum
Moundou
Doba
Koumra
Ndélé
Mt. Toussoro 1226
Sa'id Bundu

Oturkpo
Banyo
Bétaré Oya
Bouar
Bossangoa
Bozoum
Kaga Bandoro
CENTRAL AFRICAN REPUBLIC
Ippy
Yalinga

Massif de l'Adamaoua
Bamenda
Bafoussam
Foumban
Fumban
Nanga-Eboko
Bertoua
Batouri
Carnot
Bossembélé
Sibut
Bambari
Bangassou
Bakouma

Calabar
Kumba
Nkongsamba
Mt. Cameroon
Limbe
2054
CAMEROON
Yaoundé
Mbalmayo
Abong-Mbang
Yokadouma
Berbérati
Nola
Bangui
Mbaïki
Zongo
Bosobolo
Mobaye
Mobayi
Gemena
Businga
Bondo
Bili
Akети

Douala
Bioko
B. of Bon.
Kribi
Ebolowa
Sangmélima
Djoum
Souanké
Libenge
Budjala
Bombomo
Lisala
Busu Djanoa
Bumba
Congo
Yambio

EQUATORIAL GUINEA
Bata
Rio Muni
Oyem
Ouesso
Impfondo
Mbandaka
Basankusa
Yahuma
Yangambi

Libreville
Cocobeach
Makokou
Booué
Abolo
Owando
Bokoro
Bokote
Boende
Befale
Djolu
Opala

C. Lopez
Port-Gentil
Omboué
Lambaréné
GABON
Koula Moutou
Lastoursville
Ewo
Gamboma
Mai-Ndombe
Inongo
Mushie
L. Tumba
Basin
Ikela
Lomela
Monkoto

Tchibanga
Mossendjo
Sibiti
Djambala
Bolobo
Kutu
Lukenie
Dekese
CON
Lodja

Mayumba
Kindu
Madingou
Brazzaville
Kinkala
Bandundu
Oshwe
Kasaï
Sankuru
Mweka
Lusambo
(DEM. R

Loubomo
Tshela
KINSHASA
Kenge
Dibaya-Lubue
Ilebo
OF THE

Pointe-Noire
Cabinda (Angola)
Boma
Matadi
Mbanza Ngungu
Popokabaka
Idiofa
Kananga
Mbuji-Mayi
Kabind

Mbanza Congo
Damba
Maquela do Zombo
Kasongo Lunda
Loange
Tshikapa
Luiza
Gandajika
Mwene Ditu

ATLANTIC OCEAN
Nzeto
Ambriz
Songo
N'Gage
Uige
Massango
Luachimo
Lucapa
Kapanga
Sandoa

Caungula
Capenda Camulemba
Cacolo
Saurimo
Labilashi

LUANDA
Ndalatando
Malanje
Cambundi Catembo

Gunza
Gabela
Sumbe
Calulo
Andulo
ANGOLA
Luau
Dilolo

Projection : Sanson-Flamsteed's Sinusoïdal

East from Greenwich

ft   m
12 000   4000
9000   3000
6000   2000
4500   1500
3000   1000
1200   400
600   200
0   0
200   600
4000   3000
2000   6000
4000   12 000
m   ft

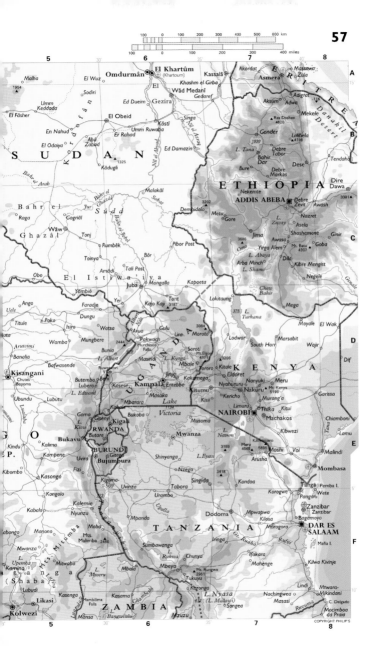

57

Scale bar: 100 0 100 200 300 400 500 600 km / 100 0 100 200 300 400 miles

SUDAN

Malha · 1954 · El Wuz · Omdurmân · El Khartûm (Khartoum) · Kassalâ · Akordat · Massawa · Zula · Asmera · **ERITREA**

Umm Keddada · Sodiri · Khashm el Girba · Gedaref · Aksúm · Adigrat · -16 · **Danakil**

El Fâsher · En Nahud · El Obeid · Ed Dueim · Umm Ruwaba · Singa · Wâd Medanî · Gezira · Adwa · Mekele

Kôdugli · 1325 · Er Rahad · Kâsti · Nil el Azraq · Ed Damazin · Gonder · Lalibela · 1320 · **Desert**

El Odaiya · Aba Zabad · L. Tana · Debre Tabor · Dese · Tendaho

Bahr el Arab · Bahr el Jebel · Malakâl · Sobat · Bahir Dar · Debre Markos · Bure

Raga · Gogriâl · **B a h r e l** · Jur · **Sûdd** · Nekemte · **ETHIOPIA** · Dire Dawa

Wâw · **G h a z â l** · Tonj · Rumbêk · Bôr · Pibor Post · 3202 · Dembidolo · ADDIS ABEBA · Debre Zeyit · Awash · 3381▲

Obo · Toinya · Tali Post · Metu · Gore · Nazret · Asela

Amadi · Juba · Mongalla · Kapoeta · Jima · Awasa · Shashemene · Ginir · Mt Batu 4307▲ · Goba

Yambió · Yei · Kajo Kaji · 3187 · Torit · Lokitaung · Omo · Yirga Alem · L. Zuqay · Dila · Kibre Mengist

Uele · Faradje · Watsa · **U G A N D A** · Gulu · Moroto · L. Turkana · 378 · Negele · **Genâle**

Ango · Isiro · Dungu · Arua · Pakwach · Lira · 3084▲ · Soroti · Mega · Moyale · El Wak

Titule · Poko · Mungbere · Bunia · Murchison Falls · Masindi · Mt Elgon 4321▲ · Lodwar · South Horn · Marsabit · Wajir · Dif

Aruwimi · Wamba · Bafwasende · Butembo · Beni · Ruwenzori · L. Kyoga · Mbale · 3296 · Kitale · Eldoret · Nanyuki · Meru · Garissa

CONGO DEM. REP. · Kisangani · Chutes Boyoma · Lubero · L. Edward · Kasese · Fort Portal · Jinja · Kakamega · Tororo · **KENYA** · Nyahururu · Mt Kenya 5199▲ · Murang'a

Ubundu · Lubutu · Goma · Kampala · Entebbe · Kisumu · Kisii · Kericho · Nakuru · Thika · Machakos · Chiamboni

Kindu · Kalima · Bukavu · Gisenyi · Kigali · **RWANDA** · Butare · Masaka · Bukoba · **Lake Victoria** · Musoma · Limuru · **NAIROBI** · Kibwezi · Lamu

Kibombo · Kampene · Kasongo · Uvira · **BURUNDI** · Gitega · Bujumbura · Mwanza · Nzega · Shinyanga · L. Eyasi · Kilimanjaro 5895 · Meru 4566▲ · 3188▲ · Arusha · Moshi · Voi · Malindi · Mombasa

Kongolo · Kalemie · Nyunzu · Kigoma-Ujiji · Uvinza · Tabora · Singida · 3418▲ · Kondoa · Korogwe · Tanga · Pemba I. · Wete · Pangani

Kabalo · Manono · Moba · Mpanda · Urambo · **Mts Mitumba** · **T A N Z A N I A** · Dodoma · Mpwapwa · Kilosa · Morogoro · Zanzibar · Zanzibar I. · Bagamoyo · **DAR ES SALAAM**

Mwanza · Fizi · **Mts Malimba** 2480 · Sumbawanga · Iringa · Gr. Ruaha · Rufiji · Mafia I.

L. Upemba · L. Mweru · Mitwaba · L. Rukwa · Chunya · Mbeya · Mt Rungwe 2961▲ · Tukuyu · Mahenge · Kilwa Kivinje

(Shaba) · Lubudi · Kamina · Kasenga · Hambilima Falls · Mansa · Kasama · Chambeshi · Kitongo · **L. Nyasa (L. Malawi)** · Sangea · Nachingwea · Lindi · Mtwara-Mikindani

Likasi · Kolwezi · **Z A M B I A** · Bangweulu · Mzuzu · Masasi · Ruvuma · C. Delgado · Mocimboa da Praia

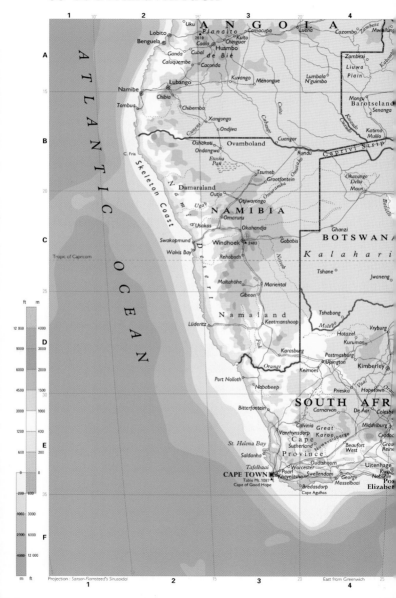

ft   m

12 000 4000

9000   3000

6000   2000

4500   1500

3000   1000

1200   400

600   200

0   0

200   600

1000   3000

2000   6000

4000   12 000

m   ft

Projection : Sasson-Flamsteed's Sinusoidal   East from Greenwich

ATLANTIC OCEAN

ANGOLA

Uku · Planalto · Camacupa · Luena · Cazombo · Zambeze · Mwibilunga
Lobito · 2619 · Kuito · Chenguar
Benguela · Caala · Huambo
Ganda · Cubal · de Bié · Caconda · Kuvango · Menongue · Lumbala · Zambezi
Caluquembe · N'guimbo · Liuwa · Plain · Kabompo
Lubango · Katima
Namibe · Chibia · Mongu · Mulilo
Tombua · Chibemba · Senanga · Barotseland

Xangongo · Cubango · Caprivi Strip
Ondjiva · Cuangar · Rundu · Kwando
Oshakati · Ovamboland · Okavango · Delta · Maun · Barotse
Ondangwa
Etosha · Tsumeb
Pan · Grootfontein · Okavango · Delta · Maun

Damaraland · Outjo · Omaruru · Otjiwarongo · Ghanzi

NAMIBIA · BOTSWANA

Ugab · Omaruru
Usakos · Okahandja
Swakopmund · Windhoek △2483 · Gobabis · Kalahari
Walvis Bay · Rehoboth · Tshane
Tropic of Capricorn

Maltahöhe · Mariental · Tshabong · Jwaneng
Gibeon · Molopo · Vryburg
Namaland · Keetmanshoop · Hotazel · Kuruman
Lüderitz · Fish · Karasburg · Postmasburg · Kimberley
Orange · Upington · Keimoes · Prieska · Hopetown
Port Nolloth · Karasburg · De Aar · Coles
Nababeep · SOUTH AFR
Bitterfontein · Carnarvon
Calvinia · Great · Middelburg · Cradoc
Vanrhynsdorp · Cape · Karoo · Graa
St. Helena Bay · Sutherland · Beaufort · Reine
Saldanha · Province · West · Uitenhage
Tafelbaai · Oudtshoorn · Kw
CAPE TOWN · Paarl · Swellendam · George · Po
Table Mt. 1087 · Khayelitsha · Mosselbaai · Elizabet
Cape of Good Hope · Bredasdorp
Cape Agulhas

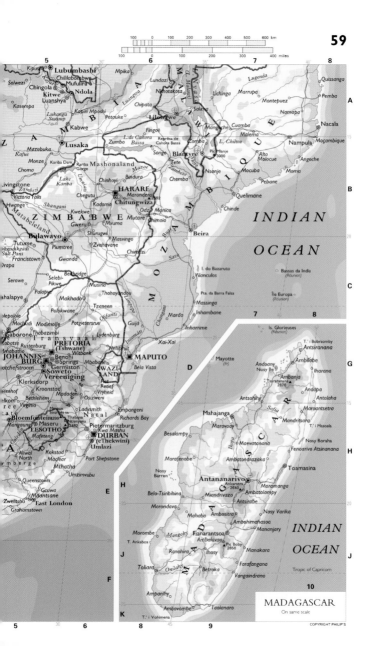

100   0   100   200   300   400   500   600 km
100   0   100   200   300   400 miles

5 30 **6** 35 **7** 40 **8**

Kipushi °Lubumbashi   Mpika°   Lundazi   Lugenda   °Quissanga
Solwezi°   Chililabombwe   °Uchinga   Marrupa   Montepuez   °Pemba
Chingola° Mufulira   Nchelatoka   Salima   Namapa
Kitwe° °Ndola   °Chipata   °Liongwe   MALAWI   Namapa A
Kasempa°   Luanshya   Petauke°   Fingoe   Mangoche °Cuamba   Nacala
Kabwe°   Lukanga   Zomba   Malema   Nampula °Moçambique 15
ZAMBIA   Swamp   Kapiri Mposhi   L. de Cahora   Represa de   L. Chilwa   Alto   °Angoche
Mazabuka°   °Lusaka   Bassa Cahora Bassa   Blantyre °Pico Milanje   Molocue   Moma
Kafue°   Zumbo°   Songo   Tete   3000   °Mocuba °Pebane
Monze°   Kariba Dam   Kariba Gorge   Mazoe   Chemba   Nsanje   °Quelimane B
Choma°   Mashonaland   °Chinhoyi   Bindura   °Chinde
Livingstone°   Lake   Chegutu   HARARE   Marondera   Manica   INDIAN
Victoria Falls   Kariba   °Kadoma   Chitungwiza   Chimoio
Hwange°   Shangani   Kwekwe°   Odzi   Mutare   °Beira   OCEAN
ZIMBABWE   °Gweru   Shurugwi   Buzi
Bulawayo°   Masvingo°   °Zvishavane   Chinezi   I. do Bazaruto
°Plumtree   °Zvishavane   Save   °Vilanculos   °Bassas da India 20
Tutume°   Gwanda°   °Massinga   Pta. da Barra Falsa   Île Europa C
Francistown°   Selebi-   Beitbridge   Marão   Inhambane   (Réunion)
Drapa   Pikwe   °Musina   Guija   Inharrime
Serowe°   Makhado°   Changane   7   8
Mahalapye°   Polokwane°   Tzaneen°   Xai-Xai
Molepolole°   Modimolle°   Potgietersrus   Is. Glorieuses   (Réunion)
Gaborone°   Thabazimbi°   Lydenburg   Mayotte   T. i Bobraomby   Antsiranana
Lobatse   Rustenburg°   Transvaal   Nelspruit   (Fr)   Andoany   Ambilobe   °Iharana G
JOHANNES-   (Tshwane)   Benoni   Nosy Be   Ambanja   °Andapa
BURG   °Springs   Mbabane   Antsohihy   Tsaratanana   Antalaha
atchefstroom   Germiston   SWAZI-   2876
Soweto   Vereeniging   LAND   Mahajanga   Sofia   °Mandritsara   T. i Masoala
Klerksdorp°   Oshiweni   Maroovoy   H
Kroonstad°   Bela Vista   Besalampy°   Maevatanana   Nosy Boraha 15
Virginia°   Mpadeni   °MAPUTO   Morafenobe°   Ambatondrazaka   Fenoarivo Atsinanana
Welkom°   Vryheid   Nosy   Antananarivo   °Toamasina
Bloemfontein°   Ladysmith°   Barren   Ankaratra   Moramanga
Mangaung   Maseru   Natal   2643
LESOTHO   Kwa Mashu   Miandrivazo   Antsirabe
Mafeteng°   Pietermaritzburg   MADAGASCAR   20
Aliwal   Kokstad°   DURBAN   Belo-Tsiribihina   Ambositra   Nosy Varika
North   (eThekwini)   Morondava°   Ambahimahasoa
mberge   Moclear°   Umlazi   Mahabo   Fianarantsoa   Mananjary
Queenstown°   Port Shepstone   Moromba°   Ambalavao   Manakara   INDIAN
Gcowa°   Mhatha   T. Ankabos   Ranohira°   Ihasy   OCEAN
Zwelitsha°   Mdantsane   Betraka°   Farafangana
°East London   Umzimvubu   Toliara°   Onilahy   Vangaindrano J
Grahamstown°   Ampanihy   Tropic of Capricorn
Ambovombe   °Taolanaro   **10**
T. i Vohimena   **MADAGASCAR** K
On same scale

5 **6** 30 **8** 45 **9**

COPYRIGHT PHILIP'S

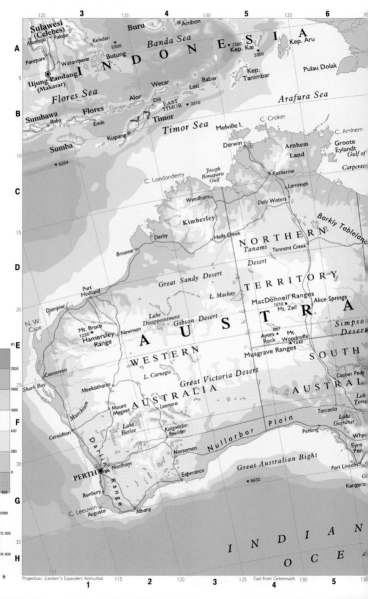

Projection: Lambert's Equivalent Azimuthal

East from Greenwich

PAPUA NEW GUINEA

New Guinea
Mount Hagen 4508 ▲Mt. Wilhelm
Lae
Fly
Owen Stanley Range
Gulf of Papua
Port Moresby
Torres Strait
C. York

New Britain
New Georgia
Solomon Sea
D'Entrecasteaux Islands
Louisiade Archipelago

2743 ▲ Mt. Balbi
9140
Bougainville
Choiseul
Santa Isabel

New Georgia
Honiara ▲2439
Guadalcanal
San Cristóbal
Rennell

SOLOMON ISLANDS
Malaita

Weipa
Cape York Peninsula

Coral Sea

P A C I F I C

Cooktown
Wellesley Is.
Mitchell
Normanton
Forsayth
1611 ▲ Cairns
Townsville
Charters Towers
Cloncurry Hughenden
Mount Isa Dajarra
Winton
Emerald
Longreach
Yaraka
Charleville
Quilpie
Thargomindah
Cunnamulla
Dirranbandi
Bourke
Walgett
Cobar

QUEENSLAND
A L I A

Barrier Reef
Great
Great Dividing Range
Diamantina

Mackay
Rockhampton
Gladstone
Bundaberg
Maryborough
Gympie
Roma
Toowoomba
BRISBANE
Ipswich
Gold Coast
Lismore
Grafton
Moree

CORAL
SEA
ISLANDS
TERRITORY

Îles Chesterfield

Îles D'Entrecasteaux

O C E A N

Tropic of Capricorn

NEW SOUTH WALES
Tamworth
Round Mt. 1615
Port Macquarie
Taree
Dubbo
Orange
Bathurst
Newcastle
SYDNEY
Wollongong
Griffith
Hay
Goulburn
Canberra A.C.T.
Mt. Kosciuszko 2230 ▲
Bombala
C. Howe

Lord Howe I. (Austral.)
▼734

Tasman Sea

Flinders Ranges
Broken Hill
Port Pirie
Port Augusta Sb.
Mildura
Murray
Swan Hill
Bendigo
Ballarat
ADELAIDE
Vincent
Encounter B.
Horsham
Mount Gambier
Warrnambool

Wagga Wagga
Albury
Wodonga
Shepparton
Snowy Mts.

VICTORIA
Sale
MELBOURNE
Geelong

▼5287

King I.
Bass Strait
Furneaux Group

Burnie
1617 ▲ Mt. Ossa
Launceston

TASMANIA
S.E.Cape
Hobart

ake Eyre
Marree
Cooper Creek
Grey Range
Warrego
Darling

COPYRIGHT PHILIP'S

SOUTH AUSTRALIA

Abminga
Pedirka
The Stevenson
Chandler
Marla
The Hamilton
Indulkana
L. Coonnie
L. Yamma
Yamma
L. Thomas
L. Coomnie
Goyder
Lagoon
Peera Peera
Poolanna L.
McGregor Ra.

Mintabie
Oodnadatta
The Alberga
The Neales
The Warburton
L. Howitt
Innamincka
Cooper Creek
Bulloo

A
Cadney Park
Lora Cr.
Peake Cr.
Warrina
Lake Eyre
(North)
Kittakittaooloo
L. Hope
Strzelecki Creek
Coober Pedy
Combay
Cadibaerrawirracanna
William
Creek
L. Florence
L. Gregory
Coward Springs
Lake Eyre
(South)
Marree
The Frome
L. Blanche
L. Callabonna
Tibooburra

30
Farina
Andamooka
Opal Fields
Leigh Creek
Lyndhurst
Arkaroola
Benbonyathe
1064
Milparinka
The Sah L.
Olympic Dam
Maldoona
Tarcoola
L. Younghusband
L. Hanson
Woomera
Pimba
Bettana
Parachilna
Lake
Frome
White Cliffs
L. Harris
Kingoonya
Island
Lagoon
Primary
Lagoon
St. Mary Pk.
1168
Hawker
Wilcannia
L. Everard
L. Acraman
L. Gairdner
L. Macfarlane
Cradock
Carrieton
472
Stephens Creek
Cockburn
Broken Hill
Koonibba
Ceduna
Denial Bay
Thevenard
Poochera
Nukey Bluff
472
Quorn
Wilmington
Yunta
Mannahill
Menindee L.
Cundelilla L.
Tandou L.
Menindee
Darling
Ratcatchers

B
Nuyts
Arch.
Smoky
Bay
C. Bauer
Minnipa
Wudinna
L. Gilles
Iron Knob
Mt. Remarkable
963
Port Germein
Peterborough
Terowie
Papilta L.
Popio L.
Travellers L.
Poincarie
Smoky Bay
Streaky Bay
Port Kenny
Kyancutta
Iron Baron
Iron Duke
Whyalla
Port Pirie
Crystal Brook
Gladstone
Jamestown
Hallett
Anna
Burra
Victoria
C. Blanche
C. Radstock
Anxious
Bay
Kopi
Rudall
Cleve
Arno
Bay
Cowell
Port Broughton
Snowtown
Mt. Bryan
934
Morgan
L. Victoria
Wentworth
Mildura
Merbein
Red Cliffs
Pitarpunga L.
Euston
Flinders I.
Investigator
Group
Elliston
Lock
Kadina
Wallaroo
Port Broughton
Balaklava
Wakefield
Hamley Bridge
Riverton
Robertstown
Milang
Angaston
Waikerie
Barmera
Meringur
Werrimull
Hattah
Ouyen
Balranald
Mount Hope
Darke Peak
Cummins
Tumby Bay
Maitland
Ardrossan
Kapunda
Nuriootpa
Truro
Morgan
Loxton
Alawoona
Underbool
Patchewollock
L. Tyrrell
Swan Hill

35
Coffin Bay Pen.
Coffin Bay
Port Lincoln
C. Carnot
Stenhouse B.
Thistle I.
C. Spencer
ADELAIDE
Gawler
Elizabeth
Brighton
Murray
Bridge
Karoonda
Lameroo
Pinnaroo
Hopetoun
Birchip
Warracknabeal
Donald
Kerang
Spencer
Gulf
Edithburgh
Yorketown
Willunga
Victor
Harbor
Strathalbyn
Tailem Bend
Coonalpyn
Tintinara
Keith
Bordertown
Nhill
L. Albacutya
Jeparit
Dimboola
Wycheproof
St. Arnaud
Cape
Jaffa
Naracoorte
Kaniva
Murtoa
Dunolly
Investigator Strait
Gulf
St. Vincent
Kingscote
Kangaroo I.
C. Borda
C. du Couedic
Gantheaume
Bay
D'Estrees
Bay
Encounter Bay
Fleurieu
Pen.
Lacepede Bay
Kingston S. E.
Robe
Lucindale
Edenhope
Horsham
Natimuk
Stawell
Maryborough
Ararat
BALLAR
Beachport
L. George
Penola
Rivoli B.
Millicent
Casterton
Coleraine
Hamilton
Maroona
Marnoo

C
Mount Gambier
C. Northumberland
Mt. Burr
Mt. Gambier
Mt. McDonnell
Discovery Bay
Port
MacDonnell
Cavendish
Portland
Heywood
Port
Campbell
Bridgewater
Warrnambool
Camperdown
Terang
Colac
Geelong
Torquai
MELBOU
Apollo Bay
C. Otway

D
C. Wickham
King Island
Currie
Stokes Pt.

Projection: Bonne
East from Greenwich

[Inset map — Tasmania / Bass Strait]

On same scale

C. Wickham
Curtis
Group
Kent Group
Deal I.
King Island
Currie
Grassy
Stokes Pt.
Bass   **Strait**
Palana
Flinders Island
C. Keraudren
Hunter I.
Three
Hummock I.
Furneaux
Group
Prime Seal I.
Robbins I.
Marrawah
Cape Barren I.
Whitemark
Arthur
Smithton
Stanley
Burnie
Wynyard
Penguin
Ulverstone
Devonport
Naturaliste
Waratah
Savage River
Zeehan
Rosebery
Mt. Ossa
1617
Mole Creek
Westbury
Deloraine
Latrobe
Launceston
Longford
Perth
Ross
Tunbridge
Campbell Town
St. Marys
Bicheno
Queenstown
Strahan
Macquarie
Harbour
Hamilton
Oatlands
Triabunna
Freycinet
Pen.
Schouten I.
Hibbs Bay
TASMANIA
New Norfolk
Bridgewater-Gagebrook
Maydena
Hobart
Maria I.
Port Davey
Bathurst Harb.
Kettering
Cygnet
Dover
South West C.
Bruny I.
South East C.
Tasman Pen.
Port Arthur

[Elevation scale — left margin]

ft	m
	1500
4500	1000
3000	600
1200	400
600	200
0	0
200	600
2000	6000
4000	12 000
m	ft

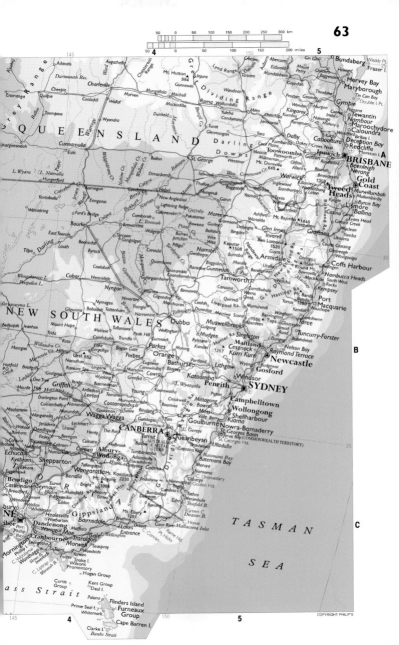

50 0 50 100 150 200 250 300 km
50 0 50 100 150 200 miles

A

B

C

QUEENSLAND

Darling Downs

BRISBANE

Gold Coast

Tweed Heads

Toowoomba

Ipswich

Warwick

Bundaberg

Fraser I.

Hervey Bay

Maryborough

Gympie

Tewantin

Noosa

Nambour

Maroochydore

Caloundra

Caboolture

Redcliffe

Deception Bay

Beenleigh

Nerang

Murwillumbah

Byron Bay

Ballina

Lismore

Casino

Grafton

Coffs Harbour

Nambucca Heads

Kempsey

Port Macquarie

Taree

Tuncurry-Forster

Nelson Bay

Raymond Terrace

Newcastle

Gosford

Maitland

Cessnock

Kurri Kurri

Singleton

Muswellbrook

Armidale

Tamworth

NEW SOUTH WALES

Dubbo

Wellington

Mudgee

Lithgow

Katoomba

Penrith

SYDNEY

Windsor

Parkes

Orange

Bathurst

Forbes

Cowra

Young

Campbelltown

Wollongong

Shellharbour

Kiama

Nowra-Bomaderry

St Georges Basin

Ulladulla

Goulburn

CANBERRA

Queanbeyan

AUSTRALIAN CAPITAL TERRITORY

(COMMONWEALTH TERRITORY)

Wagga Wagga

Griffith

Cootamundra

Junee

Leeton

Narrandera

Albury-Wodonga

Wangaratta

Mt. Kosciuszko 2230

Cooma

Eden

Batemans Bay

Moruya

Narooma

Bega

Merimbula

Echuca

Shepparton

Bendigo

Castlemaine

Seymour

Healesville

Dandenong

Cranbourne

Morwell

Traralgon

Sale

Bairnsdale

Gippsland

Orbost

Mallacoota Inlet

Pt. Hicks

TASMAN

SEA

Bass Strait

Flinders Island

Furneaux Group

Cape Barren I.

Whitemark

Clarke I.

Banks Strait

4

5

145

150

COPYRIGHT PHILIP'S

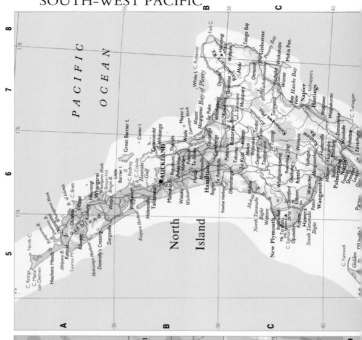

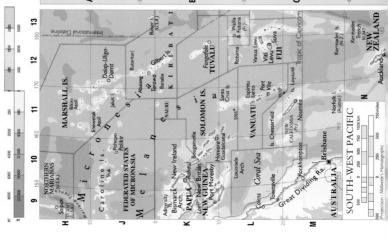

SOUTH-WEST PACIFIC

Projection : Mollweide's Homographic

km 500   0   250   500   750   1000 km

miles 500   0   250   500   750 miles

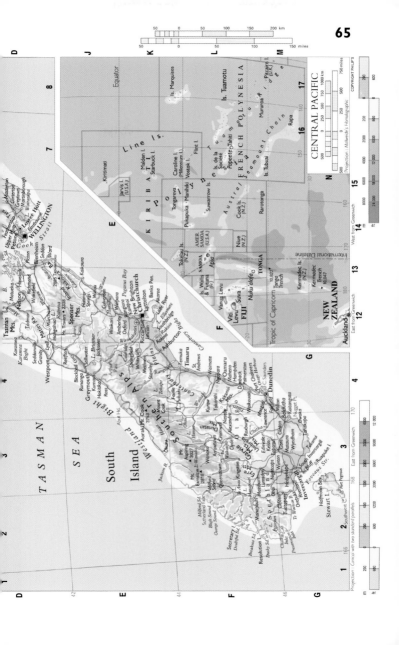

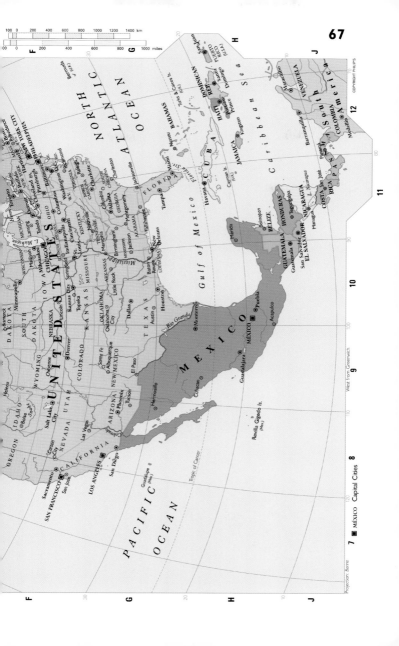

67

100 0 200 400 600 800 1000 1200 1400 km

00 0 200 400 600 800 1000 miles

F **G**

NORTH ATLANTIC OCEAN

Bermuda (U.K.)

UNITED STATES

Portland
Boston MASS.
PROVIDENCE
New Haven CONN.
NEW YORK CITY
PHILADELPHIA
Buffalo
Cleveland
Pittsburgh
Baltimore
Washington
VIRGINIA
Richmond
Raleigh
NORTH CAROLINA
Charlotte
Columbia
SOUTH CAROLINA
Charleston
GEORGIA
Atlanta
Savannah
Jacksonville
FLORIDA
Tampa
Miami
Key West

Detroit
Toledo
MICHIGAN
Lansing
OHIO
Columbus
Cincinnati
INDIANA
Indianapolis
Louisville
KENTUCKY
Nashville
TENNESSEE
Memphis
ALABAMA
Montgomery
MISSISSIPPI
Jackson
Birmingham

Milwaukee
L. Michigan
CHICAGO
WISCONSIN
Madison
ILLINOIS
Springfield
MISSOURI
St. Louis

Minneapolis
Bismarck
MINNESOTA
IOWA
Des Moines
Kansas City
NEBRASKA
Topeka
KANSAS
OKLAHOMA
Oklahoma City
Little Rock
ARKANSAS
LOUISIANA
Baton Rouge
New Orleans

SOUTH DAKOTA
NORTH DAKOTA
Helena
MONTANA
WYOMING
Cheyenne
COLORADO
Denver
NEW MEXICO
Santa Fe
Albuquerque
El Paso
Dallas
Austin
Houston
San Antonio
TEXAS
Rio Grande
Monterrey

IDAHO
Boise
OREGON
Carson City
NEVADA
Salt Lake City
UTAH
ARIZONA
Phoenix
Tucson
Las Vegas
CALIFORNIA
Sacramento
San Francisco
San Jose
LOS ANGELES
San Diego

PACIFIC OCEAN

Tropic of Cancer

Guadalupe (Mex.)

Revilla Gigedo Is. (Mex.)

MEXICO

Culiacán
Hermosillo
Guadalajara
MEXICO
Puebla
Acapulco

Gulf of Mexico

Havana
CUBA
Mérida
Cancún
BAHAMAS
Nassau
Turks & Caicos Is. (U.K.)
JAMAICA
Kingston
Cayman Is. (U.K.)

Caribbean Sea

BELIZE
Belmopan
GUATEMALA
Guatemala
HONDURAS
Tegucigalpa
EL SALVADOR
San Salvador
NICARAGUA
Managua
L. Nicaragua
COSTA RICA
San José
PANAMA
Panamá

HAITI
Port-au-Prince
DOMINICAN REP.
Santo Domingo
San Juan
PUERTO RICO (U.S.A.)

South America

COLOMBIA
Medellín
Bogotá
VENEZUELA
Maracaibo
Barranquilla

Projection: Bonne

7 ■ MÉXICO Capital Cities 8 9 10 11 12

West from Greenwich

COPYRIGHT PHILIP'S

F G H J

PACIFIC

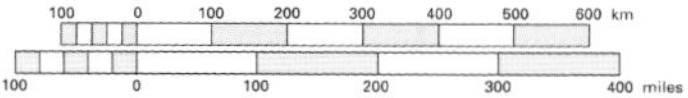

100 0 100 200 300 400 500 600 km
100 0 100 200 300 400 miles

C
D
ONTARIO
MANITOBA
SASKATCHEWAN
ALBERTA
BRITISH COLUMBIA
CANADA
UNITED STATES
MONTANA
NORTH DAKOTA
SOUTH DAKOTA
MINNESOTA
WISCONSIN
IOWA
NEBRASKA
WASHINGTON
Winnipeg
Regina
Saskatoon
Edmonton
Calgary
VANCOUVER
Victoria
SEATTLE
Olympia
Tacoma
Spokane
Bismarck
Pierre
ST. PAUL
MINNEAPOLIS
Des Moines
Omaha
Duluth
Fargo
Lake Winnipeg
L. Winnipegosis
L. Manitoba
L. of the Woods
Missouri
Selkirk Mts.
Vancouver I.
OCEAN
ALASKA
CHUKCHI SEA
BERING SEA
GULF OF ALASKA
PACIFIC OCEAN
Aleutian Is.
Anchorage
Fairbanks
Juneau
Nome
Barrow
Kodiak
Mt. McKinley 6194
Mt. Logan 5959
Brooks Range
Alaska Range
Alexander Archipelago
Queen Charlotte Is.
West from Greenwich
Projection : Bonne
COPYRIGHT PHILIP'S
1
2
3
4
5
6
9
10

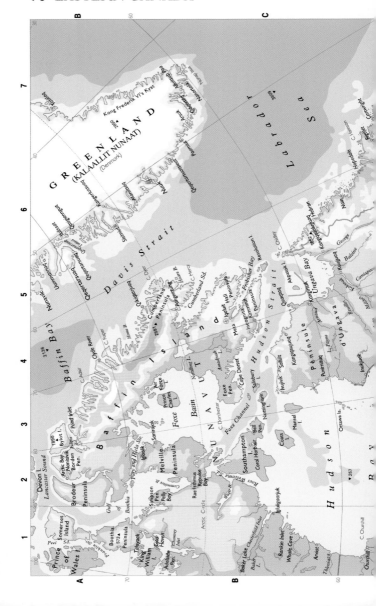

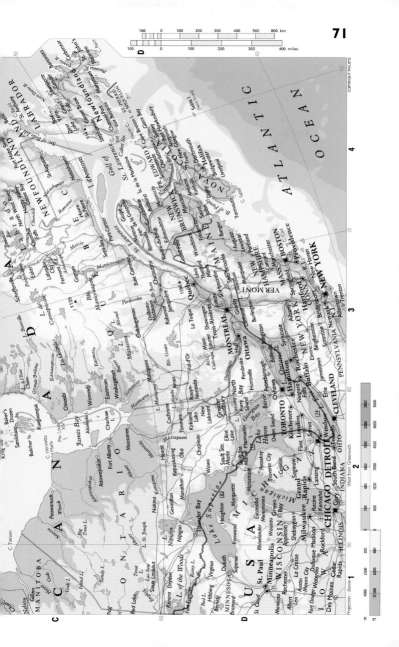

71

VANCOUVER
Vancouver
Island

Port Coquitlam
New
Westminster
Chilliwack

BRITISH CO

Ladysmith
Nanaimo

Duncan

Juan de Fuca Strait

Nooksack

Osoyoos

Grand Forks

Rossland

Trail

Crested

Battle
Bay

Neah Bay

C. Alava

Victoria
Esquimalt
Oak Bay

Abbotsford
Aldergrove
Lynden
Sumas

NORTH
CASCADES
NAT PARK

Oroville

Midway

Kettle Falls

Bonners
Ferry

La Push

Port Angeles
Port Townsend

Anacortes
Sedro-Woolley
Concrete

Winthrop

Tonasket

Republic

Colville

Newport
d'Orelle

Sandpoint

OLYMPIC
MTS.

Mt. Olympus

OLYMPIC
NAT PARK

Neilton

Bellingham
Mount Vernon
Darrington

Baker Mt.
3285

Glacier Peak
3285

Chelan

Omak
Okanogan

Franklin D.
Roosevelt L.

Deer Park

Coeur

Post Falls
d'Aleneek

Hoquiam
Aberdeen

Shelton

SEATTLE

Everett

Snohomish

Leavenworth

Brewster

Grand
Coulee
Dam

Spokane

Opportunity

St. Maries

Gray's Harbor

Bremerton

Tacoma
Renton

WASHINGTON

Wenatchee

Waterville

Coulee
City

Davenport

Cheney

Rosalia

Oakesdale

Bovill

Ocean Park

Montesano
Elma
Olympia

Puyallup
Enumclaw

Ellensburg

Ephrata

Moses Lake

Odessa

Sprague

Colfax

Pullman

Genesee
Moscow

Willapa

Raymond

Centralia

Mt. Rainier
4392

Quincy

Othello

Lind

Ritzville

Long Beach

C. Disappointment

Chehalis
Morton

Naches

Selah

Yakima

Wapato

Connell

46

Astoria
Warrenton

Toledo

Mt. St.
Helens
2549

Union Gap

Toppenish

Grandview

Sunnyside

Prosser

Richland
Pasco

Waitsburg

Pomeroy

Dayton

Clarkston
Lewiston

Asotin

Orofino

Nezperce

Seaside
Wheeler

St. Helens
Kelso

Mt. Adams
3751

Goldendale

Kennewick

Walla Walla

Milton-Freewater
Weston

Winchester

White Bird

Tillamook

Longview

PORTLAND
Vancouver
Milwaukie
Gresham

Camas
Cascade
Locks

Klickitat

Hood River

The Dalles
Mt. Hood
3427

Columbia

Arlington

Umatilla

Hermiston

Pilot Rock

Elgin

Wallowa
Enterprise

Riggins

New
Meadows
McCall

Forest Grove
Beaverton
Oregon City

Lincoln
City

McMinnville
Newberg
Canby

Wasco

Condon

Heppner

Pendleton

La Grande

Wallowa
Mts.

Council

Newport

Toledo

Dallas
Salem
Keizer
Woodburn
Stayton

Maupin

Fossil

John Day

Spray

North Powder

Baker City

Waldport

Monmouth
Corvallis

Albany
Lebanon
Brownsville

Sweet Home

Madras

Mt. Jefferson
3200

Prineville

Mitchell

Long
Creek

Haines

Brogan

Huntington

Blue

Cascade
Res.

44

Philomath

Mapleton

Florence

Junction City
Springfield

Eugene

McKenzie

Three Sisters

Cottage
Grove

Redmond

Cooked River

Dayville

Prairie City

Ontario
Payette

Nyssa

Emmett

Nampa
Caldwell
Meridian

Boise

Reedsport

North Bend
Coos Bay

Oakridge

Bend

OREGON

John
Day

Malheur
Res.

Ontario
Valley

Haines

Mountains

La Pine

Brothers

Riley

Stinkingwater

Burns

Crane

Malheur L.

Nyssa

Murphy

Jordan
Valley

Hill City

Mountain
Home

Coquille

Myrtle Point

Green

Camas
Valley

Roseburg

Silver Lake

Harney Basin

Harney L.

Owyhee

Bruneau

C. Blanco
Port
Orford

Myrtle Creek
Canyonville

Chemult

Summer
L.

Alvord

Gold
Beach

Grants Pass
Central Point
Medford

White
City

Mt.
Scott
2721

CRATER LAKE
NAT PARK

Upper
Klamath L.

Paisley

Valley
Falls

Steens Mountain
2962

Plateau

McDermitt

Owyhee

42

Brookings

Crescent
City

Happy
Camp
Hornbrook

Ashland
Dorris

Klamath Falls
Altamont

Merrill

Clear
Lake
Res.

Lakeview

Alvord
Desert

Mountain City

Contac

REDWOOD
NAT PARK

Yreka

Klamath

Canby

Alturas

Goose
L.

Lovelock

Winnemucca

Golconda

Paradise
Valley

Santa Rosa Mts.

Independence Mts.

Elko

Wells

Arcata
Eureka

Mt. Shasta
4317

Mount Shasta
McCloud

Bieber

Upper
Alkali L.

Middle
Alkali L.

Lower
Alkali L.

Battle
Mountain

Carlin

Spring
Creek

Ruby
Mts.

Franklin
L.

F

Fortuna
Scotia

CALIFORNIA

Thompson

Shasta L.

Burney

Warner

Dunphy

Rubys

Cape
Mendocino

Redding
Anderson

Lassen Peak
3187

LASSEN
VOLCANIC
NAT PARK

Eagle L.

Honey
L.

Rye Patch
Res.

Imlay

Eureka

McGill

Garberville

Red Bluff

Chester

Almanor
L.

Susanville
Westwood

Gerlach

Winnemucca L.

Trinity Range

Stillwater Range

Austin

Diamond Mts.

Ely
Schell

Laytonville

Corning

G

r

e

Willits

Orland

Paradise
Chico

Quincy

Greenville

Portola

Pyramid
L.

Wadsworth

Fernley

Carson
Sink

Shoshone Mountains

NEVADA

T o i y a b e R a

Mt. Jefferson
3599

Round
Mountain

Currant

Schell Creek Ra.

Ukiah
Hopland
Lakeport
Clear
Lake

Colusa

Oroville

Marysville

Grass
Valley

Truckee

Incline
Village

Virginia City

Sparks

Reno

Fallon

Stillwater

Hot Creek Ra.

124

Pt.
Arena

Cloverdale
Healdsburg

St. Helena

Woodland
Davis

Roseville

Auburn

Carson
City

Yerington

Walker L.

Hawthorne

Luning

Santa Rosa
Petaluma
Napa

Vacaville
Fairfield

Sacramento

Placerville

South
Lake
Tahoe

Minden

Schurz

Mt. Grant
3428

38

San
Rafael

Berkeley
Richmond

Vallejo
Concord

Lodi

Stockton

Ione

Jackson

San Andreas

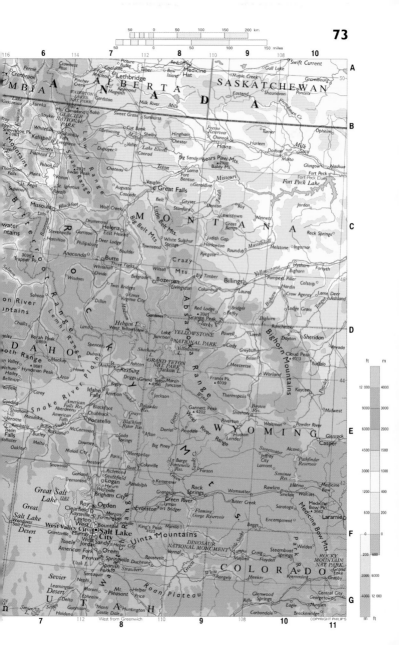

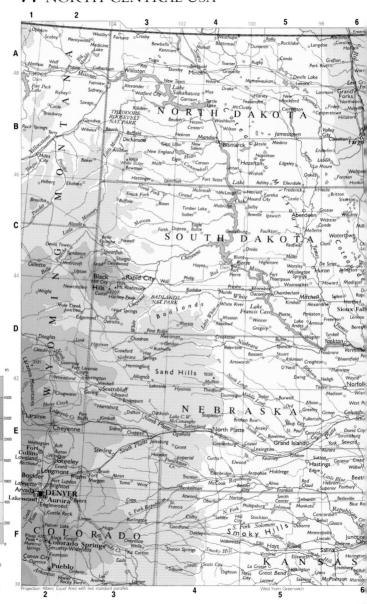

50 0 50 100 150 200 km
50 0 50 100 150 miles

CANADA

A

Lake of the Woods
Roseau Warroad
Greenbush Baudette Rainy Lake
Karlstad International Falls VOYAGEURS NAT PARK Atikokan
Thief River Falls Rainy River Fort Frances Northern Light L. Thunder Bay
Red Lake Falls Big Falls Vermilion Cloud Bay ISLE ROYALE NAT. PARK 183
Fertile Erskine Upper Red L. Lower Red L. Northome LAKE SUPERIOR Grand Portage Copper Harbor
Bagley Winnibigoshish Mountain Iron Biwabik Eagle River Keweenaw Pt. Keweenaw Pen.
Twin Valley Bemidji Cass Lake Chisholm Virginia Eveleth L'Anse Laurium Keweenaw B.
Mahnomen Detroit Lakes Leech Lake Hibbing Deer River Grand Rapids Two Harbors Apostle Is. Hancock Houghton Abbaye
Hawley Park Rapids Walker Hill City Floodwood Duluth Bayfield Ontonagon Baraga Ishpeming Marquette
Breckenridge Staples Brainerd Moose Lake Cloquet Superior Ashland Washburn Hurley Mellen Wakefield Bessemer Watersmeet Iron Mountain Negaunee
Fergus Falls Battle Lake Baxter Mille Lac L. Hinckley Solon Springs Hayward Park Falls Crandon Norway Gwinn Crystal Falls
Long Prairie Little Falls Mora Siren Spooner Phillips Rhinelander Eagle River Kingsford Powers
Wheaton Glenwood Sauk Centre Melrose Milaca Cambridge Rice Lake Ladysmith Prentice Merrill Antigo Crandon Menominee Green Bay
Morris Benson St. Cloud Sauk Rapids Barron Bloomer Wausau Oconto Falls Marinette
Ortonville Paynesville Monticello Elk River New Richmond Chippewa Falls Stevens Shawano Sturgeon Bay
Big Stone City Willmar Litchfield Brooklyn Park Blaine Hudson Eau Claire Menomonie Marshfield Wisconsin Rapids New London De Pere Algoma
Montevideo Hutchinson Coon Rapids St. Paul Menomonie Neillsville Waupaca Appleton Two Rivers
Granite Falls Glencoe Minneapolis Bloomington Hastings Red Wing Whitehall Black River Falls Wautoma Berlin Ripon Neenah Oshkosh Chilton Manitowoc
Marshall New Ulm Burnsville Lakeville Northfield Lake City Alma Sparta Necedah Adams Fond du Lac Waupun Plymouth Sheboygan
Ivanhoe Redwood Falls Le Sueur Faribault Wabasha La Crosse Tomah Mauston Portage Beaver Dam West Bend LAKE
Tyler Tracy St. Peter Owatonna Kasson Rochester Holmen Reedsburg Baraboo Watertown Hartford MICHIGAN
Sleepy Eye Mankato Waseca Stewartville La Crescent Viroqua Richland Center Madison Oconomowoc Waukesha Milwaukee Wauwatosa
Jackson Fairmont Albert Lea Blue Earth Austin Preston Decorah Waukon Prairie du Chien Dodgeville Platteville Janesville Delavan Whitewater Allis Racine
Worthington Northwood Cresco Monroe Beloit Burlington Kenosha
Sibley Emmetsburg Forest City Mason City Charles City New Hampton McGregor Lancaster Woodstock North Chicago Highland Park
Spencer Algona Sumner Oelwein Galena Freeport Rockford Belvidere Elgin Arlington Waukegan
Le Mars Cherokee Pocahontas Clarion Iowa Falls Cedar Falls Manchester Dubuque Monroe Oregon St. Charles Elmhurst Evanston
Storm Lake Fort Dodge Waterloo Independence Monticello Rochelle De Kalb CHICAGO
Sioux City Sac City Rockwell City Webster City Eldora Grundy Center Anamosa Maquoketa Sterling Dixon Aurora Cicero
South Sioux City Ida Grove Carroll **IOWA** Marshalltown Vinton Marion Clinton Rock Falls Morris Joliet
Denison Perry Ames Tama Cedar Rapids Princeton La Salle Kankakee
Blair Logan Harlan West Des Moines Des Moines Newton Grinnell Marengo Iowa City Davenport Moline Geneseo Streator Dwight
Omaha Council Bluffs Atlantic Greenfield Winterset Norwalk Montezuma Washington Rock Island Kewanee Henry Pontiac Lexington
Bellevue Glenwood Red Oak Creston Osceola Indianola Knoxville Oskaloosa Ottumwa Fairfield Burlington Mount Pleasant Galesburg Chillicothe Peoria Bloomington Normal Paxton Rantoul Champaign
Plattsmouth Shenandoah Corning Chariton Albia Fort Madison Canton Pekin Lincoln Urbana
Lincoln Clarinda Bedford Centerville Bloomfield Keokuk Macomb Carthage Mount **ILLINOIS** Clinton Decatur
Nebraska City Shubert Grant City Princeton Unionville Kahoka Beardstown Sterling Sullivan Tuscola Mattoon Shelbyville
Syracuse Rock Port Maryville Bethany Milan Kirksville Palmyra Quincy Springfield Jacksonville Lincoln Pana Effingham
Pawnee City Mound City Savannah Chillicothe Macon Monroe City Hannibal Pittsfield White Hall Taylorville Carlinville Litchfield Newton
Falls City Marysville Horton Troy St. Joseph Brunswick Moberly Louisiana Carrollton Vandalia Flora Olney
Frankfort Hiawatha Holton Excelsior Springs Carrollton Mexico Centralia Jerseyville Mount Vernon McLeansboro Benton
Little Creek L. Leavenworth Liberty Richmond Fayette Columbia Fulton St. Charles Alton Granite City Salem Centralia
Manhattan Wamego Kansas City Independence Lexington Marshall Boonville Jefferson City Hermann Washington **ST. LOUIS** St. Louis Belleville Fairfield
Topeka Overland Park Warrensburg Sedalia Mehlville Mount Vernon West Frankfort
Lawrence Olathe Harrisonville Windsor Ste. Genevieve De Soto Pinckneyville
Osage City Ottawa Paola Butler **MISSOURI** Union Sullivan Festus Du Quoin
Emporia Garnett Truman Res. Burlington

B

C

D

E

F

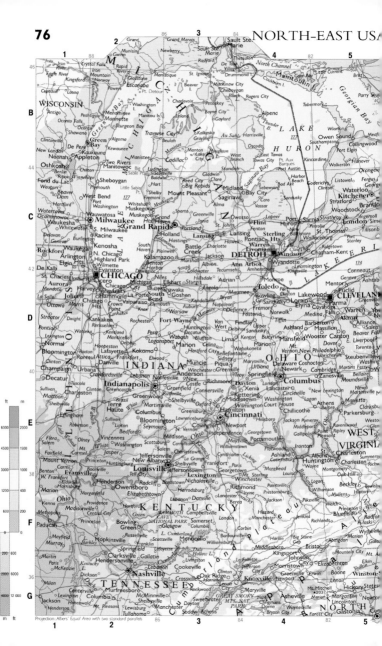

Projection: Albers' Equal Area with two standard parallels

Continuation
Eastwards
On same scale.

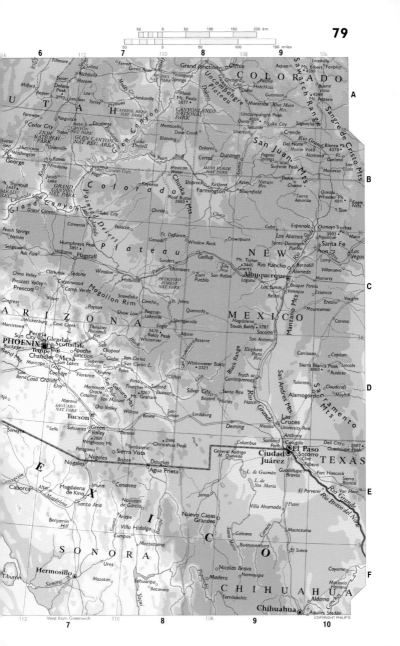

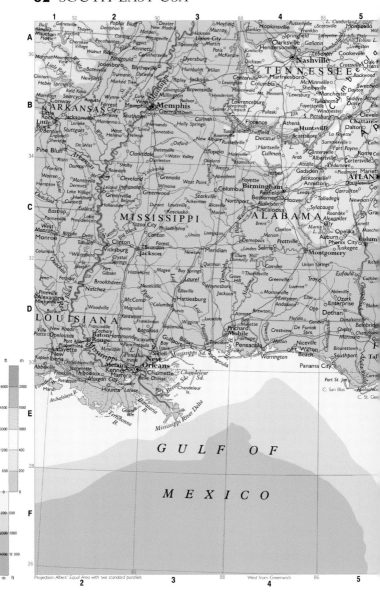

83

A

B

C

D

E

F

G

6 · 82 · 7 · 80 · 8 · 9 · 76 · 10

ATLANTIC

OCEAN

NORTH CAROLINA

SOUTH CAROLINA

GEORGIA

FLORIDA

BAHAMAS

Middlesboro · Big Stone Gap · Abingdon · Galax · Martinsville · South Boston · Danville · Reidsville · Oxford · Henderson · Roanoke Rapids · Murfreesboro · Ahoskie · Elizabeth City · Edenton

Kingsport · Bristol · Mountain City · Mt. Airy · Eden · Burlington · Woke Forest · Rocky Mount · Tarboro · Plymouth · Manteo

La Follette · Jefferson City · Greeneville · Johnson City · Elizabethton · Boone · Elkin · Yadkin · Winston-Salem · Thomasville · High Point · Siler · Durham · Chapel Hill · Raleigh · Wilson · Williamston · Washington · Bellvoir · Roanoke

Knoxville · Newport · Erwin · Lenoir · Hickory · Statesville · Salisbury · Lexington · Asheboro · Sanford · Cary · Smithfield · Greenville · Goldsboro · Hatteras

Mt. Mitchell 2037 · Morganton · Newton · Kannapolis · Albemarle · Southern Pines · Dunn · Kinston · New Bern · Pamlico Sound · C. Hatteras

Asheville · Waynesville · Brevard · Forest City · Lincolnton · Concord · CHARLOTTE · Monroe · Rockingham · Hamlet · Laurinburg · Fayetteville · Clinton · Wallace · Jacksonville · Morehead City · Onslow Bay · C. Lookout

Brasstown Bald 1458 · Seneca · Clemson · Easley · Greenville · Spartanburg · Gaffney · Rock Hill · Lancaster · Cheraw · Bennettsville · Dillon · Whiteville · Lumberton · Wilmington

Toccoa · Anderson · Hartwell · Laurens · Union · Chester · Winnsboro · Camden · Darlington · Mullins · Marion · C. Fear

Gainesville · Commerce · Greenwood · Abbeville · Newberry · Florence · Conway · North Myrtle Beach

Winder · Athens · Elberton · Clinton · Sumter · Lake City · Kingstree · Myrtle Beach · Long Bay

Lawrenceville · Thomson · Thurmond L. · Leesville · Columbia · Manning · Santee · C. Romain · Georgetown

Washington · Edgefield · Batesburg · Orangeburg · Summerton · Moncks Corner

Covington · Madison · Martinez · Aiken · Livingston · Orangeburg · Bamberg · St. George · Goose Creek · North Charleston

Eatonton · Thomson · Augusta · Barnwell · Allendale · Hampton · Walterboro · Summerville · CHARLESTON · Mount Pleasant

Griffin · Milledgeville · Waynesboro · Millen · Sylvania · Ridgeland · Burton · Beaufort

Macon · Sandersville · Statesboro · Garden City · Parris I. · Hilton Head Island

Warner Robins · Swainsboro · Dublin · Vidalia · Lyons · SAVANNAH · Hinesville

Perry · Hawkinsville · Eastman · Lyons · Ossabaw I.

Americus · Cordele · Hazlehurst · Fitzgerald · Baxley · Jesup · St. Catherines I.

Ashburn · Ocilla · Douglas · Alma · Sapelo I.

Sylvester · Tifton · Waycross · St. Simons I. · Jekyll I.

Camilla · Nashville · Adel · Okefenokee Swamp · Folkston · Kingsland · Brunswick

Moultrie · Monticello · Quitman · Jasper · Cumberland I. · St. Marys · Fernandina Beach

Thomasville · Madison · Valdosta · Live Oak · Macclenny · St. Johns · Jacksonville Beach

Perry · Apalachee B. · Lake City · Middleburg · JACKSONVILLE · St. Augustine

Starke · Green Cove Sprs. · Palm Coast

Cross City · Alachua · Gainesville · Ormond Beach

Williston · Ocala · L. George · Holly Hill · Daytona Beach · Port Orange

Crystal River · Inverness · Beverly Hills · De Land · New Smyrna Beach · Deltona

Homosassa · Leesburg · Eustis · Mt. Dora · Sanford · Titusville · C. Canaveral

Brooksville · Clermont · Winter Garden · ORLANDO · Cocoa · Merritt Island

Spring Hill · Winter Park · St. Cloud · Melbourne

New Port Richey · Dade City · Kissimmee · Haines City

Tarpon Springs · Clearwater · Largo · Dunedin · Plant City · Lakeland · Winter Haven · Lake Wales · Palm Bay

Sun City Center · Bartow · Lake Wales · Vero Beach

St. Petersburg · TAMPA · Bradenton · Avon Park · Ft. Meade · Sebring · Fort Pierce · Port St. Lucie

Longboat Key · Palmetto · Istokpoga · Okeechobee · Stuart · Hobe Sound · Grand Cay · Great Sale Cay · Little Abaco I. · Hope Town

Sarasota · Arcadia · L. Okeechobee · Pahokee

Venice · Port Charlotte · Punta Gorda · Palm Beach · Settlement Pt.

Charlotte Hbr. · Ft. La Belle · Clewiston · Belle Glade · West Palm Beach · Boynton Beach · Freeport · Grand Bahama · Marsh Harbour · Great Abaco I.

Cape Coral · Myers · Lehigh Acres · Lake Worth · Delray Beach · Moore's I.

Sanibel · Immokalee · Coral Springs · Boca Raton · Pompano Beach · Fort Lauderdale

Naples · BIG CYPRESS NAT. PRESERVE · Carol City · Hollywood · Miami Beach

Marco Island · THE EVERGLADES NAT. PARK · Hialeah · MIAMI · Coral Gables · Kendall · Biscayne B. · Southwest Pt.

36 · 34 · 32 · 30 · 28 · 26

50 · 0 · 50 · 100 · 150 · 200 km
50 · 0 · 50 · 100 · 150 miles

SAN DIEGO
Tijuana
Ensenada
Mexicali
PHOENIX
Yuma
Tucson
Casa Grande
Deming
Las Cruces
El Paso
Roswell
Lubbock
Wichita Falls
Fort Worth
Abilene

A

3078
San Felipe
Sonoita
Nogales
Douglas
Agua Prieta
Cananea
Ciudad Juárez
Pecos
Carlsbad
Odessa
San Angelo
Waco
Austin

I. Ángel de la Guarda
Caborca
Magdalena de Kino
Nacozari de García
Nuevo Casas Grandes
Ahumada
Ojinaga
Rio Grande
Fort Stockton

Bahía Sebastián Vizcaíno
Rosarito
Madera
Ciudad Acuña
Del Rio
Ciudad Acuña
Piedras Negras
Eagle Pass
SAN ANTONIO
Victoria

B
Hermosillo
Chihuahua
Cuauhtémoc
Delicias
Ciudad Camargo
Nueva Rosita
Sabinas
Monclova
San Pedro de las Colonias
Nuevo Laredo
Laredo
Falcón Res.
Corpus Christi

Guaymas
Empalme
Yaqui
Navojoa
Ciudad Obregón
Jiménez
Hidalgo del Parral
Gómez Palacio
Torreón
Sabinas Hidalgo
MONTERREY
Saltillo
Reynosa
Matamoros
Brownsville

Sta. Rosalía
Loreto
Mulegé
El Fuerte
Fuerte
Topolobampo
Los Mochis
Guamúchil
Guasave
Culiacán
Tepehuanes
Concepción del Oro
Linares
Montemorelos
San Fernando

B. Ballenas
Villa Constitución
La Paz
B. de la Paz
Durango
El Salto
Matehuala
Sombrerete
Ciudad Victoria
Ciudad Mante

C
C. San Lázaro
Mazatlán
Rosario
Escuinapa
Acaponeta
Jerez
Fresnillo
Zacatecas
Charcas
Ciudad del Maíz
Tampico

C. San Lucas
Tuxpan
Tepic
Islas Marías
Aguascalientes
San Luis Potosí
Ciudad de Valles
C. Rojo
Tampico

Puerto Vallarta
Is. de Revillagigedo (Mex.)
Aneca
GUADALAJARA
León
Guanajuato
Irapuato
Celaya
Querétaro
MEXICO
Pachuca
Tulancingo
Tuxpan
Poza Rica
Papantla

D
Ciudad Guzmán
Nevado de Colima 4339
Zamora
Morelia
Toluca
Popocatépetl 5452
PUEBLA
Pico de Orizaba 5610
Xalapa
Orizaba

Manzanillo
Colima
Uruapan
Cuernavaca
Iguala
Tlapa
Córdoba

Tecomán
Lázaro Córdenas
Balsas
Chilpancingo
Chilapa
Tlaxiaco
Oaxaca

Acapulco
Ometepec

P A C I F I C
I. Clipperton (Fr.)

O C E A N

E

F

Projection : Bonne

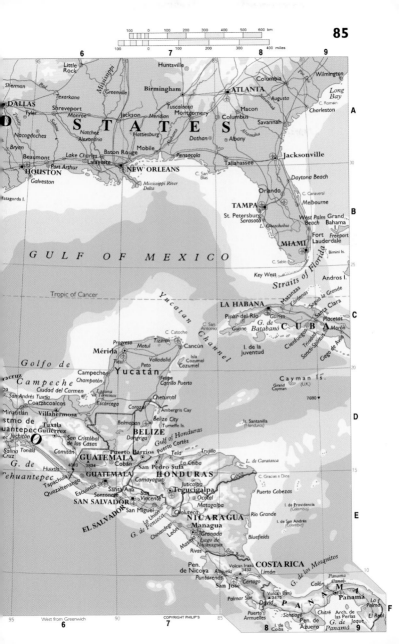

100   0   100 200 300 400   500 600 km
100   0   100   200   300   400 miles

6   **7**   **8**   **9**

Little Rock
Sherman
Texarkana
DALLAS
Tyler
Shreveport
Monroe
Huntsville
Birmingham
Greenville
Jackson
Meridian
Tuscaloosa
Montgomery
ATLANTA
Macon
Columbia
Wilmington
Columbus
Augusta
Savannah
Long Bay
C. Roman
Charleston

A

Nacogdoches
Bryan
Beaumont
Port Arthur
HOUSTON
Galveston
Matagorda I.
Natchez
Alexandria
Lake Charles
Lafayette
Baton Rouge
NEW ORLEANS
Mobile
Hattiesburg
Dothan
Pensacola
Albany
Tallahassee
Jacksonville

O   S   T   A   T   E   S

C. San Blas
Mississippi River Delta
Daytona Beach
C. Canaveral
Orlando
Melbourne
TAMPA
St. Petersburg
Sarasota
L. Okeechobee
West Palm Beach
Grand Bahama
Freeport
Fort Lauderdale
MIAMI
Bimini Is.

B

G U L F   O F   M E X I C O

C. Sable
Key West
Straits of Florida
Andros I.

Tropic of Cancer

Matanzas
Sagua la Grande
Santa Clara
LA HABANA
Pinar del Río
Güines
G. de Batabanó
Güane
C U B A
Placetas
Morón
Cienfuegos
Sancti-Spíritus
Trinidad
Ciego de Ávila

C

Yucatán Channel
C. Catoche
C. San Antonio
Progreso
Motul
Tizimín
Cancún
Mérida
Valladolid
Ticul
Peto
Isla Cozumel
Cozumel
I. de la Juventud

Golfo de
Campeche
Champotón
Campeche
Yucatán
Felipe Carrillo Puerto
Cayman Is.
Grand Cayman
(UK)
7680 ▼

D

racruz
San Andrés Tuxtla
Coatzacoalcos
Ciudad del Carmen
Laguna de Términos
Escárcega
Corozal
Chetumal
Ambergris Cay
Turneffe Is.
Belize City
Is. Santanilla
(Honduras)

pa
Minatitlán
Villahermosa
stmo de
uantepec
ec Juchitán
Tuxtla Gutiérrez
San Cristóbal de las Casas
Belmopan
BELIZE
Dangriga
Gulf of Honduras
Puerto Cortés
Trujillo

O

Salina Cruz
Tonalá
Comitán
4063
GUATEMALA
Cobán
3834
Puerto Barrios
Tela
Puerto Cortés
La Ceiba
L. de Caratasca
C. Gracias a Dios

G. de
rehuantepec
Huixtla
Tapachula
Quezaltenango
Escuintla
GUATEMALA
HONDURAS
Comayagua
Juticalpa
Tegucigalpa
Ocotal
Puerto Cabezas
I. de Providencia
(Colombia)

E

Santa Ana
Sonsonate
SAN SALVADOR
San Vicente
San Miguel
EL SALVADOR
L. de Nicaragua
G. de Fonseca
Choluteca
Matagalpa
NICARAGUA
León
Managua
Granada
Masaya
Lago de Nicaragua
Rivas
Río Grande
Bluefields
I. de San Andrés
(Colombia)

Chinandega
San Juan
Pen. de Nicoya
Abangua
Volcán Irazú
3432
COSTA RICA
Limón
G. de los Mosquitos
Colón
P A N A M
Panama
La I
Palma

F

Puntarenas
San José
Cartago
Palmar Sur
Volcán Barú
3475
David
Santiago
Chitré
Arch. de las Perlas
El Real
Puerto Armuelles
I. de Coiba
Pen. de Azuero
G. de Panamá

Projection : Bonne

West from Greenwich

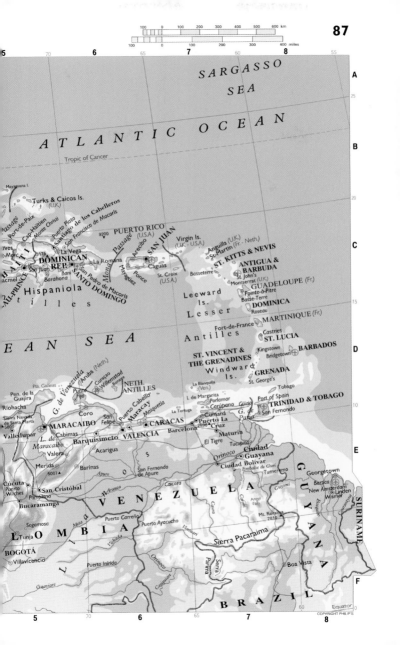

100 0 100 200 300 400 500 600 km
100 0 100 200 300 400 miles

5 70 **6** 65 **7** 60 **8** 55

A

SARGASSO
SEA

25

B

A T L A N T I C   O C E A N

Tropic of Cancer

20

Mayaguana I.

Turks & Caicos Is.
(U.K.)

Passage

Port-de-Paix
Cap-Hatien
Monte Christi
Santiago de los Caballeros
Santo Francisco de Macoris

9200
PUERTO RICO
(U.S.A.)

Virgin Is.
(U.K. - U.S.A.)

Anguilla (U.K.)
St-Martin (Fr. - Neth.)

C

Ives
Port au Prince
HAITI
3175
La Vega
DOMINICAN
REP.

Arecibo
SAN JUAN

ST. KITTS & NEVIS

ANTIGUA &
BARBUDA
St. John's

15

acmel
San Juan
Bani
Barahona

La Romana
San Pedro de Macoris
SANTO DOMINGO

Ponce
St. Croix
(U.S.A.)

Caguas
Mayaguez

Basseterre

Montserrat (U.K.)

GUADELOUPE (Fr.)
Pointe-à-Pitre
Basse-Terre

Hispaniola

n t i l l e s

Leeward
Is.
L e s s e r

DOMINICA
Roseau

Fort-de-France
MARTINIQUE (Fr.)

E A N   **S E A**

A n t i l l e s

Castries
ST. LUCIA

D

ST. VINCENT &
THE GRENADINES

Kingstown
Bridgetown
BARBADOS

Windward
Is.
GRENADA

St. George's

Pta. Gallinas

Aruba (Neth.)
Curaçao
Bonaire

NETH.
ANTILLES

La Blanquilla
(Ven.)

Tobago

Port of Spain
TRINIDAD & TOBAGO

10

Pen. de la
Guajira

Punto
Fijo
Willemstad

La Tortuga
L. de Margarita
Porlamar

Riohacha
Sierra Nevada
de Santa Marta
5800

Coro
San
Felipe

Puerto Cabello
Maracay

Maiquetia

Carúpano
Güiria
G. de
Paria
San Fernando

E

MARACAIBO
La Cabimas

Barquisimeto **VALENCIA**

CARACAS
Barcelona

Cumaná
Puerto La
Cruz

Maturín

Valledupar
L. de
Maracaibo
Valera

Acarigua

El Tigre
Tucupita
Ciudad
Guayana

Mérida
5007

Barinas

San Fernando
de Apure

Orinoco
Ciudad Bolívar

Embalse de Guri

GUYANA

Georgetown

Cúcuta
Puerto
Wilches
San Cristóbal
Pamplona

Apure

Caicara

Caura

Tumeremo

Cuyuni

New Amsterdam
Linden
Wismar

Bucaramanga

Arauca

Caroni

SURINAME

L
Sogamoso

O
Meta

M

Puerto Carreño

V E N E Z U E L A

Angel
Falls

Mt. Roraima
2810

Guaviare
Puerto Ayacucho

Ichada

Caroni

Caroni

Sierra Pacaraima

Barima
Barica
Linden

B
I
A

Puerto Inírida

Orinoco

Sierra
Parima

BOGOTÁ

Villavicencio

Guaviare

Caquetá

Boa Vista

F

B R A Z I L

Equator

0

COPYRIGHT PHILIP'S

5 70 **6** 65 **7** 60 **8**

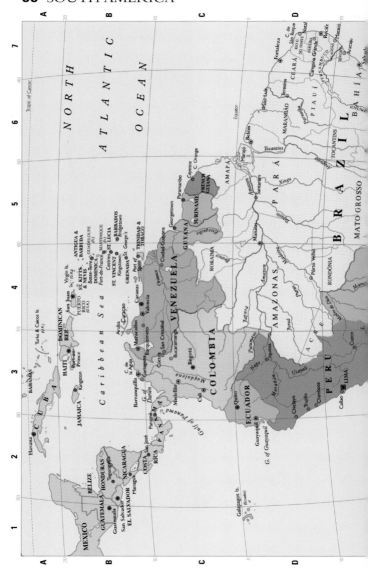

89

COPYRIGHT PHILIPS

100 0   200   400   600   800   1000 1200 1400 km
100 0   200   400   600   800   1000 miles

E

F

G

H

PACIFIC

OCEAN

Tropic of Capricorn

San Felíx
(Chile)

San Ambrosio
(Chile)

Arch. de Juan Fernández
(Chile)

Projection: Lambert's Azimuthal Equal Area

■ LIMA   Capital Cities

Arequipa

La Paz
Cochabamba
Santa Cruz
Sucre

Iquique

Antofagasta

C H I L E

San Miguel
de Tucumán

San Juan
Mendoza

Viña del Mar
Valparaíso
SANTIAGO

Concepción

Valdivia

Puerto Montt

Gulf of Penas

Magellan's Str.

Punta Arenas

Tierra del Fuego

C. Horn

GOIÁS

Brasília

MINAS GERAIS

ESPÍRITO
SANTO

Belo
Horizonte

Vitória

Campos

Juiz
de Fora

Ribeirão
Prêto

Campinas

Niterói

RIO DE
JANEIRO

SÃO PAULO

MATO GROSSO
DO SUL

Paraná

PARANÁ

Paraguay

Pilcomayo

PARAGUAY

Asunción

Curitiba

SANTA CATARINA

RIO GRANDE
DO SUL

Uruguay

Pôrto Alegre

Pelotas

URUGUAY

Montevideo

Río de la Plata

Salta

Paraná

A R G E N T I N A

Resistencia

Corrientes

Santa Fe

Rosario

Córdoba

Salado

BUENOS AIRES

La Plata

Mar del Plata

Bahía
Blanca

Negro

Colorado

Neuquén

Chubut

Comodoro Rivadavia

Gulf of San Jorge

West Falkland   FALKLAND IS.
                (U.K.)

East Falkland

Stanley

South Georgia
(U.K.)

SOUTH

ATLANTIC

OCEAN

20

30

70°West from Greenwich 60°

50

40

30

20

1   2   3   4   5   6   7

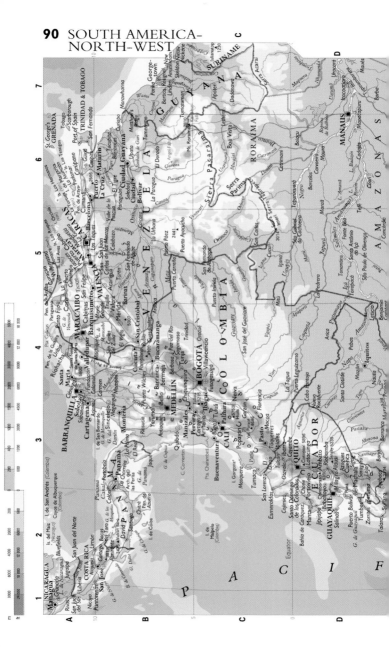

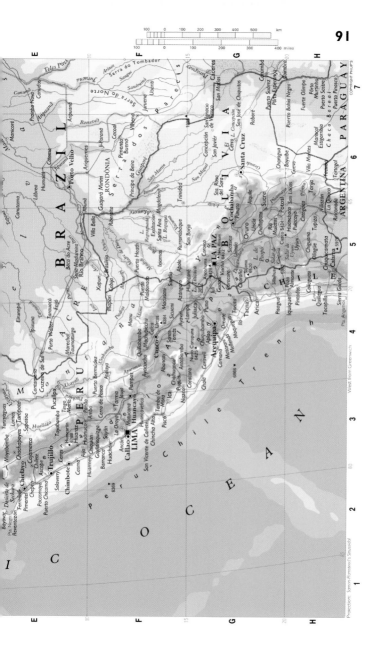

COPYRIGHT PHILIP'S

Projection: Simon Armstrong's Snazwild

West from Greenwich

PARAGUAY

ARGENTINA

BRAZIL

RONDÔNIA

Serra do Tombador

Telés Pires

Arinos

Juruena

Serra do Norte

Pareci s

Cáceres

Cuiabá

San Matias

Corumbá

Puerto Suárez

Fuerte Olimpo

Porto Sastre

Murtinho

Puerto Pinasco

Bahía Negra

C h a c o

B O L I V I A

Santa Cruz

Concepción

San Ignacio de Velasco

San José de Chiquitos

Roboré

San Javier

Cochabamba

Sucre

Potosí

Oruro

LA PAZ

Trinidad

Tarija

Villazón

La Quiaca

Uyuni

CHILE

Iquique

Tocopilla

Antofagasta

Calama

Arica

Tacna

PERU

LIMA

Callao

Trujillo

Chimbote

Huancayo

Cuzco

Arequipa

Juliaca

Puno

L. Titicaca

Puerto Maldonado

Pucallpa

Moyobamba

O C E A N

P A C I F I C

P e r u - C h i l e   T r e n c h

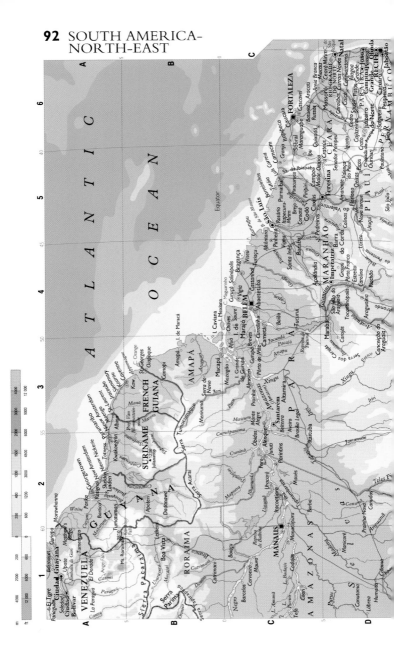

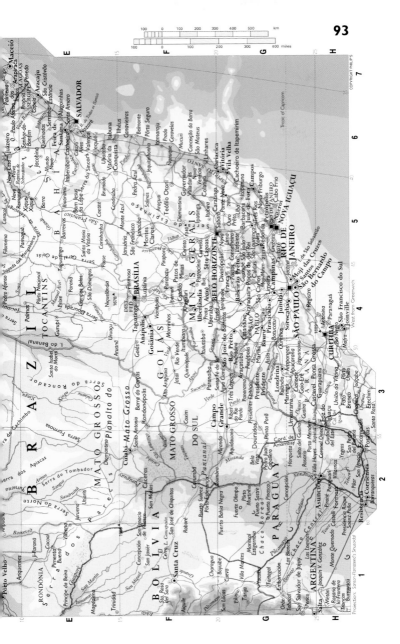

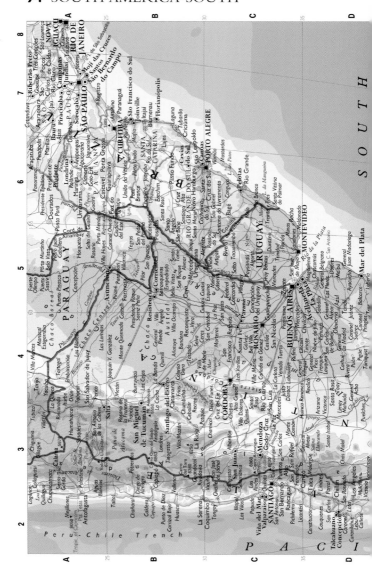

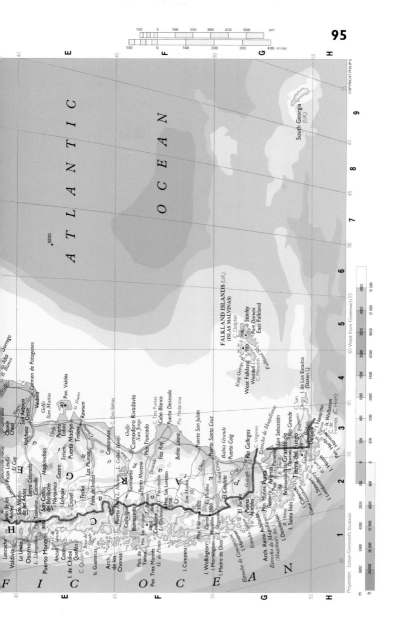

100 0 100 200 300 400 500 km
100 0 100 200 300 400 miles

COPYRIGHT PHILIPS

E   F   G   H

9
8
7
6
5
4
3
2
1

A T L A N T I C

O C E A N

South Georgia
(UK)

▲5830

Abrego
L. del Alto Blanca
El Cuy
San Antonio Oeste
Carmen de Patagones
Valcheta Viedma
Golfo San Matías
Maquinchao Puerto Lobos
Gastre Telsen Pen. Valdés
Esquel Trelew G. Nuevo
Paso de Indios Rawson
Camarones C. Dos Bahías
L. Musters Golfo San Jorge
Sarmiento Comodoro Rivadavia
Perito Moreno Tres Puntas
C. L. Buenos Pico Truncado Cabo Blanco
L. Pueyrredón Fitz Roy Puerto Deseado
L. San Martín Deseado Pta. Medanosa
Cerro Fitz Roy 3375 Pto. San Julián
Pico 3706 Chico Bahía Grande
Santa Cruz Puerto Santa Cruz
Cerro Stokes 2800 Puerto Coig
Coy Río Gallegos
Gallegos C. Vírgenes
Estrecho de Magallanes
San Sebastián
Gdor. Gregores Río Grande
Río Grande
Isla Grande de Tierra del Fuego
Ushuaia C. San Diego
I. de Los Estados
(Staten I.)
Is. Wollaston
C. de Hornos (C. Horn)

FALKLAND ISLANDS
(ISLAS MALVINAS)
(UK)
C. Dolphin
King George B.
Pebble I. 1100
Weddell I. Stanley
C. Meredith Port Darwin
West Falkland East Falkland
Falkland Sd.

Lonco che Junín de los Andes
Valdivia Piedra del Aguila
La Unión San Martín de los Andes Sierra Colorado
Osorno Collón Curá Choele Choel
L. Llanquihue 3554▲ Neuquén
Puerto Montt Zapala Valcheta
Ancud San Carlos de Bariloche Río Negro
I. de Chiloé Castro Esquel
Quellón Boca del Guafo
Is. Guaitecas

Arch. de los Chonos
Pen. de Taitao
C. Quilán
Pen. Tres Montes
G. de Penas
I. Campana
I. Wellington
I. Mornington
I. Madre de Dios
Arch. Reina Adelaida
Estrecho de Magallanes
(Magellan Str.)
Pen. Muñoz Gamero
I. Desolación
I. Santa Inés
Canal Beagle

60° West from Greenwich 55

Projection: Sanson-Flamsteed's Sinusoidal

m   ft
8000 24000
5000 18000
3000 12000
2000 6000
1000 3000

E   F   G   H
40 45 50 55

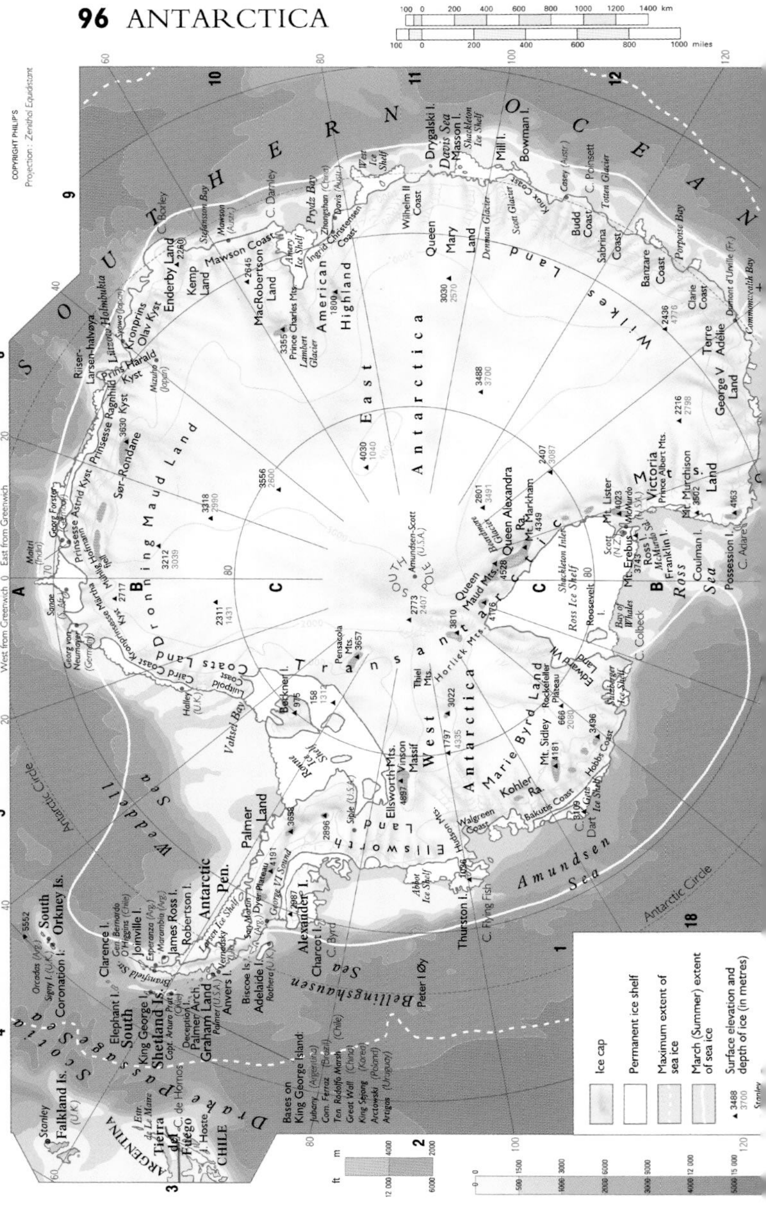

COPYRIGHT PHILIP'S
Projection: Zenithal Equidistant

100 0   200   400   600   800   1000   1200   1400 km

100 0   200   400   600   800   1000 miles

S O U T H E R N   O C E A N

Drygalski I.
Davis Sea
Masson I. (Austr.)
Mill I.
Kemp
Land

Enderby Land
MacRobertson Coast
Mawson Coast
C. Darnley
Prydz Bay

American
Highland
Bowman I.
C. Penisett
Budd
Coast
Sabrina
Coast
Banzare
Coast
Clarie
Coast
Terre
Adélie
George V
Land

Queen
Mary
Land

Wilkes Land

East
Antarctica

Dronning Maud Land

Ser-Rondane

Antarctica

Victoria
Land

Mt. Lister
Mt. Erebus
Mt. Murchison
Possession I.
C. Adare

Ross
Sea

Transantarctic Mts.

West
Antarctica

Marie Byrd Land

Ellsworth
Land

Palmer
Land

Weddell
Sea

Coats Land

Berkner I.

Amundsen-Scott
(U.S.A.)
SOUTH POLE

Queen
Maud
Land

Ross Ice Shelf

Pensacola
Mts.

Thiel
Mts.

Ronne Ice Shelf

Amundsen
Sea

Bellingshausen
Sea

Antarctic
Pen.

Alexander I.

Charcot I.

Peter I Øy
(Nor.)

Thurston I.

Antarctic Circle

Drake Passage

Scotia Sea

South
Orkney Is.

South
Shetland Is.

Coronation I.
Clarence I.
Elephant I.
King George
Graham
Land
Adelaide I.
Anvers I.
Biscoe Is.

Falkland Is.
(U.K.)
Stanley

ARGENTINA
Tierra
del
Fuego
CHILE

Antarctic Circle

Legend

- ice cap
- Permanent ice shelf
- Maximum extent of sea ice
- March (Summer) extent of sea ice
- ▲ 3488 / 3700 Surface elevation and depth of ice (in metres)

m
12 000
6000
4000
2000
0

ft

Index to Map Pages

The index contains the names of all principal places and features shown on the maps. Physical features composed of a proper name (Erie) and a description (Lake) are positioned alphabetically by the proper name. The description is positioned after the proper name and is usually abbreviated:

Erie, L. **76 C5**

Where a description forms part of a settlement or administrative name, however, it is always written in full and put in its true alphabetical position:

Lake Charles . . . **81 D7**

Names beginning St. are alphabetized under Saint, but Sankt, Sant, Santa and San are all spelt in full and are alphabetized accordingly.

The number in bold type which follows each name in the index refers to the number of the map page where that feature or place will be found. This is usually the largest scale at which the place or feature appears.

The letter and figure which are in bold type immediately after the page number give the grid square on the map page, within which the feature is situated.

Rivers are indexed to their mouths or confluences, and carry the symbol → after their names. The following symbols are also used in the index: ■ country, ☑ overseas territory or dependency, □ first order administrative area, △ national park, ⌂ nature park or reserve.

A

A Coruña	18	A1
A Estrada	18	A1
A Fonsagrada	18	A2
Aachen	14	C4
Aalborg = Ålborg	9	D7
Aalen	14	D6
Aarhus = Århus	9	D8
Aba	53	G7
Ābādān	47	E7
Ābādeh	44	D3
Abadla	52	B5
Abaetetuba	92	C4
Abakan	30	D7
Abancay	91	F4
Abarqū	44	D3
Abashiri	32	A9
Abashiri-Wan	32	B9
Ābay = Nîl el Azraq →	55	E5
Abay	29	E8
Abaya, L.	55	G6
Abbay = Nîl el Azraq →	55	E5
Abbeville	12	A4
Abbot Ice Shelf	96	B2
Abd al Kūrī	49	E5
Abéché	55	F3
Abeokuta	53	G6
Abercorn = Mbala	57	F6
Abercorn	63	A5
Aberdeen, *Australia*	63	B5
Aberdeen, *U.K.*	10	C5
Aberdeen, *S. Dak., U.S.A.*	74	C5
Aberdeen, *Wash., U.S.A.*	72	C2
Aberystwyth	11	E4
Abidjan	53	G5
Abilene	80	C4
Abitibi, L.	71	D3
Abkhazia □	25	E5
Abminga	62	A1

Åbo = Turku	9	C10
Abohar	42	D9
Abomey	53	G6
Abong-Mbang	56	D2
Abou-Deïa	55	F2
Absaroka Range	73	D9
Abū 'Alī	47	F7
Abū Dhabi = Abū Ẓaby	44	E4
Abu Hamed	55	E5
Abū Kamāl	46	D5
Abū Madd, Ra's	47	F4
Abū Zabad	55	F4
Abū Ẓaby	44	E4
Abuja	53	G7
Abunā	91	E5
Abunã →	91	E5
Abut Hd.	65	E4
Acaponeta	84	C3
Acapulco	84	D5
Acarigua	90	B5
Accra	53	G5
Achalpur	43	J10
Achill I.	11	E1
Achinsk	30	D7
Acireale	21	F5
Acklins I.	86	B5
Aconcagua, Cerro	94	C3
Aconquija, Mt.	94	B3
Acre □	91	E4
Acre →	91	E5
Ad Dahnā	47	F7
Ad Dammām	47	F7
Ad Dawādimi	47	F6
Ad Dawḥah	44	E2
Ad Dilam	47	G6
Ad Dīwānīyah	47	E6
Ada	81	B5
Adaja →	18	B3

Adam	44	F4
Adamaoua, Massif de l'	55	G1
Adamello, Mte.	20	A3
Adaminaby	63	C4
Adams, Mt.	72	C3
Adam's Bridge	43	Q11
Adana	46	C3
Adapazarı = Sakarya	46	B2
Adarama	55	E5
Adare, C.	96	B15
Adaut	37	F4
Adavale	63	A3
Adda →	20	B2
Addis Ababa = Addis Abeba	49	F2
Addis Abeba	49	F2
Adelaide	62	B2
Adelaide I.	96	A3
Adelaide Pen.	68	B10
Adélie, Terre	96	A14
Aden = Al 'Adan	49	E4
Aden, G. of	49	E4
Adi	37	E4
Adige →	20	B4
Adilabad	43	K11
Adirondack Mts.	77	C8
Admiralty I.	68	C6
Admiralty Is.	64	K9
Adonara	37	F2
Adoni	43	M10
Adour →	12	E3
Adra	18	D4
Adrano	21	F5
Adrar des Iforas	52	D6
Adriatic Sea	20	C5
Adua	37	E3
Adzhar Republic = Ajaria □	25	E5
Ægean Sea	23	E5
Aerhtai Shan	34	B4
Afghanistan ■	45	C6
'Afīf	47	G5

Name	Page	Ref
Afuá	92	C3
Afyon	46	C2
Afyonkarahisar = Afyon	46	C2
Agadez	53	E7
Agadir	52	B4
Agartala	41	F8
Agats	37	F5
Agboville	53	G5
Agde	13	E5
Agen	12	D4
Agra	42	F10
Ağri →	25	F5
Ağri →	21	D6
Ağri Dağı	46	C6
Ağri Karakose = Ağri	21	F5
Agrigento	21	F4
Agrínion	23	E3
Água Clara	93	G3
Agua Prieta	84	A3
Aguarico →	90	D3
Aguas Blancas	94	A3
Aguascalientes	84	C4
Aguilas	19	D5
Agulhas, C.	58	E4
Agung, Gunung	39	F5
Agusan →	36	C3
Ahaggar	52	D7
Ahar	46	C6
Ahipara B.	64	A5
Ahiri	43	K12
Ahmadabad	43	H8
Ahmadnagar	43	K9
Ahmadpur	42	E7
Ahmedabad = Ahmadabad	43	H8
Ahmednagar = Ahmadnagar	43	K9
Ahvāz	47	E7
Ahvenanmaa = Åland	9	C10
Aḥwar	49	E4
Aigues-Mortes	13	E6
Aihui	35	A7
Aija	91	E3
Aikawa	33	D6
Aiken	83	C7
Aimere	37	F2
Aïn Ben Tili	52	C4
Aïn Sefra	52	B5
Aïr	53	E7
Aisne →	13	B5
Aix-en-Provence	13	E6
Aix-la-Chapelle = Aachen	14	C4
Aix-les-Bains	13	D6
Aíyion	23	E4
Aizawl	41	F9
Aizuwakamatsu	33	E6
Ajaccio	13	F8
Ajanta Ra.	43	J9
Ajaria □	25	E5
Ajdābiyā	54	B3
Ajka	16	E3
'Ajmān	44	E3
Ajmer	42	F9
Ajo, C. de	18	A4
Akaroa	65	E5
Akelamo	37	D3
Aketi	56	D4
Akharnaí	23	E4
Akhelóös →	23	E3
Akhisar	23	E6
Akimiski I.	71	C2
Akita	32	D7
Akjoujt	53	E3
Akkeshi	32	B9
'Akko	46	D3
Akkol = Aqköl	29	E8
Aklavik	68	B6
Akmolinsk = Astana	29	D8
Akola	43	J10
Akordat	55	E6
Akpatok I.	70	B4
Akranes	8	C1
Akron	76	D5
Aksai Chin	42	B11
Aksaray	46	C3
Akşehir	46	C2
Aksu	34	B3
Aktogay	29	E8
Aktyubinsk = Aqtöbe	29	D6
Akure	53	G7
Akureyri	8	B2
Akyab = Sittwe	41	G9
Al 'Adan	49	E4
Al Aḥsā = Hasa □	47	F7
Al Amādīyah	46	C5
Al 'Amārah	47	E6
Al 'Aqabah	47	E3
Al 'Aramah	47	F6
Al Ashkhara	45	F4
Al Badi'	47	G6
Al Baḥral Mayyit = Dead Sea	47	E3
Al Başrah	47	E6
Al Batinah	44	F4
Al Baydā	54	B3
Al Fadīli	47	F7
Al Fallūjah	46	D5
Al Fāw	47	E7
Al Fujayrah	44	E4
Al Haddār	47	G6
Al Hāmad	47	E4
Al Ḥamar	47	G6
Al Ḥamrā'	47	F4
Al Ḥariq	47	G6
Al Ḥasakah	46	C5
Al Ḥayy	47	D6
Al Ḥillah, Iraq	47	D6
Al Ḥillah, Sí. Arabia	47	G6
Al Hoceïma	52	A5
Al Ḥudaydah	49	E3
Al Ḥufūf	47	F7
Al Ḥulwah	47	G6
Al Jāfūrah	47	F7
Al Jaghbūb	54	C3
Al Jahrah	47	E6
Al Jalāmīd	47	E4
Al Jawf, Libya	54	D3
Al Jawf, Si. Arabia	47	E4
Al Jazirah	46	D5
Al Jubayl	47	F7
Al Jubaylah	47	F6
Al Junaynah	55	F3
Al Khābūra	44	F4
Al Khalīl	47	E3
Al Kharfah	47	G6
Al Kharsāniya	47	F7
Al Khaşab	44	E4
Al Kufrah	54	D3
Al Kūt	47	D6
Al Kuwayt	47	E7
Al Lādhiqīyah	46	D3
Al Lubayyah	49	D3
Al Madīnah	47	F4
Al Majma'ah	47	F6
Al Manāmah	44	E2
Al Marj	54	B3
Al Mawşil	46	C5
Al Midhnab	47	F6
Al Mubarraz	47	F7
Al Muḥarraq	44	E2
Al Mukallā	49	E4
Al Mukhā	49	E3
Al Musayyib	47	D6
Al Muwayliḥ	47	F3
Al Qaḍīmah	47	G4
Al Qā'iyah	47	F5
Al Qāmishlī	46	C5
Al Qaşim	47	F5
Al Qaṭīf	47	F7
Al Qaṭrūn	54	D2
Al Quds = Jerusalem	47	E3
Al Qurayyat	45	F4
Al Qurnah	47	E6
Al 'Ulā	47	F4
Al 'Uqayr	47	F7
Al 'Uwaynid	47	F6
Al 'Uwayqilah	47	E5
Al 'Uyūn	47	F5
Al Wakrah	44	E2
Al Yamāmah	47	F6
Alabama □	82	C4
Alabama →	82	D4
Alaçam Dağları	23	E7
Alagoa Grande	92	D6
Alagoas □	93	D6
Alagoinhas	93	E6
Alajuela	88	D3
Alamosa	79	B10
Åland	9	C10
Alania = North Ossetia □	25	E5
Alanya	46	C2
Alapayevsk	29	D7
Alappuzha = Alleppey	43	Q10
Alaşehir	23	E7
Alaska □	69	B4
Alaska, G. of	69	C5
Alaska Peninsula	69	C4
Alaska Range	69	B4
Alatyr	24	C6
Alausi	90	D3
Alawoona	62	B3
Alba	20	B2
Albacete	19	C5
Albacutya, L.	62	C3
Albania ■	23	D3
Albany, Australia	60	H2
Albany, Ga., U.S.A.	83	D5
Albany, N.Y., U.S.A.	77	C9
Albany, Oreg., U.S.A.	72	D2
Albany →	71	C2
Albardón	94	C3
Albemarle	83	B7
Alberche →	18	C3
Albert, L., Africa	57	D6
Albert, L., Australia	62	C2
Albert Nile →	57	D6
Albertville = Kalemie	57	F5
Albertville	13	D7
Albi	12	E5
Albina	92	A3
Alborán	18	E4
Ålborg	9	D7
Alborz, Reshteh-ye Kūhhā-ye	44	B3
Albuquerque	79	C9
Albury-Wodonga	63	C4
Alcalá de Henares	18	B4
Alcalá la Real	18	D4
Álcamo	21	F4
Alcaniz	19	B5
Alcântara	92	C5
Alcántara, Embalse de	18	C2
Alcantarilla	19	D5
Alcaraz, Sierra de	19	C4
Alcaudete	18	D3
Alcázar de San Juan	18	C4
Alchevsk	25	D4
Alcira = Alzira	19	C5
Alcoy	19	C5
Aldabra Is.	51	G8
Aldan →	31	C10
Alderney	11	G5
Aleg	53	E3
Alegrete	94	B5
Aleisk	29	D9
Aleksandriya = Oleksandriya	17	C8
Alençon	12	B4
Aleppo = Ḥalab	46	C4
Alès	13	D6
Alessándria	20	B2
Ålesund	8	C7
Aleutian Is.	69	C2
Alexander Arch.	69	C6
Alexander I.	96	A3
Alexandra, Australia	63	C4

Alexandra, N.Z.	65	F3
Alexandria = El Iskandarîya	54	B4
Alexandria, *Romania*	22	C5
Alexandria, *La., U.S.A.*	81	D7
Alexandria, *Va., U.S.A.*	77	E7
Alexandrina, L.	62	C2
Alexandroúpolis	22	D5
Alga	29	E6
Algarve	18	D1
Algeciras	18	D3
Algemesí	19	C5
Alger	52	A6
Algeria ■	52	C6
Alghero	21	D2
Algiers = Alger	52	A6
Alhucemas = Al Hoceïma	52	A5
'Alī al Gharbī	47	D6
'Alī Khēl	42	C6
Aliağa	23	E6
Alicante	19	C5
Alice Springs	60	E5
Aligarh	42	F11
Alīgūdarz	46	D7
Alipur	42	E7
Alipur Duar	41	D7
Aliwal North	59	E5
Aljustrel	18	D1
Alkmaar	14	B3
All American Canal	78	D6
Allahabad	40	E3
Allegheny →	77	D5
Allegheny Mts.	77	F5
Allentown	77	D8
Alleppey	43	Q10
Aller →	14	B5
Allier →	13	C5
Allora	63	A5
Alma Ata = Almaty	29	E8
Almada	18	C1
Almadén	18	C3
Almansa	19	C5
Almanzor, Pico	18	B3
Almanzora →	19	D5
Almaty	29	E8
Almazán	19	B4
Almeirim	92	C3
Almelo	14	B4
Almendralejo	18	C2
Almería	19	D4
Almora	42	E11
Alnwick	10	D6
Alon	41	F10
Alor	37	F2
Alor Setar	38	C2
Alps	14	E5
Alsace	13	B7
Alsask	69	C9
Alsasua	19	A4
Alta Gracia	94	C4
Altai = Aerhtai Shan	34	B4
Altamira	92	C3
Altamura	21	D6
Altanbulag	35	A5
Altay	34	B3
Altea	19	C5
Alto Araguaia	93	F3
Alto Molocue	59	B7
Alton	75	F9
Altoona	77	D6
Altun Shan	34	C3
Alusi	37	F4
Alvear	94	B5
Alwar	42	F10
Alxa Zuoqi	35	C5
Alzira	19	C5
Am Timan	55	F3
Amâdi	55	G5
Amadjuak L.	70	B3
Amagasaki	33	F4
Amahai	37	E3
Amakusa-Shotō	33	G2
Amaliás	23	F3
Amalner	43	J9
Amambay, Cordillera de	94	A5
Amangeldy	29	D7
Amapá	92	B3
Amapá □	92	B3
Amarante	92	D5
Amarillo	80	B3
Amaro, Mte.	20	C5
Amasra	46	B3
Amazon = Amazonas →	92	C3
Amazonas □	90	D6
Amazonas →	92	C3
Ambala	42	D10
Ambalavao	59	J9
Ambanja	59	G9
Ambato	90	D3
Ambatolampy	59	H9
Ambatondrazaka	59	H9
Amberg	15	D6
Ambergris Cay	85	D7
Amberley	65	E5
Ambikapur	40	F4
Ambilobé	59	G9
Ambo	91	F3
Amboise	12	C4
Ambon	37	E3
Ambositra	59	J9
Amboyna Cay	38	C4
Ambriz	56	F2
Amchitka I.	69	C1
Amderma	28	C7
Ameca	84	C4
Ameland	14	B3
American Highland	96	B10
American Samoa ☑	65	L13
Americus	83	C5
Amery Ice Shelf	96	A10
Ames	75	D8
Amherst	71	D4
Amiata, Mte.	20	C3
Amiens	12	B5
Amirante Is.	26	K9
'Ammān	47	E3
Ammochostos = Famagusta	46	D3
Amorgós	23	F5
Amoy = Xiamen	35	D6
Ampanihy	59	J8
Ampenan	39	F5
Amper →	15	D6
Amravati	43	J10
Amreli	43	J7
Amritsar	42	D9
Amroha	42	E11
Amsterdam	14	B3
Amstetten	15	D8
Amudarya →	29	E6
Amundsen Gulf	68	A7
Amundsen Sea	96	B1
Amuntai	39	E5
Amur →	31	D12
Amurang	37	D2
Amyderya = Amudarya →	29	E6
An Nafūd	47	E5
An Najaf	47	D6
An Nhon	38	B3
An Nu'ayrīyah	47	F7
Anabar →	30	B9
Anaconda	73	C7
Anadolu	46	C2
'Ānah	46	D5
Anaheim	78	D4
Anakapalle	40	J4
Anambas, Kepulauan	39	D3
Anamur	46	C3
Anan	33	G4
Anantnag	42	C9
Ananyiv	17	E9
Anápolis	93	F4
Anár	44	D3
Anārak	44	C3
Anatolia = Anadolu	46	C2
Añatuya	94	B4
Anchorage	69	B5
Ancohuma, Nevada	91	G5
Ancón	91	F3
Ancona	20	C4
Ancud	95	E2
Ancud, G. de	95	E2
Andalgalá	94	B3
Andalucía □	18	D3
Andalusia	82	D4
Andaman Is.	27	H13
Andaman Sea	38	B1
Anderson	76	D3
Anderson →	68	B7
Andes, Cord. de los	91	G4
Andhra Pradesh □	43	L11
Andijon	29	E8
Andikíthira	23	G4
Andizhan = Andijon	29	E8
Andkhvoy	45	B6
Andoany	59	G9
Andorra ■	19	A6
Andorra La Vella	19	A6
Andreanof Is.	69	C2
Ándria	20	D6
Andropov = Rybinsk	24	B4
Ándros	23	F5
Andros I.	86	B4
Andújar	18	C3
Andulo	56	G3
Aneto, Pico de	19	A6
Angara →	30	D7
Angarsk	30	D8
Angaston	62	B2
Ånge	8	C9
Angeles	36	A2
Ångermanälven →	8	C9
Angers	12	C3
Ango	57	D5
Angola ■	58	A3
Angoulême	12	D4
Angoumois	12	D4
Angren	29	E8
Anguilla ☑	87	C7
Anhui □	35	C6
Anjou	12	C3
Ankang	35	C5
Ankara	46	C3
Ann Arbor	76	C4
Annaba	52	A7
Annan	11	F5
Annapolis	77	E7
Annecy	13	D7
Anning	34	D5
Anniston	82	C5
Annobón	51	G4
Anqing	35	C6
Ansbach	14	D6
Anshan	35	B7
Anshun	35	D5
Ansongo	53	E6
Ansudu	37	E5
Antabamba	91	F4
Antakya	46	C4
Antalaha	59	G10
Antalya	46	C2
Antalya Körfezi	46	C2
Antananarivo	59	H9
Antarctic Pen.	96	A4
Antarctica	96	C
Antequera	18	D3
Anti Atlas	52	C4
Antibes	13	E7
Anticosti, Î. d'	71	D4
Antigua & Barbuda ■	87	C7
Antioquia	90	B3
Antofagasta	94	A2
Antonina	94	B7
Antrim	11	D3
Antsirabe	59	H9
Antsiranana	59	G9
Antsohihy	59	G9

Antwerpen

Antwerpen	14	C3
Anupgarh	42	E8
Anvers = Antwerpen	14	C3
Anvers I.	96	A3
Anxi	34	B4
Anxious B.	62	B1
Anyang	35	C6
Anzhero-Sudzhensk	29	D9
Ánzio	20	D4
Aoga-Shima	33	G6
Aomen = Macau	35	D6
Aomori	32	C7
Aoraki Mount Cook	65	E4
Aosta	20	B1
Apalachicola →	82	E5
Apaporis →	90	D5
Aparri	36	A2
Apeldoorn	14	B3
Apennines = Appennini	20	B3
Apia	65	L13
Apiacás, Serra dos	91	E7
Aplao	91	G4
Apo, Mt.	36	C3
Apolo	91	F5
Apoteri	90	C7
Appalachian Mts.	77	F5
Appennini	20	B3
Appleton	76	B1
Aprília	20	D4
Apucarana	94	A6
Apure →	90	B5
Apurímac →	91	F4
Aqaba = Al 'Aqabah	47	E3
Aqaba, G. of	47	E3
Áqcheh	45	B6
Aqköl	29	E8
Aqmola = Astana	29	D8
'Aqrah	46	C5
Aqtöbe	29	D6
Aquidauana	93	G2
Aquitain, Bassin	12	D3
Ar Rachidiya = Er Rachidia	52	B5
Ar Ramādī	46	D5
Ar Raqqah	46	D4
Ar Rass	47	F5
Ar Rifā'ī	47	E6
Ar Riyāḍ	47	F6
Ar Ruṭbah	46	D5
Ar Ruwayḍah	47	G6
Ara	40	E5
'Arab, Bahr el →	55	G4
Arab, Shatt al →	47	E7
Arabian Desert = Es Sahrâ' Esh Sharqîya	54	C5
Arabian Gulf = Gulf, The	44	E2
Arabian Sea	26	H10
Araç	46	B3
Aracaju	93	E6
Aracati	92	C6
Araçatuba	93	G3
Aracena	18	D2
Araçuaí	93	F5
Arad	16	E5
Arafura Sea	37	F4
Aragón □	19	B5
Aragón →	19	A5
Araguacema	92	D4
Araguaia →	92	D4
Araguari	93	G3
Araguari →	92	B4
Arak	52	C6
Arakan Coast	41	H9
Arakan Yoma	41	H10
Araks = Aras, Rüd-e →	46	B7
Aral	29	E7
Aral Sea	29	E6
Aralsk = Aral	29	E7
Aralskoye More = Aral Sea	29	E6
Aran I.	10	D2
Aran Is.	11	E2
Aranda de Duero	18	B4
Aranjuez	18	B4
Arapgir	46	C4
Arapiraca	93	D6
Arapongas	94	A6
Araraquara	93	G4
Ararat	62	C3
Araripe, Chapada do	92	D6
Aras, Rüd-e →	46	B7
Arauca	90	B4
Arauca →	90	B5
Araxá	93	F4
Araya, Pen. de	90	A6
Árbatax	21	E2
Arbil	46	C6
Arbroath	10	C5
Arcachon	12	D3
Archangel = Arkhangelsk	28	C5
Arckaringa Cr. →	62	A2
Arcos de la Frontera	18	D3
Arcot	43	N11
Arctic Bay	70	A2
Arctic Red River = Tsiigehtchic	68	B6
Arda →	22	D6
Ardabīl	46	C7
Ardahan	46	B5
Ardenne	14	D3
Ardestān	44	C3
Ardlethan	63	B4
Ardmore	80	B5
Ardrossan	62	B2
Arecibo	87	C6
Areia Branca	92	C6
Arendal	9	D7
Arequipa	91	G4
Arévalo	18	B3
Arezzo	20	C3
Arganda	18	B4
Argentan	12	B3
Argentário, Mte.	20	C3
Argentina ■	94	D3
Argentino, L.	95	G2
Argeş →	22	B6
Arghandab →	42	D4
Argolikós Kólpos	23	F4
Árgos	23	F4
Argostólion	23	E3
Århus	9	D8
Ariadnoye	32	A4
Arica, Chile	91	G4
Arica, Colombia	90	D4
Arinos →	91	F7
Aripuanã	91	E6
Aripuanã →	90	E6
Ariquemes	91	E6
Arizona □	79	C7
Arizona	94	D3
Arjona	90	A3
Arkalyk = Arqalyk	29	D7
Arkansas □	81	B7
Arkansas →	81	C8
Arkansas City	80	A5
Arkhangelsk	28	C5
Arklow	11	E3
Arktícheskiy, Mys	30	A7
Arlanzón →	18	A3
Arlbergpass	14	E6
Arles	13	E6
Arlington, Va., U.S.A.	77	E7
Arlington, Wash., U.S.A.	72	B2
Arlon	14	D3
Armagh	11	D3
Armenia	90	C3
Armenia ■	25	E5
Armidale	63	B5
Arnaud →	70	B3
Arnauti, C.	46	D3
Arnhem	14	C3
Arnhem, C.	60	C4
Arnhem Land	60	C5
Arno →	20	C3
Arno Bay	62	B2
Arnsberg	14	C5
Arqalyk	29	D7
Arrah = Ara	40	E5
Arran	10	D4
Arras	13	A5
Arrecife	52	C3
Arrée, Mts. d'	12	B2
Arrowtown	65	F3
Arsenev	32	A3
Árta	23	E3
Artem	32	B3
Arthur →	62	D3
Arthur's Pass	65	E4
Artigas	94	C5
Artois	12	A5
Artsyz	17	E9
Artvin	46	B5
Aru, Kepulauan	37	F4
Arua	57	D6
Aruanã	93	E3
Aruba □	87	D6
Arunachal Pradesh □	41	C10
Arusha	57	E7
Aruwimi →	56	D4
Arviat	68	B10
Arxan	35	B6
Arys	29	E7
Arzamas	24	B5
As Saffānīyah	47	E6
As Samāwah	47	E6
As Sohar = Şuḩār	44	E4
As Sulaymānīyah, Iraq	46	D6
As Sulaymānīyah, Si. Arabia	47	F6
As Summān	47	E6
As Sūq	47	G5
As Suwaydā'	46	D4
As Suwayḥ	45	F4
As Şuwayrah	47	D6
Asahigawa	32	B8
Asansol	40	F6
Ascension I.	51	G2
Aschaffenburg	14	D5
Aschersleben	15	C6
Áscoli Piceno	20	C4
Ascope	91	E3
Aseb	49	E3
Asenovgrad	22	C5
Ash Shāmīyah	47	E6
Ash Shāriqah	44	E3
Ash Shaṭrah	47	E6
Ash Shu'bah	47	E6
Ashburton	65	E4
Asheville	83	B6
Ashford, Australia	63	A5
Ashford, U.K.	11	F7
Ashgabat	29	F6
Ashizuri-Zaki	33	G3
Ashkhabad = Ashgabat	29	F6
Ashmyany	17	A7
Ashqelon	47	E3
Ashtabula	76	D5
Ashuanipi, L.	71	C4
Asia, Kepulauan	37	D4
Asifabad	43	K11
Asinara	20	D2
Asinara, G. dell'	20	D2
Asino	29	D9
Asipovichy	17	B9
'Asīr □	48	D3
Asir, Ras	49	E5
Asmera	55	E6
Aspiring, Mt.	65	F3
Assab = Aseb	49	E3
Assam □	41	D9
Assen	14	B4
Assiniboia	69	D9
Assiniboine →	69	D10
Assis	94	A6
Assisi	20	C4
Astana	29	D8

Asti 20 B2
Astipálaia 23 F6
Astorga 18 A2
Astoria 72 C2
Astrakhan 25 D6
Asturias □ 18 A3
Asunción 94 B5
Aswân 54 D5
Aswan Dam = Sadd el Aali 54 D5
Asyût 54 C5
At Ṭafilah 47 E3
At Ṭā'if 48 C3
Atacama, Desierto de .. 94 A3
Atacama, Salar de 94 A3
Atalaya 91 F4
Atapupu 37 F2
Atâr 52 D3
Atasu 29 E8
Atauro 37 F3
'Atbara 55 E5
'Atbara, Nahr ➝ 55 E5
Atbasar 29 D7
Athabasca 69 C8
Athabasca ➝ 68 C8
Athabasca, L. 68 C8
Athens = Athínai 23 F4
Athens, Ala., U.S.A. ... 82 B4
Athens, Ga., U.S.A. ... 83 C6
Athínai 23 F4
Athlone 11 E3
Áthos 23 D5
Athy 11 E3
Ati 55 F2
Atlanta 83 C5
Atlantic City 77 E8
Atlas Mts. = Haut Atlas 52 B4
Atrek ➝ 44 B3
Atsuta 32 B7
Attapu 38 B3
Attawapiskat ➝ 71 C2
Attock 42 C8
Attopeu = Attapu 38 B3
Attur 43 P11
Atuel ➝ 94 D3
Atyraü 29 E6
Aubagne 13 E6
Aube ➝ 13 B5
Auburn 82 D6
Auburn Ra. 63 A5
Aubusson 12 D5
Auch 12 E4
Auckland 64 B6
Aude ➝ 13 E5
Augathella 63 A4
Augsburg 14 D6
Augusta, Italy 21 F5
Augusta, Ga., U.S.A. .. 83 C7
Augusta, Maine, U.S.A. 77 B11
Aunis 12 C3
Auponhia 37 E3
Aurangabad, Bihar, India 40 E5
Aurangabad, Maharashtra,
India 43 K9
Aurich 14 B4
Aurillac 12 D5
Aurora, Colo., U.S.A. .. 74 F2
Aurora, Ill., U.S.A. 76 D1
Austin, Minn., U.S.A. .. 75 D8
Austin, Tex., U.S.A. ... 80 D5
Austral Is. = Tubuai Is. 65 M16
Austral Seamount Chain 65 M16
Australia ■ 60 E6
Australian Capital
Territory □ 63 C4
Austria ■ 15 E8
Autun 13 C6
Auvergne 13 D5
Auvergne, Mts. d' 13 D5
Auxerre 13 C5
Avallon 13 C5
Aveiro, Brazil 92 C2
Aveiro, Portugal 18 B1

Åvej 46 D7
Avellaneda 94 C5
Avellino 21 D5
Aversa 21 D5
Avesta 9 C9
Avezzano 20 C4
Aviemore 10 C5
Avignon 13 E6
Ávila 18 B3
Avilés 18 A3
Avoca ➝ 62 C3
Avola 21 F5
Avranches 12 B3
Awaji-Shima 33 F4
Awash 49 F3
Awatere ➝ 65 D6
Awbārī 54 C1
Awbārī, Idehan 54 C1
Awjilah 54 C3
Axim 53 H5
Axiós ➝ 23 D4
Ayabaca 90 D3
Ayabe 33 F4
Ayacucho, Argentina .. 94 D5
Ayacucho, Peru 91 F4
Ayaguz 29 E9
Ayamonte 18 D2
Ayaviri 91 F4
Āybak 45 B7
Aydın 23 F6
Ayers Rock 60 F5
Áyios Evstrátios 23 E5
Aylmer, L. 68 B8
Ayn Dār 47 F7
Ayr 10 D4
Aytos 22 C6
Ayu, Kepulauan 37 D4
Ayvacık 23 E6
Ayvalık 23 E6
Az Zahrān 47 F7
Az Zarqā 46 D4
Az Zilfī 47 F6
Az Zubayr 47 E6
Azamgarh 40 D4
Äzärbayjan = Azerbaijan ■ 25 E6
Äzärbäyjan-e Gharbī □ . 46 C6
Äzärbäyjan-e Sharqī □ . 46 C6
Azare 53 F8
Azbine = Aïr 53 E7
Azerbaijan ■ 25 E6
Azogues 90 D3
Azores 50 C2
Azov 25 D4
Azov, Sea of 25 D4
Azuaga 18 C3
Azuero, Pen. de 86 E3
Azul 94 D5

B

Ba Don 38 A3
Baardeere = Bardera ... 49 G3
Bab el Mandeb 49 E3
Bābā, Koh-i- 42 B5
Baba Burnu 23 E6
Babadag 22 B7
Babadayhan 29 F7
Babaeski 22 D6
Babahoyo 90 D3
Babar 37 F3
Babo 37 E4
Bābol 44 B3
Bābol Sar 44 B3
Babruysk 17 B9
Babuyan Chan. 36 A2
Babylon 47 D6
Bacabal 92 C5
Bacan, Kepulauan 37 E3
Bacarra 36 A2

Bacău 17 E8
Bachelina 29 D7
Back ➝ 68 B9
Bacolod 36 B2
Bad Ischl 15 E7
Bad Kissingen 14 C6
Bad Lands 74 D3
Badagara 43 P9
Badajoz 18 C2
Badalona 19 B7
Badampahar 40 F6
Badanah 47 E5
Badarinath 42 D11
Badas, Kepulauan 39 D3
Baddo ➝ 42 E4
Bade 37 F5
Baden 15 D9
Baden-Baden 14 D5
Baden-Württemberg □ . 14 D5
Badgastein 15 E7
Bädghis □ 42 B3
Badin 43 G6
Baena 18 D3
Baeza 18 D4
Baffin B. 70 B4
Baffin I. 70 B3
Bafia 53 H8
Bafing ➝ 53 F3
Bafoulabé 53 F3
Bāfq 44 D3
Bāft 44 D4
Bafwasende 57 D5
Bagamoyo 57 F7
Baganga 36 C3
Bagansiapiapi 39 D2
Bagdarin 30 D9
Bagé 94 C6
Baghdād 46 D6
Bagheria 21 E4
Baghlān 42 A6
Baghlān □ 45 C7
Bago = Pegu 41 J11
Baguio 36 A2
Bahamas ■ 86 A4
Baharampur 40 E7
Bahawalpur 42 E7
Bahía = Salvador 93 E6
Bahía □ 93 E5
Bahía Blanca 94 D4
Bahía de Caráquez ... 90 D2
Bahía Laura 95 F3
Bahía Negra 91 H7
Bahraich 40 D3
Bahrain ■ 44 E2
Baia Mare 17 E6
Baïbokoum 55 G2
Baidoa 49 G3
Baie-Comeau 71 D4
Ba'iji 46 D5
Baikal, L. = Baykal, Oz. 30 D8
Baile Atha Cliath = Dublin 11 E3
Băileşti 22 B4
Bâ'ir 47 E4
Bairnsdale 63 C4
Baitadi 40 C3
Baiyin 35 C5
Baja 16 E4
Baja, Pta. 84 B1
Baja California 84 A1
Bajimba, Mt. 63 A5
Bakala 55 G3
Bakel 53 F3
Baker, L. 68 B10
Baker, Mt. 72 B3
Baker I. 64 J13
Baker Lake 68 B10
Bakers Dozen Is. 71 C3
Bakersfield 78 C3
Bākhtarān 46 D6
Baku 25 E6
Bakony 16 E3
Bakouma 56 C4

Baku

Baku = Bakı 25 E6
Bakutis Coast 96 B1
Baky = Bakı 25 E6
Balabac I. 38 C5
Balabac Str. 38 C5
Balabalangan, Kepulauan . 39 E5
Balaghat Ra. 43 K10
Balaguer 19 B6
Balaklava 25 E3
Balakovo 24 C6
Balashov 24 C5
Balasore = Baleshwar .. 40 G6
Balaton 16 E3
Balbina, Reprêsa de ... 90 D7
Balchik 22 C7
Balclutha 65 G3
Baleares, Is. 19 C7
Balearic Is. = Baleares, Is. . 19 C7
Baleine = Whale → 70 C4
Baler 36 A2
Baleshwar 40 G6
Bali 39 F5
Bali □ 39 F5
Baliem → 37 F5
Balıkeşir 23 E6
Balıkpapan 39 E5
Balimbing 36 C1
Balipara 41 D9
Balkan Mts. = Stara Planina 22 C4
Balkh 45 B6
Balkhash = Balqash ... 29 E8
Balkhash, Ozero = Balqash
  Köl 29 E8
Balla 41 E8
Ballarat 62 C3
Ballater 10 C5
Ballina, Australia ... 63 A5
Ballina, Ireland 11 D2
Ballinasloe 11 E2
Ballymena 11 D3
Balmaceda 95 F2
Balmoral 62 C3
Balochistan =
  Baluchistan □ 42 F4
Balonne → 63 A4
Balqash 29 E8
Balqash Köl 29 E8
Balrampur 40 D4
Balranald 62 B3
Balsas → 84 D4
Balta 17 D9
Bălți 17 E8
Baltic Sea 9 D9
Baltimore 77 E7
Baluchistan □ 42 F4
Balya 23 E6
Bam 44 D4
Bama 55 F1
Bamako 53 F4
Bambari 56 C4
Bamberg 14 D6
Bamenda 53 G8
Bāmiān □ 42 B5
Bampūr 45 E5
Ban Don = Surat Thani . 38 C1
Ban Kantang 38 C1
Ban Mê Thuôt = Buon Ma
  Thuot 38 B3
Banalia 57 D5
Bananal, I. do 93 E3
Banaras = Varanasi ... 40 E4
Bânâs, Ras 54 D6
Band-e Torkestan 45 C6
Banda, Kepulauan 37 E3
Banda Aceh 38 C1
Banda Banda, Mt. 63 B5
Banda Elat 37 F4
Banda Sea 37 F3
Bandanaira 37 E3
Bandar = Machilipatnam . 40 J3
Bandar-e Abbās 44 E4
Bandar-e Anzalī 46 C7

Bandar-e Bushehr =
  Büshehr 44 D2
Bandar-e Chārak 44 E3
Bandar-e Deylam 47 E7
Bandar-e Khomeynī 47 E7
Bandar-e Lengeh 44 E3
Bandar-e Rīg 44 D2
Bandar-e Torkeman 44 B3
Bandar Maharani = Muar . 39 D2
Bandar Penggaram = Batu
  Pahat 39 D2
Bandar Seri Begawan .. 38 D5
Bandar Sri Aman 39 D4
Bandera 94 B4
Bandırma 23 D7
Bandon 11 F2
Bandundu 56 E3
Bandung 39 F3
Banff, Canada 69 C8
Banff, U.K. 10 C5
Bang Saphan 38 B1
Bangalore 43 N10
Bangassou 56 D4
Banggai, Kepulauan ... 37 E2
Banggi 38 C5
Banghāzi 54 B3
Bangka, Sulawesi,
  Indonesia 37 D3
Bangka, Sumatera,
  Indonesia 39 E3
Bangka, Selat 39 E3
Bangkinang 39 D2
Bangko 39 E2
Bangkok 38 B2
Bangladesh ■ 41 E7
Bangong Co 42 B11
Bangor, Down, U.K. ... 11 D4
Bangor, Gwynedd, U.K. . 11 E4
Bangor, U.S.A. 77 B11
Bangued 36 A2
Bangui 56 D3
Bangweulu, L. 57 G6
Bani 87 C5
Bāniyās 46 D3
Banja Luka 20 B6
Banjarmasin 39 E4
Banjul 53 F2
Bankipore 40 E5
Banks I. 68 A7
Banks Pen. 65 E5
Banks Str. 62 D4
Bankura 40 F6
Banningville = Bandundu . 56 E3
Bannu 42 C7
Banswara 43 H9
Bantry 11 F2
Banyak, Kepulauan 39 D1
Banzare Coast 96 A13
Baoding 35 C6
Baoji 35 C5
Baoshan 34 D4
Baotou 35 B6
Bapatla 40 K3
Ba'qūbah 46 D6
Bar, Serbia & M. 22 C2
Bar, Ukraine 17 D8
Bar-le-Duc 13 B6
Barabai 39 E5
Baracoa 86 B5
Barahona 87 C5
Barail Range 41 E9
Barakaldo 19 A4
Barakhola 41 E9
Barakpur 41 F7
Baramula 42 B9
Baran 43 G10
Baranavichy 17 B8
Baranof I. 69 C6
Barapasi 37 E5
Barat Daya, Kepulauan . 37 F3
Barbacena 93 G5
Barbados ■ 87 D8

Barbastro 19 A6
Barcellona Pozzo di Gotto 21 E5
Barcelona, Spain 19 B7
Barcelona, Venezuela . 90 A6
Barcelos 90 D6
Bardaï 54 D2
Barddhaman 40 F6
Bardera 49 G3
Bardīyah 54 B4
Bareilly 42 E11
Barfleur, Pte. de 12 B3
Barhi 40 E5
Bari 20 D6
Bari Doab 42 D8
Baridī, Ra's 47 F4
Barinas 90 B4
Baring, C. 68 B8
Barisal 41 F8
Barisan, Bukit 39 E2
Barito → 39 E4
Barkly Tableland 60 D6
Bârlad → 17 F8
Barlee, L. 60 F2
Barletta 20 D6
Barmedman 63 B4
Barmer 42 G7
Barmera 62 B3
Barnaul 29 D9
Barnsley 11 E6
Barnstaple 11 F4
Baro 53 G7
Baroda = Vadodara 43 H8
Barpeta 41 D8
Barquísimeto 90 A5
Barra, Brazil 93 E5
Barra, U.K. 10 C3
Barra do Corda 92 D4
Barra Falsa, Pta. da . 59 C7
Barraba 63 B5
Barrackpur = Barakpur . 41 F7
Barraigh = Barra 10 C3
Barranca, Lima, Peru . 91 F3
Barranca, Loreto, Peru . 90 D3
Barrancabermeja 90 B4
Barrancas 90 B6
Barrancos 18 C2
Barranqueras 94 B5
Barranquilla 90 A4
Barreiras 93 E5
Barreirinhas 92 C6
Barreiro 18 C1
Barretos 93 G4
Barrier Ra. 62 B3
Barrington Tops 63 B5
Barringun 63 A4
Barrow 69 A4
Barrow-in-Furness 11 D5
Barry 11 F5
Barsi 43 K9
Barsoi 40 E6
Barstow 78 C4
Bartica 90 B7
Bartin 46 B3
Bartlesville 81 A6
Barysaw 17 A9
Bāsa'idū 44 E3
Basankusa 56 D3
Basarabeasca 17 E9
Basarabia = Bessarabiya . 17 E9
Basel 14 E4
Bashkortostan □ 29 D6
Basilan I. 36 C2
Basilan Str. 36 C2
Basildon 11 F7
Basim = Washim 43 J10
Basingstoke 11 F6
Basle = Basel 14 E4
Basoko 56 D4
Basque Provinces = Pais
  Vasco □ 19 A4
Basra = Al Başrah 47 E6
Bass Str. 61 H8

Bassano del Grappa	20	B3
Bassas da India	59	C7
Bassein	41	J10
Basseterre	87	C7
Bastak	44	E3
Bastar	40	H3
Basti	40	D4
Bastia	13	E8
Bastogne	14	C3
Bata	56	D1
Bataan □	36	B2
Batabanó, G. de	86	B3
Batac	36	A2
Batagai	31	C11
Batamay	31	C10
Batangafo	55	G2
Batangas	36	B2
Batanta	37	E4
Batdambang	38	B2
Batemans B.	63	C5
Batemans Bay	63	C5
Bath	11	F5
Bathurst = Banjul	53	F2
Bathurst, *Australia*	63	B4
Bathurst, *Canada*	71	D4
Bathurst, C.	68	C7
Bathurst Harb.	62	D4
Bathurst Inlet	68	B9
Batlow	63	C4
Batman	46	C5
Batna	52	A7
Baton Rouge	81	D8
Batouri	56	D2
Battambang = Batdambang	38	B2
Battipáglia	21	D5
Battle Creek	76	C3
Batu	49	F2
Batu, Kepulauan	39	E1
Batu Pahat	39	D2
Batuata	37	F2
Batumi	25	E5
Baturaja	39	E2
Baturité	92	C6
Bau	39	D4
Baubau	37	F2
Baucau	37	F3
Bauchi	53	F7
Bauer, C.	62	B1
Baukau = Baucau	37	F3
Bauru	93	G4
Bautzen	15	C8
Bavaria = Bayern □	15	D6
Bawdwin	41	F11
Bawean	39	F4
Bawku	53	F5
Bawlake	41	H11
Bay City	76	C4
Bay View	64	C7
Bayamo	86	B4
Bayan Har Shan	34	C4
Bayan Hot = Alxa Zuoqi	35	C5
Bayanaüyl	29	D8
Bayanhongor	35	B5
Baybay	36	B2
Baydhabo = Baidoa	49	G3
Bayern □	15	D6
Bayeux	12	B3
Bayındır	23	E6
Baykal, Oz.	30	D8
Baykonur = Bayqongyr	29	E7
Bayombong	36	A2
Bayonne	12	E3
Bayovar	91	E2
Bayqongyr	29	E7
Bayramaly	29	F7
Bayramiç	23	E6
Bayreuth	15	D6
Bayrūt	46	D3
Baytown	81	E6
Baza	19	D4
Bazaruto, I. do	59	C7
Beachport	62	C2
Beagle, Canal	95	G3
Beardmore Glacier	96	C14
Béarn	12	E3
Beauce, Plaine de la	12	B4
Beaudesert	63	A5
Beaufort	38	C5
Beaufort Sea	66	B6
Beaufort West	58	E4
Beaumont	81	D6
Beaune	13	C6
Beauvais	12	B5
Beawar →	69	C9
Beawar	42	F9
Bečej	22	B3
Béchar	52	B5
Bedford	11	E6
Beenleigh	63	A5
Be'er Sheva	47	E3
Beersheba = Be'er Sheva	47	E3
Befale	56	D4
Bega	63	C4
Behbehān	47	E7
Bei Jiang →	35	D7
Bei'an	35	B7
Beihai	35	D5
Beijing	35	C6
Beijapahi	63	B3
Beinn na Faoghla = Benbecula	10	C3
Beira	59	B6
Beirut = Bayrūt	46	D3
Beitbridge	59	C6
Beja, *Portugal*	18	C2
Beja, *Tunisia*	54	A1
Bejaïa	52	A7
Béjar	18	B3
Bejestän	44	C4
Békéscsaba	16	E5
Bela, *India*	40	E4
Bela, *Pakistan*	42	F5
Bela Crkva	22	B3
Bela Vista	94	A5
Belarus ■	24	C2
Belau = Palau ■	36	C4
Belawan	39	D1
Belaya Tserkov = Bila Tserkva	17	D10
Belcher Is.	71	C3
Beled Weyne = Belet Uen	49	G4
Belém	92	C4
Belet Uen	49	G4
Belev	24	C4
Belfast	11	D4
Belfort	13	C7
Belgaum	43	M9
Belgium ■	14	C3
Belgorod	24	C4
Belgorod-Dnestrovskiy = Bilhorod-Dnistrovskyy	25	D3
Belgrade = Beograd	22	B3
Beli Drim →	22	C3
Belinyu	39	E3
Belitung	39	E3
Belize ■	85	D7
Belize City	85	D7
Belkovskiy, Ostrov	30	B11
Bell Peninsula	70	B2
Bell Ville	94	C4
Bella Unión	94	C5
Bella Vista	94	B5
Bellary	43	M10
Bellata	63	A4
Belle-Île	12	C2
Belle Isle	71	C5
Belle Isle, Str. of	71	C5
Belleville, *Canada*	71	D3
Belleville, *U.S.A.*	75	F10
Bellin = Kangirsuk	70	C4
Bellingen	63	B5
Bellingham	72	B2
Bellingshausen Sea	96	A2
Bellinzona	13	C8
Belluno	20	A4
Belmonte	93	F6
Belmopan	85	D7
Belo Horizonte	93	F5
Belo-Tsiribihina	59	H8
Beloit	75	D10
Belokorovichi	17	C9
Belomorsk	28	C4
Belonia	41	F8
Belorussia = Belarus ■	24	C2
Belovo	29	D9
Beloye, Ozero	24	A4
Beloye More	8	B13
Belozersk	24	A4
Beltana	62	B2
Belterra	92	C3
Beltsy = Bălţi	17	E8
Belukha	29	E9
Beluran	38	C5
Belyy, Ostrov	28	B8
Belyy Yar	29	D9
Bembéréke	53	F6
Bemidji	75	B7
Ben Lomond, *N.S.W., Australia*	63	B5
Ben Lomond, *Tas., Australia*	62	D4
Ben Nevis	10	C4
Bena	53	F7
Bena-Dibele	56	E4
Benalla	63	C4
Benares = Varanasi	40	E4
Benavente	18	A3
Benbecula	10	C3
Benbonyathe	62	B2
Bend	72	D3
Bender Beila	49	F5
Bendery = Tighina	17	E9
Bendigo	63	C3
Benevento	20	D5
Bengal, Bay of	41	J7
Bengbu	35	C6
Benghazi = Banghāzī	54	B3
Bengkalis	39	D2
Bengkulu	39	E2
Bengkulu □	39	E2
Benguela	58	A2
Beni	57	D5
Beni →	91	F5
Beni Mellal	52	B4
Beni Suef	54	C5
Benidorm	19	C5
Benin ■	53	G6
Benin, Bight of	53	H6
Benin City	53	G7
Benjamin Constant	90	D4
Benoni	59	D5
Bent	44	E4
Benteng	37	F2
Benton Harbor	76	C2
Benue →	53	G7
Benxi	35	B7
Beo	36	D3
Beograd	22	B3
Beppu	33	G2
Berat	23	D2
Berau, Teluk	37	E4
Berber	55	E5
Berbera	49	E4
Berbérati	56	D3
Berbice →	90	B7
Berdichev = Berdychiv	17	D9
Berdsk	29	D9
Berdyansk	25	D4
Berdychiv	17	D9
Berebere	37	D3
Bereda	49	E5
Berehove	17	D6
Berekum	53	G5
Berestechko	17	C7
Bereza = Byaroza	17	B7

Berezhany	17	D7
Berezina = Byarezina →	17	B10
Berezniki	28	D6
Berezovo	28	C7
Berga	19	A6
Bergama	23	E6
Bérgamo	20	B2
Bergen	8	C7
Bergerac	12	D4
Berhala, Selat	39	E2
Berhampore = Baharampur	40	E7
Berhampur = Brahmapur	40	H5
Bering Sea	69	C1
Bering Strait	69	B3
Berja	19	D4
Berkeley	72	H2
Berkner I.	96	B4
Berlin	15	B7
Bermejo →, Formosa, Argentina	94	B5
Bermejo →, San Juan, Argentina	94	C3
Bermuda ☑	67	F13
Bern	14	E4
Bernburg	15	C6
Berne = Bern	14	E4
Bernina, Piz	13	C8
Beroun	16	D2
Berri	62	B3
Berry, Australia	63	B5
Berry, France	12	C5
Bershad	17	D9
Bertoua	56	D2
Berwick-upon-Tweed	10	D6
Besalampy	59	H8
Besançon	13	C7
Besar	39	E5
Bessarabiya	17	E9
Bessarabka = Basarabeasca	17	E9
Bessemer	82	C4
Betanzos	18	A1
Bétaré Oya	56	C2
Bethel	69	B3
Bethlehem, S. Africa	59	D5
Bethlehem, U.S.A.	77	D8
Béthune	13	A5
Betroka	59	J9
Bettiah	40	D5
Betul	43	J10
Betung	39	D4
Beverley	11	E6
Beverly Hills	78	C3
Beyneu	29	E6
Beypazarı	46	B2
Beyşehir Gölü	46	C2
Béziers	13	E5
Bezwada = Vijayawada	40	J3
Bhachau	43	H7
Bhadrakh	40	G6
Bhadravati	43	N9
Bhagalpur	40	E6
Bhakra Dam	42	D10
Bhamo	41	E11
Bhandara	43	J11
Bhanrer Ra.	43	H11
Bharat = India ■	43	J10
Bharatpur	42	F10
Bhatpara	41	F7
Bhavnagar	43	J8
Bhawanipatna	40	H4
Bhilsa = Vidisha	43	H10
Bhilwara	43	G9
Bhima →	43	L10
Bhind	42	F11
Bhiwandi	43	K8
Bhiwani	42	E10
Bhola	41	F8
Bhopal	43	H10
Bhubaneshwar	40	G5
Bhuj	43	H6
Bhusawal	43	J9
Bhutan ■	41	D8
Biafra, B. of = Bonny, Bight of	56	D1
Biak	37	E5
Biała Podlaska	17	B6
Białogard	16	A2
Białystok	17	B6
Biaro	37	D3
Biarritz	12	E3
Bibai	32	B7
Biberach	14	D5
Bida	53	G7
Bidar	43	L10
Biddeford	77	C10
Bié, Planalto de	58	A3
Bielefeld	14	B5
Biella	20	B2
Bielsk Podlaski	17	B6
Bielsko-Biała	16	D4
Bien Hoa	38	B3
Bienville, L.	71	C3
Big Horn Mts. = Bighorn Mts.	73	D10
Big Spring	80	C3
Big Trout L.	71	C2
Biğa	23	D6
Bigadiç	23	E7
Biggar	69	C9
Biggenden	63	A5
Bighorn →	73	C10
Bighorn Mts.	73	D10
Bihać	20	B5
Bihar	40	E5
Bihar □	40	E5
Bihor, Munţii	17	E6
Bijagós, Arquipélago dos	53	F2
Bijapur, Chhattisgarh, India	40	H3
Bijapur, Karnataka, India	43	L9
Bijär	46	D6
Bijeljina	20	B7
Bijnor	42	E11
Bikaner	42	E8
Bikini Atoll	64	H11
Bila Tserkva	17	D10
Bilara	42	F8
Bilaspur	40	F4
Bilauk Taungdan	38	B1
Bilbao	19	A4
Bilbo = Bilbao	19	A4
Bilecik	25	E3
Bilhorod-Dnistrovskyy	25	D3
Billings	73	D9
Billiton Is. = Belitung	39	E3
Bilma	55	E1
Biloxi	81	D9
Biltine	55	F3
Bima	37	F1
Bina-Etawah	43	G11
Binalbagan	36	B2
Binalong	63	B4
Binälüd, Küh-e	44	B4
Binatang = Bintangor	39	D4
Bindura	59	B6
Bingara	63	A5
Binghamton	77	C8
Bingöl	46	C5
Binh Dinh = An Nhon	38	B3
Binh Son	38	A3
Binjai	39	D1
Binnaway	63	B4
Binongko	37	F2
Bintan	39	D2
Bintangor	39	D4
Bintulu	39	D4
Bintuni	37	E4
Binzert = Bizerte	54	A1
Bioko	56	D1
Bir	43	K9
Bir Atrun	55	E4
Bîr Mogreïn	52	C3
Birchip	62	C3
Birecik	46	C4
Bireuen	38	C1
Birlik	29	E8
Birmingham, U.K.	11	E6
Birmingham, U.S.A.	82	C4
Birmitrapur	40	F5
Birni Nkonni	53	F7
Birnin Kebbi	53	F6
Birr	11	E3
Birrie →	63	A4
Birsk	29	D6
Birur	43	N9
Bisa	37	E3
Biscay, B. of	12	D2
Biscoe Is.	96	A3
Bishkek	29	E8
Biskra	52	B7
Bismarck	74	B4
Bismarck Arch.	64	K9
Bissagos = Bijagós, Arquipélago dos	53	F2
Bissau	53	F2
Bistriţa	17	E7
Bistriţa →	17	E8
Bitlis	46	C5
Bitola	22	D3
Bitolj = Bitola	22	D3
Bitterfontein	58	E3
Bitterroot Range	73	D6
Biu	55	F1
Biwa-Ko	33	F5
Biysk	29	D9
Bizerte	54	A1
Bjelovar	20	B6
Black Forest = Schwarzwald	14	D5
Black Hills	74	D3
Black Sea	25	E3
Black Volta →	53	G5
Blackball	65	E4
Blackburn	11	E5
Blackpool	11	E5
Blackwater →	11	E2
Blagodarnyy	25	D5
Blagoevgrad	22	C4
Blagoveshchensk	31	D10
Blanc, Mont	13	D7
Blanca, B.	95	D4
Blanca Peak	79	B10
Blanche, C.	62	B1
Blanche, L.	62	A2
Blanes	19	B7
Blantyre	59	B6
Blayney	63	B4
Blenheim	65	D5
Blida	52	A6
Bligh Sound	65	F2
Bloemfontein	59	D5
Bloemhof	59	D5
Blois	12	C4
Bloomington, Ill., U.S.A.	75	E10
Bloomington, Ind., U.S.A.	76	E2
Blue Mts.	72	D4
Blue Nile = Nîl el Azraq →	55	E5
Blue Ridge Mts.	83	A7
Bluefields	86	D3
Bluff	65	G3
Blumenau	94	B7
Bo	53	G3
Bo Hai	35	C6
Boa Vista	90	C6
Bobadah	63	B4
Bobbili	40	H4
Bobo-Dioulasso	53	F5
Bóbr →	16	B2
Bobraomby, Tanjon' i	59	G9
Bobruysk = Babruysk	17	B9
Bôca do Acre	91	E5
Boca Raton	83	F7
Bocaranga	55	G2
Bochum	14	C4
Bodaybo	30	D9
Boden	8	B10
Bodensee	13	C8
Bodhan	43	K10

Bodø	8	B8
Bodrog →	16	D5
Bodrum	23	F6
Boende	56	E4
Bogalusa	81	D9
Bogan Gate	63	B4
Boggabilla	63	A5
Boggabri	63	B5
Bogo	36	B2
Bogong, Mt.	63	C4
Bogor	39	F3
Bogotá	90	C4
Bogotol	29	D9
Bogra	41	E7
Bohemian Forest =		
Böhmerwald	15	D7
Böhmerwald	15	D7
Bohol □	36	C2
Bohol Sea	36	C2
Boise	72	E5
Boise City	80	A2
Bojador, C.	52	C3
Bojana →	22	D2
Bojnürd	44	B4
Bokhara →	63	A4
Bokoro	55	F2
Bolan Pass	42	E5
Bolbec	12	B4
Bole	34	B3
Bolekhiv	17	D6
Bolesławiec	16	C2
Bolhrad	17	F9
Bolivia ■	91	G6
Bollon	63	A4
Bolobo	56	E3
Bologna	20	B3
Bologoye	24	B3
Bolsena, L. di	20	C3
Bolshevik, Ostrov	30	B8
Bolshoy Begichev, Ostrov	30	B9
Bolshoy Kavkas = Caucasus		
Mountains	25	E5
Bolshoy Lyakhovskiy,		
Ostrov	31	B12
Bolton	11	E5
Bolu	25	E3
Bolvadin	46	C2
Bolzano	20	A3
Bom Jesus da Lapa	93	E5
Boma	56	F2
Bombala	63	C4
Bombay = Mumbai	43	K8
Bomboma	56	D3
Bomu →	56	D4
Bon, C.	54	A1
Bonaire	87	D6
Bonang	63	C4
Bonavista	71	D5
Bondo	56	D4
Bondoukou	53	G5
Bone, Teluk	37	E2
Bonerate	37	F2
Bonerate, Kepulauan	37	F2
Bong Son = Hoai Nhon	38	B3
Bongor	55	F2
Bonifacio	13	F8
Bonin Is.	27	G18
Bonn	14	C4
Bonney, L.	62	C3
Bonny, Bight of	56	D1
Bonoi	37	E5
Bontang	39	D5
Bonthe	53	G3
Bontoc	36	A2
Boolaboolka L.	62	B3
Booligal	63	B3
Boonah	63	A5
Boorindal	63	B4
Boorowa	63	C4
Boosaaso = Bosaso	49	E4
Boothia, Gulf of	70	A2
Boothia Pen.	68	A10
Booué	56	E2
Bor, Serbia & M.	22	B4
Bôr, Sudan	55	G5
Borås	9	D8
Borāzjān	44	D2
Borba	90	D7
Borda, C.	62	C2
Bordeaux	12	D3
Bordertown	62	C3
Bordj Fly Ste. Marie	52	C5
Bordj-in-Eker	52	D7
Bordj Omar Driss	52	C7
Borger	80	B3
Borhoyn Tal	35	B6
Borisoglebsk	24	C5
Borisov = Barysaw	17	A9
Borja	90	D3
Borkou	55	E2
Borkum	14	B4
Borley, C.	96	A9
Borneo	39	D4
Bornholm	9	D9
Borongan	36	B3
Borovichi	24	B3
Borşa	17	E7
Borüjerd	46	D7
Boryslav	17	D6
Bosa	21	D2
Bosanska Gradiška	20	B7
Bosaso	49	E4
Boshrúyeh	44	C4
Bosna →	20	B7
Bosnia-Herzegovina ■	20	B6
Bosnik	37	E5
Bosobolo	56	D3
Bosporus = İstanbul Boğazı	22	D7
Bossangoa	56	C3
Bosso	55	F1
Bosten Hu	34	B3
Boston, U.K.	11	E6
Boston, U.S.A.	77	C10
Bothnia, G. of	8	C10
Bothwell	62	D4
Botletle →	58	C4
Botoşani	17	E8
Botswana ■	58	C4
Botucatu	93	G4
Bouaké	53	G4
Bouar	56	C3
Bouârfa	52	B5
Bouca	55	G2
Bougie = Bejaïa	52	A7
Bougouni	53	F4
Boulder	74	E2
Boulder Dam = Hoover		
Dam	78	B5
Boulogne-sur-Mer	12	A4
Bouna	53	G5
Boundiali	53	G4
Bourbonnais	13	C5
Bourem	53	E5
Bourg-en-Bresse	13	C6
Bourg-St-Maurice	13	D7
Bourges	12	C5
Bourgogne	13	C6
Bourke	63	B4
Bournemouth	11	F6
Bowen Mts.	63	C4
Bowman I.	96	A12
Bowral	63	B5
Bowraville	63	B5
Boyne →	11	E3
Boyoma, Chutes	57	D5
Boz Dağları	23	E7
Bozburun	23	F7
Bozcaada	23	E6
Bozdoğan	23	F7
Bozeman	73	D8
Bozen = Bolzano	20	A3
Bozoum	56	C3
Bra	20	B1
Brač	20	C6
Bracciano, L. di	20	C4
Brach	54	C1
Bräcke	8	C9
Bradenton	83	F6
Bradford	11	E6
Braga	18	B1
Bragança, Brazil	92	C4
Bragança, Portugal	18	B2
Brahmanbaria	41	F8
Brahmani →	40	G6
Brahmapur	40	H5
Brahmaputra →	41	F7
Braidwood	63	C4
Brăila	17	F8
Branco →	90	D6
Brandenburg	15	B7
Brandenburg □	15	B7
Brandon	69	D10
Braniewo	16	A4
Bransfield Str.	96	A4
Brantford	76	C5
Brasiléia	91	F5
Brasília	93	F4
Braşov	17	F7
Brassey, Banjaran	38	D5
Bratislava	16	D3
Bratsk	30	D8
Braunau	15	D7
Braunschweig	14	B6
Bravo del Norte, Rio =		
Grande, Rio →	81	F5
Brawley	78	D5
Bray	11	E3
Bray, Pays de	12	B4
Brazil ■	93	E4
Brazos →	81	E6
Brazzaville	56	E3
Brčko	20	B3
Breaksea Sd.	65	F2
Bream B.	64	A6
Bream Hd.	64	A6
Brecon	11	F5
Breda	14	C3
Bredasdorp	58	E4
Bregenz	14	E5
Breiðafjörður	8	B1
Brejo	92	C5
Bremen	14	B5
Bremerhaven	14	B5
Bremerton	72	C2
Brennerpass	15	E6
Bréscia	20	B3
Breslau = Wrocław	16	C3
Bressanone	20	A3
Brest, Belarus	17	B6
Brest, France	12	B1
Brest-Litovsk = Brest	17	B6
Bretagne	12	B2
Brett, C.	64	A6
Brewarrina	63	A4
Brezhnev = Naberezhnyye		
Chelny	29	D6
Bria	55	G3
Briançon	13	D7
Bribie I.	63	A5
Bridgeport	77	D9
Bridgetown	87	D8
Bridgewater	71	D4
Bridgewater, C.	62	C3
Bridlington	11	D6
Bridport	62	D4
Brigham City	73	F7
Bright	63	C4
Brighton, Australia	62	C2
Brighton, U.K.	11	F6
Brindisi	21	D6
Brisbane	63	A5
Brisbane →	63	A5
Bristol, U.K.	11	F5
Bristol, U.S.A.	83	A6
Bristol B.	69	C3
Bristol Channel	11	F4

British Indian Ocean Terr. =
   Chagos Arch. 27 K11
British Isles 11 D4
British Virgin Is. ☑ 87 C7
Brittany = Bretagne 12 B2
Brive-la-Gaillarde 12 D4
Brixen = Bressanone . . . 20 A3
Brlik = Birlik 29 E8
Brno 16 D3
Brocken 14 C6
Brodeur Pen. 70 A2
Brodnica 16 B4
Brody 17 C7
Broken Hill = Kabwe . . . 59 A5
Broken Hill 62 B3
Brooks Range 69 B5
Broome 60 D3
Broughton Island =
   Qikiqtarjuaq 70 B4
Brown, Pt. 62 B1
Brownsville 80 F5
Brownwood 80 D4
Bruay-la-Buissière 13 A5
Bruce, Mt. 60 E2
Bruck an der Mur 15 E8
Bruges = Brugge 14 C2
Brugge 14 C2
Brumado 93 E5
Brunei = Bandar Seri
   Begawan 38 D5
Brunei ■ 38 D4
Brunner, L. 65 E4
Brunswick = Braunschweig 14 B6
Brunswick 83 D7
Brunswick, Pen. de 95 G2
Brussel 14 C3
Brussels = Brussel 14 C3
Bruthen 63 C4
Bruxelles = Brussel 14 C3
Bryan 81 D5
Bryan, Mt. 62 B2
Bryansk 24 C3
Bu Craa 52 C3
Buapinang 37 E2
Bucak 46 C2
Bucaramanga 90 B4
Buchach 17 D7
Buchanan 53 G3
Bucharest = Bucureşti . . 22 B6
Buckie 10 C5
Buckleboo 62 B2
Bucureşti 22 B6
Budalin 41 F10
Budapest 16 E4
Budd Coast 96 A12
Bude 11 F4
Budennovsk 25 E5
Budgewoi 63 B5
Budjala 56 D3
Buenaventura 90 C3
Buenos Aires 94 C5
Buenos Aires, L. 95 F2
Buffalo 77 C6
Bug = Buh → 25 D3
Bug → 16 B5
Buga 90 C3
Bugel, Tanjung 39 F4
Bugsuk 38 C5
Bugun Shara 35 B5
Buguruslan 29 D6
Buh → 25 D3
Buir Nur 35 B6
Bujumbura 57 E5
Bukavu 57 E5
Bukhara = Bukhoro 29 F7
Bukhoro 29 F7
Bukittinggi 39 E2
Bukoba 57 E6
Bula 37 E4
Bulahdelah 63 B5
Bulan 36 B2
Bulandshahr 42 E10

Bulawayo 59 C5
Buldan 23 E7
Bulgaria ■ 22 C5
Buli, Teluk 37 D3
Buliluyan, C. 38 C5
Bulloo → 63 A3
Bulloo L. 62 A3
Bulls 64 D6
Bulsar = Valsad 43 J8
Bulukumba 37 F2
Bulun 30 B10
Bumba 56 D4
Bumhpa Bum 41 D11
Bunbury 60 G2
Buncrana 11 D3
Bundaberg 63 A5
Bundi 43 G9
Bundoran 11 D2
Bungo Channel 33 G3
Bunia 57 D6
Bunji 42 B9
Buntok 39 E4
Bunyu 39 D5
Buol 37 D2
Buon Ma Thuot 38 B3
Buorkhaya, Mys 31 B11
Buqayq 47 F7
Bur Acaba 49 G3
Bûr Safâga 54 C5
Bûr Sa'îd 54 B5
Bûr Sûdân 55 E6
Burao 49 F4
Buraydah 47 F6
Burdur 46 C2
Burdwan = Barddhaman . 40 F6
Burgas 22 C6
Burgos 18 A4
Burgundy = Bourgogne . 13 C6
Burhaniye 23 E6
Burhanpur 43 J10
Burias I. 36 B2
Buriram 38 A2
Burkina Faso ■ 53 F5
Burlington, *Iowa, U.S.A.* 75 E9
Burlington, *N.C., U.S.A.* 83 A8
Burlington, *Vt., U.S.A.* . 77 B9
Burlyu-Tyube 29 E8
Burma ■ 41 G11
Burnie 62 D4
Burnley 11 E5
Burnside → 68 B9
Burqān 47 E6
Burra 62 B2
Burren Junction 63 B4
Burrinjuck Res. 63 C4
Burruyacú 94 B4
Bursa 23 D7
Buru 37 E3
Burundi ■ 57 E6
Bururtu 53 G7
Bury St. Edmunds 11 E7
Busan = Pusan 35 C7
Büshehr 44 D2
Büshehr ☐ 44 D2
Bushire = Büshehr 44 D2
Businga 56 D4
Buşra ash Shām 46 D4
Busto Arsizio 20 B2
Busu Djanoa 56 D4
Busuanga I. 36 B1
Buta 57 D4
Butare 57 E5
Butaritari 64 J12
Butembo 57 D5
Butha Qi 35 B7
Butte 73 C7
Butterworth 38 C2
Butuan 36 C3
Butung = Buton 37 E2
Buturlinovka 24 C5
Buur Hakaba = Bur Acaba . 49 G3

Buxtehude 14 B5
Buy 24 B5
Büyük Menderes → . . . 23 F6
Büyükçekmece 22 D7
Buzău 17 F8
Buzău → 17 F8
Buzen 33 G2
Buzi → 59 B6
Buzuluk 29 D6
Byarezina → 17 B10
Byaroza 17 B7
Bydgoszcz 16 B3
Byelorussia = Belarus ■ . 24 C2
Bykhaw 17 B10
Bykhov = Bykhaw 17 B10
Bylot I. 70 A3
Byrd, C. 96 A3
Byrock 63 B4
Byron Bay 63 A5
Byrranga, Gory 30 B8
Bytom 16 C4
Bytów 16 A3

C

Ca Mau 38 C3
Caála 58 A3
Cabanatuan 36 A2
Cabedelo 92 D7
Cabimas 90 A4
Cabinda 56 F2
Cabinda ☐ 56 F2
Cabinet Mts. 73 C6
Cabo Blanco 95 F3
Cabo Frio 93 G5
Cabo Pantoja 90 D3
Cabonga, Réservoir . . . 71 D3
Caboolture 63 A5
Cabora Bassa Dam =
   Cahora Bassa, Reprêsa
   de 59 B6
Cabot Str. 71 D5
Cabra 18 D3
Cabrera 19 C7
Cabriel → 19 C5
Čačak 22 C3
Cáceres, *Brazil* 91 G7
Cáceres, *Spain* 18 C2
Cachimbo, Serra do . . . 93 D2
Cachoeira 93 E6
Cachoeira do Sul 94 C6
Cachoeiro de Itapemirim . 93 G5
Cacólo 56 G3
Caconda 58 A3
Cadibarrawirracanna, L. . 62 A2
Cadiz, *Phil.* 36 B2
Cádiz, *Spain* 18 D2
Cádiz, G. de 18 D2
Cadney Park 62 A1
Caen 12 B3
Caetité 93 E5
Cagayan de Oro 36 C2
Cágliari 21 E2
Cágliari, G. di 21 E2
Caguas 87 C6
Cahora Bassa, Reprêsa de 59 B6
Cahors 12 D4
Cahul 17 F9
Caicara 90 B5
Caicó 92 D6
Caird Coast 96 B5
Cairns 61 D8
Cairo = El Qâhira 54 B5
Cairo 81 A9
Cajamarca 91 E3
Cajàzeiras 92 D6
Calabar 53 H7
Calábria ☐ 21 E6
Calafate 95 G2

Calahorra	19	A5
Calais	12	A4
Calama, *Brazil*	91	E6
Calama, *Chile*	94	A3
Calamar	90	A4
Calamian Group	36	B1
Calamocha	19	B5
Calang	38	D1
Calapan	36	B2
Călăraşi	22	B6
Calatayud	19	B5
Calauag	36	B2
Calavite, C.	36	B2
Calbayog	36	B2
Calca	91	F4
Calcutta = Kolkata	41	F7
Caldas da Rainha	18	C1
Caldera	94	B2
Caldwell	72	E5
Caledon →	59	E5
Calgary	69	C8
Cali	90	C3
Calicut □	43	P9
California □	78	B3
California, G. de	84	B2
Calingasta	94	C3
Callabonna, L.	62	A3
Callao	91	F3
Caloundra	63	A5
Caltagirone	21	F5
Caltanissetta	21	F5
Calulo	56	G2
Calvi	13	E8
Calviá	19	C7
Calvinia	58	E3
Camabatela	56	F3
Camacupa	58	A3
Camagüey	86	B4
Camaná	91	G4
Camargue	13	E6
Camarones	95	E3
Cambay = Khambhat	43	H8
Cambay, G. of = Khambhat, G. of	43	J8
Cambodia ■	38	B3
Cambrai	13	A5
Cambrian Mts.	11	E5
Cambridge, *N.Z.*	64	B6
Cambridge, *U.K.*	11	E7
Cambridge, *U.S.A.*	77	C10
Cambridge Bay = Ikaluktutiak	68	B9
Cambundi-Catembo	56	G3
Camden, *Ark., U.S.A.*	81	C7
Camden, *N.J., U.S.A.*	77	E8
Cameroon ■	56	C2
Cameroun, Mt.	56	D1
Cametá	92	C4
Caminha	18	B1
Camira Creek	63	A5
Camocim	92	C5
Campana, I.	95	F1
Campánia □	21	D5
Campbell Town	62	D4
Campbellton	71	D4
Campbelltown	63	B5
Campbeltown	10	D4
Campeche	85	D6
Campeche, Golfo de	85	D6
Camperdown	62	C3
Câmpina	17	F7
Campina Grande	92	D6
Campinas	94	A7
Campo Grande	93	G3
Campo Maior	92	C5
Campobasso	20	D5
Campos	93	G5
Campos Belos	93	E4
Câmpulung	17	F7
Camrose	69	C8
Çan	23	D6
Can Tho	38	B3
Canada ■	68	C8
Cañada de Gómez	94	C4
Çanakkale	23	D6
Çanakkale Boğazı	23	D6
Cananea	84	A2
Canarias, Is.	52	C2
Canary Is. = Canarias, Is.	52	C2
Canavieiras	93	F6
Canberra	63	C4
Candelo	63	C4
Candia = Iráklion	23	G5
Canea = Khaniá	23	G5
Canelones	94	C5
Cañete, *Chile*	94	D2
Cañete, *Peru*	91	F3
Cangas de Narcea	18	A2
Canguaretama	92	D6
Canguçu	94	C6
Caniapiscau →	70	C4
Caniapiscau, L. de	71	C4
Canicattì	21	F4
Çankırı	46	B3
Cann River	63	C4
Cannanore	43	P9
Cannes	13	E7
Canoas	94	B6
Canora	69	C9
Canowindra	63	B4
Cantabria □	18	A4
Cantabrian Mts. = Cantábrica, Cordillera	18	A3
Cantábrica, Cordillera	18	A3
Cantal, Plomb du	13	D5
Canterbury	11	F7
Canterbury Bight	65	F4
Canterbury Plains	65	E4
Canton = Guangzhou	35	D6
Canton	76	D5
Canudos	91	E7
Canutama	91	E6
Cap-Haïtien	87	C5
Capanaparo →	90	B5
Cape Barren I.	62	D4
Cape Breton I.	71	D4
Cape Coast	53	G5
Cape Dorset	70	B3
Cape Girardeau	81	A9
Cape Lisburne = Wevok	69	B3
Cape Town	58	E3
Cape Verde Is. ■	50	E1
Cape York Peninsula	61	C7
Capela	93	E6
Capim →	92	C4
Capraia	20	C2
Capri	21	D5
Caprivi Strip	58	B4
Captain's Flat	63	C4
Caquetá →	90	D5
Caracal	22	B5
Caracas	90	A5
Caracol	93	D5
Carajás, Serra dos	92	D3
Carangsebeş	17	F6
Caratasca, L.	86	C3
Caratinga	93	F5
Caraúbas	92	D6
Caravaca de la Cruz	19	C5
Caravelas	93	F6
Caraveli	91	G4
Carballo	18	A1
Carbonara, C.	21	E2
Carbondale	81	A9
Carbonear	71	D5
Carbónia	21	E2
Carcassonne	12	E5
Carcross	68	B6
Cardamon Hills	43	Q10
Cárdenas	86	B3
Cardiff	11	F5
Cardigan B.	11	E4
Cardston	69	D8
Carei	17	E6
Carhué	94	D4
Caria	23	F7
Cariacica	93	G5
Caribbean Sea	86	D5
Cariboo Mts.	69	C7
Carinda	63	B4
Carinhanha	93	E5
Carinthia = Kärnten □	15	E7
Caripito	90	A6
Carlisle	11	D5
Carlow	11	E3
Carlsbad	80	C1
Carmacks	68	B6
Carmarthen	11	F4
Carmaux	12	D5
Carmen	90	B3
Carmen de Patagones	95	E4
Carmona	18	D3
Carnac	12	C2
Carnarvon, *Australia*	60	E1
Carnarvon, *S. Africa*	58	E4
Carnegie, L.	60	F3
Carnot	56	D3
Carnot, C.	62	B2
Carolina	92	D4
Caroline I.	65	K15
Caroline Is.	64	J10
Caroni →	90	B6
Caronie = Nébrodi, Monti	21	F5
Caroona	63	B5
Carpathians	16	D5
Carpaţii Meridionali	17	F7
Carpentaria, G. of	60	C6
Carpentras	13	D6
Carpi	20	B3
Carrara	20	B3
Carrauntoohill	11	E2
Carrick-on-Suir	11	E3
Carrieton	62	B2
Carrizal Bajo	94	B2
Carson City	72	G4
Cartagena, *Colombia*	90	A3
Cartagena, *Spain*	19	D5
Cartago, *Colombia*	90	C3
Cartago, *Costa Rica*	86	E3
Carterton	65	D6
Carthage	81	A6
Cartwright	70	C5
Caruaru	92	D6
Carúpano	90	A6
Carvoeiro	90	D6
Carvoeiro, C.	18	C1
Casablanca	52	B4
Cascade Ra.	72	C3
Cascais	18	C1
Cascavel	94	A6
Cáscina	20	C3
Caserta	20	D5
Caseyr, Raas = Asir, Ras	49	E5
Casiguran	36	A2
Casilda	94	C4
Casino	63	A5
Casiquiare →	90	C5
Casma	91	E3
Casper	73	E10
Caspian Sea	29	E6
Castellammare di Stábia	21	D5
Castelló de la Plana	19	C5
Castelo Branco	18	C2
Castelsarrasin	12	D4
Castelvetrano	21	F4
Casterton	62	C3
Castilla-La Mancha □	18	C4
Castilla y Leon □	18	A3
Castlebar	11	E2
Castleblaney	11	D3
Castlemaine	63	C3
Castlereagh →	63	B4
Castres	12	E5
Castries	87	D7
Castro	95	E2

Castro Alves	93	E6	
Castuera	18	C3	
Cat I.	86	B4	
Catalão	93	F4	
Çatalca	22	D7	
Catalonia = Cataluña □	19	B6	
Cataluña □	19	B6	
Catamarca	94	B3	
Catanduanes □	36	B2	
Catanduva	93	G4	
Catánia	21	F5	
Catanzaro	21	E6	
Catarman	36	B2	
Cateel	36	C3	
Catoche, C.	85	C7	
Catrimani	90	C6	
Catskill Mts.	77	C8	
Cauca ➤	90	B4	
Caucaia	92	C6	
Caucasus Mountains	25	E5	
Caungula	56	F3	
Cauquenes	94	D2	
Caura ➤	90	B6	
Cauvery ➤	43	P11	
Caux, Pays de	12	B4	
Cavan	11	D3	
Cavendish	62	C3	
Caviana, I.	92	B3	
Cavite	36	B2	
Cawndilla L.	62	B3	
Cawnpore = Kanpur	40	D3	
Caxias	92	C5	
Caxias do Sul	94	B6	
Cayambe	90	C3	
Cayenne	92	A3	
Cayman Is. ☑	86	C3	
Cazombo	58	A4	
Ceanannus Mor	11	E3	
Ceará = Fortaleza	92	C6	
Ceará □	92	D6	
Ceará Mirim	92	D6	
Cebollar	94	B3	
Cebu	36	B2	
Cecil Plains	63	A5	
Cedar L.	69	C10	
Cedar Rapids	75	E9	
Cedro	92	D6	
Ceduna	62	B1	
Ceerigaabo = Erigavo	49	E4	
Cefalù	21	E5	
Cegléd	16	E4	
Celaya	84	C4	
Celebes = Sulawesi □	37	E2	
Celebes Sea	37	D2	
Celje	20	A5	
Celle	14	B6	
Celtic Sea	11	F2	
Central, Cordillera	90	C3	
Central African Rep. ■	55	G4	
Central Makran Range	42	F4	
Cephalonia = Kefallinia	23	E3	
Ceram = Seram	37	E3	
Ceram Sea = Seram Sea	37	E3	
Ceres	94	B4	
Cerignola	20	D5	
Cerigo = Kithira	23	F4	
Çerkes	46	B3	
Çerkezköy	22	D6	
Cervera	19	B6	
Cesena	20	B4	
České Budějovice	16	D2	
Českomoravská Vrchovina	16	D2	
Çeşme	23	E6	
Cessnock	63	B5	
Cetinje	22	C2	
Cetraro	21	E5	
Ceuta	18	E3	
Cévennes	13	D5	
Ceylon = Sri Lanka ■	43	R12	
Chachapoyas	91	E3	
Chachran	42	E7	
Chad ■	55	E2	
Chad, L. = Tchad, L.	55	F1	
Chadileuvú ➤	94	D3	
Chadyr-Lunga = Ciadâr-Lunga	17	E9	
Chagai Hills = Chāh Gay Hills	42	E3	
Chagos Arch.	27	K11	
Chāh Bahar	45	E5	
Chāh Gay Hills	42	E3	
Chahar Burjak	42	D3	
Chaibasa	40	F5	
Chakhānsūr	42	D3	
Chakradharpur	40	F5	
Chakwal	42	C5	
Chala	91	G4	
Chalcis = Khalkis	23	E4	
Chalhuanca	91	F4	
Chalisgaon	43	J9	
Chalky Inlet	65	G2	
Challapata	91	G5	
Chalon-sur-Saône	13	C6	
Châlons-en-Champagne	13	B6	
Chaman	42	D5	
Chamba	42	C10	
Chambal ➤	42	F11	
Chambéry	13	D6	
Chamical	94	C3	
Chamonix-Mont Blanc	13	D7	
Champagne	13	B6	
Champaign	76	D1	
Champlain, L.	77	B9	
Chañaral	94	B2	
Chandigarh	42	D10	
Chandler	62	A1	
Chandpur	41	F8	
Chandrapur	43	K11	
Chang Jiang ➤	35	C7	
Changanacheri	43	Q10	
Changane ➤	59	C6	
Changchiak'ou = Zhangjiakou	35	B6	
Ch'angchou = Changzhou	35	C6	
Changchun	35	B7	
Changde	35	D6	
Changhai = Shanghai	35	C7	
Changhua	35	D7	
Changsha	35	D6	
Changzhi	35	C6	
Changzhou	35	C6	
Chania = Khaniá	23	G5	
Channapatna	43	N10	
Channel Is.	11	G5	
Chantada	18	A2	
Chanthaburi	38	B2	
Chantrey Inlet	68	B10	
Chanute	81	A6	
Chao Phraya ➤	38	B2	
Chaozhou	35	D6	
Chapala, L. de	84	C4	
Chapayevsk	24	C6	
Chapra = Chhapra	40	E5	
Chara	31	D9	
Charagua	91	G6	
Charaña	91	G5	
Chardzhou = Chärjew	29	F7	
Charente ➤	12	D3	
Chari ➤	55	F1	
Chārīkār	42	B6	
Chärjew	29	F7	
Charleroi	14	C3	
Charles, C.	77	F8	
Charleston, S.C., U.S.A.	83	C8	
Charleston, W. Va., U.S.A.	76	E5	
Charleville	63	A4	
Charleville-Mézières	13	B6	
Charlotte	83	B7	
Charlottesville	77	E6	
Charlottetown	71	D4	
Charlton	62	C3	
Charolles	13	C6	
Charters Towers	61	E8	
Chartres	12	B4	
Chascomús	94	D5	
Châteaubriant	12	C3	
Châteaulin	12	B1	
Châteauroux	12	C4	
Châtellerault	12	C4	
Chatham = Chatham-Kent	71	D2	
Chatham = Miramichi	71	D4	
Chatham	11	F7	
Chatham-Kent	71	D2	
Chatrapur	40	H5	
Chattahoochee ➤	82	D5	
Chattanooga	82	B5	
Chaukan Pass	41	D11	
Chaumont	13	B6	
Chaves, Brazil	92	C4	
Chaves, Portugal	18	B2	
Cheb	16	C1	
Cheboksary	24	B6	
Chech, Erg	52	D5	
Chechenia □	25	E6	
Chechnya = Chechenia □	25	E6	
Cheduba I.	41	H9	
Cheepie	63	A4	
Chegga	52	C4	
Chegutu	59	B6	
Chehalis	72	C2	
Cheju do	35	C7	
Chekiang = Zhejiang □	35	D7	
Cheleken	29	F6	
Chelforó	95	D3	
Chelkar = Shalqar	29	E6	
Chelkar Tengiz, Solonchak	29	E7	
Chelm	17	C6	
Chelmno	16	B4	
Chelmsford	11	F7	
Cheltenham	11	F5	
Chelyabinsk	29	D7	
Chelyuskin, Mys	30	B8	
Chemnitz	15	C7	
Chenab ➤	42	D7	
Chengchou = Zhengzhou	35	C6	
Chengde	35	B6	
Chengdu	35	C5	
Chengjiang	34	D5	
Ch'engtu = Chengdu	35	C5	
Chennai	43	N12	
Chenzhou	35	D6	
Cheo Reo	38	B3	
Cheom Ksan	38	B2	
Chepén	91	E3	
Chepes	94	C3	
Cher ➤	12	C4	
Cherbourg	12	B3	
Cherdyn	28	C6	
Cherepanovo	29	D9	
Cherepovets	24	B4	
Chergui, Chott ech	52	B6	
Cherikov = Cherykaw	17	B10	
Cherkasy	24	D3	
Cherlak	29	D8	
Chernaya	30	B6	
Chernigov = Chernihiv	24	C3	
Chernihiv	24	C3	
Chernivtsi	17	D7	
Chernobyl = Chornobyl	17	C10	
Chernovtsy = Chernivtsi	17	D7	
Cherrapunji	41	E8	
Cherven	17	B9	
Chervonohrad	17	C7	
Cherykaw	17	B10	
Chesapeake	77	F7	
Chesapeake B.	77	E7	
Cheshskaya Guba	28	C5	
Chester, U.K.	11	E5	
Chester, U.S.A.	77	E8	
Chesterfield	11	E6	
Chesterfield, Is.	64	L10	
Chesterfield Inlet	68	B10	
Chesterton Ra.	63	A4	
Chetumal	85	D7	
Cheviot Hills	10	D5	
Chew Bahir	55	H6	

Cheyenne	74	E2
Cheyenne →	74	C4
Chhapra	40	E5
Chhatarpur	43	G11
Chhindwara	43	H11
Chi →	38	A2
Chiai	35	D7
Chiamussu = Jiamusi	35	B8
Chiávari	20	B2
Chiavenna	18	A2
Chiba	33	F7
Chibemba	58	B2
Chibia	58	B2
Chibougamau	71	D3
Chicacole = Srikakulam	40	H4
Chicago	76	D2
Chichagof I.	69	C6
Chickasha	80	B5
Chiclana de la Frontera	18	D2
Chiclayo	91	E3
Chico	72	G3
Chico →, Chubut, Argentina	95	E3
Chico →, Santa Cruz, Argentina	95	E3
Chicoutimi	71	D3
Chidambaram	43	P11
Chidley, C.	70	B4
Chiemsee	16	E7
Chiese →	20	B3
Chieti	20	C5
Chiguana	91	H5
Chihli, G. of = Bo Hai	35	C6
Chihuahua	84	B3
Chiili = Shieli	29	E7
Chik Ballapur	43	N10
Chikmagalur	43	N9
Chilapa	84	D5
Chilas	42	B9
Chilaw	43	R11
Childers	63	A5
Chile ■	94	D2
Chilete	91	E3
Chililabombwe	59	A5
Chilin = Jilin	35	B7
Chilka L.	40	H5
Chillán	94	D2
Chiloé, I. de	95	E2
Chilpancingo	84	D5
Chilung	35	D7
Chilwa, L.	59	B7
Chimbay	29	E6
Chimborazo	90	D3
Chimbote	91	E3
Chimkent = Shymkent	29	E7
Chimoio	59	B6
Chin □	41	F9
China ■	35	C5
Chinan = Jinan	35	C6
Chinandega	85	E7
Chincha Alta	91	F3
Chinchilla	63	A5
Chinchou = Jinzhou	35	B7
Chinde	59	B7
Chindwin →	41	G10
Chingola	59	A5
Ch'ingtao = Qingdao	35	C7
Chinguetti	52	D3
Chinhoyi	59	B6
Chiniot	42	D8
Chinnampo = Namp'o	35	C7
Chinon	12	C4
Chióggia	20	B4
Chíos = Khíos	23	E6
Chipata	59	A6
Chiquián	91	F3
Chiquinquira	90	B4
Chirchiq	29	E7
Chirmiri	40	F4
Chisapani Garhi	40	D5
Chişinău	17	E9
Chistopol	24	B7
Chita	30	D9
Chitral	42	B7
Chitré	86	E3
Chittagong	41	F8
Chittagong □	41	E8
Chittaurgarh	43	G9
Chittoor	43	N11
Chiusi	20	C3
Chivasso	20	B1
Chivilcoy	94	D4
Chkalov = Orenburg	29	D6
Choele Choel	95	D3
Chojnice	16	B3
Cholet	12	C3
Choluteca	85	E7
Choma	59	B5
Chomutov	16	C1
Chon Buri	38	B2
Chone	90	D3
Chŏngjin	35	B7
Chŏngju	35	C7
Chongqing	35	D5
Chŏnju	35	C7
Chonos, Arch. de los	95	F2
Chop	17	D6
Chornobyl	17	C10
Chortkiv	17	D7
Chorzów	16	C4
Chos-Malal	94	D2
Choszczno	16	B2
Chotila	43	H7
Choybalsan	35	B6
Christchurch	65	E5
Christmas I. = Kiritimati	65	J15
Chu = Shū	29	E8
Ch'uanchou = Quanzhou	35	D6
Chubut →	95	E3
Chudskoye, Ozero	24	B2
Chūgoku-Sanchi	33	F3
Chula Vista	78	D4
Chulucanas	90	E2
Chulym →	29	D9
Chumbicha	94	B3
Chumphon	38	B1
Chuna →	30	D7
Ch'unch'ŏn	35	C7
Chungking = Chongqing	35	D5
Chunya	57	F6
Chuquibamba	91	G4
Chuquicamata	94	A3
Chur	13	C8
Churachandpur	41	E9
Churchill	68	C10
Churchill →, Man., Canada	68	C10
Churchill →, Nfld. & L., Canada	71	C4
Churchill, C.	68	C10
Churchill Falls	71	C4
Churchill Pk.	69	C9
Churu	42	E9
Chushal	42	C11
Chusovoy	28	D6
Chuvashia □	24	B6
Ciadâr-Lunga	17	E9
Cícero	76	D2
Ciechanów	16	B5
Ciego de Avila	86	B4
Ciénaga	90	A4
Cienfuegos	86	B3
Cieza	19	C5
Cijara, Embalse de	18	C3
Cill Chainnigh = Kilkenny	11	E3
Cimişlia	17	E9
Cimone, Mte.	20	B3
Cinca →	19	B6
Cincar	20	C6
Cincinnati	76	E3
Çine	23	F7
Cinto, Mte.	13	E8
Circle	69	B5
Cirebon	39	F3
Citlaltépetl = Orizaba, Pico de	84	D5
Città di Castello	20	C4
Ciudad Bolívar	90	B6
Ciudad del Carmen	85	D6
Ciudad Delicias = Delicias	84	B3
Ciudad Guayana	90	B6
Ciudad Juárez	84	A3
Ciudad Madero	84	C5
Ciudad Mante	84	C5
Ciudad Obregón	84	B3
Ciudad Real	18	C4
Ciudad Rodrigo	18	B2
Ciudad Trujillo = Santo Domingo	87	C6
Ciudad Victoria	84	C5
Civitanova Marche	20	C4
Civitavécchia	20	C3
Cizre	46	C5
Clare	62	B2
Clare →, Australia	63	A5
Clarence →, N.Z.	65	E5
Clarence, I.	95	G2
Clarence I.	96	A4
Clarie Coast	96	A13
Clarke I.	62	D4
Clarksdale	81	B8
Clarksville	82	A4
Claveria	36	A2
Clear, C.	11	F2
Clearwater	83	F6
Clearwater Mts.	73	C6
Clermont-Ferrand	13	D5
Cleveland	76	D5
Clifden	65	G2
Clifton	63	A5
Clinton, N.Z.	65	G3
Clinton, U.S.A.	75	E9
Clinton Colden L.	68	B9
Clones	11	D3
Clonmel	11	E3
Clovis	80	B2
Cluj-Napoca	17	E6
Clunes	62	C3
Clutha →	65	G3
Clyde	65	F3
Clyde →	10	D4
Clyde, Firth of	10	D4
Clyde River	70	A4
Coari	90	D6
Coast Mts.	68	C7
Coast Ranges	72	F2
Coats I.	70	B2
Coats Land	96	B5
Coatzacoalcos	85	D6
Cobar	63	B4
Cobh	11	F2
Cobija	91	F5
Cobram	63	C4
Coburg	15	C6
Cocanada = Kakinada	40	J4
Cochabamba	91	G5
Cochin	43	Q10
Cochin China = Nam-Phan	38	B3
Cochrane	71	D2
Cochrane, L.	95	F2
Cockburn	62	B3
Cockburn, Canal	95	G2
Coco →	86	D3
Cocobeach	56	D1
Cod, C.	77	C10
Codajás	90	D6
Codó	92	C5
Cœur d'Alene	72	C5
Coffeyville	81	A6
Coffin B.	62	B2
Coffin Bay Peninsula	62	B2
Coffs Harbour	63	B5
Cognac	12	D3
Cohuna	63	C3
Coiba, I.	86	E3
Coig →	95	G3

Coihaique	95	F2
Coimbatore	43	P10
Coimbra, *Brazil*	91	G7
Coimbra, *Portugal*	18	B1
Coín	18	D3
Cojimíes	90	C3
Colac	62	C3
Colatina	93	F5
Colbeck, C.	96	B17
Colchester	11	F7
Coleraine, *Australia*	62	C3
Coleraine, *U.K.*	11	D3
Coleridge, L.	65	E4
Colesberg	59	E5
Colhué Huapi, L.	95	F3
Colima	84	D4
Colinas	92	D5
Coll	10	C3
Collaguasi	91	H5
Collarenebri	63	A4
Collina, Passo di	20	B3
Collingwood	64	D5
Colmar	13	B7
Colo →	63	B5
Cologne = Köln	14	C4
Colomb-Béchar = Béchar	52	B5
Colombia ■	90	C4
Colombo	43	R11
Colón, *Cuba*	86	B3
Colón, *Panama*	85	F9
Colonia del Sacramento	94	C5
Colonia Dora	94	B3
Colonsay	10	C3
Colorado □	79	A10
Colorado →, *Argentina*	95	D4
Colorado →, *N. Amer.*	78	D5
Colorado Plateau	79	B7
Colorado Springs	74	F2
Columbia, *Mo., U.S.A.*	75	F8
Columbia, *S.C., U.S.A.*	83	B7
Columbia, *Tenn., U.S.A.*	82	B4
Columbia →	72	C1
Columbia, District of □	77	E7
Columbia Basin	72	C4
Columbretes, Is.	19	C6
Columbus, *Ga., U.S.A.*	82	C5
Columbus, *Miss., U.S.A.*	82	C5
Columbus, *Ohio, U.S.A.*	76	E4
Colville →	69	A4
Colville, C.	64	B6
Colwyn Bay	11	E5
Comácchio	20	B4
Comallo	95	E2
Comilla	41	F8
Comino, C.	21	D2
Committee B.	70	B2
Commonwealth B.	96	A14
Commoron Cr. →	63	A5
Communism Pk. = Kommunizma, Pik	29	F8
Como	20	B2
Como, Lago di	20	B2
Comodoro Rivadavia	95	F3
Comorin, C.	43	Q10
Comoros ■	51	H8
Compiègne	13	B5
Comrat	17	E9
Conakry	53	G3
Conara	62	D4
Concarneau	12	C2
Conceição da Barra	93	F6
Concepción, *Bolivia*	91	G6
Concepción, *Chile*	94	D2
Concepción, *Paraguay*	94	A5
Concepción →	91	G6
Concepción del Oro	84	C4
Concepción del Uruguay	94	C5
Conchos →	84	B3
Concord, *N.C., U.S.A.*	83	B7
Concord, *N.H., U.S.A.*	77	C10
Concordia, *Argentina*	94	C5
Concórdia, *Brazil*	90	D5
Condamine	63	A5
Condeúba	93	E5
Condobolin	63	B4
Conegliano	20	B4
Confuso →	94	B5
Congo (Brazzaville) = Congo ■	56	E3
Congo (Kinshasa) = Congo, Dem. Rep. of the ■	56	E4
Congo ■	56	E3
Congo →	56	E2
Congo, Dem. Rep. of the ■	56	E4
Conjeeveram = Kanchipuram	43	N11
Conn, L.	11	D2
Connacht □	11	E2
Connecticut □	77	D9
Connecticut →	77	D9
Connemara	11	E2
Conran, C.	63	C4
Conselheiro Lafaiete	93	G5
Constance = Konstanz	14	E5
Constance, L. = Bodensee	13	C8
Constanța	22	B7
Constantine	52	A7
Constitución	94	D2
Constitución	40	G6
Contai	91	E4
Contamana	91	E4
Contas →	93	E6
Conway, L.	62	A2
Coober Pedy	62	A1
Cooch Behar = Koch Bihar	41	D7
Cook, B.	95	H2
Cook, Mt. = Aoraki Mount Cook	65	E4
Cook Inlet	69	C4
Cook Is.	65	L14
Cook Strait	65	D6
Cooktown	61	D8
Coolabah	63	B4
Cooladdi	63	A4
Coolah	63	B4
Coolamon	63	B4
Cooma	63	C4
Coonabarabran	63	B4
Coonamble	63	B4
Coondapoor	43	N9
Cooninie, L.	62	A2
Cooper Cr. →	62	A2
Coorong, The	62	C2
Cooroy	63	A5
Cootamundra	63	B4
Copenhagen = København	9	D8
Copiapó	94	B2
Copiapó →	94	B2
Coppermine = Kugluktuk	68	B8
Coppermine →	68	B8
Coquimbo	94	C2
Corabia	22	C5
Coracora	91	G4
Coral Harbour	70	B2
Coral Sea	64	L10
Corato	21	D6
Corby	11	E6
Corcaigh = Cork	11	F2
Corcubión	18	A1
Córdoba, *Argentina*	94	C4
Córdoba, *Spain*	18	D3
Córdoba, Sierra de	94	C4
Cordova	69	B5
Corfu = Kérkira	23	E2
Coria	18	C2
Corigliano Cálabro	21	E6
Corinth = Kórinthos	23	F4
Corinth, G. of = Korinthiakós Kólpos	23	E4
Corinto	93	F5
Cork	11	F2
Çorlu	22	D6
Corner Brook	71	D5
Corneşti	17	E9
Cornwall	71	D3
Corny Pt.	62	B2
Coro	90	A5
Coroatá	92	C5
Corocoro	91	G5
Coroico	91	G5
Coromandel	64	B6
Coronation Gulf	68	B8
Coronation I.	96	A4
Coronel	94	D2
Coronel Dorrego	94	D4
Coronel Suárez	94	D4
Corowa	63	C4
Corpus Christi	80	F5
Corrib, L.	11	E2
Corrientes	94	B5
Corrientes →	90	D4
Corrientes, C., *Colombia*	90	B3
Corrientes, C., *Mexico*	84	C3
Corse	13	E8
Corse, C.	13	E8
Corsica = Corse	13	E8
Corsicana	81	C5
Corte	13	E8
Çorum	46	B3
Corumbá	91	G7
Corunna = A Coruña	18	A1
Corvallis	72	D2
Cosenza	21	E6
Costa Blanca	19	C5
Costa Brava	19	B7
Costa del Sol	18	D3
Costa Dorada	19	B6
Costa Rica ■	86	E3
Cotabato	36	C2
Cotagaita	91	H5
Côte d'Azur	13	E7
Côte-d'Ivoire = Ivory Coast ■	53	G4
Cotentin	12	B3
Cotonou	53	G6
Cotopaxi	90	D3
Cotswold Hills	11	F5
Cottbus	15	C8
Couedic, C. du	62	C2
Coulman I.	96	B15
Council Bluffs	75	E7
Courantyne →	90	B7
Courtrai = Kortrijk	14	C2
Coventry	11	E6
Covilhã	18	B2
Covington	76	E3
Cowal, L.	63	B4
Cowangie	62	C3
Cowell	62	B2
Cowra	63	B4
Coxim	93	F3
Cox's Bazar	41	G8
Cozumel, Isla	85	C7
Cracow = Kraków	16	C4
Cracow	63	A5
Cradock	59	E5
Craigavon	11	D3
Crailsheim	14	D6
Craiova	22	B4
Cranbrook	69	D8
Crateús	92	D5
Crato	92	D6
Crawley	11	F6
Crazy Mts.	73	C8
Crema	20	B2
Cremona	20	B3
Cres	20	B5
Crete = Kríti	23	G5
Créteil	12	B5
Creus, C. de	19	A7
Creuse →	12	C4
Crewe	11	E5
Criciúma	94	B7
Crimean Pen. = Krymskyy Pivostriv	25	D3
Crişul Negru →	16	E5
Crna →	22	D3
Crna Gora = Montenegro □	22	C2
Crna Gora	22	C3
Croatia ■	20	B6

Crocker, Banjaran	38	C5
Croker, C.	60	C5
Cromer	11	E7
Cromwell	65	F3
Crookwell	63	B4
Cross Sound	69	C6
Crotone	21	E6
Crows Nest	63	A5
Crowsnest Pass	69	D8
Cruz Alta	94	B6
Cruz del Eje	94	C4
Cruzeiro do Sul	91	E4
Crystal Brook	62	B2
Csongrád	16	E5
Cuamba	59	A7
Cuando ➝	58	B4
Cuango = Kwango ➝	56	E3
Cuanza ➝	56	F2
Cuba ■	86	B4
Cubango ➝	58	B4
Cúcuta	90	B3
Cuddalore	43	P11
Cuddapah	43	M11
Cuenca, *Ecuador*	90	D3
Cuenca, *Spain*	19	B4
Cuenca, Serranía de	19	C5
Cuernavaca	84	D5
Cuevas del Almanzora	19	D5
Cuevo	91	H6
Cuiabá	93	F2
Cuiabá ➝	93	F2
Cuito ➝	58	B4
Culcairn	63	C4
Culgoa ➝	63	A4
Culiacán	84	C3
Culion	36	B2
Cullarin Ra.	63	B4
Cullera	19	C5
Culuene ➝	93	E3
Culverden	65	E5
Cumaná	90	A6
Cumberland	77	E6
Cumberland Pen.	70	B4
Cumberland Plateau	76	F3
Cumberland Sd.	70	B4
Cumborah	63	A4
Cumbum	43	M11
Cummins	62	B2
Cumnock	63	B4
Cunene ➝	58	B2
Cúneo	20	B1
Cunnamulla	63	A4
Cupica, G. de	90	B3
Curaçao	87	D6
Curaray ➝	90	D4
Curiapo	90	B6
Curicó	94	C2
Curitiba	94	B7
Currabubula	63	B5
Currais Novos	92	D6
Curralinho	92	C4
Currie	62	C3
Curtea de Argeş	17	F7
Curtis Group	62	C4
Curuápanema ➝	92	C2
Curuçá	92	C4
Curup	39	E2
Cururupu	92	C5
Curuzú Cuatiá	94	B5
Cuttaburra ➝	63	A3
Cuttack	40	G5
Cuvier I.	64	B6
Cuxhaven	14	B5
Cuyo	36	B2
Cuzco, *Bolivia*	91	H5
Cuzco, *Peru*	91	F4
Cwmbran	11	F5
Cyclades = Kikládhes	23	F5
Cygnet	62	D4
Cyprus ■	46	D3
Cyrenaica	54	C3
Czech Rep. ■	16	D2
Częstochowa	16	C4

D

Da Hinggan Ling	35	B7
Da Lat	38	B3
Da Nang	38	A3
Da Qaidam	34	C4
Daba Shan	35	C5
Dabo = Pasirkuning	39	E2
Dabola	53	F3
Dacca = Dhaka	41	F8
Dachau	15	D6
Dadanawa	90	C7
Dadra & Nagar Haveli □	43	J8
Dadu	42	F5
Daet	36	B2
Dagana	53	E2
Dagestan □	25	E6
Dagö = Hiiumaa	24	B1
Dagupan	36	A2
Dahod	43	H9
Dahlak Kebir	49	D3
Dahomey = Benin ■	53	G6
Daió-Misaki	33	F5
Daisetsu-Zan	32	B8
Dakar	53	F2
Dakhla	52	D2
Dakhla, El Wâhât el-	54	C4
Đakovica	22	C3
Dalälven ➝	9	C9
Dalaman ➝	23	F7
Dalandzadgad	35	B5
Dālbandīn	42	E4
Dalby	63	A5
Dali	34	D5
Dalian	35	C7
Daliang Shan	34	D5
Dallas	81	C5
Dalmacija	20	C6
Dalmatia = Dalmacija	20	C6
Dalnegorsk	32	A4
Daloa	53	G4
Dalton	82	B5
Daly Waters	60	D5
Daman	43	J8
Damanhûr	54	B5
Damar	37	F3
Damaraland	58	C3
Damascus = Dimashq	46	D4
Dāmāvand	44	C3
Dāmāvand, Qolleh-ye	44	C3
Damba	56	F3
Dâmboviţa ➝	22	B6
Dāmghān	44	B3
Damiel	18	C4
Damietta = Dumyât	54	B5
Dammam = Ad Dammām	47	F7
Damoh	43	H11
Dampier	60	E2
Dampier, Selat	37	E4
Danbury	77	D9
Dandeldhura	40	C3
Dandeli	43	M9
Dandenong	63	C4
Dandong	35	B7
Danger Is. = Pukapuka	65	L14
Dangla Shan = Tanggula Shan	34	C4
Danilov	24	B5
Dankhar Gompa	42	C11
Dannevirke	64	D7
Danube = Dunărea ➝	17	F9
Danville	83	A8
Danzig = Gdańsk	16	A4
Dao = Tobias Fornier	36	B2
Dar el Beida = Casablanca	52	B4
Dar es Salaam	57	F7
Dārāb	44	D3
Daraj	54	B1
Darband	42	B8
Darbhanga	40	D5
Dardanelles = Çanakkale Boğazı	23	D6

Dârfûr	55	F3
Dargai	42	B7
Dargan Ata	29	E7
Dargaville	64	A5
Darica	22	D7
Darién, G. del	90	B3
Darjeeling = Darjiling	40	D7
Darjiling	40	D7
Darling ➝	62	B3
Darling Downs	63	A5
Darling Ra.	60	G2
Darlington	11	D6
Darłowo	16	A3
Darmstadt	14	D5
Darnah	54	B3
Darnley, C.	96	A10
Darnley B.	68	B7
Dart, C.	96	B18
Dartmoor	11	F5
Dartmouth	71	D4
Dartmouth Res.	63	A4
Darvaza	29	E6
Darvel, Teluk = Lahad Datu, Teluk	36	D1
Darwha	43	J10
Darwin	60	C5
Daryoi Amu = Amudarya ➝	29	E6
Dās	44	E3
Dashen, Ras	57	B7
Dashhowuz	29	E6
Dasht ➝	42	G2
Datça	23	F6
Datia	43	G11
Datong	35	B6
Datu, Tanjung	39	D3
Datu Piang	36	C2
Daugava ➝	24	B1
Daugavpils	24	B2
Daulpur	42	F10
Dauphin	69	C9
Dauphiné	13	D6
Davangere	43	M9
Davao	36	C3
Davao G.	36	C3
Dävar Panāh	45	E5
Davenport	75	E9
David	86	E3
David Gorodok = Davyd Haradok	17	B8
Davis Sea	96	A11
Davis Str.	70	B5
Davos	13	C8
Davyd Haradok	17	B8
Dawei = Tavoy	38	B1
Dawna Ra.	41	J12
Dawson	68	B6
Dawson, I.	95	G2
Dax	12	E3
Daxian	35	C5
Daxue Shan	34	C5
Daylesford	62	C4
Dayr az Zawr	46	D5
Dayton	76	E3
Daytona Beach	83	E7
Dead Sea	47	E3
Deal I.	62	C4
Deán Funes	94	C4
Death Valley	78	B4
Debar	22	D3
Debre Markos	55	F6
Debrecen	16	E5
Decatur, *Ala., U.S.A.*	82	B4
Decatur, *Ill., U.S.A.*	75	F10
Deccan	43	L11
Děčín	16	C2
Dedéagach = Alexandroúpolis	22	D5
Dee ➝	10	C5
Deepwater	63	A5
Deggendorf	15	D7
Deh Bid	44	D3

Dehibat	54	B1
Dehra Dun	42	D11
Dej	17	E6
Dekese	56	E4
Delano	78	C3
Delaware □	77	E8
Delegate	63	C4
Delgado, C.	57	G8
Delgo	55	D5
Delhi	42	E10
Delice →	46	C3
Delicias	84	B3
Déline	68	B7
Delmenhorst	14	B5
Deloraine	62	D4
Delungra	63	A5
Delvinë	23	E3
Demanda, Sierra de la	18	A4
Demavend = Damávand,		
Qolleh-ye	44	C3
Dembidolo	55	G5
Demini →	90	D6
Demirci	23	E7
Demirköy	22	D6
Dempo	39	E2
Den Haag = 's-Gravenhage	14	B3
Den Helder	14	B3
Denau	29	F7
Dendang	39	E3
Denia	19	C6
Denial B.	62	B1
Deniliquin	63	C3
Denman Glacier	96	A11
Denmark ■	9	D7
Denmark Str.	66	C17
Denpasar	39	F5
Denton	80	C5
D'Entrecasteaux Is.	61	B9
Denver	74	F2
Deoghar	40	E6
Deolali	43	K8
Deoria	40	D4
Deosai Mts.	42	B9
Dera Ghazi Khan	42	D7
Dera Ismail Khan	42	D7
Derbent	25	E6
Derby, Australia	60	D3
Derby, U.K.	11	E6
Derg, L.	11	E2
Dergaon	41	D9
Derry = Londonderry	11	D3
Des Moines	75	E8
Des Moines →	75	E9
Desaguadero →	91	G5
Dese	49	E2
Desna →	17	C10
Desolación, I.	95	G2
Despeñaperros, Paso	18	C4
Dessau	15	C7
Dessye = Dese	49	E2
D'Estrees B.	62	C2
Detmold	14	C5
Detroit	76	C4
Deutsche Bucht	14	A5
Deva	17	F6
Devakottai	43	Q11
Deventer	14	B4
Devonport, Australia	62	D4
Devonport, N.Z.	64	B6
Dewas	43	H10
Deyhük	44	C4
Deyyer	44	E2
Dezfül	47	D7
Dezhneva, Mys	31	C16
Dhahran = Az Zahrän	47	F8
Dhaka	41	F8
Dhaka □	41	E8
Dhamtari	40	G3
Dhanbad	40	F6
Dhangarhi	40	C3
Dhankuta	40	D6
Dhar	43	H9

Dharmapuri	43	N11
Dhaulagiri	40	C4
Dhenkanal	40	G5
Dhíkti Óros	23	G5
Dhirfis Óros	23	E4
Dhodhekánisos	23	F6
Dhrol	43	H7
Dhuburi	41	D7
Dhule	43	J9
Diafarabé	53	F5
Diamantina	93	F5
Diamantina →	62	A2
Diamantino	93	E2
Diamond Harbour	40	F7
Dibaya-Lubue	56	E3
Dibrugarh	41	D10
Dickson = Dikson	28	B9
Didiéni	53	F4
Diefenbaker, L.	69	C9
Dieppe	12	B4
Digby	71	D4
Dighinala	41	F9
Digne-les-Bains	13	D7
Digos	36	C3
Digul →	37	F5
Dihang = Brahmaputra →	41	F7
Dijlah, Nahr →	47	E6
Dijon	13	C6
Dikson	28	B9
Dili	37	F3
Dillingham	69	C4
Dilolo	56	G4
Dimashq	46	D4
Dimboola	62	C3
Dîmbovița = Dâmbovița →	22	C5
Dimitrovgrad, Bulgaria	22	C5
Dimitrovgrad, Russia	24	C6
Dimitrovo = Pernik	22	C4
Dinagat	36	B3
Dinajpur	41	E7
Dinan	12	B2
Dinant	14	C3
Dinar	46	C2
Dinär, Küh-e	44	D2
Dinara Planina	20	B6
Dinard	12	B2
Dinaric Alps = Dinara		
Planina	20	B6
Dindigul	43	P11
Dingle	11	E1
Dingwall	10	C4
Dinosaur ○	73	F9
Dipolog	36	C2
Dir	42	B7
Dire Dawa	49	F3
Dirranbandi	63	A4
Disa	43	G8
Disappointment, L.	60	E3
Disaster B.	63	C4
Discovery B.	62	C3
Disko = Qeqertarsuaq	70	B5
Disteghil Sar	42	A9
Distrito Federal □	93	F4
Diu	43	J7
Divinópolis	93	G5
Divnoye	25	D5
Diyarbakir	46	C5
Djakarta = Jakarta	39	F3
Djambala	56	E2
Djanet	52	D7
Djawa = Jawa	39	F3
Djelfa	52	B6
Djerba, I. de	54	B1
Djerid, Chott	52	B7
Djibouti	49	E3
Djibouti ■	49	E3
Djolu	56	D4
Djoum	56	D2
Djourab, Erg du	55	E2
Dmitriya Lapteva, Proliv	31	B12
Dnepr = Dnipro →	25	D3
Dneprodzerzhinsk =		
Dniprodzerzhynsk	25	D3

Dnepropetrovsk =		
Dnipropetrovsk	25	D4
Dnestr = Dnister →	17	E10
Dnestrovski = Belgorod	24	C4
Dnieper = Dnipro →	25	D3
Dniester = Dnister →	17	E10
Dnipro →	25	D3
Dniprodzerzhynsk	25	D3
Dnipropetrovsk	25	D4
Dnister →	17	E10
Dnistrovskyy Lyman	17	E10
Dnyapro = Dnipro →	25	D3
Doba	55	G2
Doberai, Jazirah	37	E4
Dobo	37	F4
Doboj	20	B7
Dobrich	22	C6
Dobruja	17	F9
Dobrush	17	B10
Dodecanese =		
Dhodhekánisos	23	F6
Dodge City	80	A3
Dodoma	57	F7
Doha = Ad Dawhah	44	E2
Dohazari	41	F9
Doi	37	D3
Dois Irmãos, Sa.	93	D5
Dolak, Pulau	37	F5
Dolbeau-Mistassini	71	D3
Dole	13	C6
Dolomites = Dolomiti	20	A3
Dolomiti	20	A3
Dolores	94	D5
Dolphin, C.	95	G5
Dolphin and Union Str.	68	B8
Dombarovskiy	29	D6
Dominica ■	87	C7
Dominican Rep. ■	87	C5
Domodóssola	20	A2
Domville, Mt.	63	A5
Don →, Russia	25	D4
Don →, U.K.	10	C5
Don Benito	18	C3
Donald	62	C3
Donau = Dunărea →	17	F9
Donauwörth	14	D6
Doncaster	11	E6
Dondo, Teluk	37	D2
Donegal	11	D2
Donets →	25	D5
Donetsk	25	D4
Donggala	37	E1
Dongola	55	E5
Dongting Hu	35	D6
Donington, C.	62	B2
Donnelly's Crossing	64	A5
Donostia-San Sebastián	19	A5
Dora Baltea →	20	B2
Dorchester, C.	70	B3
Dordogne →	12	D3
Dordrecht	14	C3
Dori	53	F5
Dornbirn	14	E5
Dorohoi	17	E8
Döröö Nuur	34	B4
Dorrigo	63	B5
Dortmund	14	C4
Dos Bahías, C.	95	E3
Dos Hermanas	18	D3
Dosso	53	F6
Dothan	82	D5
Douai	13	A5
Douala	56	D1
Douarnenez	12	B1
Double Island Pt.	63	A5
Doubs →	13	C6
Doubtful Sd.	65	F2
Doubtless B.	64	A5
Douglas, U.K.	11	D4
Douglas, U.S.A.	79	E8
Dourados	94	A6
Douro →	18	B1

Dover, *Australia*	62	D4
Dover, *U.K.*	11	F7
Dover, Str. of	11	F7
Dovrefjell	8	C7
Dowlat Yār	45	C6
Dowlatābād	44	D4
Drăgăşani	22	B5
Dragichyn	17	B7
Dragoman, Prokhod	22	C4
Draguignan	13	E7
Drakensberg	59	E5
Dráma	22	D5
Drammen	9	D8
Drau = Drava →	20	B7
Drava →	20	B7
Dresden	15	C7
Dreux	12	B4
Drin →	22	C2
Drina →	20	B7
Drobeta-Turnu Severin	22	B4
Drochia	17	D8
Drogheda	11	E3
Drogichin = Dragichyn	17	B7
Drogobych = Drohobych	17	D6
Drohobych	17	D6
Droichead Atha = Drogheda	11	E3
Dromedary, C.	63	C5
Dronning Maud Land	96	B7
Drumheller	68	C8
Drummond Pt.	62	B2
Drut →	17	B10
Drygalski I.	96	A11
Dubā	47	F3
Dubai = Dubayy	44	E3
Dūbāsari	17	E9
Dūbāsari Vdkhr.	17	E9
Dubawnt →	68	B9
Dubawnt L.	68	B9
Dubayy	44	E3
Dubbo	63	B4
Dublin, *Ireland*	11	E3
Dublin, *U.S.A.*	83	C6
Dubno	17	C7
Dubossary = Dūbăsari	17	E9
Dubovka	24	D5
Dubréka	53	G3
Dubrovnik	20	C7
Dubrovytsya	17	C8
Dudhi	40	E4
Dudinka	30	C9
Duero = Douro →	18	B1
Dūghi Kalā	42	C3
Dugi Otok	20	B5
Duisburg	14	C4
Dujiangyan	34	C5
Dukhān	44	E2
Duki	42	D6
Dulce →	94	C4
Dulit, Banjaran	39	D4
Duluth	75	B8
Dum Duma	41	D10
Dumaguete	36	C2
Dumai	39	D2
Dumaran	36	B1
Dumfries	11	D5
Dumyât	54	B5
Dún Dealgan = Dundalk	11	D3
Dún Laoghaire	11	E3
Duna = Dunărea →	17	F9
Dunaj = Dunărea →	17	F9
Dunakeszi	16	E4
Dunărea →	17	F9
Dunaújváros	16	E4
Dunav = Dunărea →	17	F9
Dunback	65	F4
Dunbar	10	D5
Duncan	80	B5
Dundalk	11	D3
Dundee	10	C5
Dunedin	65	F4
Dunfermline	10	C5
Dungarvan	11	E3

Dungog	63	B5
Dungu	57	D5
Dunhuang	34	B4
Dunkerque	12	A5
Dunkirk = Dunkerque	12	A5
Dúnleary = Dún Laoghaire	11	E3
Dunolly	62	C3
Dunstan Mts.	65	F3
Durance →	13	E6
Durango	84	C4
Durazno	94	C5
Durazzo = Durrës	22	D2
Durban	59	D6
Düren	14	C4
Durg	40	G3
Durgapur	40	F6
Durham, *U.K.*	11	D6
Durham, *U.S.A.*	83	B8
Durmitor	22	C2
Durrës	22	D2
Dursunbey	23	E7
D'Urville, Tanjung	37	E5
D'Urville I.	65	D5
Dushak	29	F7
Dushanbe	29	F7
Dusky Sd.	65	F2
Düsseldorf	14	C4
Dutch Harbor	69	C3
Duyun	35	D5
Duzdab = Zāhedān	45	D5
Dvina, Severnaya →	28	C5
Dvinsk = Daugavpils	24	B2
Dwarka	43	H6
Dyatlovo = Dzyatlava	17	B7
Dyer, C.	70	B4
Dyer Plateau	96	B3
Dyersburg	81	A9
Dymer	17	C10
Dzamin Üüd = Borhoyn Tal	35	B6
Dzerzhinsk	24	B5
Dzhambul = Taraz	29	E8
Dzhankoy	25	D3
Dzhezkazgan = Zhezqazghan	29	E7
Dzhizak = Jizzakh	29	E7
Działdowo	16	B5
Dzierżoniów	16	C3
Dzungaria = Junggar Pendi	34	B3
Dzuumod	35	B5
Dzyarzhynsk	17	B8
Dzyatlava	17	B7

E

Earnslaw, Mt.	65	F3
East Bengal	41	E7
East Beskids = Východné Beskydy	17	D5
East C.	64	B8
East China Sea	35	C7
East Falkland	95	G5
East Kilbride	10	D4
East London	59	E5
East Main = Eastmain	71	C3
East Orange	77	D8
East St. Louis	75	F9
East Sea = Japan, Sea of	32	D4
East Toorale	63	B4
Eastbourne, *N.Z.*	65	D6
Eastbourne, *U.K.*	11	F7
Eastern Ghats	43	N11
Eastmain	71	C3
Eastmain →	71	C3
Eau Claire	75	C9
Eberswalde-Finow	15	B7
Ebetsu	32	B7
Ebolowa	56	D2
Ebro →	19	B6
Eceabat	23	D6

Ech Chéliff	52	A6
Echo Bay	68	B8
Echuca	63	C3
Ecija	18	D3
Ecuador ■	90	D3
Ed Debba	55	E5
Ed Dueim	55	F5
Eddystone Pt.	62	D4
Édéa	53	H8
Eden	63	C4
Eder →	14	C5
Édhessa	23	D4
Edievale	65	F3
Edinburg	80	F4
Edinburgh	10	D5
Edineţ	17	D8
Edirne	22	D6
Edithburgh	62	C2
Edmonton	69	C8
Edmundston	71	D4
Edremit	23	E6
Edremit Körfezi	23	E6
Edson	69	C8
Edward →	62	C3
Edward, L.	57	E5
Edward VII Land	96	C17
Edwards Plateau	80	D3
Égadi, Ísole	21	F4
Eger = Cheb	16	C1
Eger →	16	E5
Egmont, C.	64	C5
Egmont, Mt. = Taranaki, Mt.	64	C6
Eğridir	46	C2
Eğridir Gölü	46	C2
Egypt ■	54	C5
Eibar	19	A4
Eidsvold	63	A5
Eifel	14	C4
Eigg	10	C3
Eil	49	F4
Eildon, L.	63	C4
Eindhoven	14	C3
Eire = Ireland ■	11	E3
Eirunepé	91	E5
Eisenach	14	C6
Eisenerz	15	E8
Eivissa	19	C6
Eketahuna	64	D6
Ekibastuz	29	D8
El Aaiún	52	C3
El 'Alamein	54	B4
El Asnam = Ech Chéliff	52	A6
El Bayadh	52	B6
El Centro	79	K6
El Cerro	91	G6
El Cuy	95	D3
El Dere	49	G4
El Diviso	90	C3
El Djouf	53	D4
El Dorado, *Ark., U.S.A.*	81	C7
El Dorado, *Kans., U.S.A.*	80	A5
El Dorado, *Venezuela*	90	B6
El Escorial	18	B3
El Faiyûm	54	C5
El Fâsher	55	F4
El Ferrol = Ferrol	18	A1
El Fuerte	84	B3
El Gal	49	E5
El Geneina = Al Junaynah	55	F3
El Gîza	54	C5
El Homeur	52	C6
El Iskandarîya	54	B4
El Jadida	52	B4
El Khârga	54	C5
El Khartûm	55	E5
El Maestrazgo	19	B5
El Mahalla el Kubra	54	B5
El Mansûra	54	B5
El Minyâ	54	C5
El Obeid	55	F5
El Odaiya	55	F4
El Oued	52	B7

El Paso ... 79 E9
El Prat de Llobregat ... 19 B7
El Puerto de Santa María ... 18 D2
El Qâhira ... 54 B5
El Reno ... 80 B5
El Salvador ■ ... 85 E7
El Suweis ... 54 C5
El Tigre ... 90 B6
El Turbio ... 95 G2
El Uqsur ... 54 C5
El Vigía ... 90 B4
El Wak ... 57 D8
El Wuz ... 55 E5
Elat ... 47 E3
Elâzığ ... 46 C4
Elba ... 20 C3
Elbasan ... 22 D3
Elbe ⇢ ... 14 B5
Elbert, Mt. ... 79 A9
Elbeuf ... 12 B4
Elbing = Elbląg ... 16 A4
Elbląg ... 16 A4
Elbrus ... 25 E5
Elburz Mts. = Alborz,
  Reshteh-ye Kūhhā-ye ... 44 B3
Elche ... 19 C5
Elda ... 19 C5
Elde ⇢ ... 15 B6
Eldoret ... 57 D7
Elefantes ⇢ ... 59 C6
Elektrostal ... 24 B4
Elephant I. ... 96 A4
Eleuthera ... 86 A4
Elgin, U.K. ... 10 C5
Elgin, U.S.A. ... 76 C1
Elgon, Mt. ... 57 D6
Eliase ... 37 F4
Elista ... 25 D5
Elizabeth, Australia ... 62 B2
Elizabeth, U.S.A. ... 77 D8
Elizabeth City ... 83 A9
Elizabethton ... 83 A6
Elk ... 16 B6
Elkhart ... 76 D3
Elkhovo ... 22 C6
Elko ... 72 F6
Ellery, Mt. ... 63 C4
Ellesmere, L. ... 65 G5
Ellice Is. = Tuvalu ■ ... 64 K12
Elliston ... 62 B1
Ellore = Eluru ... 40 J3
Ellsworth Land ... 96 B2
Ellsworth Mts. ... 96 B2
Elmore ... 63 C3
Elmshorn ... 14 B5
Eltham ... 64 C6
Eluru ... 40 J3
Elvas ... 18 C2
Elx = Elche ... 19 C5
Ely ... 11 E7
Emâmrūd ... 44 B3
Emba ... 29 E6
Emba ⇢ ... 29 E6
Embarcación ... 94 A4
Embetsu ... 32 A7
Embi = Emba ... 29 E6
Embi = Emba ⇢ ... 29 E6
Embrun ... 13 D7
Emden ... 14 B4
Emet ... 23 E7
Emi Koussi ... 55 E2
Emine, Nos ... 22 C6
Emissi, Tarso ... 54 D2
Emmen ... 14 B4
Empalme ... 84 B2
Empangeni ... 59 D6
Empedrado ... 94 B5
Empty Quarter = Rub' al
  Khālī ... 48 D4
Ems ⇢ ... 14 B4
En Nahud ... 55 F4
Enare = Inarijärvi ... 8 B11

Enarotali ... 37 E5
Encarnación ... 94 B5
Encounter B. ... 62 C2
Ende ... 37 F2
Enderby Land ... 96 A9
Enewetak Atoll ... 64 H11
Enez ... 23 D6
Engaño, C. ... 36 A2
Engaru ... 32 A8
Engels ... 24 C6
Enggano ... 39 F2
England □ ... 11 E6
Englewood ... 74 F2
English Bazar = Ingraj Bazar ... 40 E7
English Channel ... 11 B5
Enid ... 80 A5
Enna ... 21 F5
Ennedi ... 55 E3
Enngonia ... 63 A4
Ennis ... 11 E2
Enniskillen ... 11 D3
Enns ⇢ ... 15 D8
Enschede ... 14 B4
Ensenada ... 84 A1
Entebbe ... 57 D6
Entre Ríos □ ... 94 C5
Entroncamento ... 18 C1
Enugu ... 53 G7
Eólie, Ís. ... 21 E5
Épernay ... 13 B5
Ephesus ... 23 F6
Épinal ... 13 B7
Equatorial Guinea ■ ... 56 D1
Er Rachidia ... 52 B5
Er Rahad ... 55 F5
Er Rif ... 52 A5
Erāwadi Myit =
  Irrawaddy ⇢ ... 41 K10
Erbil = Arbil ... 46 C6
Erciyaş Dağı ... 46 C3
Érd ... 16 E4
Erdek ... 23 D6
Erebus, Mt. ... 96 B15
Erechim ... 94 B6
Ereğli, Konya, Turkey ... 46 C3
Ereğli, Zonguldak, Turkey ... 46 B2
Eresma ⇢ ... 18 B3
Erfurt ... 15 C6
Ergani ... 46 C4
Érice ... 21 E4
Erie ... 77 C5
Erie, L. ... 76 C5
Erigavo ... 49 E4
Erimanthos ... 23 F3
Erimo-misaki ... 32 C8
Eritrea ■ ... 49 E2
Erlangen ... 15 D6
Ermenek ... 46 C3
Ermoúpolis = Síros ... 23 F5
Erne, Lower L. ... 11 D3
Erode ... 43 P10
Eromanga ... 63 A3
Erramala Hills ... 43 M11
Ertis = Irtysh ⇢ ... 28 C7
Erzgebirge ... 15 C7
Erzincan ... 46 C4
Erzurum ... 46 C5
Es Sahrâ' Esh Sharqîya ... 54 C5
Es Sînâ' ... 54 C5
Esan-Misaki ... 32 C7
Esashi, Hokkaidō, Japan ... 32 A8
Esashi, Hokkaidō, Japan ... 32 C7
Esbjerg ... 9 D7
Esch-sur-Alzette ... 13 B6
Escuinapa ... 84 C3
Esenguly ... 29 F6
Eşfahān ... 44 C2
Esh Sham = Dimashq ... 46 D4
Esil = Ishim ⇢ ... 29 D8
Eskilstuna ... 9 D9
Eskimo Point = Arviat ... 68 B10
Eskişehir ... 46 C2

Esla ⇢ ... 18 B2
Eslāmābād-e Gharb ... 46 D6
Eşme ... 23 E7
Esmeraldas ... 90 C3
Esperance ... 60 G3
Espichel, C. ... 18 C1
Espinazo, Sierra del =
  Espinhaço, Serra do ... 93 F5
Espinhaço, Serra do ... 93 F5
Espírito Santo □ ... 93 G5
Espoo ... 9 C10
Esquel ... 95 E2
Esquina ... 94 C5
Essaouira ... 52 B4
Essen ... 14 C4
Essequibo ⇢ ... 90 B7
Esslingen ... 14 D5
Estados, I. de Los ... 95 G4
Estância ... 93 E6
Estevan ... 69 D9
Estonia ■ ... 24 B2
Estrela, Serra da ... 18 B2
Estremoz ... 18 C2
Estrondo, Serra do ... 92 D4
Esztergom ... 16 E4
Étampes ... 12 B5
Etawah ... 42 F11
eThekwini = Durban ... 59 D6
Ethiopia ■ ... 49 F2
Etna ... 21 F5
Etosha Pan ... 58 B3
Euboea = Évvoia ... 23 E5
Eucumbene, L. ... 63 C4
Eufaula ... 82 D5
Eugene ... 72 E2
Eugowra ... 63 B4
Eulo ... 63 A4
Euphrates = Furāt, Nahr
  al ⇢ ... 47 E6
Eureka ... 72 F1
Euroa ... 63 C4
Europa, Île ... 59 J8
Europa, Picos de ... 18 A3
Europa, Pta. de ... 18 D3
Evans Head ... 63 A5
Evanston ... 76 C2
Evansville ... 76 F2
Everard, L. ... 62 B1
Everest, Mt. ... 40 C6
Everett ... 72 C2
Everglades △ ... 83 G7
Évora ... 18 C2
Évreux ... 12 B4
Évros ⇢ ... 22 D6
Évry ... 12 B5
Évvoia ... 23 E5
Ewo ... 56 E2
Exaltación ... 91 F5
Exeter ... 11 F5
Exmoor ... 11 F5
Exmouth ... 11 F5
Extremadura □ ... 18 C2
Eyasi, L. ... 57 E6
Eyre (North), L. ... 62 A2
Eyre (South), L. ... 62 A2
Eyre, L. ... 60 F6
Eyre Mts. ... 65 F3
Eyre Pen. ... 62 B2
Ezine ... 23 E6

F

F.Y.R.O.M. = Macedonia ■ ... 22 D3
Fabriano ... 20 C4
Fada ... 55 E3
Fada-n-Gourma ... 53 F6
Faddeyevskiy, Ostrov ... 31 B12
Faenza ... 20 B3
Færoe Is. = Føroyar ... 6 C4

Fāgāras 17 F7
Fagnano, L. 95 G3
Fahraj 45 D4
Fair Isle 10 B6
Fairbanks 69 B5
Fairfield, *Ala., U.S.A.* . . 82 C4
Fairfield, *Calif., U.S.A.* . 72 G2
Fairlie 65 F4
Fairweather, Mt. 69 C6
Faisalabad 42 D8
Faizabad 40 D4
Fakfak 37 E4
Falaise 12 B3
Falam 41 F9
Falconara Maríttima . . . 20 C4
Falcone, C. del 20 D2
Faleshty = Fălești 17 E8
Fălești 17 E8
Falun 9 C9
Famagusta 46 D3
Fano 20 C4
Fao = Al Fāw 47 F7
Faradje 57 D5
Farafangana 59 J9
Farāh 42 C3
Farāh □ 42 C3
Faranah 53 F3
Farasān, Jazā'ir 49 D3
Farasan Is. = Farasān,
  Jazā'ir 49 D3
Fareham 11 F6
Farewell, C. 64 D5
Farewell C. = Nunap Isua 70 C6
Farghona 29 E8
Fargo 74 B6
Farīmān 45 C4
Farina 62 B2
Faro, *Brazil* 92 C2
Faro, *Portugal* 18 D2
Farrāshband 44 D3
Färs □ 44 D3
Fársala 23 E4
Fartak, Rás 47 E3
Farvel, Kap = Nunap Isua . 70 C6
Färyäb □ 45 B6
Fasā 44 D3
Fasano 21 D6
Fastiv 17 C9
Fastov = Fastiv 17 C9
Fatagar, Tanjung 42 F11
Fatehgarh 42 F9
Fatehpur, *Raj., India* . . 42 F9
Fatehpur, *Ut. P., India* . 40 E3
Favara 21 F4
Favignana 21 F4
Faxaflói 8 C1
Faya-Largeau 55 E2
Fayd 47 F5
Fayetteville, *Ark., U.S.A.* 81 A6
Fayetteville, *N.C., U.S.A.* 83 B8
Fazilka 42 D9
Fdérik 52 D3
Feather ➤ 72 G3
Featherston 65 D6
Fécamp 12 B4
Fehmarn 15 A6
Feilding 64 D6
Feira de Santana 93 E6
Feldkirch 14 E5
Felipe Carrillo Puerto . . 85 D7
Felixstowe 11 F7
Fenyang 35 C6
Feodosiya 25 D4
Ferdows 44 C4
Ferfer 49 F4
Fergana = Farghona . . . 29 E8
Fermo 20 C4

Fernando de Noronha . . . 92 C7
Fernando Póo = Bioko . . 56 D1
Ferozepore = Firozpur . . 42 D9
Ferrara 20 B3
Ferreñafe 91 E3
Ferret, C. 12 D3
Ferrol 18 A1
Fès 52 B5
Fetești 22 B6
Fetlar 10 A6
Feuilles ➤ 70 C3
Fez = Fès 52 B5
Fezzan 54 C2
Fianarantsoa 59 J9
Fier 23 D2
Figeac 12 D5
Figueira da Foz 18 B1
Figueres 19 A7
Figuig 52 B5
Fihaonana 64 L12
Filiatrá 23 F3
Filyos Çayı ➤ 46 B3
Fíngoè 59 A6
Finike 46 C2
Finisterre, C. = Fisterra, C. 18 A1
Finland ■ 8 C11
Finland, G. of 9 D1
Finley ➤ 68 C7
Finniss, C. 62 B1
Fiora ➤ 20 C3
Firat = Furāt, Nahr al ➤ . 47 E6
Firenze 20 C3
Firozpur 42 D9
Fīrūzābād 44 D3
Fīrūzkūh 44 C3
Fish ➤ 58 D3
Fishguard 11 E4
Fisterra, C. 18 A1
Fitz Roy 95 F3
Fiume = Rijeka 20 B5
Fizi 57 E5
Flagstaff 79 C7
Flåm 8 C7
Flaming Gorge Reservoir . 73 F9
Flamingo, Teluk 37 F5
Flanders = Flandre 14 C2
Flandre 14 C2
Flathead L. 73 B7
Flattery, C. 72 B1
Flensburg 14 A5
Flers 12 B3
Flesko, Tanjung 37 D2
Flin Flon 69 C9
Flinders ➤ 61 D7
Flinders I. 62 C4
Flinders Ranges 62 B2
Flint 76 C4
Flint I. 65 L15
Florence = Firenze 20 C3
Florence, *Ala., U.S.A.* . . 82 B4
Florence, *S.C., U.S.A.* . . 83 B8
Florence, L. 62 A2
Flores 37 F2
Flores Sea 37 F2
Florești 17 E9
Florianópolis 94 B7
Florida 94 C5
Florida □ 83 F6
Florida, Straits of 86 B3
Flórina 23 D3
Florø 8 C7
Fluk 37 E3
Flushing = Vlissingen . . 14 C2
Fly ➤ 61 B7
Flying Fish, C. 96 B1
Foça 23 E6
Focșani 17 F8
Fóggia 20 D5
Föhr 14 A5

Foix 12 E4
Folda 8 B8
Foligno 20 C4
Folkestone 11 F7
Fond du Lac 75 D10
Fondi 20 D4
Fongafale 64 K12
Fonsagrada = A
  Fonsagrada 18 A2
Fonseca, G. de 85 E7
Fontainebleau 13 B5
Fonte Boa 90 D5
Fontenay-le-Comte 12 C3
Foochow = Fuzhou 35 D6
Forbes 63 B4
Ford's Bridge 63 A4
Forestier Pen. 62 D4
Forfar 10 C5
Forlì 20 B4
Formentera 19 C6
Formentor, C. de 19 C7
Fórmia 20 D4
Formosa = Taiwan ■ . . . 35 D7
Formosa 94 B5
Formosa, Serra 93 E3
Formosa B. = Ungwana B. 57 E8
Føroyar 6 C4
Forsayth 61 D7
Forst 15 C8
Fort Albany 71 C2
Fort Collins 74 E2
Fort-de-France 87 D7
Fort Dodge 75 D7
Fort Franklin = Déline . . 68 B7
Fort Good Hope 68 B7
Fort Hertz = Putao 41 D11
Fort Lauderdale 83 F7
Fort Liard 68 B7
Fort Macleod 69 D8
Fort McPherson 68 B6
Fort Myers 83 F7
Fort Norman = Tulita . . . 68 B7
Fort Peck L. 73 C10
Fort Pierce 83 F7
Fort Providence 68 B8
Fort Resolution 68 B8
Fort Rupert = Waskaganish 71 C3
Fort Scott 81 A6
Fort Shevchenko 29 E6
Fort Simpson 68 B7
Fort Smith, *Canada* . . . 68 B8
Fort Smith, *U.S.A.* 81 B6
Fort Walton Beach 82 D4
Fort Wayne 76 D3
Fort William 10 C4
Fort Worth 80 C5
Fort Yukon 69 B5
Fortaleza 92 C6
Forûr 44 E3
Foshan 35 D6
Fossano 20 B1
Fougères 12 B3
Foula 10 A5
Foúrnoi 23 F6
Fouta Djalon 53 F3
Foveaux Str. 65 G3
Foxe Basin 70 B3
Foxe Chan. 70 B2
Foxe Pen. 70 B3
Foxton 64 D6
Foz do Iguaçu 94 B6
Franca 93 G4
Francavilla Fontana 21 D6
France ■ 13 C5
Frances 62 C3
Franceville 56 E2
Franche-Comté 13 C6
Francistown 59 C5
Frankfurt, *Brandenburg,
  Germany* 15 B8
Frankfurt, *Hessen,
  Germany* 14 C5

Fränkische Alb	15	D6
Franklin B.	68	B7
Franklin I.	96	B15
Franklin Mts.	68	B7
Franklin Str.	68	A10
Frankston	63	C4
Frantsa Iosifa, Zemlya	28	A6
Fraser →	69	D7
Fraser I.	63	A5
Fraserburgh	10	C5
Fray Bentos	94	C5
Fredericksburg	77	E7
Fredericton	71	D4
Frederikshavn	9	D8
Fredrikstad	9	D8
Freeport, *Bahamas*	86	A4
Freeport, *U.S.A.*	75	D10
Freetown	53	G3
Fregenal de la Sierra	18	C2
Freiburg	14	E4
Freire	95	D2
Freising	15	D6
Freistadt	15	D8
Fréjus	13	E7
Fremont	78	B2
French Guiana ☐	92	B3
French Polynesia ☐	65	M16
Fresco →	92	D3
Freshfield, C.	96	A14
Fresnillo	84	C4
Fresno	78	B3
Freycinet Pen.	62	D4
Fria, C.	58	B2
Frías	94	B3
Friedrichshafen	14	E5
Friendly Is. = Tonga ■	65	L13
Frobisher B.	70	B4
Frobisher Bay = Iqaluit	70	B4
Frome, L.	62	B2
Frosinone	20	D4
Frunze = Bishkek	29	E8
Frutal	93	F4
Frýdek-Místek	16	D4
Fuchou = Fuzhou	35	D6
Fuchū	33	F3
Fuengirola	18	D3
Fuentes de Oñoro	18	B3
Fuerte →	84	B3
Fuerte Olimpo	91	H7
Fuerteventura	52	C3
Fuhai	34	B3
Fuji	33	F6
Fuji-San	33	F6
Fujian ☐	35	D6
Fujiyama, Mt. = Fuji-San	33	F6
Fukien = Fujian ☐	35	D6
Fukuchiyama	33	F4
Fukue-Shima	33	G1
Fukui	33	E5
Fukuoka	33	G2
Fukushima	33	E7
Fukuyama	33	F3
Fulda	14	C5
Fulda →	14	C5
Funabashi	33	F7
Funafuti = Fongafale	64	K12
Funchal	52	B2
Fundación	90	A4
Fundão	18	B2
Fundy, B. of	71	D4
Funtua	53	F7
Furāt, Nahr al →	47	E6
Furneaux Group	62	D4
Fürstenwalde	15	B8
Fürth	14	D6
Furukawa	32	D7
Fury and Hecla Str.	70	B2
Fusagasuga	90	C4
Fushun	35	B7
Futuna	64	L12
Fuxin	35	B7
Fuzhou	35	D6
Fyn	9	D8

G

Gabela	56	G2
Gabès	54	B1
Gabès, G. de	54	B1
Gabon ■	56	E2
Gaborone	59	C5
Gabrovo	22	C5
Gachsārān	44	D2
Gadag	43	M9
Gadarwara	43	H11
Gadhada	43	J7
Gadsden	82	B4
Gadwal	43	L10
Gafsa	52	B7
Gagnoa	53	G4
Gagnon	71	C4
Gaillimh = Galway	11	E2
Gainesville, *Fla.*, *U.S.A.*	83	E6
Gainesville, *Ga.*, *U.S.A.*	83	B6
Gainesville, *Tex.*, *U.S.A.*	80	C5
Gairdner, L.	62	B2
Galashiels	10	D5
Galați	17	F9
Galatina	21	D7
Galcaio	49	F4
Galdhøpiggen	8	C7
Galela	37	D3
Galesburg	75	E9
Galich	24	B5
Galicia ☐	18	A2
Galilee, Sea of = Yam		
Kinneret	46	D3
Gállego →	19	B5
Gallegos →	95	G3
Gallinas, Pta.	90	A4
Gallipoli = Gelibolu	23	D6
Gallipoli	21	D6
Gällivare	8	B10
Galloway, Mull of	11	D4
Galveston	81	E6
Gálvez	94	C4
Galway	11	E2
Galway B.	11	E2
Gambia ■	53	F2
Gambia →	53	F2
Gambier Is.	62	C2
Gamboma	56	E3
Gan Jiang →	35	D6
Ganāveh	44	D2
Gäncä	25	E6
Gand = Gent	14	C2
Ganda	58	A2
Gandak →	40	E5
Gandava	42	E5
Gander	71	D5
Gandhi Sagar	43	G9
Gandía	19	C5
Ganedidalem = Gani	37	E3
Ganga →	41	F8
Ganganagar	42	E8
Gangaw	41	F10
Gangdisê Shan	40	B3
Ganges = Ganga →	41	F8
Gangtok	41	D7
Gani	37	E3
Gansu ☐	34	C5
Ganta	53	G4
Gantheaume, C.	62	C2
Gantsevichi = Hantsavichy	17	B8
Ganyem = Genyem	37	E6
Ganzhou	35	D6
Gaoua	53	F5
Gaoual	53	F3
Gaoxiong = Kaohsiung	35	D7
Gap	13	D7
Gar	34	C2
Garabogazköl Aylagy	29	E6
Garanhuns	92	D6
Garda, L. di	20	B3
Garden City	80	A3

Gardēz	42	C6
Gardo	49	F4
Gargano, Mte.	20	D5
Garigliano →	20	D4
Garland	73	F7
Garm	29	F8
Garmisch-Partenkirchen	14	E6
Garmo, Qullai =		
Kommunizma, Pik	29	F8
Garmsär	44	C3
Garoe	49	F4
Garonne →	12	D3
Garoowe = Garoe	49	F4
Garoua	55	G1
Garrison Res. = Sakakawea,		
L.	74	B4
Garry, L.	68	B9
Garvie Mts.	65	F3
Garwa = Garoua	55	G1
Gary	76	D2
Garzê	34	C5
Garzón	90	C3
Gasan Kuli = Esenguly	29	F6
Gascogne	12	E4
Gascogne, G. de	12	D2
Gascony = Gascogne	12	E4
Gaspé	71	D4
Gaspé, C.	71	D4
Gaspésie, Pén. de la	71	D4
Gasteiz = Vitoria-Gasteiz	19	A4
Gastonia	83	B7
Gastre	95	E3
Gata, C. de	19	D4
Gata, Sierra de	18	B2
Gateshead	11	D6
Gauhati = Guwahati	41	D8
Gavāter	45	E5
Gávdhos	23	G5
Gävle	9	C9
Gawilgarh Hills	43	J10
Gawler	62	B2
Gaxun Nur	34	B5
Gaya, *India*	40	E5
Gaya, *Niger*	53	F6
Gayndah	63	A5
Gaysin = Haysyn	17	D9
Gayvoron = Hayvoron	17	D9
Gaza	47	E3
Gaziantep	46	C4
Gazimağosa = Famagusta	46	D3
Gdańsk	16	A4
Gdańska, Zatoka	16	A4
Gdov	24	B2
Gdynia	16	A4
Gebe	37	D3
Gebze	22	D7
Gedaref	55	F6
Gediz →	23	E6
Gedser	9	E8
Geelong	63	C3
Geesthacht	14	B6
Geidam	55	F1
Gejiu	34	D5
Gela	21	F5
Gelibolu	23	D6
Gelsenkirchen	14	C4
Gemena	56	D3
Gemerek	46	C4
Gemlik	23	D7
General Acha	94	D4
General Alvear,		
Buenos Aires, Argentina	94	D5
General Alvear, *Mendoza,*		
Argentina	94	D3
General Belgrano	94	D5
General Juan Madariaga	94	D5
General La Madrid	94	D4
General MacArthur	36	B3
General Pico	94	D4
General Pinedo	94	B4
General Santos	36	C3
General Villegas	94	D4

Geneva = Genève	14	E4
Geneva, L. = Léman, L.	13	C7
Genève	14	E4
Genil ➔	18	D3
Gennargentu, Mti. del	21	D2
Genoa = Génova	20	B2
Genoa	63	C4
Génova	20	B2
Génova, G. di	20	C2
Gent	14	C2
Genyem	37	E6
Georga, Zemlya	28	A5
George	58	E4
George ➔	70	C4
George, L., N.S.W., Australia	63	C4
George, L., S. Austral., Australia	62	C3
George River = Kangiqsualujjuaq	70	C4
George Sound	65	F2
George Town	38	C2
George V Land	96	A14
George VI Sound	96	B3
Georgetown = Janjanbureh	53	F3
Georgetown	90	B7
Georgia □	83	C6
Georgia ■	25	E5
Georgian B.	71	D2
Georgiu-Dezh = Liski	24	C4
Georgiyevsk	25	E5
Gera	15	C7
Geral de Goiás, Serra	93	E4
Geraldton	60	F1
Gerede	46	B3
Gereshk	42	D4
Germany ■	14	C6
Germiston	59	D5
Gernika-Lumo	19	A4
Gerona = Girona	19	B7
Geser	37	E4
Getafe	18	C4
Gettysburg	77	E7
Getxo	19	A4
Getz Ice Shelf	96	B18
Ghaghara ➔	40	E5
Ghana ■	53	G5
Ghanzi	58	C4
Ghardaïa	52	B6
Gharyān	54	B1
Ghat	54	D1
Ghawdex = Gozo	21	F5
Ghayl	47	G6
Ghazal, Bahr el ➔, Chad	55	F2
Ghazâl, Bahr el ➔, Sudan	57	C6
Ghaziabad	42	E10
Ghazipur	40	E4
Ghazni	42	C6
Ghazni □	42	C6
Ghent = Gent	14	C2
Gheorghe Gheorghiu-Dej = Oneşti	17	E8
Ghizao	42	C4
Ghowr □	42	C4
Ghugus	43	K11
Ghūriān	42	B2
Gia Lai = Plei Ku	38	B3
Giarabub = Al Jaghbūb	54	C3
Giarre	21	F5
Gibraltar ☑	18	D3
Gibraltar, Str. of	18	E3
Gibson Desert	60	E4
Giebnegáisi = Kebnekaise	8	B9
Giessen	14	C5
Gifu	33	F5
Giglio	20	C3
Gijón	18	A3
Gila ➔	78	D5
Gīlān □	46	C7
Gilbert Is.	64	J12
Gilgandra	63	B4
Gilgit	42	B9
Gilles, L.	62	B2
Gin Gin	63	A5
Ginir	49	F3
Gióna, Óros	23	E4
Giresun	46	B4
Girga	54	C5
Giridih	40	E6
Girne = Kyrenia	19	B7
Girona	12	D3
Gironde ➔	10	D4
Girvan	10	D4
Gisborne	64	C8
Gisenyi	57	E5
Gitega	57	E5
Giuba ➔	49	G3
Giurgiu	22	C5
Giza = El Gîza	54	C5
Gizycko	16	A5
Gjirokastër	23	D3
Gjoa Haven	68	B10
Glace Bay	71	D5
Gladstone, Queens., Australia	61	E9
Gladstone, S. Austral., Australia	62	B2
Glâma = Glomma ➔	9	C8
Glasgow	10	D4
Glazov	28	D6
Gleiwitz = Gliwice	16	C4
Glen Canyon △	79	B7
Glen Innes	63	A5
Glendale	78	C3
Glenelg ➔	62	C3
Glenmorgan	63	A4
Glenreagh	63	B5
Glenrothes	10	C5
Glens Falls	77	C9
Gliwice	16	C4
Głogów	16	C3
Glomma ➔	9	C8
Glorieuses, Is.	59	G9
Gloucester, Australia	63	B5
Gloucester, U.K.	11	F5
Glusk	17	B9
Gmünd	15	D8
Gmunden	15	E7
Gniezno	16	B3
Goa	43	M8
Goa □	43	M8
Goalen Hd.	63	C4
Goalpara	41	D8
Goba	49	F2
Gobabis	58	C3
Gobi	35	B6
Godavari ➔	40	J4
Godavari Pt.	40	J4
Godhra	43	H8
Gods ➔	69	C10
Gods L.	69	C10
Godthåb = Nuuk	70	B5
Godwin Austen = K2	42	B10
Goeie Hoop, Kaap die = Good Hope, C. of	58	E3
Gogra = Ghaghara ➔	40	E5
Goiânia	93	F4
Goiás	93	F3
Goiás □	93	E4
Goio-Erê	94	A6
Gojra	42	D8
Gökçeada	23	D5
Gökova Körfezi	23	F6
Gokteik	41	F11
Gold Coast	63	A5
Golden Gate	72	H2
Goldsboro	83	B9
Goleniów	16	B2
Golfo Aranci	20	D2
Golspie	10	C5
Goma	57	E5
Gomel = Homyel	17	B10
Gomera	52	C2
Gómez Palacio	84	B4
Gomogomo	37	F4
Gomoh	40	F6
Gompa = Ganta	53	G4
Gonäbäd	44	C4
Gonaïves	87	C5
Gonbad-e Kāvūs	44	B3
Gonda	40	D3
Gonder	55	F6
Gönen	23	D6
Gonghe	34	C5
Gongolgon	63	B4
Good Hope, C. of	58	E3
Goodooga	63	A4
Goolgowi	63	B4
Goondiwindi	63	A5
Gop	43	H6
Göppingen	14	D5
Gorakhpur	40	D4
Goražde	20	C7
Gordon ➔	62	D4
Gore, Ethiopia	55	G6
Gore, N.Z.	65	G3
Görgän	44	B3
Gorgona, I.	90	C3
Gorizia	20	B4
Gorkiy = Nizhniy Novgorod	24	B5
Gorkovskoye Vdkhr.	24	B5
Görlitz	15	C8
Gorlovka = Horlivka	25	D4
Gorna Dzhumayo = Blagoevgrad	22	C4
Gorna Oryakhovitsa	22	C5
Gorno-Altay □	29	D9
Gorno-Altaysk	29	D9
Gornyy	32	A3
Gorodenka = Horodenka	17	D7
Gorodok = Horodok	17	D6
Gorokhov = Horokhiv	17	C7
Gorontalo	37	D2
Gorzów Wielkopolski	16	B2
Gosford	63	B5
Goshogawara	32	C7
Goslar	14	C6
Gospič	20	B5
Göta kanal	9	D9
Göteborg	9	D8
Gotha	14	C6
Gothenburg = Göteborg	9	D8
Gotland	9	D9
Gotō-Rettō	33	G1
Göttingen	14	C5
Gottwaldov = Zlín	16	D3
Gouda	14	B3
Gouin, Rés.	71	D3
Goulburn	63	B4
Gouro	55	E2
Governador Valadares	93	F5
Goya	94	B5
Goyder Lagoon	62	A2
Goyllarisquisga	91	F3
Goz Beïda	55	F3
Gozo	21	F5
Graaff-Reinet	58	E4
Gračac	20	B5
Gracias a Dios, C.	86	D3
Grado	18	A2
Grafton	63	A5
Graham Bell, Ostrov = Greem-Bell, Ostrov	28	A7
Graham Land	96	A3
Grahamstown	59	E5
Grajaú	92	D4
Grajaú ➔	92	C5
Grampian Mts.	10	C4
Grampians, The	62	C3
Gran Canaria	52	C2
Gran Chaco	94	B4
Gran Paradiso	20	B1
Gran Sasso d'Itália	20	C4
Granada, Nic.	85	E7
Granada, Spain	18	D4
Granby	71	D3

Grand Bahama 86 A4
Grand Bassam 53 G5
Grand Canyon 79 B6
Grand Cayman 86 C3
Grand Coulee Dam .. 72 C4
Grand Forks 74 B6
Grand Island 74 E5
Grand Rapids, Canada . 69 C10
Grand Rapids, U.S.A. ... 76 C3
Grand St-Bernard, Col du . 13 D7
Grand Teton 73 E8
Grande →, Bolivia 91 G6
Grande →, Bahia, Brazil .. 93 E5
Grande →, Minas Gerais,
  Brazil 93 G3
Grande, B. 95 G3
Grande, Rio → 81 F5
Grande Baleine, R. de la → 71 C3
Granite City 75 F9
Granity 65 D4
Granja 92 C5
Granollers 19 B7
Grantham 11 E6
Granville 12 B3
Grasse 13 E7
Graulhet 12 E4
's-Gravenhage 14 B3
Gravesend 63 A5
Graz 15 E8
Great Abaco I. 86 A4
Great Australian Bight .. 60 G4
Great Barrier I. 64 B6
Great Barrier Reef 61 D8
Great Basin 72 G5
Great Bear → 68 B7
Great Bear L. 68 B7
Great Belt = Store Bælt .. 9 D8
Great Dividing Ra. 61 E8
Great Falls 73 C8
Great Inagua I. 86 B5
Great Indian Desert = Thar
  Desert 42 F7
Great Karoo 58 E4
Great Lake 62 D4
Great Ouse → 11 E7
Great Ruaha → 57 F7
Great Saint Bernard Pass =
  Grand St-Bernard, Col du 13 D7
Great Salt L. 73 F7
Great Salt Lake Desert .. 73 F7
Great Sandy Desert 60 E3
Great Sangi = Sangihe,
  Pulau 37 D3
Great Slave L. 68 B8
Great Smoky Mts. △ ... 83 B6
Great Victoria Desert .. 60 F4
Great Wall 35 C5
Great Yarmouth 11 E7
Greater Antilles 86 C5
Greater Sudbury = Sudbury 71 D2
Greater Sunda Is. 39 F4
Gredos, Sierra de 18 B3
Greece ■ 23 E4
Greeley 74 E2
Greem-Bell, Ostrov 28 A7
Green → 79 A8
Green Bay 76 B2
Green C. 63 C5
Greenland ☑ 66 C9
Greenock 10 D4
Greensboro 83 A8
Greenville, Ala., U.S.A. .. 82 D4
Greenville, Miss., U.S.A. .. 81 C8
Greenville, N.C., U.S.A. .. 83 B9
Greenville, S.C., U.S.A. .. 83 B6
Greenwood, Miss., U.S.A. .. 81 C8
Greenwood, S.C., U.S.A. .. 83 B6
Gregory, L. 62 A2
Greifswald 15 A7
Greiz 15 C7
Gremikha 28 C4
Grenada ■ 87 D7

Grenfell 63 B4
Grenoble 13 D6
Grey → 65 E4
Grey Ra. 63 A3
Greymouth 65 E4
Greytown 65 D6
Griffin 83 C5
Griffith 63 B4
Grimari 55 G3
Grimaylov = Hrymayliv . 17 D8
Grimsby 11 E6
Gris-Nez, C. 12 A4
Grodno = Hrodna 17 B6
Grodzyanka = Hrodzyanka 17 B9
Grójec 16 C5
Groningen 14 B4
Grootfontein 58 B3
Grosser Arber 15 D7
Grosseto 20 C3
Grossglockner 15 E7
Groznyy 25 E6
Grudziądz 16 B4
Gryazi 24 C4
Gryazovets 28 D5
Gua 40 F5
Guadalajara, Mexico .. 84 C4
Guadalajara, Spain ... 18 B4
Guadalcanal 64 K11
Guadalete → 18 D2
Guadalquivir → 18 D2
Guadalupe = Guadeloupe ☑ 87 C7
Guadalupe, Sierra de .. 18 C3
Guadarrama, Sierra de . 18 B4
Guadeloupe ☑ 87 C7
Guadiana → 18 D2
Guadix 18 D4
Guafo, Boca del 95 E2
Guaíra 94 A6
Guaitecas, Is. 95 E2
Guajará-Mirim 91 F5
Guajira, Pen. de la ... 90 A4
Gualeguaychú 94 C5
Guam ☑ 64 H9
Guamúchil 84 B3
Guanahani = San Salvador
  I. 86 B5
Guanajuato 84 C4
Guandacol 94 B3
Guane 86 B3
Guangdong □ 35 D6
Guangxi Zhuangzu
  Zizhiqu □ 35 D5
Guangzhou 35 D6
Guanipa → 90 B6
Guantánamo 86 B4
Guaporé → 91 F5
Guaqui 91 G5
Guarapuava 94 B6
Guarda 18 B2
Guardafui, C. = Asir, Ras .. 49 E5
Guasdualito 90 B4
Guatemala 85 E6
Guatemala ■ 85 D6
Guaviare → 90 C5
Guaxupé 93 G4
Guayama 87 C6
Guayaquil 90 D3
Guayaquil, G. de 90 D2
Guaymas 84 B2
Guddu Barrage 42 E6
Gudur 43 M11
Guecho = Getxo 19 A4
Guelph 76 C5
Guéret 12 C4
Guernica = Gernika-Lumo . 19 A4
Guernsey 11 G5
Guidónia-Montecélio .. 20 C4
Guildford 11 F6
Guilin 35 D6
Guimarães 18 B1
Guimaras □ 36 B2
Guinea ■ 53 F3
Guinea, Gulf of 51 F3

Guinea-Bissau ■ 53 F3
Guingamp 12 B2
Güiria 90 A6
Guiuan 36 B3
Guiyang 35 D5
Guizhou □ 35 D5
Gujarat □ 43 H7
Gujranwala 42 C9
Gujrat 42 C9
Gulbarga 43 L10
Gulf, The = Persian Gulf . 44 E2
Gulgong 63 B4
Güllük 23 F6
Gulshad 29 E8
Gulu 57 D6
Gümüşhane 46 B4
Gumzai 37 F4
Guna 43 G10
Gunnedah 63 B5
Gunningbar Cr. → 63 B4
Guntakal 43 M10
Guntur 40 J3
Gunungapi 37 F3
Gunungsitoli 39 D1
Gunza 56 G2
Gupis 42 A8
Gurdaspur 42 C9
Gurkha 40 C5
Gurley 63 A4
Gurupá 92 C3
Gurupá, I. Grande de .. 92 C3
Gurupi → 92 C4
Guryev = Atyraū 29 E6
Gusau 53 F7
Güstrow 15 B7
Gütersloh 14 C5
Guthrie 80 B5
Guwahati 41 D8
Guyana ■ 90 B7
Guyane française = French
  Guiana ☑ 92 B3
Guyenne 12 D4
Guyra 63 B5
Güzelyurt = Morphou .. 46 D3
Gwa 41 J10
Gwabegar 63 B4
Gwädar 42 G3
Gwalior 42 F11
Gwanda 59 C5
Gweru 59 B5
Gwydir → 63 A4
Gyandzha = Gäncä ... 25 E6
Gyaring Hu 34 C4
Gydanskiy Poluostrov .. 28 B8
Gympie 63 A5
Gyöngyös 16 E4
Győr 16 E3
Gyula 16 E5
Gyumri 25 E5
Gyzylarbat 29 F6

H

Haarlem 14 B3
Haast → 65 E3
Haboro 32 A7
Hachijō-Jima 33 G6
Hachinohe 32 C7
Hadarba, Ras 54 D6
Ḥadd, Ra's al 45 F4
Hadejia 53 F7
Hadera 46 D3
Ḥaḍramawt 49 D4
Haeju 35 C7
Haerhpin = Harbin ... 35 B7
Hafar al Bāṭin 47 E6
Hafizabad 42 C8
Haflong 41 E9
Haft Gel 47 E7

Hafun, Ras	49	E5
Hagen	14	C4
Hagerstown	77	E7
Hagi	33	F2
Hagondange	13	B7
Hague, C. de la	12	B3
Hague, The = 's-		
Gravenhage	14	B3
Haguenau	13	B7
Haifa = Ḥefa	46	D3
Haikou	35	D6
Ḥāʾil	47	F5
Hailar	35	B6
Hailuoto	8	B10
Hainan □	35	E5
Haiphong	35	D5
Haiti ■	87	C5
Haiya	55	E6
Hajdúböszörmény	16	E5
Hajnówka	17	B6
Hakodate	32	C7
Hala	42	G6
Ḥalab	46	D4
Ḥalabjah	54	D6
Halaib	15	C6
Halberstadt	64	D6
Halcombe	36	B2
Halcon	9	D8
Halden	40	F7
Haldia	42	E11
Haldwani	71	D4
Halifax, *Canada*	11	E6
Halifax, *U.K.*	44	E4
Halil →	70	B2
Hall Beach = Sanirajak	15	C6
Halle	62	B2
Hallett	9	D8
Halmahera	37	D3
Halmstad	9	D8
Hälsingborg = Helsingborg	44	E3
Ḥālūl	33	F3
Hamada	46	D7
Hamadān	46	D7
Hamadān □	46	D4
Hamāh	33	F5
Hamamatsu	8	C8
Hamar	14	B5
Hamburg	14	B5
Hämeenlinna	60	E2
Hameln	35	C7
Hamersley Ra.	34	B4
Hamhung	62	C3
Hami	71	D4
Hamilton, *Australia*	64	B6
Hamilton, *Canada*	10	D4
Hamilton, *N.Z.*	62	B2
Hamilton, *U.K.*	14	B5
Hamley Bridge	14	C4
Hamlin = Hameln	8	A10
Hamm	76	D2
Hammerfest	65	F4
Hammond	77	F7
Hampden	20	B7
Hampton	32	D7
Han Pijesak	14	C5
Hanamaki	35	C6
Hanau	34	B4
Handan	35	C7
Hangayn Nuruu	35	C7
Hangchou = Hangzhou	35	C7
Hangzhou	49	E3
Hangzhou Wan	9	D10
Ḥanish	42	C11
Hanko	65	E5
Hanle	69	C8
Hanmer Springs	75	F9
Hanna	14	B5
Hannibal	35	D5
Hannover	14	B5
Hanoi	95	G2
Hanover = Hannover		
Hanover, I.		

Hansi	42	E9
Hanson, L.	62	B2
Hantsavichy	17	B8
Hanzhong	35	C5
Haora	40	F7
Haparanda	8	B10
Happy Valley-Goose Bay	71	C4
Hapur	42	E10
Ḥaql	47	E3
Har	37	F4
Har Hu	34	C4
Har Us Nuur	34	B4
Ḥaraḍ	47	F7
Haranomachi	33	E7
Harare	59	B6
Haraz	55	F2
Harbin	35	B7
Hardangerfjorden	8	C7
Hardwar = Haridwar	42	E11
Hardy, Pen.	95	H3
Harer	49	F3
Hargeisa	49	F3
Hari →	39	E2
Haridwar	42	E11
Haringhata →	41	G7
Harirūd →	42	A2
Harlingen	80	F5
Harlow	11	F7
Harney Basin	72	E4
Härnösand	8	C9
Harris	10	C3
Harris L.	62	B2
Harrisburg	77	D7
Harrison, C.	70	C5
Harrogate	11	D6
Hart, L.	62	B2
Hartford	77	D9
Hartlepool	11	D6
Harvey	76	D2
Harwich	11	F7
Haryana □	42	E10
Haryn →	17	B8
Harz	14	C6
Hasa □	47	F7
Hassi Messaoud	52	B7
Hastings, *N.Z.*	64	C7
Hastings, *U.K.*	11	F7
Hastings, *U.S.A.*	74	E5
Hastings Ra.	63	B5
Hatay = Antalya	46	C2
Hatfield P.O.	62	B3
Hatgal	34	A5
Hathras	42	F11
Hatia	41	F8
Hattah	62	B3
Hatteras, C.	83	B10
Hattiesburg	81	D9
Hatvan	16	E4
Hau Bon = Cheo Reo	38	B3
Haugesund	9	D7
Hauraki G.	64	B6
Haut Atlas	52	B4
Havana = La Habana	86	B3
Havant	11	F6
Havel →	15	B7
Havelock	65	D5
Haverfordwest	11	F4
Havlíčkův Brod	16	D2
Havre	46	B3
Havza	78	J12
Hawai'i □	78	H12
Hawaiian Is.	65	F3
Hawea, L.	64	C6
Hawera	10	D5
Hawick	64	C7
Hawke B.	62	B2
Hawker	63	B3
Hay	68	B8
Hay River	37	E3
Haya = Tehoru	69	C10
Hayes →	22	D6
Hayrabolu		

Haysyn	17	D9
Hayvoron	17	D9
Hazārān, Kūh-e	44	D3
Hazaribag	40	F5
Healesville	63	C4
Hearst	71	D2
Hebei □	35	C6
Hebel	63	A4
Hebron = Al Khalīl	47	E3
Hebron	70	C4
Hechi	35	D5
Hechuan	35	C5
Heerlen	13	A6
Ḥefa	46	D3
Hefei	35	C6
Hegang	35	B8
Heidelberg	14	D5
Heilbronn	14	D5
Heilongjiang □	35	B7
Heimaey	8	C1
Heinze Kyun	41	K11
Hejaz = Ḥijāz □	47	F4
Hekimhan	46	C4
Hekou	34	D5
Helena, *Ark., U.S.A.*	81	B8
Helena, *Mont., U.S.A.*	73	C7
Helensville	64	B6
Helgoland	14	A4
Heligoland B. = Deutsche		
Bucht	14	A5
Hellespont = Çanakkale		
Boğazı	23	D6
Hellin	19	C5
Helmand □	42	D3
Helmand →	42	D2
Helmsdale	10	B5
Helsingborg	9	D8
Helsinki	9	C11
Helwân	54	C5
Hemel Hempstead	11	F6
Henan □	35	C6
Henares →	18	B4
Henashi-Misaki	32	C6
Henderson	83	A8
Hengyang	35	D6
Henrietta Maria, C.	71	C2
Hentiyn Nuruu	35	B5
Henty	63	C4
Henzada	41	J10
Heraklion = Iráklion	23	G5
Herät	42	B3
Herät □	42	B3
Herceg-Novi	22	C2
Hereford	11	E5
Herford	14	B5
Hermidale	63	B4
Hermite, I.	95	H3
Hermon, Mt. = Shaykh, J.		
ash	46	D3
Hermosillo	84	B2
Hernád →	16	E5
Heroica Nogales = Nogales	84	A2
's-Hertogenbosch	14	C3
Hessen □	14	C5
Hexham	62	C3
Heywood	83	G7
Hialeah	75	B8
Hibbing	62	D4
Hibbs B.	83	B7
Hickory	63	C4
Hicks, Pt.	84	B3
Hidalgo del Parral	33	E7
Higashiajima-San	33	F4
Higashiōsaka	35	B8
High Point	69	C8
High River	16	D4
High Tatra = Tatry	11	F6
High Wycombe	24	B1
Hiiumaa	47	E6
Ḥijārah, Ṣaḥrā' al	47	F4
Ḥijāz □	36	C3
Hijo = Tagum		

Hikurangi

Hikurangi, *Gisborne, N.Z.* . 64 C7
Hikurangi, *Northland, N.Z.* . 64 A6
Hildesheim 14 B5
Hillston 63 B4
Hilo 78 J13
Hilversum 14 B3
Himachal Pradesh □ 42 D10
Himalaya 40 C5
Himatnagar 43 H8
Himeji 33 F4
Himi 33 E5
Ḥimş 46 D4
Hindmarsh, L. 62 C3
Hindu Bagh 42 D5
Hindu Kush 42 B7
Hindupur 43 N10
Hinganghat 43 J11
Hingoli 43 K10
Hinna = Imi 49 F3
Hinojosa del Duque 18 C3
Hirakud Dam 40 G4
Hiroo 32 B8
Hirosaki 32 C7
Hiroshima 33 F3
Hisar 42 E9
Hispaniola 87 C5
Hitachi 33 E7
Hjälmaren 9 D9
Hkakabo Razi 41 C11
Hlyboka 17 D7
Ho Chi Minh City = Thanh
    Pho Ho Chi Minh 38 B3
Hoai Nhon 38 B3
Hoare B. 70 B4
Hobart 62 D4
Hobbs Coast 96 B18
Hodaka-Dake 33 E5
Hodeida = Al Ḩudaydah . . 49 E3
Hodgson 69 C10
Hódmezővásárhely 16 E5
Hodna, Chott el 52 A6
Hodonín 16 D3
Hoek van Holland 14 B3
Hof 15 C7
Hofsjökull 8 C2
Hōfu 33 F2
Hogan Group 62 C4
Hoggar = Ahaggar 52 D7
Hoher Rhön = Rhön 14 C5
Hohhot 35 B6
Hoi An 38 A3
Hokianga Harbour 64 A5
Hokitika 65 E4
Hokkaidō □ 32 B8
Holbrook 63 C4
Holguín 86 B4
Hollandia = Jayapura 37 E6
Hollywood 83 G7
Holman 68 A8
Holstebro 9 D7
Holyhead 11 E4
Homalin 41 E10
Hombori 53 E5
Home B. 70 B4
Homer 69 C4
Homs = Ḥimş 46 D4
Homyel 17 B10
Hon Chong 38 B2
Honan = Henan □ 35 C6
Honbetsu 32 B8
Honduras ■ 85 E7
Honduras, G. de 85 D7
Hønefoss 9 C8
Honfleur 12 B4
Hong Kong □ 35 D6
Hongjiang 35 D5
Hongshui He ➤ 35 D5
Hongze Hu 35 C6
Honiara 64 K10
Honjō 32 D7
Honolulu 78 H12
Honshū 33 F4

Hood, Mt. 72 D3
Hooghly = Hugli ➤ 40 G7
Hook of Holland = Hoek van
    Holland 14 B3
Hoorn 14 B3
Hoover Dam 78 B5
Hope, L. 62 A2
Hopedale 70 C4
Hopei = Hebei □ 35 C6
Hopetoun 62 C3
Hopetown 58 D4
Hoquiam 72 C2
Horlick Mts. 96 C1
Horlivka 25 D4
Hormoz 44 E3
Hormoz, Jaz.-ye 44 E4
Hormozgān □ 44 E3
Hormuz, Str. of 44 E4
Horn 15 D8
Horn, Cape = Hornos, C. de 95 H3
Hornavan 8 B9
Hornos, C. de 95 H3
Horodenka 17 D7
Horodok, *Khmelnytskyy,*
    Ukraine 17 D8
Horodok, *Lviv, Ukraine* . . 17 D6
Horokhiv 17 C7
Horqin Youyi Qianqi 35 B7
Horqueta 94 A5
Horsham 62 C3
Horton ➤ 68 B7
Hose, Gunung-Gunung . . . 39 D4
Hoshangabad 43 H10
Hoshiarpur 42 D9
Hospet 43 M10
Hoste, I. 95 H3
Hot Springs 81 B7
Hotan 34 C2
Houhora Heads 64 A5
Houlton 77 A12
Houma 81 E8
Houston 81 E6
Hovd 34 B4
Hövsgöl Nuur 34 A5
Howard 63 A5
Howe, C. 63 C5
Howitt, L. 62 A2
Howrah = Haora 40 F7
Høyanger 8 C7
Hoyerswerda 15 C8
Hpa-an = Pa-an 41 J11
Hpungan Pass 41 D11
Hradec Králové 16 C2
Hrodna 17 B6
Hrodzyanka 17 B9
Hrvatska = Croatia ■ 20 B6
Hrymayliv 17 D8
Hsenwi 41 F11
Hsiamen = Xiamen 35 D6
Hsian = Xi'an 35 C5
Hsinhailien = Lianyungang 35 C6
Hsüchou = Xuzhou 35 C6
Hua Hin 38 B1
Huacho 91 F3
Huai He ➤ 35 C6
Huainan 35 C6
Huallaga ➤ 90 E3
Huambo 58 A3
Huancabamba 91 E3
Huancane 91 G5
Huancavelica 91 F3
Huancayo 91 F3
Huang Hai = Yellow Sea . . 35 C7
Huang He ➤ 35 C6
Huangshan 35 D6
Huangshi 35 C6
Huánuco 91 E3
Huaraz 91 E3
Huarmey 91 F3
Huascarán 91 E3

Huasco 94 B2
Huatabampo 84 B3
Hubei □ 35 C6
Hubli 43 M9
Huddersfield 11 E6
Hudiksvall 8 C9
Hudson ➤ 77 D8
Hudson Bay 70 B2
Hudson Mts. 96 B2
Hudson Str. 70 B4
Hue 38 A3
Huelva 18 D2
Huesca 19 A5
Hughenden 61 E7
Hugli ➤ 40 G7
Huila, Nevado del 90 C3
Huinca Renancó 94 C4
Huize 34 D5
Hukawng Valley 41 D11
Ḩulayfā' 47 F5
Huld = Ulaanjirem 35 B5
Hull = Kingston upon Hull 11 E6
Hull 71 D3
Hulun Nur 35 B6
Humahuaca 94 A3
Humaitá 91 E6
Humber ➤ 11 E6
Humboldt 69 C9
Humboldt ➤ 72 F4
Hume, L. 63 C4
Hūn 54 C2
Húnaflói 8 B1
Hunan □ 35 D6
Hunedoara 17 F6
Hungary ■ 16 E4
Hungerford 63 A3
Huŋnam 35 C7
Hunsrück 14 D4
Hunter I. 62 D3
Hunter Ra. 63 B5
Hunterville 64 C6
Huntington 76 E4
Huntington Beach 78 D3
Huntly, *N.Z.* 64 B6
Huntly, *U.K.* 10 C5
Huntsville 82 B4
Huonville 62 D4
Hupeh = Hubei □ 35 C6
Huron, L. 76 B4
Hurunui ➤ 65 E5
Húsavík 8 B2
Huşi 17 E9
Hutchinson 80 A5
Hutton, Mt. 63 A4
Hvar 20 C6
Hwang Ho = Huang He ➤ . 35 C6
Hwange 59 B5
Hyargas Nuur 34 B4
Hyderabad, *India* 43 L11
Hyderabad, *Pakistan* 42 G6
Hyères 13 E7
Hyères, Is. d' 13 E7
Hyūga 33 G2

I

I-n-Gall 53 E7
Iaco ➤ 91 E5
Ialomiţa ➤ 22 B6
Iaşi 17 E8
Iba 36 A2
Ibadan 53 G6
Ibagué 90 C3
Ibar ➤ 22 C3
Ibarra 90 C3
Ibiá 93 F4
Ibiapaba, Sa. da 92 C5
Ibiza = Eivissa 19 C6
Ibonma 37 E4

Ibotirama	93	E5
Ibu	37	D3
Ibusuki	33	H2
Ica	91	F3
Iça ➔	90	D5
Içana	90	C5
Içel = Mersin	46	C3
Iceland ■	8	B2
Ich'ang = Yichang	35	C6
Ichchapuram	40	H5
Ichihara	33	F7
Ichilo ➔	91	G6
Ichinomiya	33	F5
Ichinoseki	32	D7
Idaho □	73	D7
Idaho Falls	73	E7
Idar-Oberstein	14	D4
Idfû	54	D5
Ídhi Óros	23	G5
Ídhra	23	F4
Idi	38	C1
Idiofa	56	E3
Idlib	46	D4
Ierápetra	23	G5
Iesi	20	C4
Ife	53	G6
Iforas, Adrar des	52	E6
Igarapava	93	G4
Igarka	28	C9
Iglésias	21	E2
Igloolik	70	B2
Igluligaarjuk = Chesterfield		
Inlet	68	B10
Iglulik = Igloolik	70	B2
İğneada Burnu	22	D7
Igoumenítsa	23	E3
Iguaçu ➔	94	B6
Iguaçu, Cat. del	94	B6
Iguala	84	D5
Igualada	19	B6
Iguassu = Iguaçu ➔	94	B6
Iguatu	92	D6
Iharana	59	G10
Ihosy	59	J9
Iida	33	F5
Iisalmi	8	C11
Ijebu-Ode	53	G6
IJsselmeer	14	B3
Ikaluktutiak	68	B9
Ikaría	23	F6
Ikeda	33	F3
Ikela	56	E4
Iki	33	G1
Ikparjuk = Arctic Bay	70	A2
Ilagan	36	A2
Ilâm	46	D6
Iława	16	B4
Île ➔	29	E8
Île-de-France □	12	B5
Ilebo	56	E4
Ilesha	53	G6
Ilhéus	93	E6
Ili = Ile ➔	29	E8
Iligan	36	C2
Illampu = Ancohuma,		
Nevada	91	G5
Illana B.	36	C2
Illapel	94	C2
Iller ➔	14	D5
Illimani, Nevado	91	G5
Illium = Troy	23	E6
Ilmen, Ozero	24	B3
Ilo	91	G4
Iloilo	36	B2
Ilorin	53	G6
Ilwaki	37	F3
Imabari	33	F3
Imandra, Ozero	28	C4
Imari	33	G1
Imatra	8	C11
imeni 26 Bakinskikh		
Komissarov = Neftçala	46	C7
Imeri, Serra	90	C5
Imi	49	F3
Ímola	20	B3
Imperatriz	92	D4
Impéria	20	C2
Imperial Dam	78	D5
Impfondo	56	D3
Imphal	41	E9
Imroz = Gökçeada	23	D5
Imuruan B.	36	B1
In Salah	52	C6
Ina	33	F5
Inangahua	65	D4
Inanwatan	37	E4
Iñapari	91	F5
Inari	8	B11
Inarijärvi	8	B11
Inca	19	C7
Ince Burun	46	B3
Inch'ŏn	35	C7
Incirliova	23	F6
Incomáti ➔	59	D6
Indalsälven ➔	8	C9
Indaw	41	E11
Independence, Kans.,		
U.S.A.	81	A6
Independence, Mo., U.S.A.	75	F7
India ■	43	J10
Indian ➔	83	F7
Indiana □	76	D3
Indianapolis	76	E2
Indigirka ➔	31	B12
Indira Gandhi Canal	42	F8
Indonesia ■	39	E4
Indore	43	H9
Indravati ➔	40	H3
Indre ➔	12	C4
Indus ➔	43	G5
İnebolu	46	B3
Inglewood, Queens.,		
Australia	63	A5
Inglewood, Vic., Australia	62	C3
Inglewood, N.Z.	64	C6
Ingolstadt	15	D6
Ingraj Bazar	40	E7
Ingrid Christensen Coast	96	A10
Ingulec = Inhulec	25	D3
Inhambane	59	C7
Inharrime	59	C7
Inhulec	25	D3
Ining = Yining	34	B3
Inírida ➔	90	C5
Injune	63	A4
Inland Kaikoura Ra.	65	D5
Inland Sea	33	F3
Inle L.	41	G11
Inn ➔	15	D7
Innamincka	62	A3
Inner Hebrides	10	C3
Inner Mongolia = Nei		
Monggol Zizhiqu □	35	B6
Innsbruck	15	E6
Inongo	56	E3
Inoucdjouac = Inukjuak	70	C3
Inowrocław	16	B4
Insein	41	J11
International Falls	75	A8
Inukjuak	70	C3
Inútil, B.	95	G2
Inuvik	68	B6
Invercargill	65	G3
Inverell	63	A5
Invergordon	10	C4
Inverness	10	C4
Inverurie	10	C5
Investigator Group	62	B1
Investigator Str.	62	C2
Inya	29	D9
Inza	24	C6
Ioánnina	23	E3
Ionian Is. = Iónioi Nísoi	23	E3
Ionian Sea	21	F6
Iónioi Nísoi	23	E3
Íos	23	F5
Iowa □	75	D8
Iowa City	75	E9
Ipameri	93	F4
Ipatinga	93	F5
Ipiales	90	C3
Ipin = Yibin	35	D5
Ipixuna	91	E4
Ipoh	38	D2
Ippy	56	C4
Ipsala	22	D6
Ipswich, Australia	63	A5
Ipswich, U.K.	11	E7
Ipu	92	C5
Iqaluit	70	B4
Iquique	91	H4
Iquitos	90	D4
Iracoubo	92	A3
Iráklion	23	G5
Iran ■	44	C3
Iran, Gunung-Gunung	39	D4
Īrānshahr	45	E5
Irapuato	84	C4
Iraq ■	46	D5
Ireland ■	11	E3
Irian Jaya = Papua □	37	E5
Iringa	57	F7
Iriri ➔	92	C3
Irish Republic = Ireland ■	11	E3
Irish Sea	11	E4
Irkutsk	30	D8
Irö-Zaki	33	F6
Iron Baron	62	B2
Iron Gate = Portile de Fier	22	B4
Iron Knob	62	B2
Ironwood	75	B9
Irpin	17	C10
Irrara Cr. ➔	63	A4
Irrawaddy □	41	J10
Irrawaddy ➔	41	K10
Irrawaddy, Mouths of the	41	K10
Irtysh ➔	28	C7
Irún	19	A5
Irunea = Pamplona	19	A5
Irvine	10	D4
Irymple	62	B3
Isabela	36	C2
Ísafjörður	8	B1
Isahaya	33	G2
Ísar ➔	15	D7
Ischia	21	D4
Ise-Wan	33	F5
Isère ➔	13	D6
Isérnia	20	D5
Isfahan = Eşfahān	44	C2
Ishikari-Gawa ➔	32	B7
Ishikari-Wan	32	B7
Ishim ➔	29	D8
Ishinomaki	32	D7
Ishkuman	42	A8
Isil Kul	29	D8
Isiro	57	D5
Iskenderun	46	C4
İskůr ➔	22	C5
Islamabad	42	C8
Island L.	69	C10
Island Lagoon	62	B2
Islay	10	D3
Isle ➔	12	D3
Isle of Wight □	11	F6
Ismail = Izmayil	17	F9
Ismâ'ilîya	47	E3
Ísparta	46	C2
Íspica	21	F5
Israel ■	46	E3
Issoire	13	D5
Issyk-Kul, Ozero = Ysyk-Köl	29	E8
İstanbul	22	D7
İstanbul Boğazı	22	D7
Istiaia	23	E4
Istra	20	B4

Istres

Istres 13 E6
Istria = Istra 20 B4
Itaberaba 93 E5
Itabira 93 F5
Itabuna 93 E6
Itaipú, Reprêsa de 94 B6
Itaituba 92 C2
Itajaí 94 B7
Italy ■ 20 C4
Itapecuru-Mirim 92 C5
Itaperuna 93 G5
Itapicuru →, Bahia, Brazil . 93 E6
Itapicuru →, Maranhão,
  Brazil 92 C5
Itapípoca 92 C6
Itaquí 94 B5
Ithaca = Itháki 23 E3
Itháki 23 E3
Itô 33 F6
Itonamas → 91 F6
Ituiutaba 93 F4
Itumbiara 93 F4
Iturbe 94 A3
Itzehoe 14 B5
Ivanava 17 B7
Ivanhoe 63 B3
Ivano-Frankivsk 17 D7
Ivanovo = Ivanava 17 B7
Ivanovo 24 B5
Ivatsevichy 17 B7
Ivory Coast ■ 53 G4
Ivrea 20 B1
Ivujivik 70 B3
Iwaizumi 32 D7
Iwaki 33 E7
Iwakuni 33 F3
Iwamizawa 32 B7
Iwanai 32 B7
Iwata 33 F5
Iwate-San 32 D7
Iwo 53 G6
Ixiamas 91 F5
Izhevsk 28 D6
Izmayil 17 F9
Izmir 23 E6
Izmit = Kocaeli 25 E2
Iznik Gölü 23 D7
Izu-Shotō 33 F7
Izumi-Sano 33 F4
Izumo 33 F3
Izyaslav 17 C8

J

Jabalpur 43 H11
Jablah 46 D4
Jablonec nad Nisou 16 C2
Jaboatão 92 D6
Jaca 19 A5
Jacareí 94 A7
Jackson, Mich., U.S.A. . . . 76 C3
Jackson, Miss., U.S.A. . . . 81 C8
Jackson, Tenn., U.S.A. . . . 82 B3
Jackson B. 65 E4
Jacksons 65 E4
Jacksonville, Fla., U.S.A. . 83 D7
Jacksonville, Ill., U.S.A. .. 75 F9
Jacksonville, N.C., U.S.A. . 83 B9
Jacmel 87 C5
Jacobabad 42 E6
Jacobina 93 E5
Jacundá → 92 C3
Jadotville = Likasi 57 G5
Jaén, Peru 91 E3
Jaén, Spain 18 D4
Jaffa = Tel Aviv-Yafo 46 D3
Jaffa, C. 62 C2
Jaffna 43 Q12
Jagadhri 42 D10

Jagdalpur 40 H3
Jagodina 22 B3
Jagraon 42 D9
Jagtial 43 K11
Jaguariaíva 94 A7
Jaguaribe → 92 C6
Jahrom 44 D3
Jailolo 37 D3
Jailolo, Selat 37 D3
Jaipur 42 F9
Jakarta 39 F3
Jalālābād 42 B7
Jalapa Enríquez = Xalapa . 84 D5
Jalgaon 43 J9
Jalna 43 K9
Jalón → 19 B5
Jalpaiguri 41 D7
Jaluit I. 64 J11
Jamaica ■ 86 C4
Jamalpur, Bangla. 41 E7
Jamalpur, India 40 E6
Jamanxim → 92 C2
Jambi 39 E2
Jambi □ 39 E2
James → 74 D6
James B. 71 C2
James Ross I. 96 A4
Jamestown, Australia 62 B2
Jamestown, N. Dak., U.S.A. 74 B5
Jamestown, N.Y., U.S.A. . . 77 C6
Jamkhandi 43 L9
Jammu 42 C9
Jammu & Kashmir □ 42 B10
Jamnagar 43 H7
Jamshedpur 40 F6
Jand 42 C8
Jandaq 44 C3
Jandowae 63 A5
Janesville 75 D10
Janjanbureh 53 F3
Januária 93 F5
Jaora 43 H9
Japan ■ 33 F5
Japan, Sea of 32 D4
Japen = Yapen 37 E5
Japurá → 90 D5
Jaú 90 B3
Jarama → 18 B4
Jargalant = Hovd 34 B4
Jarvis I. 65 K15
Jarwa 40 D4
Jåsk 44 E4
Jasper 82 C4
Jászberény 16 E4
Jatai 93 F3
Játiva = Xátiva 19 C5
Jaú 93 G4
Jauja 91 F3
Jaunpur 40 E4
Java = Jawa 39 F3
Java Sea 39 E3
Jawa 39 F3
Jaya, Puncak 37 E5
Jayanti 41 D7
Jayapura 37 E6
Jayawijaya, Pegunungan . 37 E5
Jaynagar 40 D6
Jebel, Bahr el → 55 G5
Jedburgh 10 D5
Jedda = Jiddah 47 G4
Jędrzejów 16 C5
Jefferson City 75 F8
Jega 53 F6
Jelenia Góra 16 C2
Jelgava 24 B1
Jembongan 38 C5
Jena 15 C6
Jeparit 62 C3
Jequié 93 E5
Jequitinhonha 93 F5
Jequitinhonha → 93 F6
Jérémie 86 C5

Jerez de la Frontera 18 D2
Jerez de los Caballeros . . . 18 C2
Jerid, Chott el = Djerid,
  Chott 52 B7
Jerilderie 63 C4
Jersey 11 G5
Jersey City 77 D8
Jerusalem 47 E3
Jervis B. 63 C5
Jesi = Iesi 20 C4
Jesselton = Kota Kinabalu . 38 C5
Jessore 41 F7
Jeypore 40 H4
Jhal Jhao 42 F4
Jhalawar 43 G10
Jhang Maghiana 42 D8
Jhansi 43 G11
Jharsuguda 40 G5
Jhelum 42 C8
Jhelum → 42 D8
Jhunjhunu 42 E9
Jiamusi 35 B8
Ji'an 35 D6
Jiangmen 35 D6
Jiangsu □ 35 C6
Jiangxi □ 35 D6
Jiao Xian = Jiaozhou 35 C7
Jiaozhou 35 C7
Jiaxing 35 C7
Jiayi = Chiai 35 D7
Jibuti = Djibouti ■ 49 E3
Jiddah 47 G4
Jido 41 C10
Jihlava 16 D3
Jihlava → 16 D3
Jijiga 49 F3
Jilin 35 B7
Jilong = Chilung 35 D7
Jima 55 G6
Jiménez 84 B4
Jinan 35 C6
Jindabyne 63 C4
Jindřichův Hradec 16 D2
Jingdezhen 35 D6
Jinggu 34 D5
Jinhua 35 D6
Jining,
  Nei Monggol Zizhiqu,
  China 35 B6
Jining, Shandong, China . 35 C6
Jinja 57 D6
Jinnah Barrage 42 C7
Jinzhou 35 B7
Jiparaná → 91 E6
Jipijapa 90 D2
Jiu → 22 C4
Jiujiang 35 D6
Jixi 35 B8
Jizzakh 29 E7
Joaçaba 94 B6
João Pessoa 92 D7
Joaquín V. González 94 B4
Jodhpur 42 F8
Joensuu 8 C11
Jogjakarta = Yogyakarta . 39 F4
Johannesburg 59 D5
Johnson City 83 A6
Johnston Falls =
  Mambilima Falls 57 G5
Johnstown 77 D6
Johor Baharu 39 D2
Joinville 94 B7
Joinville I. 96 A4
Joliet 76 D1
Joliette 71 D3
Jolo 36 C2
Jonesboro 81 B8
Jönköping 9 D8
Jonquière 71 D3
Joplin 81 A6
Jordan ■ 47 E4
Jorhat 41 D10

Jorong 39 E4
Jos 53 G7
Jotunheimen 8 C7
Jowzjān □ 45 B6
Juan de Fuca Str. 72
Juan Fernández, Arch. de . 89 G3
Juárez 94 D5
Juàzeiro 93 D5
Juàzeiro do Norte 92 D6
Juba = Giuba → 49 G3
Jubbulpore = Jabalpur .. 43 H11
Juby, C. 52 C3
Júcar = Xúquer → 19 C5
Juchitán 85 D5
Jugoslavia = Serbia &
  Montenegro ■ 22 B3
Juiz de Fora 93 G5
Juli 91 G5
Juliaca 91 G4
Julianehåb = Qaqortoq .. 70 B6
Jullundur 42 D9
Jumilla 19 C5
Jumla 40 C4
Jumna = Yamuna → 40 E3
Junagadh 43 J7
Jundiai 94 A7
Juneau 69 C6
Junee 63 B4
Junggar Pendi 34 B3
Junin 94 C4
Junin de los Andes 95 D2
Juniyah 46 D3
Jur, Nahr el → 55 G4
Jura = Jura, Mts. du 13 C7
Jura = Schwäbische Alb . 14 D5
Jura 10 D4
Jura, Mts. du 13 C7
Juruá → 90 D5
Juruena → 91 E7
Juruti 92 C3
Justo Daract 94 C3
Jutland = Jylland 9 D7
Juventud, I. de la 86 B3
Jylland 9 D7
Jyväskylä 8 C11

K

K2 .... 42 B10
Kaapstad = Cape Town .. 58 E3
Kabaena 37 F2
Kabala 53 G3
Kabale 57 E6
Kabalo 57 F5
Kabanjahe 39 D1
Kabarai 37 E4
Kabardino-Balkaria □ ... 25 E5
Kabarega Falls = Murchison
  Falls 57 D6
Kabasalan 36 C2
Kabompo → 58 A4
Kabongo 57 F5
Kabūd Gonbad 44 B4
Kābul 42 B6
Kābul □ 42 B6
Kābul → 42 C8
Kaburuang 37 D3
Kabwe 59 A5
Kachchh, Gulf of 43 H6
Kachchh, Rann of 43 G6
Kachin □ 41 D11
Kachiry 29 D8
Kaçkar 25 E5
Kadan Kyun 38 B1
Kadina 62 B2
Kadiyevka = Stakhanov . 25 D4
Kadoma 59 B5
Kādugli 55 F4
Kaduna 53 F7

Kaédi 53 E3
Kaesŏng 35 C7
Käf 47 E4
Kafan = Kapan 25 F6
Kafanchan 53 G7
Kafirévs, Ákra 23 E5
Kafue 59 B5
Kaga Bandoro 56 C3
Kagan 29 F7
Kağızman 46 B5
Kagoshima 33 H2
Kagul = Cahul 17 F9
Kahayan → 39 E4
Kahnūj 44 E4
Kaho'olawe 78 H12
Kahramanmaraş 46 C4
Kai, Kepulauan 37 F4
Kai Besar 37 F4
Kai Kecil 37 F4
Kaiapoi 65 E5
Kaifeng 35 C6
Kaikohe 64 A5
Kaikoura 65 E5
Kaimana 37 E4
Kaimanawa Mts. 64 C6
Kainji Res. 53 F6
Kaipara Harbour 64 B6
Kaironi 37 E4
Kairouan 54 A1
Kaiserslautern 14 D4
Kaitaia 64 A5
Kaitangata 65 G3
Kajaani 8 C11
Kajabbi 61 D6
Kajo Kaji 55 H5
Kakamega 57 D6
Kakanui Mts. 65 F4
Kakhovka 25 D3
Kakhovske Vdskh. 25 D3
Kakinada 40 J4
Kalaallit Nunaat =
  Greenland ☑ 66 C9
Kalabagh 42 C7
Kalabahi 37 F2
Kalach 24 C5
Kaladan → 41 G9
Kalahari 58 C4
Kalakan 31 D9
Kálamai 23 F4
Kalamata = Kálamai ... 23 F4
Kalamazoo 76 C3
Kalan 46 C4
Kalao 37 F2
Kalaotoa 37 F2
Kalat 42 E5
Kalce 20 B5
Kale 23 F7
Kalegauk Kyun 41 K11
Kalemie 57 F5
Kalewa 41 F10
Kalgan = Zhangjiakou .. 35 B6
Kalgoorlie-Boulder 60 G3
Kaliakra, Nos 22 C7
Kalibo 36 B2
Kalima 57 E5
Kalimantan 39 E4
Kalimantan Barat □ 39 D4
Kalimantan Selatan □ .. 39 E5
Kalimantan Tengah □ .. 39 E4
Kalimantan Timur □ ... 39 D5
Kálimnos 23 F6
Kalinin = Tver 24 B4
Kaliningrad 24 C1
Kalinkavichy 17 B9
Kalispell 73 B6
Kalisz 16 C4
Kallsjön 8 C8
Kalmar 9 D9
Kalmykia □ 25 D6
Kalocsa 16 E4

Kaluga 24 C4
Kalush 17 D7
Kalutara 43 R11
Kama → 29 D6
Kamaishi 32 D7
Kamarān 49 D3
Kamchatka, Poluostrov . 31 D13
Kamchatka Pen. =
  Kamchatka, Poluostrov . 31 D13
Kamchiya → 22 C6
Kamen 29 D9
Kamen-Rybolov 32 A3
Kamenjak, Rt 20 B4
Kamenka Bugskaya =
  Kamyanka-Buzka 17 C7
Kamensk Uralskiy 29 D7
Kamin-Kashyrskyy 17 C7
Kamina 57 F5
Kamloops 69 C7
Kampala 57 D6
Kampar → 39 D2
Kampen 14 B3
Kampong Chhnang 38 B2
Kampong Saom 38 B2
Kampot 38 B2
Kampuchea = Cambodia ■ 38 B3
Kampungbaru = Tolitoli . 37 D2
Kamrau, Teluk 37 E4
Kamui-Misaki 32 B7
Kamyanets-Podilskyy .. 17 D8
Kamyanka-Buzka 17 C7
Kamyshin 24 C6
Kanagi 32 C7
Kananga 56 F4
Kanash 24 B6
Kanastraíon, Ákra =
  Palioúrion, Ákra 23 E4
Kanazawa 33 E5
Kanchanaburi 38 B1
Kanchenjunga 40 D7
Kanchipuram 43 N11
Kandahar = Qandahār .. 42 D4
Kandalaksha 8 B12
Kandangan 39 E5
Kandi 53 F6
Kandla 43 H7
Kandos 63 B4
Kandy 43 R12
Kangaroo I. 62 C2
Kangâvar 46 D7
Kangean, Kepulauan ... 39 F5
Kangerlussuaq 70 B5
Kangiqliniq = Rankin Inlet . 68 B10
Kangiqsualujjuaq 70 C4
Kangiqsujuaq 70 B3
Kangiqtugaapik = Clyde
  River 70 A4
Kangirsuk 70 C4
Kangnŭng 35 C7
Kangto 41 D9
Kaniapiskau =
  Caniapiscau → 70 C4
Kaniapiskau, L. =
  Caniapiscau, L. de ... 71 C4
Kanin, Poluostrov 28 C5
Kanin Nos, Mys 28 C5
Kaniva 62 C3
Kankakee 76 D2
Kankan 53 F4
Kankendy = Xankändi .. 25 F6
Kanker 40 G3
Kannapolis 83 B7
Kannauj 42 F11
Kannod 43 H10
Kano 53 F7
Kanowit 39 D4
Kanoya 33 H2
Kanpetlet 41 G9
Kanpur 40 D3
Kansas □ 74 F5
Kansas City, *Kans.*, U.S.A. 75 F7
Kansas City, *Mo.*, U.S.A. . 75 F7

Kansk

Kansk	30	D7
Kansu = Gansu □	34	C5
Kanye	59	C5
Kaohsiung	35	D7
Kaolack	53	F2
Kapan	25	F6
Kapanga	56	F4
Kapchagai = Qapshaghay	29	E8
Kapela = Velika Kapela	20	B5
Kapfenberg	15	E8
Kapiri Mposhi	59	A5
Käpisä □	45	C7
Kapit	39	D4
Kapoeta	55	H5
Kaposvár	16	E3
Kaptai L.	41	F9
Kapuas →	39	E3
Kapuas Hulu, Pegunungan	39	D4
Kapunda	62	B2
Kapuni	64	C6
Kaputar	63	B5
Kara	28	C7
Kara Bogaz Gol, Zaliv = Garabogazköl Aylagy	29	E6
Kara Kalpak Republic = Qoraqalpoghistan □	29	E6
Kara Kum	29	E6
Kara Sea	28	B8
Karabiğa	23	D6
Karabük	46	B3
Karaburun	23	E6
Karabutak = Qarabutaq	29	E7
Karacabey	23	D7
Karacasu	23	F7
Karachi	43	G5
Karad	43	L9
Karaganda = Qaraghandy	29	E8
Karagayly	29	E8
Karaikal	43	P11
Karaikkudi	43	P11
Karakalpakstan = Qoraqalpoghistan □	29	E6
Karakelong	36	D3
Karakitang	37	D3
Karaklis = Vanadzor	25	E5
Karakol	29	E8
Karakoram Pass	42	B10
Karakoram Ra.	42	B10
Karalon	30	D9
Karaman	46	C3
Karamay	34	B3
Karambu	39	E5
Karamea Bight	65	D4
Karasburg	58	D3
Karasino	28	C9
Karasuk	29	D8
Karatau, Khrebet = Qarataū	29	E7
Karatsu	33	G2
Karawanken	20	A5
Karazhal	29	E8
Karbalā'	47	D6
Karcag	16	E5
Kardhítsa	23	E3
Karelia □	8	C12
Kargasok	29	D9
Kargat	29	D9
Kargil	42	B10
Kariba, L.	59	B5
Kariba Dam	59	B5
Kariba Gorge	59	B5
Karimata, Kepulauan	39	E3
Karimata, Selat	39	E3
Karimnagar	43	K11
Karimunjawa, Kepulauan	39	F4
Karin	49	E4
Karkaralinsk = Qarqaraly	29	E8
Karkinitska Zatoka	25	D3
Karkinitskiy Zaliv = Karkinitska Zatoka	25	D3
Karl-Marx-Stadt = Chemnitz	15	C7
Karlovac	20	B5
Karlovo	22	C5
Karlovy Vary	16	C1
Karlsbad = Karlovy Vary	16	C1
Karlskrona	9	D9
Karlsruhe	14	D5
Karlstad	9	D8
Karnal	42	E10
Karnali →	40	C3
Karnaphuli Res. = Kaptai L.	41	F9
Karnataka □	43	N10
Kärnten □	15	E7
Karonga	57	F6
Karoonda	62	C2
Karora	55	E6
Kárpathos	23	G6
Kars	46	B5
Karsakpay	29	E7
Karshi = Qarshi	29	F7
Karufa	37	E4
Karungu	57	E6
Karvina	16	D4
Karwar	43	M9
Kasai →	56	E3
Kasama	57	G6
Kasaragod	43	N9
Kasba L.	68	B9
Kasempa	59	A5
Kasenga	57	G5
Käshän	44	C2
Kashgar = Kashi	34	C2
Kashi	34	C2
Kashk-e Kohneh	42	B3
Käshmar	44	C4
Kashun Noerh = Gaxun Nur	34	B5
Kasimov	24	C5
Kasiruta	37	E3
Kasongo	57	E5
Kasongo Lunda	56	F3
Kásos	23	G6
Kassalâ	55	E6
Kassel	14	C5
Kastamonu	46	B3
Kasur	42	D9
Katanga □	57	F4
Katangi	43	J11
Katerini	23	D4
Katha	41	E11
Kathiawar	43	H7
Kathmandu = Katmandu	40	D5
Katihar	40	E6
Katima Mulilo	58	B4
Katingan = Mendawai →	39	E4
Katiola	53	G4
Katmandu	40	D5
Katoomba	63	B5
Katowice	16	C4
Katsina	53	F7
Kattegat	9	D8
Kaua'i	78	G11
Kaunas	9	C1
Kavalerovo	32	A4
Kaválla	22	D5
Kavir, Dasht-e	44	C3
Kaw	92	B3
Kawagoe	33	F6
Kawaguchi	33	F6
Kawardha	40	G3
Kawasaki	33	F6
Kawasi	37	E3
Kawerau	64	C7
Kawhia Harbour	64	C6
Kawio, Kepulauan	36	D3
Kawnro	41	F12
Kawthoolei = Kayin □	41	H11
Kawthule = Kayin □	41	H11
Kaya	53	F5
Kayah □	41	H11
Kayan →	39	D5
Kayeli	37	E3
Kayes	53	F3
Kayin □	41	H11
Kayoa	37	D3
Kayseri	46	C3
Kazachye	31	B11
Kazakhstan ■	29	E7
Kazan	24	B6
Kazanlŭk	22	C5
Kazatin = Kozyatyn	17	D9
Käzerün	44	D2
Kazym →	28	C7
Kéa	23	F5
Kebnekaise	8	B9
Kebri Dehar	49	F3
Kecskemét	16	E4
Kediri	39	F4
Keeling = Chilung	35	D7
Keetmanshoop	58	D3
Kefallinía	23	E3
Kefamenanu	37	F2
Keffi	53	G7
Keflavik	8	C1
Keighley	11	E6
Keith	62	C3
Kekri	42	G9
Kelang	39	D2
Kells = Ceanannus Mor	11	E3
Kelowna	69	D8
Kelso	65	F3
Keluang	39	D2
Kem	28	C4
Kema	37	D3
Kemah	46	C4
Kemerovo	29	D9
Kemi	8	B10
Kemi älv = Kemijoki →	8	B10
Kemijärvi	8	B11
Kemijoki →	8	B10
Kemp Land	96	A9
Kempsey	63	B5
Kempten	14	E6
Kendal	39	F4
Kendall	63	B5
Kendari	37	E2
Kendawangan	39	E4
Kendrapara	40	G6
Kenema	53	G3
Keng Tawng	41	G12
Keng Tung	41	G12
Kenitra	52	B4
Kennedy, Mt.	41	F9
Kennewick	72	C4
Kenogami →	71	C2
Kenosha	76	C2
Kent Group	62	C4
Kent Pen.	68	B9
Kentau	29	E7
Kentucky □	76	F3
Kentville	71	D4
Kenya ■	57	D7
Kenya, Mt.	57	E7
Kepi	37	F5
Kerala □	43	P10
Kerang	62	C3
Kerch	25	D4
Kericho	57	E7
Kerinci	39	E2
Kerki	29	F7
Kérkira	23	E2
Kermadec Is.	64	M13
Kermadec Trench	65	N13
Kermän	44	D4
Kermän □	44	D4
Kermänshäh = Bäkhtarän	46	D6
Kerrobert	69	C9
Kerulen →	35	B6
Kerzaz	52	C5
Keşan	23	D6
Kesennuma	32	D7
Kestenga	28	C4
Ket →	29	D9
Ketapang	39	E4
Ketchikan	69	C6
Kętrzyn	16	A5
Key West	86	B3
Khabarovsk	31	E11

124

Khābūr →	46	D5
Khairpur	42	F6
Khakassia □	30	D6
Khalkhāl	46	C7
Khalkis	23	E4
Khalmer-Sede = Tazovskiy	28	C8
Khalmer Yu	28	C7
Khalturin	24	B6
Khalūf	48	C6
Khambhat	43	H8
Khambhat, G. of	43	J8
Khamir	49	D3
Khānābād	45	B7
Khānaqin	46	D6
Khandwa	43	J10
Khanewal	42	D7
Khaniá	23	G5
Khanion, Kólpos	23	G4
Khanka, L.	32	A3
Khankendy = Xankändi	25	F6
Khanty-Mansiysk	29	C7
Khapcheranga	30	E9
Kharagpur	40	E4
Kharan Kalat	42	E4
Kharānaq	44	C3
Kharda	43	K9
Kharg = Khārk, Jazireh-ye	47	E7
Khārga, El Wâhât-el	54	C5
Khargon	43	J9
Khārk, Jazireh-ye	47	E7
Kharkiv	24	D4
Kharkov = Kharkiv	24	D4
Kharovsk	24	B5
Kharta	22	D7
Khartoum = El Khartûm	55	E5
Khasan	32	B4
Khāsh	42	E2
Khashm el Girba	55	F6
Khaskovo	22	D5
Khatanga	30	B8
Khatanga →	30	B8
Khaybar, Ḥarrat	47	F4
Khed Brahma	43	G8
Khemmarat	38	A3
Khenchela	52	A7
Kherson	25	D3
Kheta →	30	B8
Khilok	30	D9
Khíos	23	E6
Khiuma = Hiiumaa	24	B1
Khiva	29	E7
Khīyāv	46	C6
Khmelnik	17	D8
Khmelnytskyy	17	D8
Khmer Rep. = Cambodia ■	38	B3
Khodoriv	17	D7
Khodzent = Khŭjand	29	E7
Khojak Pass	42	D5
Kholm, Afghan.	45	B6
Kholm, Russia	24	B3
Khomeyn	44	C2
Khon Kaen	38	A2
Khóra Sfakion	23	G5
Khorat = Nakhon		
Ratchasima	38	B2
Khorramābād	46	D7
Khorrāmshahr	47	E7
Khotyn	17	D8
Khouribga	52	B4
Khowst	42	C6
Khoyniki	17	C9
Khu Khan	38	B2
Khudzhand = Khŭjand	29	E7
Khŭgiāni	42	D4
Khŭjand	29	E7
Khulna	41	F7
Khulna □	41	F7
Khūr	44	C4
Khūriyā Mūriyā, Jazā'ir	48	D6
Khush	42	C3
Khushab	42	C8
Khust	17	D6

Khuzdar	42	F5
Khvor	44	C3
Khvormūj	44	D2
Khvoy	46	C6
Khyber Pass	42	B7
Kiama	63	B5
Kiamba	36	C2
Kiangsi = Jiangxi □	35	D6
Kiangsu = Jiangsu □	35	C6
Kibombo	57	E5
Kibwezi	57	E7
Kicking Horse Pass	69	C8
Kidal	53	E6
Kidnappers, C.	64	C7
Kiel	14	A6
Kiel Canal = Nord-Ostsee-		
Kanal	14	A5
Kielce	16	C5
Kieler Bucht	14	A6
Kiev = Kyyiv	17	C10
Kiffa	53	E3
Kifri	46	D6
Kigali	57	E6
Kigoma-Ujiji	57	E5
Kii-Channel	33	B3
Kikinda	22	B2
Kikládhes	23	F5
Kikwit	56	E3
Kilcoy	63	A5
Kilifi	57	E7
Kilimanjaro	57	E7
Kilis	46	C4
Kiliya	17	F9
Kilkenny	11	E3
Kilkis	23	D4
Killarney, Australia	63	A5
Killarney, Ireland	11	E2
Killeen	80	D5
Killíni	23	F4
Kilmarnock	10	D4
Kilmore	63	C3
Kilosa	57	F7
Kilrush	11	E2
Kilwa Kivinje	57	F7
Kimaam	37	F5
Kimba	62	B2
Kimberley, Australia	60	D4
Kimberley, S. Africa	58	D4
Kimmirut	70	B4
Kimry	24	B4
Kinabalu, Gunong	38	C5
Kindia	53	F3
Kindu	57	E5
Kineshma	24	B5
King George B.	95	G4
King George I.	96	A4
King George Is.	71	C2
King I. = Kadan Kyun	38	B1
King I.	62	C3
King William I.	68	B10
Kingait = Cape Dorset	70	B3
Kingaok = Bathurst Inlet	68	B9
Kingaroy	63	A5
Kingoonya	62	B2
Kings Canyon △	78	B3
King's Lynn	11	E7
Kingscote	62	C2
Kingsport	83	A6
Kingston, Canada	71	D3
Kingston, Jamaica	86	C4
Kingston, N.Z.	65	F3
Kingston South East	62	C2
Kingston upon Hull	11	E6
Kingstown	87	D7
Kingsville	80	F5
Kınık	23	E6
Kinkala	56	E2
Kinleith	64	C6
Kinsale	11	F2
Kinsha = Chang Jiang →	35	C7
Kinshasa	56	E3
Kinston	83	B9
Kiparissía	23	F3

Kiparissiakós Kólpos	23	F3
Kipushi	59	A5
Kirghizia = Kyrgyzstan ■	29	E8
Kiribati ■	64	K12
Kırıkkale	46	C3
Kirillov	24	B4
Kirin = Jilin	35	B7
Kirinyaga = Kenya, Mt.	57	E7
Kiritimati	65	J15
Kirkcaldy	10	C5
Kirkcudbright	11	D4
Kirkee	43	K8
Kirkland Lake	71	D2
Kırklareli	22	D6
Kirkūk	46	D6
Kirkwall	10	B5
Kirov	28	D5
Kirovabad = Gäncä	25	E6
Kirovakan = Vanadzor	25	E5
Kirovohrad	25	D3
Kirovsk = Babadayhan	29	F7
Kirovskiy	32	A3
Kırşehir	25	G5
Kirthar Range	42	F5
Kiruna	8	B10
Kiryū	33	E6
Kisangani	57	D5
Kisar	37	F3
Kishanganj	40	D7
Kishangarh	42	F7
Kishb, Ḥarrat al	47	G5
Kishinev = Chişinău	17	E9
Kishtwar	42	C9
Kisii	57	E6
Kiskőrös	16	E4
Kiskunfélegyháza	16	E4
Kiskunhalas	16	E4
Kislovodsk	25	E5
Kiso-Gawa →	33	F5
Kissidougou	53	G3
Kisumu	57	E6
Kita	53	F4
Kitaibaraki	33	E7
Kitakyūshū	33	G2
Kitale	57	D7
Kitami	32	B8
Kitchener	71	D2
Kitega = Gitega	57	E5
Kíthira	23	F4
Kíthnos	23	F5
Kittakittaooloo, L.	62	A2
Kitui	57	E7
Kitwe	59	A5
Kivertsi	17	C7
Kivu, L.	57	E5
Kiyev = Kyyiv	17	C10
Kiyevskoye Vdkhr. =		
Kyyivske Vdskh.	17	C10
Kızıl Irmak →	25	E4
Kizlyar	25	E6
Kizyl-Arvat = Gyzylarbat	29	F6
Kladno	16	C2
Klagenfurt	15	E8
Klaipėda	24	B1
Klamath Falls	72	E3
Klamath Mts.	72	F2
Klarälven →	9	C8
Klatovy	16	D1
Klerksdorp	59	D5
Kletsk = Klyetsk	17	B8
Kłodzko	16	C3
Klouto	53	G6
Kluane L.	68	B6
Kluczbork	16	C4
Klyetsk	17	B8
Knossós	23	G5
Knox Coast	96	A12
Knoxville	83	B6
Koartac = Quaqtaq	70	B4
Koba	37	F4
Kobarid	20	A4

Kobdo = Hovd	34	B4
Köbe	33	F4
København	9	D8
Koblenz	14	C4
Kobroor	37	F4
Kobryn	17	B7
Kocaeli	25	E2
Kočani	22	D4
Koch Bihar	41	D7
Kochi = Cochin	43	Q10
Kōchi	33	G3
Kochiu = Gejiu	34	D5
Kodiak	69	C4
Kodiak I.	69	C4
Kofiau	37	E3
Koforidua	53	G5
Kōfu	33	F6
Kohat	42	C7
Kohima	41	E10
Kohkīlūyeh va Būyer Aḥmadi □	44	D2
Kohler Ra.	96	B1
Kokand = Qŭqon	29	E8
Kokas	37	E4
Kokchetav = Kökshetaü	29	K9
Koko Kyunzu	41	K9
Kokomo	76	D2
Kökshetaü	29	D7
Koksoak →	70	C4
Kokstad	59	E5
Kola	37	F4
Kola Pen. = Kolskiy Poluostrov	8	B13
Kolaka	37	E2
Kolar	43	N11
Kolar Gold Fields	43	N11
Kolayat	42	F8
Kolchugino = Leninsk-Kuznetskiy	29	D9
Kolepom = Dolak, Pulau	37	F5
Kolguyev, Ostrov	28	C5
Kolhapur	43	L9
Kolín	16	C2
Kolkata	41	F7
Kollam = Quilon	43	Q10
Köln	14	C4
Koło	16	B4
Kołobrzeg	16	A2
Kolomna	24	B4
Kolomyya	17	D7
Kolonodale	37	E2
Kolosib	41	E9
Kolpashevo	29	D9
Kolpino	24	B3
Kolskiy Poluostrov	8	B13
Kolwezi	57	G5
Kolyma →	31	C13
Komatsu	33	E5
Komi □	28	C6
Kommunarsk = Alchevsk	25	D4
Kommunizma, Pik	29	F8
Komodo	37	F1
Komoran, Pulau	37	F5
Komotini	22	D5
Kompong Cham	38	B3
Kompong Chhnang = Kampong Chhnang	38	B2
Kompong Som = Kampong Saom	38	B2
Komrat = Comrat	17	E9
Komsomolets, Ostrov	30	A7
Kon Tum	38	B3
Konarhā □	42	B7
Konch	42	G11
Kondoa	57	E7
Köneürgench	29	E6
Kong	53	G5
Kong, Koh	38	B2
Konglu	41	D11
Kongolo	57	F5
Königsberg = Kaliningrad	24	C1
Konin	16	B4
Konjic	20	C6
Konosha	28	C5
Konotop	24	C3
Końskie	16	C5
Konstanz	14	E5
Kontagora	53	F7
Konya	46	C3
Konya Ovası	46	C3
Koonibba	62	B1
Koorawatha	63	B4
Kootenay L.	69	D8
Kopaonik	22	C3
Koper	20	B4
Kopi	62	B2
Koprivnica	20	A6
Kopychyntsi	17	D7
Korab	22	D3
Korçë	23	D3
Korčula	20	C6
Kordestan = Kurdistan	46	D5
Kordestān □	46	D6
Kordofân	55	F4
Korea, North ■	35	C7
Korea, South ■	35	C7
Korea Bay	35	C7
Korea Strait	35	C7
Korets	17	C8
Korhogo	53	G4
Korinthiakós Kólpos	23	E4
Kórinthos	23	F4
Kōriyama	33	E7
Korneshty = Corneşti	17	E9
Koro	53	G4
Korogwe	57	F7
Koror	36	C4
Körös →	16	E5
Korosten	17	C9
Korostyshev	17	C9
Kortrijk	14	C2
Kos	23	F6
Kościan	16	B3
Kosciuszko, Mt.	63	C4
Kosha	54	D5
K'oshih = Kashi	34	C2
Koshiki-Rettō	33	H1
Košice	16	D5
Kosovo □	22	C3
Kosovska Mitrovica	22	C3
Kôstî	55	F5
Kostopil	17	C8
Kostroma	24	B5
Kostrzyn	16	B2
Koszalin	16	A3
Kota	43	G9
Kota Baharu	38	C2
Kota Belud	38	C5
Kota Kinabalu	38	C5
Kota Kubu Baharu	39	D2
Kota Tinggi	39	D2
Kotaagung	39	F2
Kotabaru	39	E5
Kotabumi	39	E2
Kotamobagu	37	D2
Kotelnich	24	B6
Kotelnyy, Ostrov	31	B11
Kotka	9	C11
Kotlas	28	C5
Kotor	22	C2
Kotovsk	17	E9
Kotturu	43	M10
Kotuy →	30	B8
Kotzebue	69	B3
Koudougou	53	F5
Kouilou →	56	E2
Koula Moutou	56	E2
Koulen = Kulen	38	B2
Koumra	55	G2
Kounradskiy	29	E8
Kousséri	55	F1
Kouvola	8	C11
Kovel	17	C7
Kovrov	24	B5
Köyceğiz	23	F7
Kozan	46	C3
Kozáni	23	D3
Kozhikode = Calicut	43	P9
Kozyatyn	17	D9
Kra, Isthmus of = Kra, Kho Khot	38	B1
Kra, Kho Khot	38	B1
Kracheh	38	B3
Kragujevac	22	B3
Krajina	20	B6
Krakatau = Rakata, Pulau	39	F3
Kraków	16	C4
Kraljevo	22	C3
Kramatorsk	25	D4
Kranj	20	A5
Kraśnik	16	C6
Krasnoarmeysk	29	D5
Krasnodar	25	D4
Krasnoperekopsk	25	D3
Krasnoselkup	28	C9
Krasnoturinsk	28	D7
Krasnovodsk = Türkmenbashi	29	E6
Krasnoyarsk	30	D7
Krasnýy Luch	25	D4
Krasnyy Yar	25	D6
Kratie = Kracheh	38	B3
Krau	37	E6
Krefeld	14	C4
Kremen	20	B5
Kremenchuk	24	D3
Kremenchuksk Vdskh.	24	D3
Kremenets	17	C7
Krems	15	D8
Kribi	56	D1
Krichev = Krychaw	17	B10
Krishna →	40	K3
Krishnanagar	41	F7
Kristiansand	9	D7
Kristiansund	8	C2
Kríti	23	G5
Krivoy Rog = Kryvyy Rih	25	D3
Krk	20	B5
Kronprins Olav Kyst	96	A9
Kronshtadt	24	B2
Kroonstad	59	D5
Kropotkin	25	D5
Krotoszyn	16	C3
Krung Thep = Bangkok	38	B2
Krupki	17	A9
Kruševac	22	C3
Krychaw	17	B10
Krymskyy Pivostriv	25	D3
Kryvyy Rih	25	D3
Ksar el Kebir	52	B4
Ksar es Souk = Er Rachidia	52	B5
Kuala Lipis	39	D2
Kuala Lumpur	39	D2
Kuala Sepetang	38	D2
Kuala Terengganu	38	C2
Kualajelai	39	E4
Kualakapuas	39	E4
Kualakurun	39	E4
Kualapembuang	39	E4
Kualasimpang	39	D1
Kuandang	37	D2
Kuangchou = Guangzhou	35	D6
Kuantan	39	D2
Kuba = Quba	25	E6
Kuban →	25	D4
Kuching	39	D4
Kucing = Kuching	39	D4
Kuda	43	H7
Kudat	38	C5
Kudymkar	28	D6
Kueiyang = Guiyang	35	D5
Kufra Oasis = Al Kufrah	54	D3
Kufstein	15	E7
Kugaaruk = Pelly Bay	70	B2
Kugluktuk	68	B8

Kūhak 42 F3
Kūhhā-ye-Bashākerd 45 E4
Kūhpāyeh 44 C3
Kuito 58 A3
Kuji 32 C7
Kukës 22 C3
Kula 23 E7
Kulasekarappattinam ... 43 Q11
Kuldja = Yining 34 B3
Kulen 38 B2
Kŭlob 29 F7
Kulsary 29 E6
Kulunda 29 D8
Kulwin 62 C3
Kulyab = Kŭlob 29 F7
Kuma ➔ 25 E6
Kumagaya 33 F9
Kumai 39 E4
Kumamba, Kepulauan ... 37 E5
Kumamoto 33 G2
Kumanovo 22 C3
Kumara 65 E4
Kumasi 53 G5
Kumayri = Gyumri 25 E5
Kumba 56 D1
Kumbakonam 43 P11
Kumbarilla 63 A5
Kumon Bum 41 D11
Kungrad = Qŭnghirot ... 29 E6
Kungur 29 D6
Kunlong 41 F12
Kunlun Shan 34 C3
Kunming 34 D5
Kunsan 35 C7
Kunya-Urgench =
  Köneürgench 29 E6
Kuopio 8 C11
Kupa ➔ 20 B6
Kuqa 34 B3
Kür ➔ 25 E6
Kura = Kür ➔ 25 E6
Kurdistan 46 D5
Kŭrdzhali 22 D5
Kure 33 F3
Kurgan 29 D7
Kuria Maria Is. = Khuriyā
  Muriyā, Jazā'ir 48 D6
Kurigram 41 E7
Kuril Is. = Kurilskiye
  Ostrova 31 E12
Kurilskiye Ostrova 31 E12
Kurnool 43 L11
Kurow 65 F4
Kurri Kurri 63 B5
Kursk 24 C4
Kuruktag 34 B3
Kuruman 58 D4
Kurume 33 G2
Kus Gölü 23 D6
Kuşadasi 23 F6
Kushiro 32 B9
Kushtia 41 F7
Kuskokwim B. 69 C3
Kustanay = Qostanay ... 29 D7
Kütahya 46 C2
Kutaisi 25 E5
Kutaraja = Banda Aceh ... 38 C1
Kutch, Gulf of = Kachchh,
  Gulf of 43 H6
Kutch, Rann of = Kachchh,
  Rann of 43 G6
Kutno 16 B4
Kutu 56 E3
Kutum 55 F3
Kuujjuaq 70 C4
Kuusamo 8 B11
Kuwait = Al Kuwayt ... 47 E7
Kuwait ■ 47 E6
Kuybyshev = Samara ... 24 C7
Kuybyshev 29 D8
Kuybyshevskoye Vdkhr. ... 24 B6

Kuyumba 30 C7
Kuzey Anadolu Dağları ... 46 B3
Kuznetsk 24 C6
Kvarner 20 B5
Kvarnerič 20 B5
Kwakoegron 92 A2
Kwando ➔ 58 B4
Kwangju 35 C7
Kwangsi-Chuang = Guangxi
  Zhuangzu Zizhiqu □ ... 35 D5
Kwangtung =
  Guangdong □ 35 D6
Kwatisore 37 E4
Kweichow = Guizhou □ ... 35 D5
Kwekwe 59 B5
Kwidzyn 16 B4
Kwoka 37 E4
Kyabra Cr. ➔ 63 A3
Kyabram 63 C4
Kyancutta 62 B2
Kyaukpadaung 41 G10
Kyaukpyu 41 H9
Kyaukse 41 G11
Kyneton 63 C3
Kyō-ga-Saki 33 F4
Kyoga, L. 57 D6
Kyogle 63 A5
Kyongpyaw 41 J10
Kyōto 33 F4
Kyrenia 46 D3
Kyrgyzstan ■ 29 E8
Kystatyam 30 C10
Kyunhla 41 F10
Kyūshū 33 G2
Kyustendil 22 C4
Kyusyur 30 B10
Kyyiv 17 C10
Kyyivske Vdskh. ... 17 C10
Kyzyl Kum 29 E7
Kyzyl-Kyya 29 E8
Kyzyl-Orda = Qyzylorda ... 29 E7

L

La Alcarria 19 B4
La Asunción 94 A6
La Banda 94 B3
La Carlota 94 C4
La Ceiba 85 D7
La Cocha 94 B3
La Coruña = A Coruña ... 18 A1
La Crosse 75 D9
La Estrada = A Estrada ... 18 A1
La Grange 82 C5
La Guaira 90 A5
La Habana 86 B3
La Línea de la Concepción ... 18 D3
La Mancha 19 C4
La Palma 52 C2
La Palma del Condado ... 18 D2
La Paragua 90 B6
La Paz, Entre Rios,
  Argentina 94 C5
La Paz, San Luis, Argentina ... 94 C3
La Paz, Bolivia 91 G5
La Paz, Mexico 84 C2
La Pedrera 90 D5
La Plata 94 D5
La Quiaca 94 A3
La Rioja 94 B3
La Rioja □ 18 A4
La Robla 18 A3
La Roche-sur-Yon ... 12 C3
La Rochelle 12 C3
La Roda 19 C4
La Romana 87 C6
La Serena 94 B2

La Seu d'Urgell 19 A6
La Seyne-sur-Mer ... 13 E6
La Spézia 20 B2
La Tortuga 87 D6
La Tuque 71 D3
La Unión 95 E2
La Urbana 90 B5
La Vall d'Uixó 19 C5
La Vega 87 C5
Laas Caanood = Las Anod ... 49 F4
Labe = Elbe ➔ 14 B5
Labé 53 F3
Laboulaye 94 C4
Labrador 71 C4
Lábrea 91 E6
Labuan 38 C5
Labuan, Pulau 38 C5
Labuha 37 E3
Labuhanbajo 37 F2
Labuk, Telok 38 C5
Labyrinth, L. 62 B2
Labytnangi 28 C7
Lac La Biche 69 C8
Lac la Martre = Wha Ti ... 68 B8
Lacanau 12 D3
Laccadive Is. =
  Lakshadweep Is. ... 26 H11
Lacepede B. 62 C2
Lachlan ➔ 63 B3
Lacombe 69 C8
Ladakh Ra. 42 B10
Lädiz 45 D5
Ladoga, L. = Ladozhskoye
  Ozero 8 C12
Ladozhskoye Ozero ... 8 C12
Ladysmith 59 D5
Lae 61 B8
Lafayette 81 D7
Lafia 53 G7
Laghmān □ 45 C7
Laghouat 52 B6
Lagonoy G. 36 B2
Lagos, Nigeria 53 G6
Lagos, Portugal ... 18 D1
Laguna 94 B7
Lagunas 90 E3
Lahad Datu 36 C1
Lahad Datu, Teluk ... 36 D1
Lahat 39 E2
Lahewa 39 D1
Lähijän 46 C7
Lahn ➔ 14 C4
Lahore 42 D9
Lahti 8 C11
Lahtis = Lahti 8 C11
Laï 55 G2
Laila = Layla 47 G6
Lairg 10 B4
Laizhou 35 C6
Lajes 94 B6
Lake Cargelligo ... 63 B4
Lake Charles 81 D7
Lake City 83 D6
Lake Harbour = Kimmirut ... 70 B4
Lake Worth 83 F7
Lakeland 83 E7
Lakes Entrance ... 63 C4
Lakewood 76 D5
Lakonikós Kólpos ... 23 F4
Lakor 37 F3
Lakota 53 G4
Lakshadweep Is. ... 26 H11
Lalaghat 41 E9
L'Albufera 19 C5
Lalín 18 A1
Lalitapur 40 D5
Lamaing 41 K11
Lamas 91 E3
Lambaréné 56 E2
Lambert Glacier ... 96 B10
Lamego 18 B2
Lameroo 62 C3

Lamía	23	E4
Lamon B.	36	B2
Lampa	91	G4
Lampedusa	21	G4
Lampione	21	G4
Lampung □	39	F2
Lamu	57	E8
Lāna'i	78	H12
Lanak La	42	B11
Lancaster, *U.K.*	11	D5
Lancaster, *U.S.A.*	77	D7
Lancaster Sd.	70	A2
Lanchow = Lanzhou	35	C5
Lanciano	20	C5
Landeck	14	E6
Landes	12	D3
Landi Kotal	42	B7
Land's End	11	F4
Landshut	15	D7
La'nga Co	40	B3
Langjökull	8	C2
Langkawi, Pulau	38	C1
Langkon	38	C5
Langreo	18	A3
Langres	13	C6
Langres, Plateau de	13	C6
Langsa	38	D1
Languedoc	13	E5
Lannion	12	B2
Lansdowne	63	B5
Lansing	76	C3
Lanusei	21	E2
Lanzarote	52	C3
Lanzhou	35	C5
Laoag	36	A2
Laoang	36	B3
Laohekou	35	C6
Laon	13	B5
Laos ■	38	A3
Lappland	8	B10
Lapseki	23	D6
Laptev Sea	30	B10
L'Áquila	20	C4
Lär	44	E3
Laramie	74	E2
Larantuka	37	F2
Larat	37	F4
Laredo	80	F4
Lariang	37	E1
Lárisa	23	E4
Larnaca	46	D3
Larne	11	D4
Larrimah	60	D5
Larsen Ice Shelf	96	A3
Larvik	9	D8
Las Anod	49	F4
Las Cruces	79	D9
Las Flores	94	D5
Las Lajas	94	D2
Las Lomitas	94	A4
Las Palmas	52	C2
Las Plumas	95	E3
Las Varillas	94	C4
Las Vegas	78	B5
Lash-e Joveyn	42	D2
Lashio	41	F11
Lassen Pk.	72	F3
Lastoursville	56	E2
Lastovo	20	C6
Latacunga	90	D3
Latakia = Al Lädhiqiyah	46	D3
Latina	20	D4
Latium = Lazio □	20	C4
Latrobe	62	D4
Latvia ■	24	B1
Lauchhammer	15	C7
Launceston	62	D4
Laurel	81	D9
Lauria	21	D5
Lausanne	14	E4
Laut	38	D3
Laut Kecil, Kepulauan	39	E5
Laval	12	B3
Lávrion	23	F5
Lawas	38	D5
Lawele	37	F2
Lawng Pit	41	E11
Lawrence, *N.Z.*	65	F3
Lawrence, *U.S.A.*	75	F7
Lawton	80	B4
Layla	47	G6
Lazio □	20	C4
Lazo	32	B3
Le Creusot	13	C6
Le Havre	12	B4
Le Mans	12	C4
Le Mont-St-Michel	12	B3
Le Puy-en-Velay	13	D5
Le Touquet-Paris-Plage	12	A4
Le Tréport	12	A4
Le Verdon-sur-Mer	12	D3
Leamington Spa = Royal		
Leamington Spa	11	E6
Leavenworth	75	F7
Lebak	36	C2
Lebanon ■	46	D3
Lebork	16	A3
Lebrija	18	D2
Lebu	94	D2
Lecce	23	D2
Lecco	20	B2
Lech →	14	D6
Łęczyca	16	B4
Leeds	11	E6
Leer	14	B4
Leeton	63	B4
Leeuwarden	14	B3
Leeuwin, C.	60	G2
Leeward Is.	87	C7
Leganés	18	B4
Legazpi	36	B2
Leghorn = Livorno	20	C3
Legionowo	16	B5
Legnago	20	B3
Legnica	16	C3
Leh	42	B10
Leicester	11	E6
Leiden	14	B3
Leie →	14	C2
Leine →	14	B5
Leinster □	11	E3
Leipzig	15	C7
Leiria	18	C1
Leitrim	11	D2
Leizhou Bandao	35	D6
Lékva Óros	23	G5
Leleque	95	E2
Léman, L.	13	C7
Lemhi Ra.	73	D7
Lena →	30	B10
Leninabad = Khüjand	29	E7
Leninakan = Gyumri	25	E5
Leningrad = Sankt-		
Peterburg	24	B3
Leninogorsk	29	D9
Leninsk	25	D6
Leninsk-Kuznetskiy	29	D9
Lenmalu	37	E4
Lens	13	A5
Lentini	21	F5
Leoben	15	E8
Leodhas = Lewis	10	B3
León, *Mexico*	84	C4
León, *Nic.*	85	E7
León, *Spain*	18	A3
León, Montes de	18	A2
Leongatha	63	C4
Leova	17	E9
Lepel = Lyepyel	24	C2
Lérida = Lleida	19	B6
Lerwick	10	A6
Les Cayes	86	C5
Les Sables-d'Olonne	12	C3
Lesbos = Lésvos	23	E6
Leskovac	22	C3
Lesotho ■	59	D5
Lesozavodsk	32	A3
Lesser Antilles	87	D7
Lesser Sunda Is.	37	F2
Lésvos	23	E6
Leszno	16	C3
Lethbridge	69	D8
Leti, Kepulauan	37	F3
Leticia	90	D4
Letpadan	41	J10
Letpan	41	H10
Letterkenny	11	D3
Leuser, G.	39	D1
Leuven	14	C3
Levádhia	23	E4
Levanger	8	C8
Levin	64	D6
Lévis	71	D3
Levkás	23	E3
Levkôsia = Nicosia	46	D3
Levskigrad = Karlovo	22	C5
Lewis	10	B3
Lewisporte	71	D5
Lewiston, *Idaho, U.S.A.*	72	C5
Lewiston, *Maine, U.S.A.*	77	B10
Lexington, *Ky., U.S.A.*	76	E3
Lexington, *N.C., U.S.A.*	83	B7
Leyte □	36	B2
Lezhë	22	D2
Lhasa	34	D4
Lhazê	34	D3
Lhokkruet	38	D1
Lhokseumawe	38	C1
L'Hospitalet de Llobregat	19	B7
Lianga	36	C3
Lianyungang	35	C6
Liaoning □	35	B7
Liaoyuan	35	B7
Liard →	68	B7
Libau = Liepāja	24	B1
Libenge	56	D3
Liberal	80	A3
Liberec	16	C2
Liberia ■	53	G4
Lîbîya, Sahrâ'	54	C4
Libobo, Tanjung	37	E3
Libourne	12	D3
Libreville	56	D1
Libya ■	54	C2
Libyan Desert = Lîbîya,		
Sahrâ'	54	C4
Licantén	94	D2
Licata	21	F4
Lichinga	59	A7
Lida	17	B7
Liechtenstein ■	14	E5
Liège	14	C3
Liegnitz = Legnica	16	C3
Lienyünchiangshih =		
Lianyungang	35	C6
Lienz	15	E7
Liepāja	24	B1
Liffey →	11	E3
Lifford	11	D3
Lightning Ridge	63	A4
Liguria □	20	B2
Ligurian Sea	20	C2
Lijiang	34	D5
Likasi	57	G5
Lille	13	A5
Lillehammer	8	C8
Lilongwe	59	A6
Liloy	36	C2
Lim →	20	C7
Lima, *Indonesia*	37	E3
Lima, *Peru*	91	F3
Lima, *U.S.A.*	76	D3
Lima →	18	B1
Limassol	46	D3
Limay Mahuida	94	D3
Limbang	38	D5

Limbe	56	D1
Limburg	14	C5
Limeira	93	G4
Limerick	11	C2
Limfjorden	9	D7
Limia = Lima →	18	B1
Limnos	23	E5
Limoges	12	D4
Limón	86	E3
Limousin	12	D4
Limoux	12	E5
Limpopo →	59	D6
Limuru	57	E7
Linares, Chile	94	D2
Linares, Mexico	84	C5
Linares, Spain	18	C4
Lincoln, Argentina	94	C4
Lincoln, N.Z.	65	E5
Lincoln, U.K.	11	E6
Lincoln, U.S.A.	75	A6
Linden	90	B6
Lindesnes	9	D7
Líndhos	23	F7
Lindi	57	F7
Lingayen	36	A2
Lingayen G.	36	A2
Lingen	14	B4
Lingga	39	E2
Lingga, Kepulauan	39	E2
Linguère	53	E2
Linhai	35	D7
Linhares	93	F5
Linköping	9	D9
Linosa	21	G4
Lins	93	G4
Linxia	34	C5
Linz	15	D8
Lion, G. du	13	E6
Lipa	36	B2
Lipari	21	E5
Lipcani	17	D8
Lipetsk	24	C4
Lipkany = Lipcani	17	D8
Lipovcy Manzovka	32	A3
Lipovets	17	D9
Lippe →	14	C4
Liptrap C.	63	C4
Lira	57	D6
Liria = Lliria	19	C5
Lisala	56	D4
Lisboa	18	C1
Lisbon = Lisboa	18	C1
Lisburn	11	D3
Lisichansk = Lysychansk	25	D4
Lisieux	12	B4
Liski	24	C4
Lismore	63	A5
Lister, Mt.	96	B15
Liston	63	A5
Listowel	11	E2
Litani →	46	D3
Lithgow	63	B5
Lithínon, Ákra	23	G5
Lithuania ■	24	B1
Litoměřice	16	C2
Little Barrier I.	64	B6
Little Missouri →	74	B3
Little River	65	E5
Little Rock	81	B7
Liukang Tenggaja = Sabalana, Kepulauan	37	F1
Liuwa Plain	58	A4
Liuzhou	35	D5
Liverpool, Canada	71	D4
Liverpool, U.K.	11	E5
Liverpool Plains	63	B5
Liverpool Ra.	63	B5
Livingstone	59	B5
Livny	24	C4
Livorno	20	C3
Ljubljana	20	A5
Llancanelo, Salina	94	D3
Llanelli	11	F4
Llanes	18	A3
Llano Estacado	80	C2
Llanos	90	C4
Lleida	19	B6
Lliria	19	C5
Llobregat →	19	B7
Lloret de Mar	19	B7
Llucmajor	19	C7
Llullaillaco, Volcán	94	A3
Loa →	94	A2
Lobatse	59	D5
Loberia	94	D5
Lobito	58	A2
Lock	62	B2
Loch Garman = Wexford	11	E3
Loches	12	C4
Lockhart	62	B3
Lod	46	D3
Lodhran	42	E7
Lodi, Italy	20	B2
Lodi, U.S.A.	72	G3
Lodja	56	E4
Lodwar	57	D7
Łódź	16	C4
Lofoten	8	B9
Logan	73	F8
Logan, Mt.	68	B5
Logone →	55	F2
Logroño	19	A4
Lohardaga	40	F5
Loi-kaw	41	H11
Loir →	12	C3
Loire →	12	C2
Loja, Ecuador	90	D3
Loja, Spain	18	D3
Loji = Kawasi	37	E3
Lokitaung	57	D7
Lokkan tekojärvi	8	B11
Lokoja	53	G7
Lom	22	C4
Lomami →	56	D4
Lombárdia □	20	B2
Lomblen	37	F2
Lombok	39	F5
Lomé	53	G6
Lomela	56	E4
Lomela →	56	E4
Lomond, L.	10	C4
Lompobatang	37	F1
Łomża	16	B6
Loncoche	95	D2
Londa	43	M9
London	11	F6
Londonderry	11	D3
Londonderry, C.	60	C4
Londonderry, I.	95	H2
Long Beach	78	D3
Long I., Bahamas	86	B4
Long I., U.S.A.	77	D9
Long Xuyen	38	B3
Longford, Australia	62	D4
Longford, Ireland	11	E3
Longiram	39	E5
Longnawan	39	D4
Longreach	61	E7
Longview, Tex., U.S.A.	81	C6
Longview, Wash., U.S.A.	72	C2
Lons-le-Saunier	13	C6
Lop Nur	34	B4
Lopez, C.	56	E1
Lora →	42	D4
Lora, Hämün-i-	42	E4
Lora Cr. →	62	A2
Lora del Río	18	D3
Lorain	76	D4
Loralai	42	D6
Lorca	19	D5
Lorestán □	46	D6
Loreto	92	D4
Lorient	12	C2
Lorne	62	C3
Lorraine □	13	B7
Los Alamos	79	C9
Los Andes	94	C2
Los Angeles, Chile	94	D2
Los Angeles, U.S.A.	78	C3
Los Blancos	94	A4
Los Hermanos Is.	90	A6
Los Mochis	84	B3
Los Roques Is.	90	A5
Los Testigos, Is.	90	A6
Los Vilos	94	C2
Lošinj	20	B5
Lot →	12	D4
Lota	94	D2
Loubomo	56	E2
Louga	53	E2
Louis Trichardt	59	C5
Louis XIV, Pte.	71	C3
Louisiade Arch.	61	C9
Louisiana □	81	D8
Louisville	76	E3
Loulé	18	D1
Lourdes	12	E3
Louth, Australia	63	B4
Louth, U.K.	11	E6
Louvain = Leuven	14	C3
Lovech	22	C5
Lowell	77	C10
Lower California = Baja California	84	A1
Lower Hutt	65	D6
Lower Saxony = Niedersachsen □	14	B5
Lower Tunguska = Tunguska, Nizhnyaya →	30	C6
Lowestoft	11	E7
Lowgar □	45	C7
Łowicz	16	B4
Loxton	62	B3
Loyalty Is. = Loyauté, Îs.	64	M11
Loyang = Luoyang	35	C6
Loyauté, Îs.	64	M11
Loyew	17	C10
Luachimo	56	F4
Lualaba →	57	D5
Luanda	56	F2
Luangwa →	59	A6
Luanshya	59	A5
Luapula →	57	F5
Luarca	18	A2
Luau	56	G4
Lubang Is.	36	B2
Lubbock	80	C3
Lübeck	15	B6
Lubero = Luofu	57	E5
Lubin	16	C3
Lublin	17	C6
Lubuklinggau	39	E2
Lubuksikaping	39	D2
Lubumbashi	59	A5
Lubutu	57	E5
Lucca	20	C3
Lucena, Phil.	36	B2
Lucena, Spain	18	D3
Lucerne = Luzern	13	C8
Luckenwalde	15	B7
Lucknow	40	D3
Lüda = Dalian	35	C7
Lüderitz	58	D3
Ludhiana	42	D9
Ludwigsburg	14	D5
Ludwigshafen	14	D5
Lufira →	57	F5
Lufkin	81	D6
Luga	24	B2
Lugano	13	C8
Lugansk = Luhansk	25	D4
Lugh Ganana	49	G3
Lugo, Italy	20	B3
Lugo, Spain	18	A2
Lugoj	17	F5
Lugovoy = Qulan	29	E8

Luhansk 25 D4
Luimneach = Limerick . . 11 E2
Luís Correia 92 C5
Luitpold Coast 96 B5
Luiza 56 F4
Lukanga Swamp 59 A5
Lukenie → 56 E3
Łuków 17 C6
Lule älv → 8 B10
Luleå 8 B10
Lüleburgaz 22 D6
Lulonga → 56 D3
Lulua → 56 E4
Lumbala N'guimbo 58 A4
Lumsden 65 F3
Lumut, Tanjung 39 E3
Lund 8 D8
Lundazi 59 A6
Lundu 39 D3
Lüneburg 14 B6
Lüneburger Heide 14 B6
Lunéville 13 B7
Lunglei 41 F9
Luni 42 G8
Luni → 43 G7
Luninyets 17 B8
Luofu 57 E5
Luoyang 35 C6
Lurgan 11 D3
Lusaka 59 B5
Lusambo 56 E4
Lushnjë 23 D2
Luta = Dalian 35 C7
Lutherstadt Wittenberg . . 15 C7
Luton 11 F6
Łutselk'e 68 B8
Lutsk 17 C7
Lützow Holmbukta 96 A8
Luuq = Lugh Ganana 49 G3
Luwuk 37 E2
Luxembourg 13 B7
Luxembourg ■ 14 D4
Luxor = El Uqsur 54 C5
Luza 24 A6
Luzern 13 C8
Luzhou 35 D5
Luziânia 93 F4
Luzon 36 A2
Lviv 17 D7
Lvov = Lviv 17 D7
Lyakhavichy 17 B8
Lyakhovskiye, Ostrova . . . 31 B12
Lyallpur = Faisalabad 42 D8
Lydenburg 59 D6
Lydia 23 E7
Lyell 65 D5
Lyepyel 24 C2
Łyna → 16 A5
Lynchburg 77 F6
Lynd Ra. 63 A4
Lyndhurst 62 B2
Lynn Lake 69 C9
Lyon 13 D6
Lyonnais 13 D6
Lys = Leie → 14 C2
Lysychansk 25 D4
Lyttelton 65 E5
Lyubertsy 24 B4
Lyuboml 17 C7

M

Ma'än 47 E3
Ma'anshan 35 C6
Ma'arrat an Nu'mān 46 D4
Maas → 14 C3
Maastricht 13 A6
McAllen 80 F4
Macao = Macau 35 D6

Macapá 92 B3
Macau, Brazil 92 D6
Macau, China 35 D6
M'Clintock Chan. 68 A9
McComb 81 D8
MacDonnell Ranges 60 E5
Macedonia =
    Makedhonía □ 23 D4
Macedonia ■ 22 D3
Maceió 93 D6
Macerata 20 C4
Macfarlane, L. 62 B2
Macgillycuddy's Reeks . . 11 F2
McGregor Ra. 62 A3
Mach 42 E5
Machado = Jiparaná → . . 91 E6
Machakos 57 E7
Machala 90 D3
Machilipatnam 40 J3
Machiques 90 A4
Machintyre → 63 A5
Mackay 61 E8
Mackay, L. 60 E4
Mackenzie → 68 B6
Mackenzie City = Linden . 90 B7
Mackenzie Mts. 68 B6
McKinley, Mt. 69 B4
McKinney 81 C5
Macksville 63 B5
Maclean 63 A5
Maclear 59 E5
Macleay → 63 B5
McMurdo Sd. 96 B15
Mâcon, France 13 C6
Macon, U.S.A. 83 C6
McPherson Ra. 63 A5
Macquarie Harbour 62 D4
McRobertson Land 96 B10
Madagascar ■ 59 J9
Madã'in Sälih 47 F4
Madama 54 D1
Madang 61 B8
Madaripur 41 F8
Madauk 41 J11
Madaya 41 F11
Maddalena 20 D2
Madeira 52 B2
Madeira → 90 D7
Madha 43 L9
Madhya Pradesh □ 43 H10
Madikeri 43 N9
Madimba 56 E3
Madingou 56 E2
Madison 75 D10
Madiun 39 F4
Madras = Chennai 43 N12
Madras = Tamil Nadu □ . . 43 P10
Madre, Laguna 80 F5
Madre, Sierra 36 A2
Madre de Dios → 91 F5
Madre de Dios, I. 95 G1
Madre Occidental, Sierra . 84 B3
Madrid 18 B4
Madurai 43 Q11
Madurantakam 43 N11
Mae Sot 38 A1
Maebashi 33 E6
Maevatanana 59 H9
Maffra 63 C4
Mafia I. 57 F7
Mafra, Brazil 94 B7
Mafra, Portugal 18 C1
Magadan 31 D13
Magallanes, Estrecho de . 95 G2
Magangué 90 B4
Magdalena, Argentina . . . 94 D5
Magdalena, Bolivia 91 F6
Magdalena → 90 A4
Magdeburg 15 B6
Magelang 39 F4
Magellan's Str. =
    Magallanes, Estrecho de 95 G2

Maggiore, Lago 20 B2
Magnetic Pole (South) . . . 96 A13
Magnitogorsk 29 D6
Magosa = Famagusta . . . 46 D3
Maguarinho, C. 92 C4
Maġusa = Famagusta . . . 46 D3
Magwe 41 G10
Mahābād 46 C6
Mahabo 59 J8
Mahajanga 59 H9
Mahakam → 39 E5
Mahalapye 59 C5
Maḩallāt 44 C2
Mahanadi → 40 G6
Maharashtra □ 43 J9
Mahbubnagar 43 L10
Mahdia 54 A1
Mahenge 57 F7
Maheno 65 F4
Mahesana 43 H8
Mahia Pen. 64 C7
Mahilyow 17 B10
Mahón = Maó 19 C8
Mai-Ndombe, L. 56 E3
Maicurú → 92 C3
Maidstone 11 F7
Maiduguri 55 F1
Majdi 41 F8
Maikala Ra. 40 G3
Main → 14 D5
Maine 12 C3
Maingkwan 41 D11
Mainit, L. 36 C3
Mainland, Orkney, U.K. . . 10 B5
Mainland, Shet., U.K. . . . 10 A6
Mainz 14 C5
Maipú 94 D5
Maiquetía 90 A5
Mairabari 41 D9
Maitland, N.S.W., Australia 63 B5
Maitland, S. Austral.,
    Australia 62 B2
Maizuru 33 F4
Majene 37 E1
Majorca = Mallorca 19 C7
Makale 37 E1
Makarikari = Makgadikgadi
    Salt Pans 59 C5
Makasar = Ujung Pandang 37 F1
Makasar, Selat 37 E1
Makasar, Str. of = Makasar,
    Selat 37 E1
Makat 29 E6
Makedhonía □ 23 D4
Makedonija = Macedonia ■ 22 D3
Makeyevka = Makiyivka . . 25 D4
Makgadikgadi Salt Pans . 59 C5
Makhachkala 25 E6
Makian 37 D3
Makinsk 29 D8
Makiyivka 25 D4
Makkah 47 G4
Makó 16 E5
Makokou 56 D2
Makrai 43 H10
Makran 45 E5
Makran Coast Range 42 G4
Mākū 46 C6
Makurazaki 33 H2
Makurdi 53 G7
Malabar Coast 43 P9
Malabo = Rey Malabo . . . 56 D1
Malacca, Str. of 38 D1
Maladzyechna 17 A8
Málaga 18 D3
Malagasy Rep. =
    Madagascar ■ 59 J9
Malakal 55 G5
Malakand 42 B7
Malang 39 F4
Malanje 56 F3
Mälaren 9 D9

Malargüe 94 D3
Malaryta 17 C7
Malatya 46 C4
Malawi ■ 59 A6
Malawi, L. = Nyasa, L. ... 59 A6
Malay Pen. 38 C2
Malaybalay 36 C3
Malåyer 46 D7
Malaysia ■ 38 D4
Malazgirt 46 C5
Malbooma 62 B1
Malbork 16 A4
Malden I. 65 K15
Maldives ■ 26 J11
Maldonado 94 C6
Maléa, Ákra 23 F4
Malegaon 43 J9
Malema 59 A7
Malha 55 E4
Mali ■ 53 E5
Mali → 41 E11
Maliku 37 E2
Malili 37 E2
Malin Hd. 10 D3
Malindi 57 E8
Malines = Mechelen ... 14 C3
Malino 37 D2
Malita 36 C3
Malkara 22 D6
Mallacoota Inlet 63 C4
Mallaig 10 C4
Mallawi 54 C5
Mallorca 19 C7
Mallow 11 E2
Malmö 9 D8
Malolos 36 B2
Malpelo, I. de 90 C2
Malta ■ 21 G5
Maltahöhe 58 C3
Maluku 37 E3
Maluku □ 37 E3
Maluku Sea = Molucca Sea 37 E2
Malvan 43 L8
Malvinas, Is. = Falkland
  Is. ☑ 95 G5
Malyn 17 C9
Malyy Lyakhovskiy, Ostrov 31 B12
Mamanguape 92 D6
Mamasa 37 E1
Mamberamo → 37 E5
Mambilima Falls 57 G5
Mamburao 36 B2
Mamoré → 91 F5
Mamou 53 F3
Mamuju 37 E1
Man 53 G4
Man, I. of 11 D4
Man Na 41 F11
Manaar, G. of = Mannar, G.
  of 43 Q11
Manacapuru 90 D6
Manacor 19 C7
Manado 37 D2
Managua 85 E7
Manakara 59 J9
Manama = Al Manämah ... 44 E2
Mananjary 59 J9
Manaos = Manaus 90 D7
Manapouri 65 F2
Manapouri, L. 65 F2
Manas 34 B3
Manas → 41 D8
Manaung 41 H9
Manaus 90 D7
Manchester, U.K. 11 E5
Manchester, U.S.A. 77 C10
Mand → 44 D3
Mandal 9 D7
Mandala, Puncak 37 E6
Mandalay 41 F11
Mandalī 46 D6
Mandar, Teluk 37 E1

Mandaue 36 B2
Mandi 42 D10
Mandimba 59 A7
Mandioli 37 E3
Mandla 40 F3
Mandritsara 59 H9
Mandsaur 43 G9
Mandvi 43 H6
Mandya 43 N10
Manfalût 54 C5
Manfredónia 20 D5
Mangalia 22 C7
Mangalore 43 N9
Mangaweka 64 C6
Manggar 39 E3
Manggawitu 37 E4
Mangkalihat, Tanjung ... 37 D1
Mangla Dam 42 C8
Mangnai 34 C4
Mango 53 F6
Mangoche 59 A7
Mangole 37 E3
Mangonui 64 A5
Mangueira, L. da 94 C6
Mangyshlak Poluostrov ... 29 E6
Manica 59 B6
Manicoré 91 E6
Manicouagan → 71 D4
Manifah 47 F7
Manihiki 65 L14
Manila 36 B2
Manila B. 36 B2
Manilla 63 B5
Manipur □ 41 E9
Manipur → 41 F10
Manisa 23 E6
Manitoba □ 69 C10
Manitoba, L. 69 C10
Manitowoc 76 B2
Manizales 90 B3
Manjhand 42 G6
Manjra → 43 K10
Manmad 43 J9
Manna 39 E2
Mannahill 62 B3
Mannar 43 Q11
Mannar, G. of 43 Q11
Mannar I. 43 Q11
Mannheim 14 D5
Mannum 62 B2
Manokwari 37 E4
Manono 57 F5
Manosque 13 E6
Manresa 19 B6
Mansa 57 G5
Mansel I. 70 B2
Mansfield, Australia 63 C4
Mansfield, U.K. 11 E6
Mansfield, U.S.A. 76 D4
Manta 90 D2
Mantalingajan, Mt. 38 C5
Mantes-la-Jolie 12 B4
Manthani 43 K11
Mántova 20 B3
Manu 91 F4
Manuel Alves → 93 E4
Manui 37 E2
Manych-Gudilo, Ozero ... 25 D5
Manzai 42 C7
Manzanares 18 C4
Manzanillo, Cuba 86 B4
Manzanillo, Mexico 84 D4
Manzhouli 35 B6
Mao, Chad 55 F2
Maó, Spain 19 C8
Maoke, Pegunungan 37 E5
Maoming 35 D6
Mapam Yumco 40 B3
Mapia, Kepulauan 37 D4
Mapuera → 90 D7
Maputo 59 D6
Maqnä 47 E3

Maquan He =
  Brahmaputra → 41 F7
Maquela do Zombo 56 F3
Maquinchao 95 E3
Mar Chiquita, L. 94 C4
Mar del Plata 94 D5
Mar Menor 19 D5
Maraã 90 D5
Marabá 92 D4
Maracá, I. de 92 B3
Maracaibo 90 A4
Maracaibo, L. de 90 B4
Maracay 90 A5
Maradi 53 F7
Marägheh 46 C6
Maräh 47 F6
Marajó, I. de 92 C4
Marand 46 C6
Maranguape 92 C6
Maranhão = São Luís ... 92 C5
Maranhão □ 92 D4
Maranoa → 63 A4
Marañón → 90 D4
Marão 59 C6
Maraş = Kahramanmaraş 46 C4
Maratua 37 D1
Marbella 18 D3
Marburg 14 C5
Marche 12 C4
Marchena 18 D3
Mardan 42 B8
Mardin 46 C5
Marek = Stanke Dimitrov 22 C4
Margarita, I. de 90 A6
Margaritovo 32 B4
Margate 11 F7
Margilan 29 E8
Märgow, Dasht-e 42 D3
Mari El □ 24 B6
Maria I. 62 D4
Maria van Diemen, C. ... 64 A5
Mariana Trench 64 H9
Maribor 20 A5
Marie Byrd Land 96 B18
Mariecourt = Kangiqsujuaq 70 B3
Mariental 58 C3
Mariinsk 29 D9
Marília 93 G3
Marin 18 A1
Marinduque 36 B2
Maringá 94 A6
Marion 81 A9
Mariscal Estigarribia ... 91 H6
Maritimes, Alpes 13 D7
Maritsa = Évros → 22 D6
Mariupol 25 D4
Marivän 46 D6
Marka = Merca 49 G3
Markham, Mt. 96 C15
Marks 24 C6
Marla 62 A1
Marmagao 43 M8
Marmara 23 D6
Marmara Denizi 23 D7
Marmaris 23 F7
Marmolada, Mte. 20 A3
Marne → 12 B5
Maroantsetra 59 H9
Marondera 59 B6
Maroni → 92 A3
Maroochydore 63 A5
Maroona 62 C3
Maroua 55 F1
Marovoay 59 H9
Marquises, Is. 65 K17
Marrakech 52 B4
Marrawah 62 D3
Marree 62 A2
Marrowie Cr. → 63 B4
Marrupa 59 A7
Marsá Matrûh 54 B4
Marsabit 57 D7

Marsala	21	F4
Marsden	63	B4
Marseille	13	E6
Marshall	81	C6
Marshall Is. ■	64	J12
Marshalltown	75	D8
Martaban	41	J11
Martaban, G. of	41	J11
Martapura, *Kalimantan, Indonesia*	39	E4
Martapura, *Sumatera, Indonesia*	39	E2
Martigues	13	E6
Martinborough	65	D6
Martinique ☑	87	D7
Martinsville	83	A8
Marton	64	D6
Martos	18	D4
Marudi	39	D4
Maruf	42	D5
Marugame	33	F3
Marwar	42	G8
Mary	29	F7
Maryborough = Port Laoise	11	E3
Maryborough, *Queens., Australia*	63	A5
Maryborough, *Vic., Australia*	62	C3
Maryland ☐	77	E7
Marzūq	54	C1
Marzūq, Idehan	54	D1
Masaka	57	E6
Masalembo, Kepulauan	39	F4
Masalima, Kepulauan	39	F5
Masamba	37	E2
Masan	35	C7
Masandam, Ra's	44	E4
Masasi	57	G7
Masaya	85	E7
Masbate	36	B2
Mascara	52	A6
Masela	37	F3
Maseru	59	D5
Mashābih	47	F4
Mashhad	44	B4
Māshkel, Hāmūn-i-	42	E3
Mashki Chāh	42	E3
Masindi	57	D6
Masjed Soleyman	47	E7
Mask, L.	11	E2
Maskin	44	F4
Masohi = Amahai	37	E3
Mason City	75	D8
Masqat	45	F4
Massa	20	B3
Massachusetts ☐	77	C9
Massakory	55	F2
Massangena	59	C6
Massena	77	B8
Massénya	55	F2
Massif Central	13	D5
Massinga	59	C7
Masson I.	96	A11
Mastanli = Momchilgrad	22	D5
Masterton	65	D6
Mastuj	42	A8
Mastung	42	E5
Masty	17	B7
Masuda	33	F2
Masvingo	59	C6
Matadi	56	F2
Matagalpa	85	E7
Matagami, L.	71	D3
Matak	39	D3
Matam	53	E3
Matamoros, *Coahuila, Mexico*	84	B4
Matamoros, *Tamaulipas, Mexico*	84	B5
Ma'ṭan as Sarra	54	D3
Matane	71	D4
Matanzas	86	B3
Matapan, C. = Taínaron, Ákra	23	F4
Mataram	39	F5
Matarani	91	G4
Mataró	19	B7
Mataura	65	G3
Matehuala	84	C4
Matera	21	D6
Mathráki	23	E2
Mathura	42	F10
Mati	36	C3
Matíri Ra.	65	D5
Mato Grosso ☐	93	E3
Mato Grosso, Planalto do	93	F3
Mato Grosso do Sul ☐	93	F3
Matochkin Shar	28	B6
Matosinhos	18	B1
Maṭruḥ	45	F4
Matsue	33	F3
Matsumae	32	C7
Matsumoto	33	E6
Matsusaka	33	F5
Matsuyama	33	G3
Mattagami ➡	71	C2
Mattancheri	43	Q10
Matthew's Ridge	90	B6
Matucana	91	F3
Matún = Khowst	42	C6
Maturín	90	B6
Mau Ranipur	43	G11
Maubeuge	13	A5
Maude	63	B3
Maudin Sun	41	K10
Maués	90	D7
Mauganj	40	E3
Maui	78	H12
Maulamyaing = Moulmein	41	J11
Maumere	37	F2
Maun	58	B4
Maungmagan Kyunzu	41	K11
Mauritania ■	53	E3
Mauritius ■	51	H9
Mawk Mai	41	G11
Mawlaik	41	F10
Mawlamyine = Moulmein	41	J11
Mawson Coast	96	A10
Mayaguana	87	B5
Mayagüez	87	C6
Maydena	62	D4
Mayenne ➡	12	C3
Maykop	25	E5
Mayo	68	B6
Mayo Volcano	36	B2
Mayor I.	64	B7
Mayu	37	D3
Mazabuka	59	B5
Mazagán = El Jadida	52	B4
Mazagão	92	C3
Mazán	90	D4
Māzandarān ☐	44	B3
Mazar-e Sharif	45	B6
Mazara del Vallo	21	F4
Mazarrón	19	D5
Mazaruni ➡	90	B7
Mazatlán	84	C3
Māzhān	44	C4
Mazinān	44	B4
Mazoe ➡	59	B6
Mazurski, Pojezierze	16	B5
Mazyr	17	C9
Mbabane	59	D6
Mbaïki	56	D3
Mbala	57	F6
Mbale	57	D6
Mbalmayo	56	D2
Mbamba Bay	57	G6
Mbandaka	56	D3
Mbanza Congo	56	F2
Mbanza Ngungu	56	F2
Mbarara	57	E6
Mbeya	57	F6
Mbini = Río Muni ☐	56	D2
Mbour	53	F2
Mbuji-Mayi	56	F4
Mead, L.	78	B5
Mearim ➡	92	C5
Meaux	13	B5
Mecca = Makkah	47	G4
Mechelen	14	C3
Mecheria	52	B5
Mecklenburg	15	B6
Mecklenburger Bucht	15	A6
Medan	39	D1
Medanosa, Pta.	95	F3
Médéa	52	A6
Medellín	90	B3
Medford	72	E2
Medgidia	22	B7
Medicine Bow Ra.	73	F10
Medicine Hat	69	C8
Medina = Al Madīnah	47	F4
Medina del Campo	18	B3
Medina Sidonia	18	D3
Medinipur	40	F6
Mediterranean Sea	50	C5
Médoc	12	D3
Medveditsa ➡	24	D5
Medvezhyegorsk	28	C4
Meekatharra	60	F2
Meerut	42	E10
Mégara	23	F4
Meghalaya ☐	41	E8
Meiktila	41	G10
Meissen	15	C7
Meizhou	35	D6
Mejillones	94	A2
Mekhtar	42	D6
Meknès	52	B4
Mekong ➡	41	H9
Mekongga	37	E2
Mekvari = Kür ➡	25	E6
Melagiri Hills	43	N10
Melaka	39	D2
Melalap	38	C5
Melanesia	64	K10
Melbourne, *Australia*	63	C3
Melbourne, *U.S.A.*	83	E7
Mélèzes ➡	70	C3
Melfort	69	C9
Melilla	19	E4
Melitopol	25	D4
Melk	15	D8
Melo	94	C6
Melolo	37	F2
Melrose	63	B4
Melun	13	B5
Melville	69	C9
Melville I.	60	C5
Melville Pen.	70	B2
Memboro	37	F1
Memel = Klaipėda	24	B1
Memmingen	14	E6
Mempawah	39	D3
Memphis, *Tenn., U.S.A.*	82	B3
Memphis, *Tex., U.S.A.*	80	B3
Ménaka	53	E6
Menan = Chao Phraya ➡	38	B2
Mendawai ➡	39	E4
Mende	13	D5
Mendocino, C.	72	F1
Mendoza	94	C3
Mene Grande	90	B4
Menemen	23	E6
Menggala	39	E3
Mengzi	34	D5
Menindee	62	B3
Menindee L.	62	B3
Meningie	62	C2
Menominee	76	B2
Menongue	58	A3
Menorca	19	C7
Mentawai, Kepulauan	39	E1
Menton	14	E7
Meppel	14	B4
Merabéllou, Kólpos	23	G5

Merano 20 A3
Merauke 37 F6
Merbein 62 B3
Merca 49 G3
Merced 78 B2
Mercedes, Buenos Aires,
  Argentina 94 C5
Mercedes, Corrientes,
  Argentina 94 B4
Mercedes, San Luis,
  Argentina 94 C3
Mercedes, Uruguay 94 C5
Mercer 64 B6
Mercy, C. 70 B4
Meredith, C. 95 G4
Mergui Arch. = Myeik
  Kyunzu 38 B1
Mérida, Mexico 85 C7
Mérida, Spain 18 C2
Mérida, Venezuela 90 B4
Meridian 82 C5
Merirumã 92 B3
Merriwa 63 B5
Merseburg 15 C6
Mersin 46 C3
Mersing 39 D2
Merthyr Tydfil 11 F5
Mértola 18 D2
Meru 57 D7
Mesa 79 D7
Meshed = Mashhad 44 B4
Mesolóngion 23 E3
Mesopotamia = Al Jazirah 21 E5
Messina 21 E5
Messina, Str. di 21 E5
Messini 23 F4
Messiniakós Kólpos 23 F4
Mesta → 22 D5
Meta → 90 B5
Metairie 81 E8
Metán 94 B4
Methven 65 E4
Metlakatla 69 C6
Metz 13 B7
Meulaboh 39 D1
Meureudu 38 C1
Meuse → 13 A6
Mexiana, I. 92 C4
Mexicali 84 A1
México 84 D5
Mexico ■ 84 C4
Mexico, G. of 85 C7
Meymaneh 42 B4
Mezen 28 C5
Mezen → 28 C5
Mézenc, Mt. 13 D6
Mezőkövesd 16 E5
Mezőtúr 16 E5
Mhow 43 H9
Miami 83 G7
Miami Beach 83 G7
Miàndowāb 46 C6
Miandrivazo 59 H9
Miàneh 46 C6
Mianwali 42 C7
Miass 29 D7
Michigan □ 76 C2
Michigan, L. 76 C2
Michurin 22 C6
Michurinsk 24 C5
Micronesia, Federated
  States of ■ 64 J10
Middelburg 58 E5
Middlesbrough 11 D6
Midi, Canal du → 12 E4
Midland 80 D3
Midyat 46 C5
Midzŏr 22 C4
Międzychód 16 B2
Międzyrzec Podlaski ... 17 C6
Mielec 16 C5
Mieres 18 A3

Mikhaylovgrad = Montana 22 C4
Mikonos 23 F5
Milagro 90 D3
Milan = Milano 20 B2
Milano 20 B2
Milâs 23 F6
Milazzo 21 E5
Mildura 62 B3
Miles 63 A5
Miletus 23 F6
Milford Haven 11 F4
Milford Sd. 65 F2
Milḥ, Baḥr al 47 D5
Mill I. 96 A12
Millau 13 D5
Millennium I. = Caroline I. 65 K15
Millicent 62 C3
Millinocket 77 B11
Millmerran 63 A5
Milos 23 F5
Milparinka 62 A3
Milton 65 G3
Milton Keynes 11 E6
Milwaukee 76 C2
Min Jiang →, Fujian, China 35 D6
Min Jiang →, Sichuan,
  China 35 D5
Mina Su'ud 47 E7
Mina'al Aḥmadī 47 E7
Minamata 33 G2
Minas 94 C5
Minas Gerais □ 93 F4
Minbu 41 G10
Mindanao 36 C2
Mindanao Sea = Bohol Sea 36 C2
Mindanao Trench 36 B3
Minden 14 B5
Mindiptana 37 F6
Mindoro 36 B2
Mindoro Str. 36 B2
Mingäçevir Su Anbarı .. 25 E6
Mingin 41 F10
Mingteke Daban = Mintaka
  Pass 42 A9
Minho = Miño → 18 B1
Minho 18 B1
Minna 53 G7
Minneapolis 75 C8
Minnesota □ 75 B7
Minnipa 62 B2
Miño → 18 B1
Minorca = Menorca 19 C7
Minot 74 A4
Minsk 24 C2
Mińsk Mazowiecki 16 B5
Mintaka Pass 42 A9
Minutang 41 C11
Mira 20 B4
Miraj 43 L9
Miram Shah 42 C7
Miramichi 71 D4
Miranda 93 G2
Miranda de Ebro 19 A4
Miranda do Douro 18 B2
Miri 38 D4
Mirim, L. 94 C6
Mirpur Khas 42 G6
Mirzapur 40 E4
Mish'āb, Ra's al 47 E7
Mishan 35 B8
Miskolc 16 D5
Misool 37 E4
Miṣrātah 54 B2
Missinaibi → 71 C2
Mississippi □ 81 C9
Mississippi → 81 E9
Mississippi River Delta 81 E9
Missoula 73 C7
Missouri □ 75 F8
Missouri → 75 F9
Mistassini, L. 71 C3
Misurata = Miṣrātah ... 54 B2

Mitchell, Australia ... 63 A4
Mitchell, U.S.A. 74 D5
Mitchell → 61 D7
Mitilini 23 E6
Mito 33 E7
Mitrovica = Kosovska
  Mitrovica 22 C3
Mittagong 63 B5
Mittimatalik = Pond Inlet 70 A3
Mitú 90 C4
Mitumba, Mts. 57 F5
Mitwaba 57 F5
Miyake-Jima 33 F6
Miyako 32 D7
Miyakonojŏ 33 H2
Miyazaki 33 H2
Miyet, Bahr el = Dead Sea 47 E3
Mizdah 54 B1
Mizoram □ 41 F9
Mjøsa 8 C8
Mladá Boleslav 16 C2
Mława 16 B5
Mljet 20 C6
Mmabatho 59 D5
Mo i Rana 8 B8
Moa 37 F3
Moabaye 56 D4
Moabayi 56 D4
Mobile 82 D3
Mobutu Sese Seko, L. =
  Albert, L. 57 D6
Moçambique 59 H8
Moçâmedes = Namibe 58 B2
Mochudi 59 C5
Mocimboa da Praia 57 G8
Mocoa 90 C3
Mocuba 59 B7
Modane 13 D7
Módena 20 B3
Modesto 78 B2
Módica 21 F5
Moe 63 C4
Moengo 92 A3
Mogadishu = Muqdisho .. 49 G4
Mogador = Essaouira ... 52 B4
Mogami-Gawa → 32 D7
Mogaung 41 E11
Mogi das Cruzes 94 A7
Mogilev = Mahilyow 17 B10
Mogilev-Podolskiy =
  Mohyliv-Podilskyy ... 17 D8
Mogok 41 F11
Mohács 16 F4
Moḥammadābād 44 B4
Mohyliv-Podilskyy 17 D8
Moisie → 71 C4
Mojave Desert 78 C4
Mokai 64 C6
Mokokchung 41 D10
Mokra Gora 22 C3
Molchanovo 29 D9
Moldavia = Moldova ■ .. 17 E9
Molde 8 C7
Moldova ■ 17 E9
Moldoveanu, Vf. 17 F7
Molepolole 59 C5
Molfetta 20 D6
Moline 75 E9
Mollendo 91 G4
Molodechno =
  Maladzyechna 17 A8
Moloka'i 78 H12
Molong 63 B4
Molopo → 58 D4
Molotov = Perm 29 D6
Molu 37 F4
Molucca Sea 37 E2
Moluccas = Maluku 37 E3
Moma 37 E3
Mombasa 57 E7
Mombetsu 32 A8
Momchilgrad 22 D5

Mompós	90	B4
Mona Passage	87	C6
Monaco ■	13	E7
Monahans	80	D2
Monastir = Bitola	22	D3
Moncayo, Sierra del	19	B5
Mönchengladbach	14	C4
Monchique	18	D1
Monclova	84	B4
Mondego ➤	18	B1
Mondeodo	37	E2
Mondovì	20	B1
Monforte de Lemos	18	A2
Mông Hsu	41	G12
Mong Kung	41	G11
Mong Nai	41	G11
Mong Pawk	41	F12
Mong Ton	41	G12
Mong Wa	41	G13
Mong Yai	41	F12
Mongalla	55	G5
Monghyr = Munger	40	E6
Mongibello = Etna	21	F4
Mongo	55	F2
Mongolia ■	35	B5
Mongu	58	B4
Monkoto	56	E4
Monópoli	21	D6
Monroe, La., U.S.A.	81	C7
Monroe, N.C., U.S.A.	83	B7
Monrovia	53	G3
Mons	14	C2
Monse	37	E2
Mont-de-Marsan	12	E3
Mont-St-Michel, Le	12	B3
Montalbán	19	B5
Montana	22	C4
Montana □	73	C9
Montargis	13	C5
Montauban	12	D4
Montbéliard	13	C7
Montceau-les-Mines	13	C6
Monte Alegre	92	C3
Monte Azul	93	F5
Monte-Carlo	20	C1
Monte Caseros	94	C4
Monte Comán	94	C3
Monte Santu, C. di	21	D2
Montecristo	20	C3
Montego Bay	86	C4
Montélimar	13	D6
Montemorelos	84	B5
Montenegro □	22	C2
Montepuez	59	A7
Monterey	78	B2
Montería	90	B3
Monterrey	84	B4
Montes Claros	93	F5
Montesilvano	20	C5
Montevideo	94	C5
Montgomery = Sahiwal	42	D8
Montgomery	82	C4
Montilla	18	D3
Montluçon	13	C5
Montmorillon	12	C4
Montoro	18	C3
Montpellier	13	E5
Montréal	71	D3
Montrose, U.K.	10	C5
Montrose, U.S.A.	79	A9
Montserrat ☑	87	C7
Monywa	41	F10
Monza	20	B2
Monze	59	B5
Monze, C.	43	G5
Monzón	19	B6
Moonie	63	A5
Moonie ➤	63	A4
Moonta	62	B2
Moose Jaw	69	C9
Moosomin	69	C9
Moosonee	71	C2
Mopti	53	F5
Moqor	42	C5
Moquegua	91	G4
Mora	8	C8
Moradabad	42	E11
Morafenobe	59	H8
Moramanga	59	H9
Moratuwa	43	R11
Morava ➤, Serbia & M.	22	B3
Morava ➤, Slovak Rep.	16	D3
Moravian Hts. = Českomoravská Vrchovina	16	D2
Morawhanna	90	B7
Moray Firth	10	C5
Morden	69	D10
Mordvinia □	24	C5
Moree	63	A4
Morelia	84	D4
Morella	19	B5
Morena, Sierra	18	C3
Moreton I.	63	A5
Morgan City	81	E8
Morioka	32	D7
Morlaix	12	B2
Mornington	63	C4
Mornington, I.	95	F1
Moro G.	36	C2
Morocco ■	52	B4
Morogoro	57	F7
Morombe	59	J8
Morón	86	B4
Morón de la Frontera	18	D3
Morondava	59	J8
Morotai	37	D3
Moroto	57	D6
Morphou	46	D3
Morrinhos	93	F4
Morrinsville	64	B6
Morristown	83	A6
Morshansk	24	C5
Morteros	94	C4
Mortlake	62	C3
Morundah	63	B4
Moruya	63	C5
Morvan	13	C6
Morven	63	A4
Morwell	63	C4
Moscos Is.	41	L11
Moscow = Moskva	24	B4
Moscow	72	C5
Mosel ➤	13	A7
Moselle = Mosel ➤	13	A7
Mosgiel	65	F4
Moshi	57	E7
Mosjøen	8	B8
Moskva	24	B4
Mosonmagyaróvár	16	E3
Mosquera	90	C3
Moss Vale	63	B5
Mossburn	65	F3
Mosselbaai	58	E4
Mossendjo	56	E2
Mossgiel	63	B3
Mossoró	92	D6
Most	16	C1
Mostaganem	52	A6
Mostar	20	C6
Mostardas	94	C6
Mosty = Masty	17	B7
Mostyska	17	D6
Mosul = Al Mawşil	46	C5
Motihari	40	D5
Motril	18	D4
Motueka	65	D5
Motueka ➤	65	D5
Moúdhros	23	E5
Mouila	56	E2
Moulamein	63	C3
Moulins	13	C5
Moulmein	41	J11
Moundou	55	G2
Mount Barker	62	C2
Mount Cook	65	E4
Mount Gambier	62	C3
Mount Hope, N.S.W., Australia	63	B4
Mount Hope, S. Austral., Australia	62	B2
Mount Isa	61	E6
Mount Lofty Ra.	62	B2
Mount Maunganui	64	B7
Mount Perry	63	A5
Moura, Brazil	90	D6
Moura, Portugal	18	C2
Mourdi, Dépression du	55	E3
Moussoro	55	F2
Moutong	37	D2
Moyale	57	D7
Moyen Atlas	52	B4
Moyo	39	F5
Moyyero ➤	30	C8
Moyynty	29	E8
Mozambique = Moçambique	59	H8
Mozambique ■	59	B7
Mozambique Chan.	51	H8
Mozdok	25	E5
Mozyr = Mazyr	17	C9
Mpanda	57	F6
Mpika	59	A6
Mpwapwa	57	F7
Mthatha	59	E5
Mu Us Shamo	35	C5
Muar	39	D2
Muarabungo	39	E2
Muaraenim	39	E2
Muarajuloi	39	E4
Muarakaman	39	E5
Muaratebo	39	E2
Muaratembesi	39	E2
Muaratewe	39	E4
Mubarraz = Al Mubarraz	47	F7
Mubi	55	F1
Muckadilla	63	A4
Mucuri	93	F6
Mudanjiang	35	B7
Mudanya	23	D7
Mudgee	63	B4
Mufulira	59	A5
Mugi	33	G4
Muğla	23	F7
Mugu	40	C4
Muhammad Qol	54	D6
Mühlhausen	14	C6
Mühlig Hofmann fjell	96	B7
Mujnak = Muynak	29	E6
Mukacheve	17	D6
Mukah	39	D4
Mukden = Shenyang	35	B7
Mukomuko	39	E2
Muktsar	42	D9
Mukur = Moqor	42	C5
Mula	19	C5
Mulchén	94	D2
Mulde ➤	15	C7
Mulhacén	18	D4
Mulhouse	13	C7
Mull	10	C4
Muller, Pegunungan	39	D4
Mullingar	11	E3
Mullumbimby	63	A5
Multan	42	D7
Mumbai	43	K8
Muna	37	F2
München	15	D6
Munchen-Gladbach = Mönchengladbach	14	C4
Muncie	76	D3
Münden	14	C5
Mundo Novo	93	E5
Mungallala	63	A4
Mungallala Cr. ➤	63	A4
Mungbere	57	D5

Munger	40	E6
Munich = München	15	D6
Muñoz Gamero, Pen.	95	G2
Münster	14	C4
Munster □	11	E2
Muntok	39	E3
Muqdisho	49	G4
Murallón, Cerro	95	F2
Murang'a	57	E7
Murashi	24	B6
Muratlı	22	D6
Murchison ➔	60	F1
Murchison, Mt.	96	B15
Murchison Falls	57	D6
Murcia	19	C5
Murcia □	19	D5
Mureş ➔	22	A3
Murfreesboro	82	B4
Murgab = Murghob	29	F8
Murghob	29	F8
Murgon	63	A5
Müritz	15	B7
Murmansk	8	B12
Murom	24	B5
Muroran	32	B7
Muroto	33	G4
Muroto-Misaki	33	G4
Murray ➔	62	C2
Murray Bridge	62	C2
Murrumbidgee ➔	62	B3
Murrumburrah	63	B5
Murrurundi	62	C3
Murtoa	62	C3
Murwara	40	F3
Murwillumbah	63	A5
Mürzzuschlag	15	E8
Muş	46	C5
Mûsa, Gebel	47	E3
Musa Khel	42	D6
Mûsa Qal'eh	42	C4
Musala, *Bulgaria*	22	C4
Musala, *Indonesia*	39	D1
Muscat = Masqat	47	C6
Muscat & Oman = Oman ■	48	C6
Muscatine	75	E9
Musgrave Ranges	60	F5
Mushie	56	E3
Musi ➔	39	E2
Musina	59	C6
Muskogee	81	B6
Musoma	57	E6
Mussoorie	42	D11
Mustafakemalpaşa	23	D7
Mustang	40	C4
Musters, L.	95	F3
Muswellbrook	63	B5
Mût, *Egypt*	54	C4
Mut, *Turkey*	46	C3
Muzhi	28	C7
Mvuma	59	B6
Mwanza, *Dem. Rep. of*		
the Congo	57	F5
Mwanza, *Tanzania*	57	E6
Mweka	56	E4
Mweru, L.	57	F5
Mwinilunga	58	A4
My Tho	38	B3
Myanaung	41	H10
Myanmar = Burma ■	41	G11
Myaungmya	41	J10
Mycenæ	23	F4
Myeik Kyunzu	38	B1
Myingyan	41	G10
Myitkyina	41	E11
Mykolayiv	25	D3
Mymensingh	41	E8
Myrdalsjökull	8	C2
Mysia	23	E6
Mysore = Karnataka □	43	N10
Mysore	43	N10
Myszków	16	C4
Mytishchi	24	B4

N

Na Hearadh = Harris	10	C3
Naab ➔	15	D7
Naberezhnyye Chelny	29	D6
Nabeul	54	A1
Nabire	37	E5
Nâblus = Nābulus	46	D3
Nābulus	46	D3
Nachingwea	57	G7
Nacogdoches	81	D6
Nacozari de García	84	A3
Nadiad	43	H8
Nadüshan	44	C3
Nadvirna	17	D7
Nadym	28	C8
Nadym ➔	28	C8
Nafud Desert = An Nafūd	47	E5
Naga	36	B2
Nagaland □	41	E10
Nagano	33	E6
Nagaoka	33	E6
Nagappattinam	43	P11
Nagar Parkar	43	G7
Nagasaki	33	G1
Nagaur	42	F8
Nagercoil	43	Q10
Nagineh	44	C4
Nagoya	33	F5
Nagpur	43	J11
Nagykanizsa	16	E3
Nagykőrös	16	E4
Naha	35	D7
Nahāvand	46	D7
Nain, *Canada*	70	C4
Nā'īn, *Iran*	44	C3
Nairn	10	C5
Nairobi	57	E7
Najafābād	44	C2
Najd	47	F5
Najibabad	42	E11
Nakamura	33	G3
Nakashibetsu	32	B9
Nakhfar al Buşayyah	47	E6
Nakhichevan = Naxçıvan	25	F6
Nakhichevan Rep. =		
Naxçıvan □	25	F6
Nakhodka	32	B3
Nakhon Phanom	38	A2
Nakhon Ratchasima	38	B2
Nakhon Sawan	38	A2
Nakhon Si Thammarat	38	C2
Nakina	71	C2
Nakuru	57	E7
Nal ➔	42	G4
Nalchik	25	E5
Nalgonda	43	L11
Nallamalai Hills	43	M11
Nam Co	34	C4
Nam-Phan	38	B3
Namak, Daryācheh-ye	44	C3
Namak, Kavir-e	44	C4
Namaland	58	C3
Namangan	29	E8
Namapa	59	A7
Namber	37	E4
Nambour	63	A5
Nambucca Heads	63	B5
Namib Desert	58	C2
Namibe	58	B2
Namibia ■	58	C3
Namlea	37	E3
Namoi ➔	63	B4
Nampa	72	E5
Namp'o	35	C7
Nampō-Shotō	33	H7
Nampula	59	B7
Namrole	37	E3
Namse Shankou	40	C4
Namtu	41	F11
Namur	14	C3
Nan-ch'ang = Nanchang	35	D6
Nanaimo	69	D7
Nanango	63	A5
Nanao	33	E5
Nanchang	35	D6
Nanching = Nanjing	35	C6
Nanchong	35	C5
Nancy	13	B7
Nanda Devi	42	D11
Nanded	43	K10
Nandewar Ra.	63	B5
Nandurbar	43	J9
Nandyal	43	M11
Nanga-Eboko	56	D2
Nanga Parbat	42	B9
Nangapinoh	39	E4
Nangarhār □	42	B7
Nangatayap	39	E4
Nanjing	35	C6
Nanking = Nanjing	35	C6
Nanning	35	D5
Nanping	35	D6
Nansei-Shotō = Ryūkyū-		
rettō	35	D7
Nantes	12	C3
Nantucket I.	77	D10
Nanuque	93	F5
Nanusa, Kepulauan	36	D3
Nanyang	35	C6
Nanyuki	57	D7
Nao, C. de la	19	C6
Napa	72	G2
Napier	64	C7
Naples = Nápoli	21	D5
Naples	83	F7
Napo ➔	90	D4
Nápoli	21	D5
Nara	53	E4
Naracoorte	62	C3
Naradhan	63	B4
Narasapur	40	J3
Narathiwat	38	C2
Narayanganj	41	F8
Narayanpet	43	L10
Narbonne	13	E5
Nardò	23	D2
Narew ➔	16	B5
Narin	42	A6
Narmada ➔	43	J8
Narodnaya	28	C7
Narooma	63	C5
Narrabri	63	B4
Narran ➔	63	A4
Narrandera	63	B4
Narromine	63	B4
Narsimhapur	43	H11
Naruto	33	F4
Narva	24	B2
Narvik	8	B9
Naryan-Mar	28	C6
Narym	29	D9
Naryn	29	E8
Naseby	65	F4
Naser, Buheirat en	54	D5
Nashville	82	A4
Nasik	43	K8
Nasirabad	42	F9
Nassarawa	53	G7
Nassau	86	A4

Nassau, B. 95 H3
Nasser, L. = Naser, Buheirat
  en 54 D5
Natal, *Brazil* 92 D6
Natal, *Indonesia* 39 D1
Naṭanz 44 C2
Natashquan 71 C4
Natashquan → 71 C4
Natchez 81 D8
Nathalia 63 C4
Nathdwara 43 G8
Natitingou 53 F6
Natkyizin 41 K11
Natron, L. 57 E7
Natuna Besar, Kepulauan . 39 D3
Natuna Selatan, Kepulauan 39 D3
Naturaliste, C. 62 D4
Naujaat = Repulse Bay .. 70 B2
Naumburg 15 C6
Nauru ■ 64 K11
Naushahra = Nowshera . 42 B8
Nauta 90 D4
Nautanwa 40 D4
Navahrudak 17 B7
Navalmoral de la Mata .. 18 C3
Navarino, I. 95 H3
Navarra □ 19 A5
Năvodari 22 B7
Navoi = Nawoiy 29 E7
Navojoa 84 B3
Návpaktos 23 E3
Návplion 23 F4
Navsari 43 J8
Nawabshah 42 F6
Nawakot 40 D5
Nawalgarh 42 F9
Nawāsif, Ḥarrat 47 G5
Nawoiy 29 E7
Naxçivan 25 F6
Naxçivan □ 25 F6
Náxos 23 F5
Nãy Band 44 E3
Nayoro 32 A8
Nazas → 84 B4
Nazili 23 F7
Ndalatando 56 F2
Ndélé 56 C4
Ndjamena 55 F1
Ndola 59 A5
Neagh, Lough 11 D3
Near Is. 69 C1
Neath 11 F5
Nebitdag 29 F6
Nebraska □ 74 F6
Nébrodi, Monti 21 F5
Neckar → 14 D5
Necochea 94 D5
Neemuch = Nimach ... 43 G9
Neepawa 69 C10
Neftçala 46 C7
Negapatam =
  Nagappattinam 43 P11
Negele 49 F2
Negombo 43 R11
Negotin 22 B4
Negrais C. = Maudin Sun . 41 K10
Negro →, *Argentina* 95 E4
Negro →, *Brazil* 90 D6
Negro →, *Uruguay* 94 C5
Negros 36 C2
Nei Monggol Zizhiqu □ . 35 B6
Neijiang 35 D5
Neiva 90 C3
Nejd = Najd 47 F5
Nellore 43 M11
Nelson, *Canada* 69 D8
Nelson, *N.Z.* 65 D5
Nelson → 69 C10
Nelson, C. 62 C3
Nelson, Estrecho 95 G2
Nelspruit 59 D6

Néma 53 E4
Neman = Nemunas → . 24 B1
Nemunas → 24 B1
Nemuro 32 B9
Nemuro Str. 32 B9
Nenagh 11 E2
Nenjiang 35 B7
Nepal ■ 40 D5
Nepalganj 40 C3
Neretva → 20 C6
Ness, L. 10 C4
Nesterov 17 C6
Nesvizh = Nyasvizh ... 17 B8
Netherlands ■ 14 B3
Netherlands Antilles ☒ .. 87 D6
Nettilling L. 70 B3
Neubrandenburg 15 B7
Neumünster 14 A5
Neunkirchen 14 D4
Neuquén 94 D3
Neuruppin 15 B7
Neustrelitz 15 B7
Neva → 24 B3
Nevada □ 72 G5
Nevers 13 C5
Nevertire 63 B4
Nevinnomyssk 25 E5
Nevşehir 46 C3
New Amsterdam 90 B7
New Angledool 63 A4
New Bedford 77 D10
New Bern 83 B9
New Brighton 65 E5
New Britain, *Papua N. G.* . 64 K10
New Britain, *U.S.A.* ... 77 D9
New Brunswick □ 71 D4
New Caledonia ☒ 64 M11
New Castile = Castilla-La
  Mancha □ 18 C4
New Delhi 42 E10
New England Ra. 63 B5
New Glasgow 71 D4
New Hampshire □ ... 77 C10
New Haven 77 D9
New Hebrides = Vanuatu ■ 64 L11
New Ireland 64 K10
New Jersey □ 77 E10
New London 77 D9
New Mexico □ 79 C9
New Norfolk 62 D4
New Orleans 81 E8
New Plymouth 64 C6
New Providence I. ... 86 A4
New Siberian Is. =
  Novosibirskiye Ostrova . 31 B12
New South Wales □ .. 63 B4
New York 77 D9
New York □ 77 C8
Newark 77 D8
Newburgh 77 D8
Newbury 11 F6
Newcastle 63 B5
Newcastle-upon-Tyne .. 11 D6
Newfoundland &
  Labrador □ 71 C5
Newman 60 E2
Newport, *I. of W., U.K.* .. 11 F6
Newport, *Newp., U.K.* ... 11 F5
Newport, *U.S.A.* 77 D10
Newport News 77 F7
Newquay 11 F4
Newry 11 D3
Neya 24 B5
Neyriz 44 D3
Neyshābūr 44 B4
Nezhin = Nizhyn 24 C3
Ngabang 39 D3
Ngabordamlu, Tanjung . 37 F4
Nganglong Kangri 40 A3
Ngaoundéré 56 C2
Ngapara 65 F4

Ngoring Hu 34 C4
Nguigmi 55 F1
Nha Trang 38 B3
Nhill 62 C3
Niagara Falls, *Canada* .. 71 D3
Niagara Falls, *U.S.A.* ... 77 C6
Niah 39 D4
Niamey 53 F6
Nias 39 D1
Nicaragua ■ 85 E7
Nicaragua, L. de 85 E7
Nicastro 21 E6
Nice 13 E7
Nichinan 33 H2
Nicobar Is. 27 J13
Nicosia 46 D3
Nicoya, Pen. de 85 F7
Niedersachsen □ 14 B5
Niemen = Nemunas → .. 24 B1
Nienburg 14 B5
Nieuw Amsterdam ... 92 A2
Nieuw Nickerie 92 A2
Niğde 46 C3
Niger ■ 53 E7
Niger → 53 G7
Nigeria ■ 53 G7
Nightcaps 65 F3
Nii-Jima 33 F6
Niigata 33 E6
Ni'ihau 78 H10
Niitsu 33 E6
Nijmegen 14 C3
Nikiniki 37 F2
Nikolayev = Mykolayiv .. 25 D3
Nikolayevsk 24 C6
Nikopol 25 D3
Nikshahr 45 E5
Nikšić 22 C2
Nîl, Nahr en → 54 B5
Nîl el Abyad → 55 E5
Nîl el Azraq → 55 E5
Nile = Nîl, Nahr en → .. 54 B5
Nimach 43 G9
Nîmes 13 E6
Nimfaíon, Ákra = Pínnes,
  Ákra 23 D5
Nimmitabel 63 C4
Nimrūz □ 45 D5
Ninawá 46 C5
Nindigully 63 A4
Nineveh = Ninawá ... 46 C5
Ningbo 35 D7
Ningxia Huizu Zizhiqu □ . 35 C5
Niobrara → 74 D5
Nioro du Sahel 53 E4
Niort 12 C3
Nipawin 69 C9
Nipigon, L. 71 D2
Niquelândia 93 E4
Nirmal 43 K11
Nirmali 40 D6
Niš 22 C3
Nişāb, *Si. Arabia* ... 47 E6
Nişāb, *Yemen* 49 E4
Nistru = Dnister → ... 17 E10
Niterói 93 G5
Niue 65 L14
Niut 39 D4
Nivernais 13 C5
Nizamabad 43 K11
Nizamghat 41 C10
Nizhnevartovsk 29 C8
Nizhniy Novgorod ... 24 B5
Nizhniy Tagil 29 D6
Nizhyn 24 C3
Nkhotakota 59 A6
Nkongsamba 56 D1
Nmai → 41 E11
Noakhali = Maijdi ... 41 F8
Nobeoka 33 H2
Nocera Inferiore 21 D5
Nogales, *Mexico* ... 84 A2

Nogales, *U.S.A.*	79	E7
Nōgata	33	G2
Noginsk	30	C7
Noires, Mts.	12	B2
Noirmoutier, Î. de	12	C2
Nojima-Zaki	33	F6
Nok Kundi	42	E3
Nola	56	D3
Nome	69	B3
Nong Khai	38	A2
Noranda = Rouyn-Noranda	71	D3
Nord-Ostsee-Kanal	14	A5
Norderney	14	B4
Norderstedt	14	B5
Nordfriesische Inseln	14	A5
Nordhausen	14	C6
Nordkapp	8	A11
Nordrhein-Westfalen □	14	C4
Nordvik	30	B9
Norfolk	77	F7
Norfolk I.	64	M11
Norilsk	30	C6
Norman	80	B5
Norman Wells	68	B7
Normandie	12	B4
Normanton	61	D7
Norquinco	95	E2
Norrköping	9	D9
Norrland	8	C9
Norseman	60	G3
North Battleford	69	C9
North Bay	71	D3
North Bend	72	E1
North C.	64	A5
North Cape = Nordkapp	8	A11
North Carolina □	83	B7
North Channel	11	D4
North Dakota □	74	B4
North East Frontier Agency = Arunachal Pradesh □	41	C10
North Frisian Is. = Nordfriesische Inseln	14	A5
North I.	64	B5
North Korea ■	35	C7
North Lakhimpur	41	D10
North Minch	10	B4
North Ossetia □	25	E5
North Platte	74	E4
North Platte →	74	E4
North Rhine Westphalia = Nordrhein-Westfalen □	14	C4
North Saskatchewan →	69	C8
North Sea	10	D8
North Sporades = Vóriai Sporádhes	23	E4
North Taranaki Bight	64	C6
North Thompson →	69	C7
North Uist	10	C3
North West C.	60	E1
North West Frontier □	42	B8
North West Highlands	10	C4
North West River	71	C4
Northampton	11	E6
Northern Circars	40	J4
Northern Ireland □	11	D3
Northern Marianas ⊘	64	H9
Northern Territory □	60	D5
Northland □	64	A5
Northumberland, C.	62	C3
Northumberland Str.	71	D4
Northwest Territories □	68	B9
Norton Sd.	69	B3
Norway ■	8	C8
Norway House	69	C10
Norwegian Sea	6	B5
Norwich	11	E7
Noshiro	32	C7
Nogratābād	45	D4
Nossob →	58	D4
Nosy Be	59	G9
Nosy Boraha	59	H9
Nosy Varika	59	J9
Noteć →	16	B2
Notre Dame B.	71	D5
Notre-Dame-de-Koartac = Quaqtaq	70	B4
Notre-Dame-d'Ivugivic = Ivujivik	70	B3
Nottaway →	71	C3
Nottingham	11	E6
Nouâdhibou	52	D2
Nouâdhibou, Ras	52	D2
Nouakchott	53	E2
Nouméa	64	M11
Nouveau Comptoir = Wemindji	71	C3
Nouvelle-Calédonie = New Caledonia ⊘	64	M11
Nova Casa Nova	93	D5
Nova Friburgo	93	G5
Nova Gaia = Cambundi-Catembo	56	G3
Nova Iguaçu	93	G5
Nova Iorque	92	D5
Nova Lima	93	F5
Nova Lisboa = Huambo	58	A3
Nova Scotia □	71	D4
Nova Venécia	93	F5
Nova Zagora	22	C5
Novara	20	D7
Novaya Ladoga	24	A3
Novaya Lyalya	29	D7
Novaya Zemlya	28	B6
Novgorod	24	B3
Novhorod-Siverskyy	24	C3
Novi Lígure	20	B2
Novi Pazar	22	C3
Novi Sad	22	B2
Novo Mesto	20	B5
Novo Remanso	93	D5
Novoataysk	29	D9
Novocherkassk	25	D5
Novogrudok = Navahrudak	17	B7
Novohrad-Volynskyy	17	C8
Novokachalinsk	32	A3
Novokazalinsk = Zhangaqazaly	29	E7
Novokuybyshevsk	24	C6
Novokuznetsk	29	D9
Novomoskovsk	24	C4
Novorossiysk	25	E4
Novorybnoye	30	B8
Novoselytsya	17	D8
Novoshakhtinsk	25	D4
Novosibirsk	29	D9
Novosibirskiye Ostrova	31	B12
Novotroitsk	29	D6
Novouzensk	24	C6
Novovolynsk	17	C7
Novska	20	B6
Novyy Port	28	C8
Nowa Sól	16	C2
Nowgong	41	D9
Nowra	63	B5
Nowshera	42	B8
Nowy Targ	16	D5
Nowy Tomyśl	16	B3
Noyon	13	B5
Nsanje	59	B7
Nubian Desert = Nûbîya, Es Sahrâ en	54	D5
Nûbîya, Es Sahrâ en	54	D5
Nuboai	37	E5
Nuéltin L.	68	B10
Nueva Rosita	84	B4
Nuéve de Julio	94	D4
Nuevitas	86	B4
Nuevo, G.	95	E4
Nuevo Laredo	84	B5
Nugget Pt.	65	G3
Nuhaka	64	C7
Nukey Bluff	62	B2
Nuku'alofa	65	M13
Nukus	29	E6
Nullarbor Plain	60	G4
Numalla, L.	63	A3
Numan	55	G1
Numazu	33	F6
Numfoor	37	E4
Numurkah	63	C4
Nunap Isua	70	C6
Nuneaton	11	E6
Nunivak I.	69	B3
Nunkun	42	C10
Núoro	21	D2
Nuremberg = Nürnberg	15	D6
Nuriootpa	62	B2
Nürnberg	15	D6
Nurran, L. = Terewah, L.	63	A4
Nusa Tenggara Barat □	39	F5
Nusa Tenggara Timur □	37	F2
Nushki	42	E5
Nuuk	70	B5
Nuwakot	40	C4
Nuweveldberge	58	E4
Nuyts Arch.	62	B1
Nyahururu	57	D7
Nyainqentanglha Shan	34	C4
Nyâlâ	55	F3
Nyasa, L.	59	A6
Nyasvizh	17	B8
Nyda	28	C8
Nyíregyháza	17	E5
Nylstroom	59	C5
Nymagee	63	B4
Nyngan	63	B4
Nyoman = Nemunas →	24	B1
Nysa	16	C3
Nysa →	16	B2
Nyurba	30	C9
Nzega	57	E6
Nzérékoré	53	G4
Nzeto	56	F2

O

Ō-Shima	33	F6
Oahe, L.	74	C4
O'ahu	78	H12
Oak Ridge	83	A5
Oakey	63	A5
Oakland	78	B1
Oamaru	65	F4
Oates Land	96	A15
Oaxaca	84	D5
Ob →	28	C7
Oba	71	D2
Oban	10	C4
Obbia	49	F4
Oberhausen	14	C4
Oberon	63	B4
Obi	37	E3
Óbidos	92	C2
Obihiro	32	B8
Obilatu	37	E3
Obo	57	C5
Obozerskiy	28	C5
Obskaya Guba	28	C8
Obuasi	53	G5
Ocala	83	E6
Ocaña	18	C4
Occidental, Cordillera	90	C3
Oceanside	78	D4
Ocniţa	17	D8
Ōda	33	F3
Odate	32	C7
Odawara	33	F6
Ödemiş	23	E7
Odense	9	D8
Oder →	15	B8
Odesa	25	D3
Odessa	80	D2

Odienné	53	G4
Odintsovo	24	B4
Odra = Oder →	15	B8
Oeiras	92	D5
Ofanto →	20	D6
Offa	53	G6
Offenbach	14	C5
Offenburg	14	D4
Oga	32	D6
Oga-Hantō	32	D6
Ōgaki	33	F5
Ogbomosho	53	G6
Ogden	73	F7
Ogdensburg	77	B8
Oglio →	20	B3
Ogooué →	56	E1
Ohai	65	F2
Ohakune	64	C6
Ohanet	52	C7
Ohata	32	C7
Ohau, L.	65	F3
Ohio □	76	D4
Ohio →	76	F1
Ohře →	16	C2
Ohrid	22	D3
Ohridsko Jezero	23	D3
Oise →	12	B5
Ōita	33	G2
Oiticica	92	D5
Ojos del Salado, Cerro	94	B3
Oka →	28	D5
Okaba	37	F5
Okahandja	58	C3
Okanogan →	72	B4
Okara	42	D8
Okavango Delta	58	B4
Okayama	33	F3
Okazaki	33	F5
Okeechobee, L.	83	F7
Okefenokee Swamp	83	D6
Okhotsk, Sea of	31	D12
Oki-Shotō	33	E3
Okinawa-Jima	35	D7
Oklahoma □	80	B5
Oklahoma City	80	B5
Okmulgee	81	B6
Oknitsa = Ocniţa	17	D8
Oksibil	37	E6
Oktyabrsk	29	E6
Oktyabrskiy = Aktsyabrski	17	B9
Oktyabrskoy Revolyutsii, Ostrov	30	B7
Okuru	65	E3
Okushiri-Tō	32	B6
Öland	9	D9
Olary	62	B3
Olavarría	94	D4
Oława	16	C3
Ólbia	20	D2
Old Castile = Castilla y Leon □	18	A3
Old Crow	68	B6
Oldenburg	14	B5
Oldham	11	E5
Olekma →	31	C10
Olekminsk	31	C10
Oleksandriya	17	C8
Olenek	30	C9
Olenek →	30	B10
Oléron, Î. d'	12	D3
Oleśnica	16	C3
Olevsk	17	C8
Olhão	18	D2
Olifants = Elefantes →	59	C6
Ólimbos, Óros	23	D4
Olinda	92	D7
Olivenza	18	C2
Ollagüe	91	H5
Olomouc	16	D3
Olongapo	36	B2
Olot	19	A7
Olsztyn	16	B5
Olt →	22	C5
Olteniţa	22	B6
Olympia, Greece	23	F3
Olympia, U.S.A.	72	C2
Olympic Mts.	72	C2
Olympus, Mt. = Ólimbos, Óros	23	D4
Olympus, Mt. = Uludağ	23	D7
Om →	29	D8
Ōmagari	32	D7
Omagh	11	D3
Omaha	75	E7
Oman ■	48	C6
Oman, G. of	45	E4
Omaruru	58	C3
Omate	91	G4
Ombai, Selat	37	F2
Omboué	56	E1
Ombrone →	20	C3
Omdurmân	55	E5
Ometepec	84	D5
Omo →	55	G6
Omsk	29	D8
Ōmu	32	A8
Omul, Vf.	17	F7
Omuramba Omatako →	58	B4
Ōmuta	33	G2
Onang	37	E1
Onda	19	C5
Ondangwa	58	B3
Onega	28	C4
Onega, L. = Onezhskoye Ozero	8	C13
Oneşti	17	E8
Onezhskoye Ozero	8	C13
Ongarue	64	C6
Onilahy →	59	J8
Onitsha	53	G7
Ontario □	71	D2
Ontario, L.	77	C7
Oodnadatta	62	A2
Oostende	14	C2
Ootacamund = Udagamandalam	43	P10
Opala	56	E4
Opava	16	D3
Opole	16	C3
Oporto = Porto	18	B1
Opotiki	64	C7
Opua	64	A6
Opunake	64	C5
Oradea	17	E5
Öræfajökull	8	C2
Orai	42	G11
Oral = Zhayyq →	29	E6
Oral	24	C7
Oran	52	A5
Orange, Australia	63	B4
Orange, France	13	D6
Orange, U.S.A.	81	D7
Orange →	58	D3
Orange, C.	92	B3
Orangeburg	83	C7
Oranienburg	15	B7
Oranje = Orange →	58	D3
Oras	36	B3
Oraşul Stalin = Braşov	17	F7
Orbetello	20	C3
Orbost	63	C4
Orchila, I.	90	A5
Ordos = Mu Us Shamo	35	C5
Ordu	46	B4
Ordzhonikidze = Vladikavkaz	25	E5
Ore Mts. = Erzgebirge	15	C7
Örebro	9	D9
Oregon □	72	E3
Orekhovo-Zuyevo	24	B4
Orel	24	C4
Ören	23	F6
Orenburg	29	D6
Orense = Ourense	18	A2
Orepuki	65	G2
Orgaz	18	C4
Orgeyev = Orhei	17	E9
Orhaneli	23	E7
Orhangazi	23	D7
Orhei	17	E9
Orhon Gol →	35	A5
Oriental, Cordillera	90	B4
Orihuela	19	C5
Orinoco →	90	B6
Orissa □	40	G5
Oristano	21	E2
Oristano, G. di	21	E2
Orizaba	84	D5
Orizaba, Pico de	84	D5
Orkney Is.	10	B5
Orlando	83	E7
Orléanais	12	C5
Orléans	12	C4
Ormara	42	G4
Ormoc	36	B2
Ormond	64	C7
Örnsköldsvik	8	C9
Orocué	90	C4
Orol Dengizi = Aral Sea	29	E6
Oroquieta	36	C2
Orosháza	16	E5
Ororoo	62	B2
Orsha	24	C3
Orsk	29	D6
Orşova	22	B4
Ortaca	23	F7
Ortegal, C.	18	A2
Orthez	12	E3
Ortigueira	18	A2
Ortles	20	A3
Ortón →	91	F5
Orūmīyeh	46	C6
Orūmīyeh, Daryācheh-ye	46	C6
Oruro	91	G5
Oruzgān □	42	C5
Orvieto	20	C4
Oryakhovo	22	C4
Ōsaka	33	F4
Ösel = Saaremaa	24	B1
Osh	29	E8
Oshawa	71	D3
Oshkosh	74	E3
Oshmyany = Ashmyany	17	A7
Oshogbo	53	G6
Oshwe	56	E3
Osijek	20	B7
Osipenko = Berdyansk	25	D4
Osipovichi = Asipovichy	17	B9
Oskarshamn	9	D9
Ōskemen	29	E9
Oslo	9	D8
Oslofjorden	9	D8
Osmanabad	43	K10
Osmaniye	46	C4
Osnabrück	14	B5
Osorno	95	E2
Ossa, Mt.	62	D4
Óssa, Óros	23	E4
Ostend = Oostende	14	C2
Oster	17	C10
Österdalälven	8	C8
Östersund	8	C8
Ostfriesische Inseln	14	B4
Ostrava	16	D4
Ostróda	16	B4
Ostrołęka	16	B5
Ostrów Mazowiecka	16	B5
Ostrów Wielkopolski	16	C3
Ostrowiec-Świętokrzyski	16	C5
Ostuni	21	D6
Osuna	18	D3
Oswego	77	C7
Otago □	65	F3
Otago Harbour	65	F4
Otaki	64	D6

Otaru 32 B7
Otaru-Wan = Ishikari-Wan 32 B7
Otavalo 90 C3
Otjiwarongo 58 C3
Otoineppu 32 A8
Otorohanga 64 C6
Otranto 23 D2
Otranto, C. d' 23 D2
Otranto, Str. of 23 D2
Ōtsu 33 F4
Ottawa 71 D3
Ottawa Is. 70 C2
Ottumwa 75 E8
Oturkpo 53 G7
Otway, B. 95 G2
Otway, C. 62 C3
Otwock 16 B5
Ouachita Mts. 81 B6
Ouadda 55 G3
Ouagadougou 53 F5
Ouahran = Oran 52 A5
Ouallene 52 D6
Ouanda Djallé 55 G3
Ouargla 52 B7
Ouarzazate 52 B4
Oubangi → 56 E3
Oudtshoorn 58 E4
Ouessant, Î. d' 12 B1
Ouesso 56 D3
Ouezzane 52 B4
Oujda 52 B5
Oulu 8 B11
Oulujärvi 8 C11
Oulujoki → 8 B11
Oum Chalouba 55 E3
Oum Hadjer 55 F2
Ounianga Sérir 55 E3
Ourense 18 A2
Ouricuri 92 D5
Ouro Prêto 93 G5
Outer Hebrides 10 C3
Outjo 58 C3
Ouyen 62 C3
Ovalle 94 C2
Ovamboland 58 B3
Oviedo 18 A3
Ovruch 17 C9
Owaka 65 G3
Owambo = Ovamboland . 58 B3
Owase 33 F5
Owbeh 42 B3
Owen Sound 71 D3
Owen Stanley Ra. 61 B8
Owo 53 G7
Owyhee → 72 E5
Oxford, N.Z. 65 E5
Oxford, U.K. 11 F6
Oxnard 78 C3
Oxus = Amudarya → .. 29 E6
Oya 39 D4
Oyama 33 E6
Oyem 56 D2
Oyo 53 G6
Ozamiz 36 C2
Ozark Plateau 81 A8
Ōzd 16 D5

P

Pa-an 41 J11
Paarl 58 E3
Pab Hills 42 F5
Pabianice 16 C4
Pabna 41 E7
Pacaja → 92 C3
Pacaraima, Sa. 90 C6
Pacasmayo 91 E3
Pachpadra 42 G8
Pachuca 84 C5

Padaido, Kepulauan ... 37 E5
Padang 39 E2
Padangpanjang 39 E2
Padangsidempuan 39 D1
Paderborn 14 C5
Pádova 20 B3
Padua = Pádova 20 B3
Paducah 76 F1
Paeroa 64 B6
Pag 20 B5
Pagadian 36 C2
Pagai Selatan, Pulau .. 39 E2
Pagai Utara, Pulau ... 39 E2
Pagalu = Annobón ... 51 G4
Pagastikós Kólpos 23 E4
Pagatan 39 E5
Pahiatua 64 D6
Päijänne 8 C11
Painan 39 E2
Paint Hills = Wemindji . 71 C3
Painted Desert 79 C7
País Vasco □ 19 A4
Paisley 10 D4
Paita 90 E2
Pajares, Puerto de ... 18 A3
Pakistan ■ 42 E7
Pakokku 41 G10
Paktiā □ 42 C6
Pakxe 38 A3
Pala 55 G2
Palagruža 20 C6
Palam 43 K10
Palampur 42 C10
Palana 62 C4
Palanan 36 A2
Palanan Pt. 36 A2
Palangkaraya 39 E4
Palani Hills 43 P10
Palanpur 43 G8
Palapye 59 C5
Palau ■ 36 C4
Palawan 38 C5
Palayankottai 43 Q10
Paleleh 37 D2
Palembang 39 E2
Palencia 18 A3
Palermo 21 E4
Palestine 81 D6
Paletwa 41 G9
Palghat 43 P10
Pali 42 G8
Palioúrion, Ákra 23 E4
Palitana 43 J7
Palk Bay 43 Q11
Palk Strait 43 Q11
Pallanza = Verbánia .. 20 B2
Palm Springs 78 D4
Palma, B. de 19 C7
Palma de Mallorca ... 19 C7
Palmares 92 D6
Palmas, C. 53 H4
Pálmas, G. di 21 E2
Palmeira dos Índios .. 93 D6
Palmer 69 B5
Palmer Arch. 96 A3
Palmer Land 96 B3
Palmerston 65 F4
Palmerston North 64 D6
Palmi 21 E5
Palmira 90 C3
Palmyra = Tudmur ... 46 D4
Palopo 37 E2
Palos, C. de 19 D5
Palu, Indonesia 37 E1
Palu, Turkey 46 C5
Pamiers 12 E4
Pamir 29 F8
Pamlico Sd. 83 B10
Pampa 80 B3
Pampanua 37 E2
Pampas, Argentina ... 94 D4
Pampas, Peru 91 F4

Pamplona, Colombia .. 90 B4
Pamplona, Spain 19 A5
Panaji 43 M8
Panamá 85 F9
Panama ■ 86 E4
Panamá, G. de 86 E4
Panama Canal 86 E4
Panama City 82 D5
Panão 91 E3
Panay 36 B2
Panay, G. 36 B2
Pančevo 22 B3
Pandan 36 B2
Pandharpur 43 L9
Pando, L. = Hope, L. . 62 A2
Panevėžys 24 B1
Panfilov 29 E8
Pang-Long 41 F12
Pang-Yang 41 F12
Pangani 57 F7
Pangfou = Bengbu ... 35 C6
Pangkajene 37 E1
Pangkalanbrandan ... 39 D1
Pangkalanbuun 39 E4
Pangkalpinang 39 E3
Pangnirtung 70 B4
Panguitaran Group ... 36 C2
Panjgur 42 F4
Panjim = Panaji 43 M8
Panjinad Barrage 42 E7
Pannirtuuq = Pangnirtung 70 B4
Panorama 94 A6
Pantar 37 F2
Pante Macassar 37 F2
Pantelleria 21 F3
Paoting = Baoding ... 35 C6
Paot'ou = Baotou 35 B6
Paoua 56 C3
Pápa 16 E3
Papakura 64 B6
Papantla 84 C5
Papar 38 C5
Papeete 65 L16
Papua □ 37 E5
Papua New Guinea ■ . 61 B8
Papudo 94 C2
Papun 41 H11
Pará = Belém 92 C4
Pará □ 92 C3
Paracatu 93 F4
Paracel Is. 38 A4
Parachilna 62 B2
Paradip 40 G6
Parado 37 F1
Paragua → 90 B6
Paraguaçu → 93 E6
Paraguaná, Pen. de .. 90 A4
Paraguarí 94 B5
Paraguay ■ 94 A5
Paraguay → 94 B5
Paraíba = João Pessoa 92 D7
Paraíba □ 92 D6
Parakou 53 G6
Paramaribo 92 A2
Paraná, Argentina ... 94 C4
Paraná, Brazil 93 E4
Paraná □ 94 A6
Paraná → 94 C5
Paranaguá 94 B7
Paranaíba 93 F3
Paranaíba → 93 G3
Paranapanema → 94 A6
Paranas 36 B3
Parang, Maguindanao, Phil. 36 C2
Parang, Sulu, Phil. .. 36 C2
Parângul Mare, Vf. ... 17 F6
Paratinga 93 E5
Parbhani 43 K10
Parchim 15 B6
Pardo →, Bahia, Brazil 93 F6
Pardo →, Mato Grosso,
  Brazil 93 G3

Pardubice

Pardubice	16	C2
Parecis, Serra dos	91	F7
Parepare	37	E1
Párga	23	E3
Pariaguán	90	B6
Parigi	37	E2
Parika	90	B7
Parima, Serra	90	C6
Parinari	90	D4
Parintins	92	C2
Pariparit Kyun	41	K9
Paris, France	12	B5
Paris, U.S.A.	81	C6
Park Range	73	G10
Parkersburg	76	E5
Parkes	63	B4
Parla	18	B4
Parma	20	B3
Parnaguá	93	E5
Parnaíba	92	C5
Parnaíba →	92	C5
Parnassós	23	E4
Pärnu	24	B1
Paroo →	63	B3
Páros	23	F5
Parral	94	D2
Parry Sound	71	D3
Partínico	21	E4
Paru →	92	C3
Parván □	42	B6
Parvatipuram	40	H4
Pasadena, Calif., U.S.A.	78	C3
Pasadena, Tex., U.S.A.	81	E6
Pascagoula	81	D9
Paşcani	17	E8
Pasco	72	C4
Pasco, Cerro de	91	F3
Pashmakli = Smolyan	22	D5
Pasirkuning	39	E2
Pašman	20	C5
Pasni	42	G3
Paso de Indios	95	E3
Passau	15	D7
Passero, C.	21	F5
Passo Fundo	94	B6
Passos	93	G4
Pastaza →	90	D3
Pasto	90	C3
Patagonia	95	F3
Patan = Lalitapur	40	D5
Patan	43	H8
Patani	37	D3
Patchewollock	62	C3
Patea	64	C6
Paternò	21	F5
Paterson	77	D8
Pathankot	42	C9
Pathein = Bassein	41	J10
Patiala	42	D10
Patkai Bum	41	D10
Pátmos	23	F6
Patna	40	E5
Patos, L. dos	94	C6
Patos de Minas	93	F4
Patquía	94	C3
Pátrai	23	E3
Pátraikós Kólpos	23	E3
Patras = Pátrai	23	E3
Patrocínio	93	F4
Pattani	38	C2
Patuakhali	41	F8
Pau	12	E3
Pauk	41	G10
Paulis = Isiro	57	D5
Paulistana	92	D5
Paulo Afonso	93	D6
Pavia	20	B2
Pavlodar	29	D8
Pavlohrad	25	D4
Pavlovo	24	B5
Pavlovsk	24	C5
Pawtucket	77	D10

Paxoí	23	E3
Payakumbuh	39	E2
Payne Bay = Kangirsuk	70	C4
Paysandú	94	C5
Paz, B. de la	84	C2
Pazar	46	B5
Pazardzhik	22	C5
Peace →	68	C8
Peak Hill	63	B4
Peake Cr. →	62	A2
Pebane	59	B7
Pebas	90	D4
Peć	22	C3
Pechenga	28	C4
Pechenizhyn	17	D7
Pechora →	28	C6
Pechorskaya Guba	28	C6
Pecos →	80	E3
Pécs	16	E4
Pedder, L.	62	D4
Pedirka	62	A2
Pedra Azul	93	F5
Pedreiras	92	C5
Pedro Afonso	93	D4
Pedro Juan Caballero	94	A5
Peebinga	62	B3
Peel →, Australia	63	B5
Peel →, Canada	68	B6
Peera Peera Poolanna L.	62	A2
Pegasus Bay	65	E5
Pegu	41	J11
Pegu Yoma	41	H10
Pehuajó	94	D4
Peine	14	B6
Peip'ing = Beijing	35	C6
Peipus, L. = Chudskoye, Ozero	24	B2
Peixe	93	E4
Pekalongan	39	F3
Pekanbaru	39	D2
Pekin	75	E10
Peking = Beijing	35	C6
Pelagie, Is.	21	G4
Pelaihari	39	E4
Peleaga, Vf.	17	F6
Peleng	37	E2
Pelješac	20	C6
Pelly →	68	B6
Pelly Bay	70	B2
Peloponnese = Pelopónnisos □	23	F4
Pelopónnisos □	23	F4
Pelorus Sd.	65	D5
Pelotas	94	C6
Pelvoux, Massif du	13	D7
Pematangsiantar	39	D1
Pemba I.	57	F7
Pembroke, Canada	71	D3
Pembroke, U.K.	11	F4
Penang = Pinang	38	C2
Penápolis	94	A6
Peñarroya-Pueblonuevo	18	C3
Peñas, C. de	18	A3
Penas, G. de	95	F2
Pench'i = Benxi	35	B7
Pend Oreille, L.	72	C5
Pendembu	53	G3
Pendleton	72	D4
Penedo	93	E6
Penguin	62	D4
Peniche	18	C1
Penida, Nusa	39	F5
Peninsular Malaysia □	39	D2
Penmarch, Pte. de	12	C1
Pennines	11	D5
Pennsylvania □	77	D7
Penola	62	C3
Penong	60	G5
Penrith	63	B5
Pensacola	82	D4
Pensacola Mts.	96	C4
Penshurst	62	C3

Penticton	69	D8
Pentland Firth	10	B5
Penza	24	C6
Penzance	11	F4
Peoria	75	E10
Perabumulih	39	E2
Perche, Collines du	12	B4
Perdido, Mte.	19	A6
Perdu, Mt. = Perdido, Mte.	19	A6
Pereira	90	C3
Pereyaslav-Khmelnytskyy	24	C3
Pergamino	94	C4
Péribonka →	71	D3
Perico	94	A3
Périgueux	12	D4
Perijá, Sierra de	90	B4
Perlas, Arch. de las	86	E4
Perm	29	D6
Pernambuco = Recife	92	D7
Pernatty Lagoon	62	B2
Pernik	22	C4
Perpendicular Pt.	63	B5
Perpignan	13	E5
Persepolis	44	D3
Pershotravensk	17	C8
Persia = Iran ■	44	C3
Persian Gulf	44	E2
Perth, Australia	60	G2
Perth, U.K.	10	C5
Perth Amboy	77	D8
Peru ■	90	C3
Perúgia	20	C4
Pervomaysk	25	D3
Pervouralsk	29	D6
Pésaro	20	C4
Pescara	20	C4
Peshawar	42	B7
Peshkopi	22	D3
Pesqueira	92	D6
Petah Tiqwa	46	D3
Petauke	59	A6
Peter I.s Øy	96	A2
Peterborough, Australia	62	B2
Peterborough, Canada	71	D3
Peterborough, U.K.	11	E6
Peterhead	10	C6
Petersburg, Alaska, U.S.A.	69	C6
Petersburg, Va., U.S.A.	77	F7
Petitsikapau L.	71	C4
Petlad	43	H8
Peto	85	C7
Petone	65	D6
Petra Velikogo, Zaliv	32	B3
Petrich	22	D4
Petrikov = Pyetrikaw	17	B9
Petrograd = Sankt-Peterburg	24	B3
Petrolândia	93	D6
Petrolina	92	D5
Petropavl	29	D7
Petropavlovsk-Kamchatskiy	31	D13
Petrópolis	93	G5
Petroşani	17	F6
Petrovaradin	22	B2
Petrovsk	24	C6
Petrozavodsk	8	C12
Peureulak	38	D1
Pforzheim	14	D5
Phagwara	42	D9
Phalodi	42	F8
Phan Rang	38	B3
Phangan, Ko	38	C2
Phangnga	38	C1
Phatthalung	38	C2
Phetchabun	38	A2
Philadelphia	77	E8
Philippines ■	36	B2
Philippopolis = Plovdiv	22	C5
Phillip I.	63	C4
Phitsanulok	38	A2
Phnom Dangrek	38	B2
Phnom Penh	38	B2

Phoenix 79 D6
Phra Nakhon Si Ayutthaya 38 B2
Phuket 38 C1
Piacenza 20 B2
Pian Cr. ➤ 63 B4
Pianosa 20 C3
Piatra Neamţ 17 E8
Piauí □ 92 D5
Piave ➤ 20 B2
Pibor Post 55 G5
Picardie 13 B5
Pichilemu 94 C2
Pico Truncado 95 F3
Picton, *Australia* 63 B5
Picton, *N.Z.* 65 D6
Picún Leufú 95 D3
Piedmont = Piemonte □ . 20 B2
Piedras, R. de las ➤ 91 F5
Piedras Negras 84 B4
Pielinen 8 C11
Piemonte □ 20 B1
Piet Retief 59 D6
Pietermaritzburg 59 D6
Pietersburg 59 C5
Pietrosul, Vf., *Maramureş,*
   Romania 17 E7
Pietrosul, Vf., *Suceava,*
   Romania 17 E7
Pigüe 94 D4
Piła 16 B3
Pilar 94 B5
Pilcomayo ➤ 42 E11
Pilibhit 16 C5
Pilica ➤ 16 C5
Pilos 23 F3
Pilsen = Plzeň 16 D1
Pimba 62 B2
Pimenta Bueno 91 F6
Pimentel 91 E3
Pinang 38 C2
Pinar del Río 86 B3
Pınarhisar 22 D6
Pińczów 16 C5
Pindos Óros 23 E3
Pindus Mts. = Pindos Óros 23 E3
Pine Bluff 81 B7
Pine Point 68 B8
Pinega ➤ 28 C5
Pinerolo 20 B1
Ping ➤ 38 A2
Pingdong 35 D7
Pingliang 35 C5
Pingxiang 35 D5
Pinhel 18 B2
Pini 39 D1
Piniós ➤ 23 E4
Pinnaroo 62 C3
Pinnes, Ákra 23 D5
Pinrang 37 E1
Pinsk 17 B8
Pintados 91 H5
Pinyug 24 A6
Piombino 20 C3
Pioner, Ostrov 30 B7
Piorini, L. 90 D6
Piotrków Trybunalski 16 C4
Pip 45 E5
Piquiri ➤ 94 A6
Piracicaba 94 A7
Piracuruca 92 C5
Piraeus = Piraiévs 23 F4
Piraiévs 23 F4
Pirané 94 B5
Pirapora 93 F5
Pirgos 23 F3
Pirin Planina 22 D4
Pirineos = Pyrénées 19 A6
Piripiri 92 C5
Pirmasens 14 D4
Pirot 22 C4
Piru 37 E3
Pisa 20 C3

Pisagua 91 G4
Pisco 91 F3
Písek 16 D2
Pishan 34 C2
Pising 37 F2
Pistóia 20 C3
Pisuerga ➤ 18 B3
Pitarpunga, L. 62 B3
Pitcairn I. 65 M17
Piteå 8 B10
Piteşti 22 B5
Pithapuram 40 J4
Pittsburg 81 A6
Pittsburgh 77 D5
Pittsworth 63 A5
Piura 90 E2
Placentia 71 D5
Placentia B. 71 D5
Plainview 80 B3
Pláka, Ákra 23 G6
Plasencia 18 B2
Plastun 32 A5
Plata, Río de la ➤ 94 C5
Plátani ➤ 21 F4
Platte ➤ 75 F7
Plauen 15 C7
Plei Ku 38 B3
Plenty, B. of 64 B7
Pleven 22 C5
Plevlja 22 C2
Płock 16 B4
Plöckenstein 15 D7
Ploiești 22 B6
Plovdiv 22 C5
Plumtree 59 C5
Plymouth 11 F4
Plzeň 16 D1
Po ➤ 20 B4
Po Hai = Bo Hai 35 C6
Pobedy, Pik 29 E8
Pocatello 73 E7
Poços de Caldas 93 G4
Podgorica 22 C2
Podilska Vysochyna 17 D8
Podolsk 24 B4
Poh 37 E2
Pohnpei 64 J10
Poinsett, C. 87 C7
Pointe-à-Pitre 88 C7
Pointe-Noire 56 E2
Poitiers 12 C4
Poitou 12 C3
Pokaran 42 F7
Pokataroo 63 A4
Pokrovsk = Engels 24 C6
Pola = Pula 20 B4
Polan 45 E5
Polatsk 24 B3
Poltava 24 D3
Polunochnoye 28 C7
Polynesia 65 L15
Polynésie française =
   French Polynesia ⌧ 65 M16
Pombal 18 C1
Pomézia 20 D4
Pomorskie, Pojezierze . . . 16 B3
Ponape = Pohnpei 64 J10
Ponca City 80 A5
Ponce 87 C6
Pond Inlet 70 A3
Pondicherry 43 P11
Ponferrada 18 A2
Ponnani 43 P9

Ponta Grossa 94 B6
Ponta Pora 94 A5
Pontarlier 13 C7
Pontchartrain L. 81 D8
Ponte Nova 93 G5
Pontevedra 18 A1
Pontiac 76 C4
Pontianak 39 E3
Pontine Is. = Ponziane, Ísole 21 D4
Pontine Mts. = Kuzey
   Anadolu Dağları 46 B3
Pontivy 12 B2
Pontoise 12 B5
Ponziane, Ísole 21 D4
Poochera 62 B1
Poole 11 F6
Poona = Pune 43 K8
Pooncarie 62 B3
Poopelloe L. 63 B3
Poopó, L. de 91 G5
Popayán 90 C3
Popilla L. 62 B3
Poplo L. 62 B3
Poplar Bluff 81 A8
Popocatépetl, Volcán 84 D5
Popokabaka 56 F3
Porbandar 43 J6
Porcupine ➤ 69 B5
Pordenone 20 B4
Pori 8 C10
Porlamar 90 A6
Poroshiri-Dake 32 B8
Porpoise B. 96 A13
Port Alberni 69 D7
Port Angeles 72 B2
Port Arthur, *Australia* . . . 62 D4
Port Arthur, *U.S.A.* 81 E7
Port-au-Prince 87 C5
Port Augusta 62 B2
Port Broughton 62 B2
Port-Cartier 71 C7
Port Chalmers 65 F4
Port Darwin 95 G5
Port Davey 62 D4
Port Dickson 39 D2
Port Elizabeth 59 E5
Port Etienne = Nouâdhibou 52 D2
Port Fairy 62 C3
Port-Gentil 56 E1
Port Harcourt 53 H7
Port Harrison = Inukjuak . 70 C3
Port Hawkesbury 71 C4
Port Hedland 60 E2
Port Huron 76 C4
Port Kenny 62 B1
Port Lairge = Waterford . . 11 E3
Port Laoise 11 E3
Port Lincoln 62 B2
Port Loko 53 G3
Port Louis 51 J9
Port MacDonnell 62 C3
Port Macquarie 63 B5
Port Moresby 61 B8
Port Nolloth 58 D3
Port Nouveau-Québec =
   Kangiqsualujjuaq 70 C4
Port of Spain 87 D7
Port Pegasus 65 G2
Port Phillip B. 63 C3
Port Pirie 62 B2
Port Radium = Echo Bay . 68 B8
Port Safaga = Bûr Safâga 54 C5
Port Said = Bûr Sa'îd 54 B5
Port Shepstone 59 E6
Port Stanley = Stanley . . . 95 G5
Port Sudan = Bûr Sûdân . 55 E6
Port Talbot 11 F5
Port-Vendres 13 E5
Port Wakefield 62 B2
Port Weld = Kuala
   Sepetang 38 D2
Porta Orientalis 22 B4

Portadown	11	D3
Portage la Prairie	69	D10
Portalegre	18	C2
Portbou	19	A7
Portile de Fier	22	B4
Portimão	18	D1
Portland, *N.S.W., Australia*	63	B4
Portland, *Vic., Australia*	62	C3
Portland, *Maine, U.S.A.*	77	C10
Portland, *Oreg., U.S.A.*	72	D2
Portland B.	62	C3
Porto	18	B1
Pôrto Alegre	94	C6
Porto Amboim = Gunza	56	G2
Pôrto de Móz	92	C3
Porto Empédocle	21	F4
Pôrto Esperança	91	G7
Pôrto Franco	92	D4
Pôrto Mendes	94	A6
Pôrto Murtinho	91	H7
Pôrto Nacional	93	E4
Porto-Novo	53	G6
Porto Santo, I. de	52	B2
Porto Seguro	93	F6
Pôrto Tôrres	20	D2
Pôrto União	94	B6
Pôrto Válter	91	E4
Porto-Vecchio	13	F8
Pôrto Velho	91	E6
Portoferráio	20	C3
Portoscuso	21	E2
Portoviejo	90	D2
Portree	10	C3
Portsmouth, *U.K.*	11	F6
Portsmouth, *U.S.A.*	77	F7
Porttipahtan tekojärvi	8	B11
Portugal ■	18	C1
Porvenir	95	G2
Posadas	94	B5
Poso	37	E2
Posse	93	E4
Possession I.	96	B15
Postojna	20	B5
Potchefstroom	59	D5
Potenza	21	D5
Poteriteri, L.	65	G2
Potgietersrus	59	C5
Poti	25	E5
Potomac →	77	E7
Potosí	91	G5
Pototan	36	B2
Potrerillos	94	B3
Potsdam	15	B7
Poughkeepsie	77	D9
Považská Bystrica	16	D4
Poverty B.	64	C8
Póvoa de Varzim	18	B1
Powder →	74	B2
Powell, L.	79	B7
Poyang Hu	35	D6
Požarevac	22	B3
Poznań	16	B3
Pozo Almonte	91	H5
Pozoblanco	18	C3
Pozzuoli	21	D5
Prachuap Khiri Khan	38	B1
Prado	93	F6
Prague = Praha	16	C2
Praha	16	C2
Prainha, *Amazonas, Brazil*	91	E6
Prainha, *Pará, Brazil*	92	C3
Prapat	39	D1
Prata	93	F4
Prato	20	C3
Pravia	18	A2
Praya	39	F5
Preobrazheniye	32	B3
Preparis North Channel	41	K9
Preparis South Channel	41	K9
Přerov	16	D3
Preservation Inlet	65	G2
Presidencia Roque Saenz Peña	94	B4
Presidente Epitácio	93	G3
Presidente Prudente	93	G3
Prespansko Jezero	23	D3
Presque Isle	77	A11
Preston	11	E5
Pretoria	59	D5
Préveza	23	E3
Příbram	16	D2
Prichard	82	D3
Prieska	58	D4
Prilep	22	D3
Priluki = Prylyky	24	C3
Prime Seal I.	62	D4
Prince Albert	69	C9
Prince Albert Mts.	96	B15
Prince Albert Pen.	68	A8
Prince Albert Sd.	68	A8
Prince Charles I.	70	B3
Prince Charles Mts.	96	B10
Prince Edward I. □	71	D4
Prince of Wales I., *Canada*	68	A10
Prince of Wales I., *U.S.A.*	69	C6
Principe da Beira	91	F6
Prins Harald Kyst	96	B8
Prinsesse Astrid Kyst	96	B7
Prinsesse Ragnhild Kyst	96	B8
Pripet = Prypyat →	17	C10
Pripet Marshes	17	B9
Priština	22	C3
Privas	13	D6
Privolzhskaya Vozvyshennost	24	C6
Prizren	22	C3
Proddatur	43	M11
Progreso	85	C7
Prokopyevsk	29	D9
Prokuplje	22	C3
Prome	41	H10
Propr[i]á	93	E6
Prosna →	16	B3
Prostějov	16	D3
Proston	63	A5
Provence	13	E6
Providence	77	D10
Providencia, I. de	86	D3
Provins	13	B5
Provo	73	F8
Pruszków	16	B5
Prut →	17	F9
Pruzhany	17	B7
Prydz B.	96	A10
Pryluky	24	C3
Prypyat →	17	C10
Przhevalsk = Karakol	29	E8
Psará	23	E5
Pskov	24	B2
Ptsich →	17	B9
Puán	94	D4
Pucallpa	91	E4
Puduchcheri = Pondicherry	43	P11
Pudukkottai	43	P11
Puebla	84	D5
Pueblo	74	F2
Puelches	94	D3
Puente Alto	94	C2
Puente-Genil	18	D3
Puerto Aisén	95	F2
Puerto Ayacucho	90	B5
Puerto Barrios	85	D7
Puerto Bermúdez	91	F4
Puerto Bolívar	90	D3
Puerto Cabello	90	A5
Puerto Cabezas	86	D3
Puerto Carreño	90	B5
Puerto Chicama	91	E3
Puerto Coig	95	G3
Puerto Cortés	85	D7
Puerto Cumarebo	90	A5
Puerto Deseado	95	F3
Puerto Heath	91	F5
Puerto La Cruz	90	A6
Puerto Leguízamo	90	D4
Puerto Lobos	95	E3
Puerto Madryn	95	E3
Puerto Maldonado	91	F5
Puerto Montt	95	E2
Puerto Natales	95	G2
Puerto Páez	90	B5
Puerto Pinasco	94	A5
Puerto Plata	87	C5
Puerto Princesa	36	C1
Puerto Rico ☑	87	C6
Puerto Sastre	91	H7
Puerto Suárez	91	G7
Puerto Wilches	90	B4
Puertollano	18	C3
Pueyrredón, L.	95	F2
Pugachev	24	C6
Puget Sound	72	C2
Puigcerdà	19	A6
Pukaki, L.	65	F4
Pukapuka	65	L14
Pukekohe	64	B6
Pula	20	B4
Pulandian	35	C7
Puławy	16	C5
Pullman	72	C5
Pulog, Mt.	36	A2
Pułtusk	16	B5
Puná, I.	90	D2
Punakha	41	D7
Punata	91	G5
Punch	42	C9
Pune	43	K8
Punjab □, *India*	42	D9
Punjab □, *Pakistan*	42	D9
Puno	91	G4
Punta Alta	94	D4
Punta Arenas	95	G2
Punta de Díaz	94	B2
Puntarenas	86	E3
Punto Fijo	90	A4
Puquio	91	F4
Pur →	28	C8
Purace, Vol.	90	C3
Puralia = Puruliya	40	F6
Puri	40	H5
Purnia	40	E6
Purukcahu	39	E4
Puruliya	40	F6
Purus →	90	D6
Pusan	35	C7
Pushkino	24	C6
Putao	41	D11
Putaruru	64	C6
Putignano	21	D6
Puting, Tanjung	39	E4
Putorana, Gory	30	C7
Puttalam	43	Q11
Puttgarden	15	A6
Putumayo →	90	D5
Putussibau	39	D4
Puy-de-Dôme	13	D5
Pwllheli	11	E4
Pyapon	41	J10
Pyasina →	30	B6
Pyatigorsk	25	E5
Pyè = Prome	41	H10
Pyetrikaw	17	B9
Pyinmana	41	H11
P'yŏngyang	35	C7
Pyrénées	19	A6
Pyu	41	H11

Q

Qã'emshahr	44	B3
Qahremānshahr = Bākhtarān	46	D6
Qaidam Pendi	34	C4
Qal'at al Akhdar	47	E4
Qalāt-i-Ghilzai	45	C6

Qamani'tuaq = Baker Lake   68   B10
Qamruddin Karez   42   D6
Qandahār   42   D4
Qandahār □   42   D4
Qapshaghay   29   E8
Qaqortoq   70   B6
Qarabutaq   29   E7
Qaraghandy   29   E8
Qarataū, *Kazakhstan*   29   E8
Qarataū, *Kazakhstan*   29   E7
Qardho = Gardo   49   F4
Qarqan He →   34   C3
Qarqaraly   29   E8
Qarshi   29   F7
Qaşr-e Qand   45   E5
Qasr Farâfra   54   C4
Qatar ■   44   E2
Qattâra, Munkhafed el   54   C4
Qattâra Depression =
  Qattâra, Munkhafed el   54   C4
Qâyen   44   C4
Qazaqstan = Kazakhstan ■   29   E7
Qazvin   46   C7
Qena   54   C5
Qeqertarsuaq   70   B5
Qeshm   44   E4
Qikiqtarjuaq   70   B4
Qila Safed   42   E2
Qila Saifullāh   42   D6
Qilian Shan   34   C4
Qingdao   35   C7
Qinghai □   34   C4
Qinghai Hu   34   C5
Qinhuangdao   35   C6
Qinzhou   35   D5
Qiqihar   35   B7
Qitai   34   B3
Qom   44   C2
Qomolangma Feng =
  Everest, Mt.   40   C6
Qomsheh   44   C2
Qondūz   45   B7
Qondūz □   45   B7
Qoraqalpoghistan □   29   D7
Qostanay   29   D7
Quambatook   62   C3
Quambone   63   B4
Quan Long = Ca Mau   38   C3
Quang Ngai   38   A3
Quanzhou   35   D6
Quaqtaq   70   B4
Quartu Sant'Élena   21   E2
Quba   25   E6
Qūchān   44   B4
Queanbeyan   63   C4
Québec   71   D3
Québec □   71   D3
Queen Alexandra Ra.   96   C15
Queen Charlotte Is.   68   C6
Queen Charlotte Sd.   69   C7
Queen Elizabeth Is.   66   B9
Queen Mary Land   96   B11
Queen Maud G.   68   B9
Queen Maud Land =
  Dronning Maud Land   96   C16
Queen Maud Mts.   96   C3
Queenscliff   63   C3
Queensland □   61   E7
Queenstown, *Australia*   62   D4
Queenstown, *N.Z.*   65   F3
Queenstown, *S. Africa*   59   E5
Queimadas   93   E6
Quelimane   59   B7
Quelpart = Cheju do   35   C7
Querétaro   84   C4
Quetta   42   D5
Quezon City   36   B2
Qui Nhon   38   B3
Quibaxe   56   F2
Quibdo   90   B3
Quiberon   12   C2
Quilán, C.   95   E2
Quillabamba   91   F4

Quillagua   91   H5
Quillota   94   C2
Quilon   43   Q10
Quilpie   63   A3
Quimilí   94   B4
Quimper   12   B1
Quimperlé   12   C2
Quincy   75   F9
Quines   94   C3
Quintanar de la Orden   18   C4
Quirindi   63   B5
Quissanga   59   G8
Quito   90   D3
Quixadá   92   C6
Qulan   29   E8
Qŭnghirot   29   E6
Quorn   62   B2
Qŭqon   29   E8
Quseir   54   C5
Quzhou   35   D6
Qyzylorda   29   E7

R

Raahe   8   C10
Raba   37   F1
Rába →   16   E3
Rabat, *Malta*   21   G5
Rabat, *Morocco*   52   B4
Rabaul   64   K10
Rābigh   47   G4
Rābniţa   17   E9
Race, C.   71   D5
Rach Gia   38   B3
Racine   76   C2
Rădăuţi   17   E7
Radekhiv   17   C7
Radom   16   C5
Radomsko   16   C4
Radomyshl   17   C9
Radstock, C.   62   B1
Rae   68   B8
Rae Bareli   40   D3
Rae Isthmus   70   B2
Raetihi   64   C6
Rafaela   94   C4
Rafḥā   47   E5
Rafsanjān   44   D4
Ragachow   17   B10
Ragama   43   R11
Raglan   64   B6
Ragusa   21   F5
Raha   37   E2
Rahimyar Khan   42   E7
Raichur   43   L10
Raigarh   40   G4
Railton   62   D4
Rainier, Mt.   72   C3
Raipur   40   G3
Ra'is   47   G4
Raj Nandgaon   40   G3
Raja, Ujung   39   D1
Raja Ampat, Kepulauan   37   E3
Rajahmundry   40   J3
Rajang →   39   D4
Rajapalaiyam   43   Q10
Rajasthan □   42   F8
Rajasthan Canal = Indira
  Gandhi Canal   42   F8
Rajgarh   43   G10
Rajkot   43   H7
Rajpipla   43   J8
Rajshahi   41   E7
Rakaia   65   E5
Rakaia →   65   E5
Rakan, Ra's   44   E2
Rakaposhi   42   A9
Rakata, Pulau   39   F3
Rakhiv   17   D7
Rakitnoye   32   A4

Raleigh   83   B8
Ramanathapuram   43   Q11
Rame Hd.   63   C4
Ramechhap   40   D6
Ramgarh, *Jharkhand, India*   40   F5
Ramgarh, *Raj., India*   42   F7
Ramnad =
  Ramanathapuram   43   Q11
Râmnicu Sărat   17   F8
Râmnicu Vâlcea   17   F7
Rampur   42   E11
Rampur Hat   40   E6
Ramree I.   41   H9
Ramtek   43   J11
Ranaghat   41   F7
Ranau   38   C5
Rancagua   94   C2
Ranchi   40   F5
Randers   9   D8
Rangaunu B.   64   A5
Rangia   41   D8
Rangiora   65   E5
Rangitaiki →   64   B7
Rangitata →   65   E4
Rangon →   41   J11
Rangoon   41   J11
Rangpur   41   E7
Ranibennur   43   M9
Raniganj   40   F6
Raniwara   43   G8
Rankin Inlet   68   B10
Rankins Springs   63   B4
Ranong   38   C1
Ransiki   37   E4
Rantauprapat   39   D1
Rantemario   37   E1
Rapa   65   M16
Rapallo   20   B2
Räpch   45   E4
Rapid City   74   C3
Rarotonga   65   M14
Ra's al Khaymah   44   E4
Ra's Lānūf   54   B2
Rasht   46   C7
Rat Islands   69   C1
Ratangarh   42   E9
Rathenow   15   B7
Ratlam   43   H9
Ratnagiri   43   L8
Raukumara Ra.   64   C7
Rauma   8   C10
Raurkela   40   F5
Rausu-Dake   32   A9
Rava-Ruska   17   C6
Rāvar   44   D4
Ravenna   20   B4
Ravensburg   14   E5
Ravi →   42   D7
Rawalpindi   42   C8
Rawāndūz   46   C6
Rawene   64   A5
Rawlins   73   F10
Rawson   95   E3
Rawu, C.   71   D5
Rayadurg   43   M10
Rayagada   40   H4
Raz, Pte. du   12   B1
Razdel'naya = Rozdilna   17   E10
Razgrad   22   C6
Razim, Lacul   22   B7
Ré, Î. de   12   C3
Reading, *U.K.*   11   F6
Reading, *U.S.A.*   77   D8
Realicó   94   D4
Rebi   37   F4
Rebiana   54   D3
Rebun-Tō   32   A7
Rechytsa   17   B10
Recife   92   D7
Reconquista   94   B5
Recreo   94   B3
Red →, *La., U.S.A.*   81   D8
Red →, *N. Dak., U.S.A.*   74   A6

Red Cliffs 62 B3
Red Deer 69 C8
Red Sea 48 C2
Red Tower Pass = Turnu
  Roşu, P. 17 F7
Redcar 11 D6
Redcliffe 63 A5
Redding 72 F2
Redditch 11 E6
Redon 12 C2
Redondela 18 A1
Redwood City 78 B1
Ree, L. 11 E3
Reefton 65 E4
Regensburg 15 D7
Reggâne = Zaouiet
  Reggâne 52 C6
Réggio di Calábria 21 E5
Réggio nell'Emília 20 B3
Reghin 17 E7
Regina 69 C9
Rehoboth 58 C3
Rehovot 46 E3
Reichenbach 15 C7
Reidsville 83 A8
Reigate 11 F6
Reims 13 B6
Reina Adelaida, Arch. .. 95 G2
Reindeer L. 69 C9
Reinga, C. 64 A5
Reinosa 18 A3
Remarkable, Mt. 62 B2
Remeshk 45 E4
Rendsburg 14 A5
Rengat 39 E2
Reni 17 F9
Renmark 62 B3
Rennes 12 B3
Reno 72 G4
Reno → 20 B4
Rentería 19 A5
Republican → 74 F6
Repulse Bay 70 B2
Requena, Peru 90 E4
Requena, Spain 19 C5
Reşadiye = Datça 23 F6
Resht = Rasht 46 C7
Resistencia 94 B5
Reşiţa 17 F5
Resolution I., Canada .. 70 B4
Resolution I., N.Z. 65 F2
Réthímnon 23 G5
Réunion ☑ 51 J9
Reus 19 B6
Reutlingen 14 D5
Revelstoke 69 C8
Revillagigedo, Is. de .. 84 D2
Rewa 40 E3
Rewari 42 E10
Rey Bouba 55 G1
Rey Malabo 56 D1
Reykjavík 8 C1
Reynosa 84 B5
Rhein → 14 C4
Rhein-Main-Donau-Kanal . 15 D6
Rheine 14 B4
Rheinland-Pfalz ☐ 14 C4
Rhine = Rhein → 14 C4
Rhineland-Palatinate =
  Rheinland-Pfalz ☐ ... 14 C4
Rhode Island ☐ 77 D10
Rhodes = Ródhos 23 F7
Rhodope Mts. = Rhodopi
  Planina 22 D5
Rhodopi Planina 22 D5
Rhön 14 C5
Rhondda 11 F5
Rhône → 13 E6
Rhum 10 C3
Riachão 92 D4
Riasi 42 C9
Riau ☐ 39 E2
Riau, Kepulauan 39 D2

Ribadeo 18 A2
Ribeirão Prêto 93 G4
Riberalta 91 F5
Riccarton 65 E5
Richland 72 C4
Richmond, N.Z. 65 D5
Richmond, Calif., U.S.A. 72 H2
Richmond, Va., U.S.A. .. 77 F7
Richmond Ra. 63 A5
Ridder = Leninogorsk .. 29 D9
Ried 15 D7
Riesa 15 C7
Rieti 20 C4
Rif = Er Rif 54 A5
Riga 24 B1
Riga, G. of 24 B1
Rigestān 42 D4
Rigolet 70 C5
Riiser-Larsen-halvøya .. 96 A8
Rijeka 20 B5
Rimah, Wadi ar → 47 F5
Rímini 20 B4
Rimouski 71 D4
Rinca 37 F1
Rinconada 94 A3
Rinjani 39 F5
Rio Branco, Brazil 91 E5
Río Branco, Uruguay 94 C6
Río Cuarto 94 C4
Rio de Janeiro 93 G5
Rio de Janeiro ☐ 93 G5
Rio do Sul 94 B7
Río Gallegos 95 G3
Rio Grande, Argentina .. 95 G3
Rio Grande, Brazil 94 C6
Rio Grande, U.S.A. 81 F5
Rio Grande de Santiago → 84 C3
Rio Grande do Norte ☐ . 92 D6
Rio Grande do Sul ☐ ... 94 B6
Río Largo 93 D6
Río Mulatos 91 G5
Río Muni ☐ 56 D2
Rio Negro 94 B7
Rio Verde 93 F3
Ríohacha 90 A4
Riosucio, Caldas, Colombia 90 B3
Riosucio, Choco, Colombia 90 B3
Rishiri-Tō 32 A7
Riva del Garda 20 B3
Rivadavia 94 B2
Rivera 94 C5
Riverside 78 D4
Riverton, Australia 62 B2
Riverton, N.Z. 65 G2
Riviera di Levante 20 B2
Riviera di Ponente 20 B2
Rivière-du-Loup 71 D4
Rivne 17 C8
Rívoli 20 B1
Rivoli B. 62 C3
Riyadh = Ar Riyāḍ 47 F6
Rize 46 B5
Rizzuto, C. 21 E6
Roanne 13 C6
Roanoke 77 F6
Robbins I. 62 A4
Robertson I. 96 A4
Robertson 58 C3
Robinvale 62 B3
Roboré 91 G7
Robson, Mt. 69 C8
Roca, C. da 18 C1
Rocas, I. 92 C7
Rocha 94 C6
Rochefort 12 D3
Rochester, Minn., U.S.A. 75 C8
Rochester, N.Y., U.S.A. . 77 C7
Rock Hill 83 B7
Rock Island 75 E9
Rock Springs 73 F9
Rockefeller Plateau ... 96 C18
Rockford 75 D10

Rockhampton 61 E9
Rocky Mount 83 B9
Rocky Mts. 68 C7
Rod 42 E3
Rodez 13 D5
Ródhos 23 F7
Rodney, C. 64 B6
Roes Welcome Sd. 70 B2
Rogachev = Ragachow ... 17 B10
Rogaguá, L. 91 F5
Rogatyn 17 D7
Rogoaguado, L. 91 F5
Rohri 42 F6
Rohtak 42 E10
Roi Et 38 A2
Rojo, C. 84 C5
Rokan → 39 D2
Rolândia 94 A6
Roma, Australia 63 A4
Roma, Italy 20 D4
Roman 17 E8
Romang 37 F3
Romania ■ 22 B5
Romanovka =
  Basarabeasca 17 E9
Romans-sur-Isère 13 D6
Romblon 36 B2
Rome = Roma 20 D4
Rome 82 B5
Romorantin-Lanthenay .. 12 C4
Roncador, Serra do 93 E3
Ronda 18 D3
Rondônia ☐ 91 F6
Rondonópolis 93 F3
Ronge, L. la 69 C9
Ronne Ice Shelf 96 B3
Roorkee 42 E10
Roosevelt → 91 E6
Roosevelt I. 96 B16
Roquetas de Mar 19 D4
Roraima ☐ 90 C6
Roraima, Mt. 90 B6
Rosa, Monte 13 D7
Rosario, Argentina 94 C4
Rosário, Brazil 92 C5
Rosario, Mexico 84 C3
Rosario, Paraguay 94 A5
Rosario de la Frontera 94 B3
Rosário do Sul 94 C6
Roscommon 11 E2
Roseau, Dominica 87 C7
Roseau, U.S.A. 75 A7
Rosebery 62 D4
Roseburg 72 E2
Rosenheim 15 E7
Roses, G. de 19 A7
Rosetown 69 C9
Roseville 72 G3
Rosewood 63 A5
Rosignano Maríttimo ... 20 C3
Rosignol 90 B7
Roşiori de Vede 22 B5
Roslavl 24 C3
Ross, Australia 62 D4
Ross, N.Z. 65 E4
Ross I. 96 B15
Ross Ice Shelf 96 C16
Ross Sea 96 B15
Rossano 21 E6
Rosslare 11 E3
Rosso 53 E2
Rossosh 24 C4
Rostock 15 A7
Rostov, Don, Russia ... 25 D4
Rostov, Yaroslavl, Russia 24 B4
Roswell 80 C1
Rotherham 11 E6
Roto 63 B4
Rotondo, Mte. 13 E8
Rotorua 64 C7
Rotorua, L. 64 C7
Rotterdam 14 C3
Rottweil 14 D5

Rotuma 64 L12
Roubaix 13 A5
Rouen 12 B4
Round Mt. 63 B5
Roussillon 13 E5
Rouyn-Noranda 71 D3
Rovaniemi 8 B11
Rovereto 20 B3
Rovigo 20 B3
Rovinj 20 B4
Rovno = Rivne 17 C8
Rovuma = Ruvuma → .. 57 G8
Rowena 63 A4
Roxas 36 B2
Roxburgh 65 F3
Royal Leamington Spa .. 11 E6
Royan 12 D3
Rozdilna 17 E10
Rozhyshche 17 C7
Rtishchevo 24 C5
Ruahine Ra. 64 C6
Ruapehu 64 C6
Ruapuke I. 65 G3
Rub' al Khālī 48 D4
Rubio 90 B4
Rubtsovsk 29 D9
Rudall 62 B2
Rudolfa, Ostrov 28 A6
Rufiji → 57 F7
Rufino 94 C4
Rugby 11 E6
Rügen 15 A7
Ruhr → 14 C4
Rukwa, L. 57 F6
Rum = Rhum 10 C3
Rumāh 47 F6
Rumania = Romania ■ .. 22 B5
Rumbêk 55 G4
Rumia 16 A4
Rumoi 32 B7
Runanga 65 E4
Runaway, C. 64 B7
Ruoqiang 34 C3
Rupa 41 D9
Rupat 39 D2
Rupert → 71 C3
Rupert House =
  Waskaganish 71 C3
Rurrenabaque 91 F5
Ruse 22 C5
Russas 92 C6
Russellkonda 40 H5
Rustavi 25 E6
Rustenburg 59 D5
Ruteng 37 F2
Ruvuma → 57 G8
Ruwenzori 57 D5
Rwanda ■ 57 E6
Ryazan 24 C4
Ryazhsk 24 C5
Rybachye 29 E9
Rybinsk 24 B4
Rybinskoye Vdkhr. 24 B4
Rybnitsa = Rãbnița 17 E9
Rylstone 63 B4
Ryōtsu 32 D6
Rypin 16 B4
Ryūkyū Is. = Ryūkyū-rettō .. 35 D7
Ryūkyū-rettō 35 D7
Rzeszów 16 C5
Rzhev 24 B3

S

Sa Dec 38 B3
Sa'ādatābād 44 D3
Saale → 15 C6
Saalfeld 15 C6
Saar → 13 B7
Saarbrücken 14 D4

Saaremaa 24 B1
Šabac 22 B2
Sabadell 19 B7
Sabah □ 38 C5
Şabāḥ, Wadi → 47 G7
Sabalán, Kūhhā-ye 46 C6
Sabalana, Kepulauan ... 37 F1
Sábanalarga 90 A4
Sabang 38 C1
Sabará 93 F5
Saberania 37 E5
Sabhah 54 C1
Sabinas 84 B4
Sabinas Hidalgo 84 B4
Sablayan 36 B2
Sable, C., Canada 71 D4
Sable, C., U.S.A. 86 A3
Sable I. 71 D5
Sabrina Coast 96 A12
Sabulubbek 39 E1
Sabzevār 44 B4
Sabzvārān 44 D4
Săcele 17 F7
Sachsen □ 15 C7
Sachsen-Anhalt □ 15 C7
Sacramento 72 G3
Sacramento → 72 G3
Sacramento Mts. 79 D10
Sadd el Aali 54 D5
Sado 32 E6
Sadon 41 E11
Safi 52 B4
Safid Kūh 42 B3
Saga 33 G2
Sagar 43 M9
Saginaw 76 C4
Saglouc = Salluit 70 B3
Sagua la Grande 86 B3
Sagunt 19 C5
Sahagún 18 A3
Sahand, Kūh-e 46 C6
Sahara 52 D6
Saharanpur 42 E10
Saharien, Atlas 52 B6
Sahiwal 42 D8
Sa'id Bundas 55 G3
Sa'īdābād = Sirjān 44 D3
Sa'īdīyeh 46 C7
Saidpur 41 E7
Saidu 42 B8
Saigon = Thanh Pho Ho Chi
  Minh 38 B3
Saikhoa Ghat 41 D10
Saiki 33 G2
Sailolof 37 E4
Saimaa 8 C11
St. Andrews 10 C5
St. Arnaud 62 C3
St-Augustin 71 C5
St. Augustine 83 E7
St. Austell 11 F4
St-Brieuc 12 B2
St. Catharines 77 C6
St-Chamond 13 D6
St. Christopher-Nevis = St.
  Kitts & Nevis ■ 87 C7
St. Cloud 75 C7
St. Croix 87 C7
St-Denis 12 B5
St-Dizier 13 B6
St. Elias, Mt. 68 B5
St-Étienne 13 D6
St-Flour 13 D5
St-Gaudens 12 E4
St. George 63 A4
St-Georges 92 B3
St. George's 87 D7
St. George's Channel ... 11 F3
St. Georges Hd. 63 C5
St. Gotthard P. = San
  Gottardo, P. del 13 C8
St. Helena 51 H3

St. Helena B. 58 E3
St. Helens 62 D4
St. Helier 11 G5
St-Hyacinthe 71 D3
St. John 71 D4
St. John's, Antigua & B. .. 87 C7
St. John's, Canada 71 D5
St. Johns → 83 D7
St. Joseph 75 F7
St. Joseph, L. 71 C1
St. Kilda, N.Z. 65 F4
St. Kilda, U.K. 10 C2
St. Kitts & Nevis ■ 87 C7
St-Laurent 92 A3
St. Lawrence → 71 D4
St. Lawrence, Gulf of .. 71 D4
St. Lawrence I. 69 B2
St-Lô 12 B3
St. Louis, Senegal 53 E2
St. Louis, U.S.A. 75 F9
St. Lucia ■ 87 D7
St-Malo 12 B2
St-Marc 87 C5
St. Mary Pk. 62 B2
St. Marys 62 D4
St-Mathieu, Pte. 12 B1
St. Matthews, I. = Zadetkyi
  Kyun 38 C1
St-Nazaire 12 C2
St-Omer 12 A5
St. Paul 75 C8
St. Peter Port 11 G5
St. Petersburg = Sankt-
  Peterburg 24 B3
St. Petersburg 83 F6
St-Pierre et Miquelon □ . 71 D5
St-Quentin 13 B5
St-Tropez 13 E7
St. Vincent, G. 62 C2
St. Vincent & the
  Grenadines ■ 87 D7
Saintes 12 D3
Saintonge 12 D3
Saipan 64 H9
Sairang 41 F9
Sajama 91 G5
Sajószentpéter 16 D5
Sakākah 47 E5
Sakakawea, L. 74 B4
Sakarya 46 B2
Sakata 32 D6
Sakhalin 31 D12
Sakon Nakhon 38 A2
Sala 9 D9
Sala Consilina 21 D5
Saladillo 94 D5
Salado →, Buenos Aires,
  Argentina 94 D5
Salado →, La Pampa,
  Argentina 94 D3
Salado →, Santa Fe,
  Argentina 94 C4
Salaga 53 G5
Salālah 49 D5
Salamanca, Chile 94 C2
Salamanca, Spain 18 B3
Salamís 23 F4
Salar de Atacama 94 A3
Salar de Uyuni 91 H5
Salaverry 91 E3
Salawati 37 E4
Salayar 37 F2
Saldanha 58 E3
Sale, Australia 63 C4
Salé, Morocco 52 B4
Salekhard 28 C7
Salem, India 43 P11
Salem, U.S.A. 72 D2
Salerno 21 D5
Salgótarján 16 D4
Salihli 23 E7
Salihorsk 17 B8

Salima	59	A6	San Carlos, *Chile*	94	D2	San Sebastián	95	G3
Salina, *Italy*	21	E5	San Carlos, *Phil.*	36	B2	San Severo	20	D5
Salina, *U.S.A.*	74	F6	San Carlos, *Amazonas,*			San Valentin, Mte.	95	F2
Salina Cruz	85	D5	*Venezuela*	90	C5	San Vicente de la Barquera	18	A3
Salinas, *Brazil*	93	F5	San Carlos, *Cojedes,*			Sana'	49	D3
Salinas, *Ecuador*	90	D2	*Venezuela*	90	B5	Sana →	20	B2
Salinas, *U.S.A.*	78	B2	San Carlos de Bariloche	95	E2	Sanaga →	56	D1
Salinas Grandes	94	C3	San Carlos del Zulia	90	B4	Sanana	37	E3
Salinópolis	92	C4	San Cristóbal, *Argentina*	94	C4	Sanandaj	46	D6
Salisbury = Harare	59	B6	San Cristóbal, *Venezuela*	90	B4	Sancti Spíritus	86	B4
Salisbury, *U.K.*	11	F6	San Cristóbal de la Casas	85	D6	Sancy, Puy de	13	D5
Salisbury, *U.S.A.*	83	B7	San Diego	78	D4	Sandakan	38	C5
Salliq = Coral Harbour	70	B2	San Diego, C.	95	G3	Sandanski	22	D4
Salluit	70	B3	San Felipe, *Chile*	94	C2	Sanday	10	B5
Salmãs	46	C6	San Felipe, *Venezuela*	90	A5	Sandia	91	F5
Salmon →	72	D5	San Fernando, *Chile*	94	C2	Sandıklı	46	C2
Salmon River Mts.	73	D6	San Fernando, *La Union,*			Sandoa	56	F4
Salon-de-Provence	13	E6	*Phil.*	36	A2	Sandomierz	16	C5
Salonica = Thessaloníki	23	D4	San Fernando, *Pampanga,*			Sandoway	41	H10
Salonta	16	E5	*Phil.*	36	A2	Sandusky	76	D4
Salsk	25	D5	San Fernando, *Spain*	18	D2	Sandy C.	62	D3
Salso →	21	F4	San Fernando, *Trin. & Tob.*	87	D7	Sandy L.	69	C10
Salt Lake City	73	F8	San Fernando, *U.S.A.*	78	C3	Sanford, *Fla., U.S.A.*	83	E7
Salta	94	A3	San Fernando de Apure	90	B5	Sanford, *N.C., U.S.A.*	83	B8
Saltillo	84	B4	San Fernando de Atabapo	90	C5	Sanford, Mt.	69	B5
Salto	94	C5	San Francisco, *Argentina*	94	C4	Sanga →	56	E3
Salto →	20	C4	San Francisco, *U.S.A.*	78	B1	Sangamner	43	K9
Salton Sea	78	D5	San Francisco de Macorís	87	C5	Sangar	31	C10
Salûm	54	B4	San Gottardo, P. del	13	C8	Sangeang	37	F1
Salur	40	H4	San Ignacio, *Bolivia*	91	G6	Sangerhausen	15	C6
Salvador	93	E6	San Ignacio, *Paraguay*	94	B5	Sanggau	39	D4
Salween →	41	J11	San Ildefonso, C.	36	A2	Sangihe, Pulau	37	D3
Salyan	25	F6	San Javier	91	G6	Sangkapura	39	F4
Salzach →	15	D7	San Joaquin →	78	A2	Sangli	43	L9
Salzburg	15	E7	San Jorge, G.	95	F3	Sangmélima	56	D2
Salzgitter	14	B6	San José, *Costa Rica*	86	E3	Sangre de Cristo Mts.	80	A1
Salzwedel	15	B6	San Jose, *Mind. Occ., Phil.*	36	B2	Sanirajak	70	B2
Sama de Langreo =			San Jose, *Nueva Ecija, Phil.*	36	A2	Sanjo	32	A6
Langreo	18	A3	San Jose, *U.S.A.*	78	B2	Sankt Gallen	13	C8
Samales Group	36	C2	San José de Chiquitos	91	G6	Sankt Moritz	13	C8
Samangân □	45	B7	San José de Jáchal	94	C3	Sankt-Peterburg	24	B3
Samani	32	B8	San José de Mayo	94	C5	Sankt Pölten	15	D8
Samar	36	B3	San José del Guaviare	90	C4	Sankuru →	56	E4
Samara	24	C7	San Juan, *Argentina*	94	C3	Sanliurfa	46	C4
Samarinda	39	E5	San Juan, *Puerto Rico*	87	C6	Sanlúcar de Barrameda	18	D2
Samarkand = Samarqand	29	F7	San Juan →	86	D3	Sanmenxia	35	C6
Samarqand	29	F7	San Juan de los Morros	90	B5	Sannicandro Gargánico	20	D5
Sāmarrā	46	D5	San Juan Mts.	79	B9	Sant Antoni Abat	19	C6
Sambalpur	40	G5	San Justo	94	C4	Sant Feliu de Guíxols	19	B7
Sambar, Tanjung	39	E4	San Leandro	78	B1	Sant Jordi, G. de	19	B6
Sambas	39	D3	San Lorenzo	90	C3	Santa Ana, *Bolivia*	91	F5
Sambhal	42	E11	San Lorenzo, Mte.	95	F2	Santa Ana, *El Salv.*	85	E7
Sambhar	42	F9	San Lucas	91	H5	Santa Ana, *U.S.A.*	78	D4
Sambiase	21	E6	San Lucas, C.	84	C2	Sant' Antíoco	21	E2
Sambir	17	D6	San Luis	94	C3	Santa Barbara	78	C3
Samoa ■	65	L13	San Luis Obispo	78	C2	Santa Catalina I.	78	D3
Samokov	22	C4	San Luis Potosí	84	C4	Santa Catarina □	94	B7
Sámos	23	F6	San Marino	20	C4	Santa Clara	86	B4
Samothráki = Mathráki	23	E2	San Marino ■	20	C4	Santa Clotilde	90	D4
Samothráki	23	D5	San Martín, L.	95	F2	Santa Coloma de Gramenet	19	B7
Sampit	39	E4	San Matías	91	G7	Santa Cruz, *Argentina*	95	G3
Sampit, Teluk	39	E4	San Matías, G.	95	E4	Santa Cruz, *Bolivia*	91	G6
Samsun	46	B4	San Miguel	85	E7	Santa Cruz, *Phil.*	36	B2
Samui, Ko	38	C2	San Miguel →	91	F6	Santa Cruz, *U.S.A.*	78	B1
Samut Prakan	38	B2	San Miguel de Tucumán	94	B3	Santa Cruz →	95	G3
Samut Songkhram →	38	B2	San Nicolás de los Arroyos	94	C4	Santa Cruz de Tenerife	52	C2
San	53	F5	San Pedro	53	H4	Santa Cruz do Sul	94	B6
San Agustin, C.	36	C3	San Pedro de las Colonias	84	B4	Santa Cruz Is.	64	L11
San Andrés, I. de	86	D3	San Pedro de Macorís	87	C6	Santa Fe, *Argentina*	94	C4
San Andrés Tuxtla	85	D5	San Pedro del Paraná	94	B5	Santa Fe, *U.S.A.*	79	C10
San Angelo	80	D3	San Pedro Sula	85	D7	Santa Filomena	93	D4
San Antonio, *Chile*	94	C2	San Pietro	21	E2	Santa Inés, I.	95	G2
San Antonio, *U.S.A.*	80	E4	San Rafael, *Argentina*	94	C3	Santa Isabel = Rey Malabo	56	D1
San Antonio, C.	84	D5	San Rafael, *U.S.A.*	72	H2	Santa Isabel	94	D3
San Antonio Oeste	95	E4	San Remo	20	C1	Santa Isabel do Morro	93	E3
San Benedetto del Tronto	20	C4	San Roque, *Argentina*	94	B5	Santa Lucia Range	78	C2
San Bernardino	78	C4	San Roque, *Spain*	18	D3	Santa Maria, *Brazil*	94	B6
San Bernardino Str.	36	B2	San Rosendo	94	D2	Santa Maria, *U.S.A.*	78	C2
San Bernardo	94	C2	San Salvador	85	E7	Santa María →	84	A3
San Bernardo, I. de	90	B3	San Salvador de Jujuy	94	A4	Santa María da Vitória	93	E5
San Borja	91	F5	San Sebastián	86	B5	Santa Maria di Léuca, C.	23	E2
San Carlos, *Argentina*	94	C3	San Sebastián = Donostia-			Santa Marta	90	A4
			San Sebastián	19	A5			

Santa Marta, Sierra Nevada de 90 A4
Santa Maura = Levkás 23 E3
Santa Rosa, *La Pampa, Argentina* 94 D4
Santa Rosa, *San Luis, Argentina* 94 C3
Santa Rosa, *Brazil* 94 B6
Santa Rosa, *U.S.A.* 72 G2
Santa Vitória do Palmar 94 C6
Santai 35 C5
Santana, Coxilha de 94 C5
Santana do Livramento 94 C5
Santander 18 A4
Santarém, *Brazil* 92 C3
Santarém, *Portugal* 18 C1
Santiago, *Brazil* 94 B6
Santiago, *Chile* 94 C2
Santiago → 90 D3
Santiago de Compostela 18 A1
Santiago de Cuba 86 C4
Santiago de los Cabelleros 87 C5
Santiago del Estero 94 B4
Santo Amaro 93 E6
Santo Ângelo 94 B6
Santo Antônio do Leverger 93 F2
Santo Domingo 87 C6
Santo Tomás 91 F4
Santo Tomé 94 B5
Santo Tomé de Guayana = Ciudad Guayana 90 B6
Santoña 18 A4
Santoríni = Thíra 23 F5
Santos 94 A7
São Bernardo do Campo 93 G4
São Borja 94 B5
São Carlos 94 A7
São Cristóvão 93 E6
São Domingos 93 E4
São Francisco 93 F5
São Francisco → 93 E6
São Francisco do Sul 94 B7
São Gabriel 94 C6
São João da Madeira 18 B1
São João del Rei 93 G5
São João do Araguaia 92 D4
São João do Piauí 92 D5
São José do Rio Prêto 93 G4
São Leopoldo 94 B6
São Lourenço 93 G4
São Lourenço → 93 F2
São Luís 92 C5
São Marcos → 93 F4
São Marcos, B. de 92 C5
São Mateus 93 F6
São Paulo 94 A7
São Paulo □ 94 A7
São Roque, C. de 92 D6
São Sebastião, I. de 94 A7
São Tomé & Principe ■ 51 F4
São Vicente, C. de 18 D1
Saône → 13 D6
Saonek 37 E4
Saparua 37 E3
Sapele 53 G7
Saposoa 91 E3
Sapporo 32 B7
Sapulpa 81 B5
Saqqez 46 C6
Sar-e Pol 45 B6
Sar-e Pol □ 45 B6
Sar Planina 22 C3
Sarāb 46 C6
Saragossa = Zaragoza 19 B5
Saraguro 90 D3
Sarajevo 20 C7
Saran, Gunung 39 E4
Sarangani B. 36 C3
Sarangani Is. 36 C3
Sarangarh 40 G4
Saransk 24 C6
Sarapul 29 D6
Sarasota 83 F6
Saratov 24 C6
Saravane 38 A3
Sarawak □ 39 D4
Saray 22 D6
Sarayköy 23 F7
Sarbāz 45 E5
Sarbīsheh 45 C4
Sarda → 40 D3
Sardarshahr 42 E9
Sardegna □ 21 D2
Sardinia = Sardegna □ 21 D2
Sardis 23 E7
Sargodha 42 C8
Sarh 55 G2
Sārī 44 B3
Sarıgöl 23 E7
Sarikamiş 46 B5
Sarikei 39 D4
Sark 11 G5
Şarköy 23 D6
Sarlat-la-Canéda 12 D4
Sarmi 37 E5
Sarmiento 95 F3
Sarnia 71 D2
Sarolangun 39 E2
Saronikós Kólpos 23 F4
Sarre = Saar → 13 B7
Sarreguemines 13 B7
Sarthe → 12 C3
Sarvestān 44 D3
Sary-Tash 29 F8
Saryshagan 29 E8
Sasaram 40 E5
Sasebo 33 G1
Saser 42 B10
Saskatchewan □ 69 C9
Saskatchewan → 69 C9
Saskatoon 69 C9
Saskylakh 30 B9
Sasovo 24 C5
Sassandra 53 H4
Sassandra → 53 H4
Sássari 21 D2
Sassnitz 15 A7
Sassuolo 20 B3
Sasyk, Ozero 17 F9
Sata-Misaki 33 H2
Satadougou 53 F3
Satara 43 L8
Satmala Hills 43 J9
Satna 40 E3
Sátoraljaújhely 16 D5
Satpura Ra. 43 J10
Satu Mare 17 E6
Satui 39 E5
Saturnina → 91 F7
Sauðarkrókur 8 B2
Saudi Arabia ■ 47 F6
Sauerland 14 C4
Sault Ste. Marie, *Canada* 71 D2
Sault Ste. Marie, *U.S.A.* 76 A3
Saumlaki 37 F4
Saumur 12 C3
Saunders, C. 65 F4
Saurimo 56 F4
Sava → 22 B3
Savage I. = Niue 65 L14
Savalou 53 G6
Savannah 83 C7
Savannah → 83 C7
Savannakhet 38 A2
Save → 59 C6
Sāveh 46 D7
Savelugu 53 G5
Savoie □ 13 D7
Savona 20 B2
Savonlinna 8 C11
Savoy = Savoie □ 13 D7
Sawahlunto 39 E2
Sawai 37 E3
Sawai Madhopur 42 F10
Sawatch Range 79 A9
Sawu 37 F2
Sawu Sea 37 F2
Saxony = Sachsen □ 15 C7
Saxony, Lower = Niedersachsen □ 14 B5
Sayán 91 F3
Sayan, Zapadnyy 30 D7
Saydā 46 D3
Sayghān 45 C6
Sayḩūt 49 D5
Saylac = Zeila 49 E3
Saynshand 35 B6
Sazanit 23 D2
Sázava → 16 D2
Sazin 42 B8
Scandicci 20 C3
Scandinavia 8 C8
Scarborough 11 D6
Scebeli, Wabi → 49 G3
Schaffhausen 13 C8
Schefferville 71 C4
Schelde → 14 C3
Schenectady 77 C9
Schiermonnikoog 14 B4
Schio 20 B3
Schleswig 14 A5
Schleswig-Holstein □ 14 A5
Schouten I. 62 D4
Schouten Is. = Supiori 37 E5
Schwäbische Alb 14 D5
Schwaner, Pegunungan 39 E4
Schwarzwald 14 D5
Schwedt 15 B8
Schweinfurt 14 C6
Schwenningen = Villingen-Schwenningen 14 D5
Schwerin 15 B6
Schwyz 13 C8
Sciacca 21 F4
Scilla 21 E5
Scilly, Isles of 11 G3
Scone 63 B5
Scotland □ 10 C4
Scott Glacier 96 A12
Scottsbluff 74 E3
Scottsdale 62 D4
Scranton 77 D8
Scunthorpe 11 E6
Scutari = Shkodër 22 C2
Seaspray 63 C4
Seattle 72 C2
Sebastopol = Sevastopol 25 E3
Sebha = Sabhah 54 C1
Şebinkarahisar 46 B4
Sebta = Ceuta 18 E3
Sebuku 39 E5
Sebuku, Teluk 39 D5
Secretary I. 65 F2
Secunderabad 43 L11
Sedalia 75 F8
Sedan 13 B6
Seddon 65 D6
Seddonville 65 D5
Sédhiou 53 F2
Sedova, Pik 28 B6
Seferihisar 23 E6
Segamat 39 D2
Segesta 21 F4
Seget 37 E4
Ségou 53 F4
Segovia = Coco → 86 D3
Segovia 18 B3
Segre → 19 B6
Séguéla 53 G4
Segura → 19 C5
Sehore 43 H10
Seinäjoki → 8 C10
Seine → 12 B4
Seistan = Sīstān 45 D5
Sekayu 39 E2
Sekondi-Takoradi 53 H5

Selaru

Selaru 37 F4
Selçuk 23 F6
Sele → 21 D5
Selenga = Selenge
  Mörön → 35 A5
Selenge Mörön → 35 A5
Seletan, Tanjung 39 E4
Sélibabi 53 E3
Selîma, El Wâhât el 54 D4
Selkirk 69 C10
Selkirk Mts. 69 C8
Selma 83 B8
Selpele 37 E4
Selu 37 F4
Selva 94 B4
Selvas 91 E5
Seman → 23 D2
Semarang 39 F4
Semey 29 D9
Semipalatinsk = Semey . 29 D9
Semirara Is. 36 B2
Semitau 39 D4
Semiyarka 29 D8
Semmering P. 15 E8
Semnān 44 C3
Semnān □ 44 C3
Semporna 36 D1
Semuda 39 E4
Sena Madureira 91 E5
Senador Pompeu 92 D6
Senanga 58 B4
Sendai, Kagoshima, Japan 33 H2
Sendai, Miyagi, Japan .. 32 D7
Sendai-Wan 32 D7
Senegal ■ 53 F3
Sénégal → 53 E2
Senge Khambab = Indus → 43 G5
Senhor-do-Bonfim 93 E6
Senigállia 20 C4
Senj 20 B5
Senja 8 B9
Senlis 13 B5
Senmonorom 38 B3
Sens 13 B5
Senta 22 B3
Sentani 37 E6
Seo de Urgel = La Seu
  d'Urgell 19 A6
Seoul = Sŏul 35 C7
Sept-Îles 71 C4
Sequoia △ 78 B3
Seram 37 E3
Seram Sea 37 E3
Serasan 39 D3
Serbia □ 22 C3
Serbia & Montenegro ■ . 22 B3
Serdobsk 24 C5
Seremban 39 D2
Sereth = Siret → 17 F9
Sergipe □ 93 E6
Sergiyev Posad 24 B4
Seria 38 D4
Serian 39 D4
Seribu, Kepulauan 39 F3
Sérifos 23 F5
Sermata 37 F3
Serov 28 D7
Serowe 59 C5
Serpukhov 24 C4
Sérrai 22 D4
Serrinha 93 E6
Serua 37 F4
Serui 37 E5
Sesepe 37 E3
Setana 32 B6
Sète 13 E5
Sete Lagôas 93 F5
Sétif 52 A7
Settat 52 B4
Setúbal 18 C1
Setúbal, B. de 18 C1
Sevana Lich 25 E6

Sevastopol 25 E3
Severn →, Canada 71 C2
Severn →, U.K. 11 F5
Severnaya Zemlya 30 B7
Severnyye Uvaly 24 B6
Severo-Yeniseyskiy 30 C7
Severodvinsk 28 C4
Sevilla 18 D2
Sevlievo 22 C5
Seward 69 B5
Seward Peninsula 69 B3
Sewer 37 F4
Seychelles ■ 26 K9
Seyðisfjörður 8 B3
Seymour 63 C4
Sfântu Gheorghe 17 F7
Sfax 54 B1
Shaanxi □ 35 C5
Shaba = Katanga □ 57 F4
Shaballe = Scebeli, Wabi → 49 G3
Shache 34 C2
Shackleton Ice Shelf ... 96 A11
Shackleton Inlet 96 C15
Shadrinsk 29 D7
Shahdād 44 D4
Shahdād, Namakzār-e .. 44 D4
Shahdadkot 42 F5
Shahgarh 42 F6
Shahjahanpur 42 F11
Shahr-e Kord 44 C2
Shahrig 42 D5
Shajapur 43 H10
Shakhty 25 D5
Shakhunya 24 B6
Shaki 53 G6
Shalqar 29 E6
Shām, Bādiyat ash 47 D4
Shām, J. ash 44 F4
Shamil 44 E4
Shammar, Jabal 47 F5
Shamo = Gobi 35 B6
Shamo, L. 55 G6
Shan □ 41 G12
Shandong □ 35 C6
Shanghai 35 C7
Shangqiu 35 C6
Shangrao 35 D6
Shangshui 35 C6
Shannon 64 D6
Shannon → 11 E2
Shansi = Shanxi □ 35 C6
Shantou 35 D6
Shantung = Shandong □ . 35 C6
Shanxi □ 35 C6
Shaoguan 35 D6
Shaoxing 35 C7
Shaoyang 35 D6
Shaqra', Si. Arabia ... 47 F6
Shaqrā', Yemen 49 E4
Shari 32 B9
Sharjah = Ash Shāriqah . 44 E7
Sharon 76 D5
Sharya 24 B6
Shashi 35 C6
Shasta, Mt. 72 F2
Shatt al'Arab → 47 E7
Shawinigan 71 D3
Shaykh, J. ash 24 B4
Shcherbakov = Rybinsk . 24 B4
Shchuchinsk 29 D8
Shebele = Scebeli, Wabi → 49 G3
Sheboygan 76 C2
Sheffield 11 E6
Shekhupura 42 D8
Shelby 83 B7
Shelbyville 82 B4
Shellharbour 63 B5
Shenandoah → 77 E7
Shendam 53 G7
Shendī 55 E5
Shensi = Shaanxi □ ... 35 C5
Shenyang 35 B7

Sheopur Kalan 42 G10
Shepetivka 17 C8
Shepparton 63 C4
Sherbro I. 53 G3
Sherbrooke 71 D3
Sheridan 73 D10
Sherman 81 C5
Shetland Is. 10 A6
Shibām 49 D4
Shibata 33 E6
Shibecha 32 B9
Shibetsu 32 A8
Shieli 29 E7
Shijiazhuang 35 C6
Shikarpur 42 F6
Shikoku □ 33 G3
Shiliguri 40 D7
Shillong 41 E9
Shimoga 43 N9
Shimonoseki 33 G2
Shindand 42 C3
Shingū 33 G4
Shinyanga 57 E6
Shio-no-Misaki 33 G4
Shipchenski Prokhod . 22 C5
Shiquan He = Indus → . 43 G5
Shir Kūh 44 D3
Shiragami-Misaki ... 32 C7
Shīrāz 44 D3
Shire → 59 B7
Shiriya-Zaki 32 C7
Shīrvān 44 B4
Shirwa, L. = Chilwa, L. . 59 B7
Shivpuri 43 G10
Shizuoka 33 F6
Shklow 17 A10
Shkodër 22 C2
Shkumbini → 23 D2
Shmidta, Ostrov 30 A7
Sholapur = Solapur .. 43 L9
Shoshone Mts. 72 G5
Shreveport 81 C7
Shrewsbury 11 E5
Shrirampur 40 F7
Shū 29 E8
Shuangyashan 35 B8
Shule 34 C2
Shumagin Is. 69 C4
Shumen 22 C6
Shūr → 44 D3
Shurugwi 59 B5
Shūsf 45 D5
Shūshtar 47 D7
Shwebo 41 F10
Shwegu 41 E11
Shweli → 41 F11
Shymkent 29 E7
Shyok 42 B11
Shyok → 42 B9
Si Kiang = Xi Jiang → . 35 D6
Si-ngan = Xi'an 35 C5
Siahan Range 42 F4
Siaksriindrapura 39 D2
Sialkot 42 C9
Siam = Thailand ■ .. 38 A2
Sian = Xi'an 35 C5
Siantan 39 D3
Siargao I. 36 C3
Siasi 36 C2
Siau 37 D3
Šiauliai 24 B1
Šibenik 20 C5
Siberia 30 C8
Siberut 39 E1
Sibi 42 E5
Sibil = Oksibil 37 E6
Sibiti 56 E2
Sibiu 17 F7
Sibolga 39 D1
Sibsagar 41 D10
Sibu 39 D4
Sibuco 36 C2

Sibuguey B. 36 C2
Sibut 56 C3
Sibutu 36 D1
Sibutu Passage 36 D1
Sibuyan I. 36 B2
Sibuyan Sea 36 B2
Sichuan □ 34 C5
Sicilia 21 F5
Sicily = Sicilia 21 F5
Sicuani 91 F4
Siddipet 43 K11
Sidi-bel-Abbès 52 A5
Sidi Ifni 52 C3
Sidley, Mt. 96 B18
Sidon = Saydā 46 D3
Sidra, G. of = Surt, Khalīj . . 54 B2
Siedlce 17 B6
Sieg → 14 C4
Siegen 14 C5
Siemreab 38 B2
Siena 20 C3
Sieradz 16 C4
Sierra Colorada 95 E3
Sierra Gorda 94 A3
Sierra Leone ■ 53 G3
Sierra Nevada, Spain 18 D4
Sierra Nevada, U.S.A. 72 G3
Sifnos 23 F5
Sighetu-Marmației 17 E6
Sigli 38 C1
Siglufjörður 8 B2
Sigsig 90 D3
Sigüenza 19 B4
Siguiri 53 F4
Sihanoukville = Kampong
    Saom 38 B2
Sikar 42 F9
Sikasso 53 F4
Sikhote Alin, Khrebet 32 A5
Síkinos 23 F5
Sikkim □ 40 D7
Sikotu-Ko 32 B7
Sil → 18 A2
Silchar 41 E9
Silesia = Śląsk 16 C3
Silgarhi Doti 40 C3
Silghat 41 D9
Silifke 46 C3
Siliguri = Shiliguri 40 D7
Siling Co 34 C3
Silistra 22 B6
Silivri 22 D7
Sillajhuay, Cordillera 91 G5
Silva Porto = Kuito 58 A3
Simanggang = Bandar Sri
    Aman 39 D4
Simav 23 E7
Simbirsk 24 C6
Simeria 17 F6
Simeulue 39 D1
Simferopol 25 E3
Simi 23 F6
Simikot 40 C3
Simla 42 D10
Simpson Desert 60 F6
Sinabang 39 D1
Sinadogo 49 F4
Sinai = Es Sînâ´ 54 C5
Sinai, Mt. = Mûsa, Gebel . . 47 E3
Sinaloa de Leyva 84 B3
Sincelejo 90 B3
Sincora, Serra do 93 E5
Sind □ 42 F6
Sind Sagar Doab 42 D7
Sindangan 36 C2
Sindh = Sind □ 42 F6
Sines 18 D1
Sines, C. de 18 D1
Singa 55 F5
Singapore ■ 39 D2
Singaraja 39 F5
Singida 57 E6

Singitikós Kólpos 23 D5
Singkaling Hkamti 41 E10
Singkang 37 E2
Singkawang 39 D3
Singleton 63 B5
Singora = Songkhla 38 C2
Sinjai 37 F2
Sinjär 46 C5
Sinkat 55 E6
Sinkiang Uighur = Xinjiang
    Uygur Zizhiqu □ 34 B3
Sinni → 21 D6
Sinop 46 B3
Sintang 39 D4
Sintra 18 C1
Siocon 36 C2
Siófok 16 E4
Sioux City 75 D6
Sioux Falls 74 D6
Sioux Lookout 69 C10
Siping 35 B7
Sipura 39 E1
Siquijor 36 C2
Siracusa 21 F5
Sirajganj 41 E7
Sirdaryo = Syrdarya → . . . 29 E7
Siret → 17 F9
Sirjän 44 D3
Sirohi 43 G8
Sironj 43 G10
Síros 23 F5
Sirsa 42 E9
Sisak 20 B6
Sisaket 38 A2
Sisophon 38 B2
Sīstān 45 D5
Sīstān, Daryācheh-ye 45 D5
Sīstān va Balūchestān □ . . 45 E5
Sitapur 40 D3
Sitges 19 B6
Sitía 23 G6
Sitka 69 C6
Sittang Myit → 41 J11
Sittoung = Sittang Myit → . 41 J11
Sittwe 41 G9
Siuri 40 F6
Sivas 46 C4
Siverek 46 C4
Sivrihisar 46 C2
Sîwa 54 C4
Siwalik Range 40 D4
Siwan 40 D5
Sjælland 9 D8
Sjumen = Shumen 22 C6
Skadarsko Jezero 22 C2
Skagen 9 D7
Skagerrak 9 D7
Skagway 69 C6
Skala-Podilska 17 D8
Skalat 17 D7
Skardu 42 B9
Skarżysko-Kamienna 16 C5
Skeena → 68 C6
Skegness 11 E7
Skeldon 90 B7
Skellefte älv → 8 C10
Skellefteå 8 C10
Skiathos 23 E4
Skien 9 D7
Skierniewice 16 C5
Skikda 52 A7
Skíros 23 E5
Skole 17 D6
Skópelos 23 E4
Skopje 22 C3
Skvyra 17 D9
Skye 10 C3
Skyros = Skíros 23 E5
Śląsk 16 C3
Slatina 22 B5
Slave → 68 B8
Slavgorod 29 D8

Slavonski Brod 20 B7
Slavuta 17 C8
Slavyanka 32 B2
Slavyansk = Slovyansk . . . 25 D4
Slawharad 17 B10
Sleaford B. 62 B2
Sleeper Is. 70 C2
Sligeach = Sligo 11 D2
Sligo 11 D2
Sliven 22 C6
Slobodskoy 24 B7
Slobozia 22 B6
Slonim 17 B7
Slough 11 F6
Slovak Rep. ■ 16 D4
Slovakian Ore Mts. =
    Slovenské Rudohorie . . 16 D4
Slovenia ■ 20 B5
Slovenské Rudohorie 16 D4
Slovyansk 25 D4
Sluch → 17 C8
Słupsk 16 A3
Slutsk 17 B8
Smarhon 17 A8
Smederevo 22 B3
Smithton 62 D4
Smoky Bay 62 B1
Smolensk 24 C3
Smolikas, Óros 23 D3
Smolyan 22 D5
Smorgon = Smarhon 17 A8
Smyrna = İzmir 23 E6
Snake → 72 C4
Snake I. 63 C4
Snake River Plain 73 E7
Sneek 14 B3
Snežka 16 C2
Snøhetta 8 C7
Snowdon 11 E4
Snowdrift = Łutselk'e 68 B8
Snowtown 62 B2
Snowy → 63 C4
Snowy Mts. 63 C4
Snyatyn 17 D7
Snyder 80 C3
Sobat, Nahr → 55 G5
Sobral 92 C5
Soc Trang 38 C3
Soch'e = Shache 34 C2
Sochi 25 E4
Société, Is. de la 65 L15
Society Is. = Société, Is. de
    la 65 L15
Socompa, Portezuelo de . . 94 A3
Socotra 49 E5
Söderhamn 8 C9
Sodiri 55 F4
Sofia = Sofiya 22 C4
Sofia → 59 H9
Sofiya 22 C4
Sogamoso 90 B4
Sognefjorden 8 C7
Sohâg 54 C5
Soissons 13 B5
Sokal 17 C7
Söke 23 F6
Sokhumi 25 E5
Sokodé 53 G6
Sokol 24 B5
Sokółka 17 B6
Sokołów Podlaski 17 B6
Sokoto 53 F7
Solano 36 A2
Solapur 43 L9
Soledad 90 B6
Soligalich 24 B5
Soligorsk = Salihorsk 17 B8
Solikamsk 29 D6
Solimões = Amazonas → . 92 C3
Solingen 14 C4
Sóller 19 C7
Sologne 12 C4

Name	Page	Grid
Solok	39	E2
Solomon Is. ■	64	K10
Solomon Sea	61	B9
Solon	35	B7
Solor	37	F2
Šolta	20	C6
Solţānābād	44	B4
Solunska Glava	22	D3
Solwezi	59	A5
Sōma, *Japan*	32	E7
Soma, *Turkey*	23	E6
Somali Rep. ■	49	F4
Sombor	22	B2
Sombrerete	84	C4
Somerset I.	68	A10
Someş →	17	E6
Somme →	12	A4
Somosierra, Puerto de	18	B4
Somport, Puerto de	12	E3
Søndre Strømfjord = Kangerlussuaq	70	B5
Sóndrio	20	A2
Sonepur	40	G4
Song Cau	38	B3
Songea	57	G7
Songhua Jiang →	35	B8
Songkhla	38	C2
Songpan	34	C5
Sonipat	42	E10
Sonmiani	42	G5
Sono →	93	D4
Sonora →	84	B2
Sonsonate	85	E7
Soochow = Suzhou	35	C7
Sopi	37	D3
Sopot	16	A4
Sopron	16	E3
Sør-Rondane	96	B8
Sorel-Tracy	71	D3
Sórgono	21	D2
Soria	19	B4
Sorkh, Kuh-e	44	C4
Soroca	17	D9
Sorocaba	94	A7
Soroki = Soroca	17	D9
Sorong	37	E4
Soroti	57	D6
Sørøya	8	A10
Sorsogon	36	B2
Sosnowiec	16	C4
Souanké	56	D2
Soúdhas, Kólpos	23	G5
Sŏul	35	C7
Sources, Mt. aux	59	D5
Soure	92	C4
Souris →	69	D10
Sousa	92	D6
Sousse	54	A1
South Africa ■	58	E4
South Australia □	62	B2
South Bend	76	D2
South Carolina □	83	C7
South China Sea	38	C4
South Dakota □	74	C4
South East C.	62	D4
South Horr	57	D7
South I.	65	E3
South Invercargill	65	G3
South Korea ■	35	C7
South Magnetic Pole	96	A13
South Nahanni →	68	B7
South Orkney Is.	96	A4
South Platte →	74	E4
South Pole	96	C
South Ronaldsay	10	B5
South Saskatchewan →	69	C9
South Shetland Is.	96	A4
South Shields	11	D6
South Taranaki Bight	64	C6
South Uist	10	C3
South West C.	62	D4
Southampton	11	F6
Southampton I.	70	B2
Southbridge	65	E5
Southend-on-Sea	11	F7
Southern Alps	65	E4
Southern Indian L.	69	C10
Southern Ocean	96	A9
Southern Uplands	10	D5
Southport	63	A5
Southwest C.	65	G2
Sovetsk, *Kaliningrad, Russia*	24	B1
Sovetsk, *Kirov, Russia*	24	B6
Sozh →	17	C10
Spain ■	18	C4
Spalding	62	B2
Spanish Town	86	C4
Sparta = Spárti	23	F4
Spartanburg	83	B7
Spárti	23	F4
Spartivento, C., *Calabria, Italy*	21	F6
Spartivento, C., *Sard., Italy*	21	E2
Spassk Dalniy	32	A3
Spátha, Ákra	23	G4
Spence Bay = Taloyoak	68	B10
Spencer, C.	62	C2
Spencer G.	62	B2
Spenser Mts.	65	E5
Spey →	10	C5
Speyer	14	D5
Spitzbergen = Svalbard	26	B5
Split	20	C6
Spokane	72	C5
Spoleto	20	C4
Sporyy Navolok, Mys	28	B7
Spratly Is.	38	C4
Spree →	15	B7
Springfield, *N.Z.*	65	E4
Springfield, *Ill., U.S.A.*	75	F10
Springfield, *Mass., U.S.A.*	77	C9
Springfield, *Mo., U.S.A.*	81	A7
Springfield, *Ohio, U.S.A.*	76	E4
Springfield, *Oreg., U.S.A.*	72	D2
Springs	59	D5
Srbija = Serbia □	22	C3
Sre Ambel	38	B2
Srebrenica	20	B7
Sredinnyy Khrebet	31	D14
Śrem	16	B3
Sremska Mitrovica	22	B2
Sri Lanka ■	43	R12
Srikakulam	40	H4
Srinagar	42	B9
Stade	14	B5
Stafford	11	E5
Stakhanov	25	D4
Stalingrad = Volgograd	25	D5
Staliniri = Tskhinvali	25	E5
Stalino = Donetsk	25	D4
Stalinogorsk = Novomoskovsk	24	C4
Stalowa Wola	17	C6
Stamford	77	D9
Stanislav = Ivano-Frankivsk	17	D7
Stanke Dimitrov	22	C4
Stanley, *Australia*	62	D4
Stanley, *Falk. Is.*	95	G5
Stanovoy Khrebet	31	D10
Stanthorpe	63	A5
Stara Planina	22	C4
Stara Zagora	22	C5
Starachowice	16	C5
Staraya Russa	24	B3
Starbuck I.	65	K15
Stargard Szczeciński	16	B2
Staritsa	24	B3
Starogard Gdański	16	B4
Starokonstyantyniv	17	D8
Staryy Chartoriysk	17	C7
Staryy Oskol	24	C4
State College	77	D7
Staten, I. = Estados, I. de Los	95	G4
Statesville	83	B7
Stavanger	9	D7
Staveley	65	E4
Stavropol	25	D5
Stawell	62	C3
Steenkool = Bintuni	37	E4
Stefanie L. = Chew Bahir	55	H6
Stefansson Bay	96	A9
Steiermark □	15	E8
Steinkjer	8	C8
Stendal	15	B6
Steornabhaigh = Stornoway	10	B3
Stepanakert = Xankändi	25	F6
Stephens Creek	62	B3
Stepnoi = Elista	25	D6
Sterlitamak	29	D6
Stettin = Szczecin	16	B2
Stettiner Haff	15	B8
Stettler	69	C8
Steubenville	76	D5
Stevenage	11	F6
Stewart →	68	B6
Stewart L. = Chew	95	G2
Stewart I.	65	G2
Steyr	15	D8
Stillwater, *N.Z.*	65	E4
Stillwater, *U.S.A.*	80	A5
Štip	22	D4
Stirling	10	C5
Stockerau	15	D9
Stockholm	9	D9
Stockport	11	E5
Stockton	78	B2
Stockton-on-Tees	11	D6
Stoeng Treng	38	B3
Stoke-on-Trent	11	E5
Stokes Pt.	62	D3
Stolac	20	C6
Stolbovoy, Ostrov	30	B11
Stolbtsy = Stowbtsy	17	B8
Stolin	17	C8
Stonehaven	10	C5
Stony Tunguska = Tunguska, Podkamennaya →	30	C7
Stora Lulevatten	8	B9
Storavan	8	B9
Store Bælt	9	D8
Storm B.	62	D4
Stormberge	59	E5
Stornoway	10	B3
Storozhynets	17	D7
Storsjön	8	C8
Storuman	8	B9
Stowbtsy	17	B8
Strahan	62	D4
Stralsund	15	A7
Stranraer	11	D4
Strasbourg	13	B7
Stratford, *Canada*	77	C5
Stratford, *N.Z.*	64	C6
Strathalbyn	62	C2
Straubing	15	D7
Streaky B.	62	B1
Streaky Bay	62	B1
Strelka	30	D7
Strezhevoy	29	C8
Strimón →	23	D4
Strimonikós Kólpos	23	D5
Strómboli	21	E5
Stronsay	10	B6
Stroud Road	63	B5
Struica	22	D4
Stryy	17	D6
Strzelecki Cr. →	62	A2
Stuart Ra.	62	A1
Stung Treng = Stoeng Treng	38	B3
Stuttgart	14	D5
Styria = Steiermark □	15	E8
Suakin	55	E6
Subansiri →	41	D9

Subi	39	D3
Subotica	16	E4
Suceava	17	E8
Suchou = Suzhou	35	C7
Süchow = Xuzhou	35	C6
Sucre	91	G5
Sudan ■	55	E4
Sudbury	71	D2
Südd	55	G4
Sudeten Mts. = Sudety	16	C3
Sudety	16	C3
Sudirman, Pegunungan	37	E5
Sueca	19	C5
Suez = El Suweis	54	C5
Suez, G. of = Suweis, Khalîg el	54	C5
Sugluk = Salluit	70	B3
Şuḥār	44	E4
Şuhl	14	C6
Suihua	35	B7
Sukadana	39	E3
Sukagawa	33	E7
Sukaraja	39	E4
Sukarnapura = Jayapura	37	E6
Sukhona →	28	C5
Sukhumi = Sokhumi	25	E5
Sukkur	42	F6
Sukkur Barrage	42	F6
Sukumo	33	G3
Sula, Kepulauan	37	E3
Sulaiman Range	42	D6
Sulawesi □	37	E2
Sulawesi Sea = Celebes Sea	37	D2
Sulima	53	G3
Sulina	17	F9
Sullana	90	D2
Sultanpur	40	D4
Sulu Arch.	36	C2
Sulu Sea	36	C2
Suluq	54	B3
Sulzberger Ice Shelf	96	B17
Sumalata	37	D2
Sumatera □	39	D2
Sumatra = Sumatera □	39	D2
Sumba	37	F1
Sumba, Selat	37	F1
Sumbawa	39	F5
Sumbawa Besar	39	F5
Sumbe	56	G2
Sumen = Shumen	22	C6
Sumgait = Sumqayît	25	E6
Summerside	71	D4
Šumperk	16	D3
Sumqayît	25	E6
Sumter	83	C7
Sumy	24	C3
Sunbury	63	C3
Sunda, Selat	39	F3
Sunda Str. = Sunda, Selat	39	F3
Sundarbans	41	G7
Sundargarh	40	F5
Sunderland	11	D6
Sundsvall	8	C9
Sungaigerong	39	E2
Sungailiat	39	E3
Sungaipenuh	39	E2
Sungari = Songhua Jiang	35	B8
Sungurlu	46	B3
Sunnyvale	78	B1
Suntar	30	C9
Supaul	40	D6
Superior	75	B8
Superior, L.	71	D2
Suphan Daği	46	C5
Supiori	37	E5
Suquṭra = Socotra	49	E5
Şūr, Lebanon	46	D3
Şūr, Oman	45	F4
Şura →	24	B6
Surabaya	39	F4
Surakarta	39	F4
Surat, Australia	63	A4
Surat, India	43	J8
Surat Thani	38	C1
Suratgarh	42	E8
Surgut	29	C8
Suriapet	43	L11
Surigao	36	C3
Suriname ■	92	B2
Suriname →	92	A2
Surt	54	B2
Surt, Khalîj	54	B2
Surtsey	8	C1
Suruga-Wan	33	F6
Süsangerd	47	E7
Susanville	72	F3
Susquehanna →	77	E7
Susques	94	A3
Susunu	37	E4
Susurluk	23	E7
Sutherland Falls	65	F2
Sutlej →	42	E7
Suttsu	32	B7
Suva	64	L12
Suva Planina	22	C4
Suvorov Is. = Suwarrow Is.	65	L14
Suwałki	17	A6
Suwarrow Is.	65	L14
Suweis, Khalîg el	54	C5
Suzdal	24	B5
Suzhou	35	C7
Suzu	33	E5
Suzu-Misaki	33	E5
Svalbard	26	B5
Svealand □	9	D7
Sverdlovsk = Yekaterinburg	29	D7
Svetlogorsk = Svyetlahorsk	17	B9
Svishtov	22	C5
Svislach	17	B7
Svyetlahorsk	17	B9
Swabian Alps = Schwäbische Alb	14	D5
Swakopmund	58	C2
Swan Hill	62	C3
Swansea	11	F5
Swatow = Shantou	35	D6
Swaziland ■	59	D6
Sweden ■	9	D9
Sweetwater	80	C3
Swellendam	58	E4
Świdnica	16	C3
Świdnik	17	C6
Świebodzin	16	B2
Świecie	16	B4
Swift Current	69	C9
Swindon	11	F6
Swinemünde = Świnoujście	16	B2
Świnoujście	16	B2
Switzerland ■	13	C8
Sydney, Australia	63	B5
Sydney, Canada	71	D4
Sydra, G. of = Surt, Khalîj	54	B2
Syktyvkar	28	C6
Sylhet	41	E8
Sylt	14	A5
Sym	29	C9
Syracuse	77	C7
Syrdarya →	29	E7
Syria ■	46	D4
Syrian Desert = Shâm, Bâdiyat ash	47	D4
Syzran	24	C6
Szczecin	16	B2
Szczecinek	16	B3
Szczeciński, Zalew = Stettiner Haff	15	B8
Szczytno	16	B5
Szechwan = Sichuan □	34	C5
Szeged	16	E5
Székesfehérvár	16	E4
Szekszárd	16	E4
Szentes	16	E5
Szolnok	16	E5
Szombathely	16	E3

T

Tabacal	94	A4
Tabaco	36	B2
Ṭābah	47	F5
Ṭabas, Khorāsān, Iran	44	C4
Ṭabas, Khorāsān, Iran	45	C5
Tabatinga, Serra da	93	E5
Tablas I.	36	B2
Table B.	58	E3
Table Mt.	58	E3
Tábor	16	D2
Tabora	57	F6
Tabou	53	H4
Tabriz	46	C6
Tabūk	47	E4
Tacheng	34	B3
Tacloban	36	B2
Tacna	91	G4
Tacoma	72	C2
Tacuarembó	94	C5
Tademaït, Plateau du	52	C6
Tadjoura	49	E3
Tadmor	65	D5
Tadzhikistan = Tajikistan ■	29	F8
Taegu	35	C7
Taejŏn	35	C7
Tafalla	19	A5
Tafelbaai = Table B.	58	E3
Tafermaar	37	F4
Taft	36	B3
Taftān, Kūh-e	45	D5
Taga Dzong	41	D7
Taganrog	25	D4
Tagbilaran	36	C2
Tagliamento →	20	B4
Taguatinga	93	E5
Tagum	36	C3
Tagus = Tejo →	18	C1
Tahakopa	65	G3
Tahan, Gunong	38	D2
Tahat	52	D7
Tāherī	44	E3
Tahiti	65	L16
Tahoe, L.	72	G3
Tahoua	53	F7
Tahta	54	C5
Tahulandang	37	D3
Tahuna	37	D3
Taibei = T'aipei	35	D7
T'aichung	35	D7
Taieri →	65	G4
Taihape	64	C6
Tailem Bend	62	C2
Taimyr Peninsula = Taymyr, Poluostrov	30	B7
Tain	10	C4
T'ainan	35	D7
Tainaron, Ákra	23	F4
T'aipei	35	D7
Taiping	38	D2
Taitao, Pen. de	95	F1
Taiwan ■	35	D7
Taïyetos Óros	23	F4
Taiyuan	35	C6
Taizhong = T'aichung	35	D7
Ta'izz	49	E3
Tajikistan ■	29	F8
Tajima	33	E6
Tajo = Tejo →	18	C1
Tak	38	A1
Takada	33	E6
Takaka	65	D5
Takamatsu	33	F4
Takaoka	33	E5
Takapuna	64	B6
Takasaki	33	E6
Takayama	33	E5
Takefu	33	F5
Takengon	38	D1
Tākestān	46	D7

Takev	38	B2
Takhâr □	45	B7
Takikawa	32	B7
Taklamakan Shamo	34	C3
Talara	90	D2
Talas	29	E8
Talaud, Kepulauan	36	D3
Talavera de la Reina	18	C3
Talayan	36	C2
Talbragar ➔	63	B4
Talca	94	D2
Talcahuano	94	D2
Talcher	40	G5
Taldyqorghan	29	E8
Tâlesh, Kūhhā-ye	46	C7
Tali Post	55	G5
Talibon	36	B2
Taliwang	39	F5
Tall 'Afar	46	C5
Talladega	82	C4
Tallahassee	83	D5
Tallangatta	63	C4
Tallinn	24	B1
Taloyoak	68	B10
Taltal	94	B2
Talwood	63	A4
Talyawalka Cr. ➔	62	B3
Tamale	53	G5
Tamanrasset	52	D7
Tambacounda	53	F3
Tambelan, Kepulauan	39	D3
Tambo de Mora	91	F3
Tambora	39	F5
Tambov	24	C5
Tâmega ➔	18	B1
Tamenglong	41	E9
Tamil Nadu □	43	P10
Tammerfors = Tampere	8	C10
Tamo Abu, Pegunungan	39	D5
Tampa	83	F6
Tampere	8	C10
Tampico	84	C5
Tamu	41	E10
Tamworth	63	B5
Tana ➔, *Kenya*	57	E8
Tana ➔, *Norway*	8	A11
Tana, L.	55	F6
Tanabe	33	G4
Tanahbala	39	E1
Tanahgrogot	39	E5
Tanahjampea	37	F2
Tanahmasa	39	E1
Tanahmerah	37	F6
Tanakura	33	E7
Tanami Desert	60	D5
Tanana ➔	69	B4
Tananarive = Antananarivo	59	H9
Tánaro ➔	20	B2
Tandag	36	C3
Tandil	94	D5
Tando Adam	42	G6
Tandou L.	62	B3
Taneatua	64	C7
Tanen Tong Dan = Dawna Ra.	41	J12
Tanezrouft	52	D6
Tanga	57	F7
Tanganyika, L.	57	F5
Tanger	52	A4
Tanggula Shan	34	C4
Tangier = Tanger	52	A4
Tangshan	35	C6
Tanimbar, Kepulauan	37	F4
Taninthari = Tenasserim	38	B1
Tanjay	36	C2
Tanjore = Thanjavur	43	P11
Tanjung	39	E5
Tanjungbalai	39	D1
Tanjungbatu	39	D5
Tanjungkarang Telukbetung	39	F3
Tanjungpandan	39	E3
Tanjungpinang	39	D2
Tanjungredeb	39	D5
Tanjungselor	39	D5
Tanout	53	F7
Tanta	54	B5
Tantung = Dandong	35	B7
Tanunda	62	B2
Tanzania ■	57	F6
Taolanaro	59	K9
Taoudenni	52	D5
Tapa Shan = Daba Shan	35	C5
Tapajós ➔	92	C3
Tapaktuan	39	D1
Tapanui	65	F3
Tapauá ➔	91	E6
Tapeta	53	G4
Tapi ➔	43	J8
Tapirapecó, Serra	90	C6
Tapuaenuku	65	D5
Tapul Group	36	C2
Taquari ➔	91	G7
Tara, *Australia*	63	A5
Tara, *Russia*	29	D8
Tara ➔	22	C2
Tarābulus, *Lebanon*	46	D3
Tarābulus, *Libya*	54	B1
Tarakan	39	D5
Taranaki □	64	C6
Taranaki, Mt.	64	C6
Tarancón	19	B4
Táranto	21	D6
Táranto, G. di	21	D6
Tarapacá	90	D5
Tararua Ra.	64	D6
Tarashcha	17	D10
Tarauacá	91	E4
Tarauacá ➔	91	E5
Tarawera	64	C7
Tarawera, L.	64	C7
Taraz	29	E8
Tarazona	19	B5
Tarbagatay, Khrebet	29	E9
Tarbela Dam	42	B8
Tarbes	12	E4
Tarcoola	62	B1
Tarcoon	63	B4
Taree	63	B5
Tarfaya	52	C3
Târgovişte	22	B5
Târgu-Jiu	17	F6
Târgu Mureş	17	E7
Tarifa	18	D3
Tarija	94	A4
Tariku ➔	37	E5
Tarim Basin = Tarim Pendi	34	C3
Tarim He ➔	34	C3
Tarim Pendi	34	C3
Taritatu ➔	37	E5
Tarkhankut, Mys	25	D3
Tarko Sale	28	C8
Tarkwa	53	G5
Tarlac	36	A2
Tarma	91	F3
Tarn ➔	12	D4
Tarnobrzeg	16	C5
Tarnów	16	C5
Tarnowskie Góry	16	C4
Taroom	63	A4
Taroudannt	52	B4
Tarragona	19	B6
Tarrasa = Terrassa	19	B7
Tarsus	46	C3
Tartagal	94	A4
Tartu	24	B2
Ţarţūs	46	D3
Tarutung	39	D1
Tash-Kömür	29	E8
Tashauz = Dashhowuz	29	E6
Tashi Chho Dzong = Thimphu	41	D7
Tashkent = Toshkent	29	E7
Tashtagol	29	D9
Tasman B.	65	D5
Tasman Mts.	65	D5
Tasman Pen.	62	D4
Tasmania □	62	D4
Tatabánya	16	E4
Tatarbunary	17	E9
Tatarsk	29	D8
Tatarstan □	29	D6
Tateyama	33	F6
Tathra	63	C4
Tatra = Tatry	16	D4
Tatry	16	D4
Tatta	43	G5
Tat'ung = Datong	35	B6
Tatvan	46	C5
Taubaté	94	A7
Tauern	15	E7
Taumarunui	64	C6
Taumaturgo	91	E4
Taungdwingyi	41	G10
Taunggyi	41	G11
Taungup	41	H10
Taungup Taunggya	41	H9
Taunton	11	F5
Taunus	14	C5
Taupo	64	C7
Taupo, L.	64	C6
Tauranga	64	B7
Tauranga Harb.	64	B7
Taurianova	21	E6
Taurus Mts. = Toros Dağları	46	C3
Tavda	29	D7
Tavda ➔	29	D7
Taveuni	64	L12
Tavira	18	D2
Tavoy	38	B1
Tavua	38	D5
Tawitawi	36	C2
Tay ➔	10	C5
Tayabamba	91	E3
Taylakova	29	D8
Taymā	47	F4
Taymyr, Oz.	30	B8
Taymyr, Poluostrov	30	B7
Taytay	36	B1
Taz ➔	28	C8
Taza	52	B5
Tazovskiy	28	C8
Tbilisi	25	E5
Tchad = Chad ■	55	E2
Tchad, L.	55	F1
Tch'eng-tou = Chengdu	35	C5
Tchibanga	56	E2
Tch'ong-k'ing = Chongqing	35	D5
Tczew	16	A4
Te Anau, L.	65	F2
Te Aroha	64	B6
Te Awamutu	64	C6
Te Kuiti	64	C6
Te Puke	64	B7
Te Waewae B.	65	G2
Tebakang	39	D4
Tébessa	52	A7
Tebicuary ➔	94	B5
Tebingtinggi	39	D1
Tecuci	22	B6
Tedzhen = Tejen	29	F7
Tefé	90	D6
Tegal	39	F3
Tegucigalpa	85	E7
Tehachapi	78	C3
Teheran = Tehrān	44	C2
Tehoru	37	E3
Tehrān	44	C2
Tehuantepec	85	D5
Tehuantepec, G. de	85	D5
Tehuantepec, Istmo de	85	D6
Tejen	29	F7
Tejo ➔	18	C1
Tekapo, L.	65	E4
Tekeli	29	E8
Tekirdağ	22	D6
Tekkali	40	H5

Name	Page	Grid
Tel Aviv-Yafo	46	D3
Tela	85	D7
Telanaipura = Jambi	39	E2
Telavi	25	E6
Telekhany = Tsyelyakhany	17	B7
Teles Pires →	91	E7
Telford	11	E5
Tellicherry	43	P9
Telsen	95	E3
Teluk Anson = Teluk Intan	39	D2
Teluk Betung = Tanjungkarang Telukbetung	39	F3
Teluk Intan	39	D2
Telukbutun	39	D3
Telukdalem	39	D1
Tema	53	G5
Temerloh	39	D2
Temir	29	E6
Temirtau, *Kazakhstan*	29	D8
Temirtau, *Russia*	29	D9
Tempe	79	D7
Temple	80	D7
Temuco	94	D2
Temuka	65	F4
Tenali	40	J3
Tenasserim	38	B1
Tenda, Colle di	20	B3
Tendaho	49	E3
Tenerife	52	C2
Tengah □	37	D2
Tengah, Kepulauan	39	F5
Tengchong	34	D4
Tenggara □	37	E2
Tenggarong	39	E5
Tengiz, Ozero	29	D7
Tenkasi	43	Q10
Tennessee □	82	B4
Tennessee →	76	F1
Tenom	38	C5
Tenterfield	63	A5
Teófilo Otoni	93	F5
Tepa	37	F3
Tepic	84	C4
Teplice	16	C1
Ter →	19	A7
Téramo	20	C4
Terang	62	C3
Terebovlya	17	D7
Terek →	25	E6
Teresina	92	D5
Terewah, L.	63	A4
Teridgerie Cr. →	63	B4
Términi Imerese	21	F4
Termiz	29	F7
Térmoli	20	C5
Ternate	37	D3
Terney	32	A5
Terni	20	C4
Ternopil	17	D7
Terowie	62	B2
Terracina	20	D4
Terralba	21	E2
Terranova = Ólbia	20	D2
Terrassa	19	B7
Terre Haute	76	E2
Terschelling	14	B3
Teruel	19	B5
Teryaweyna L.	62	B3
Teshio	32	A7
Teshio-Gawa →	32	A7
Tesiyn Gol →	34	A4
Teslin	68	B6
Tessalit	52	D6
Tetas, Pta.	94	A2
Tete	59	B6
Teterev →	17	C10
Teteven	22	C5
Tetiyev	17	D9
Tétouan	52	A4
Tetovo	22	C3
Teuco →	94	B4

Name	Page	Grid
Teun	37	F3
Teutoburger Wald	14	B5
Tevere →	20	D4
Tewantin	63	A5
Texarkana	81	C6
Texas	63	A5
Texas □	80	D4
Texas City	81	E6
Texel	14	B3
Teyvareh	45	C6
Tezpur	41	D9
Thabana Ntlenyana	59	D5
Thabazimbi	59	C5
Thailand ■	38	A2
Thailand, G. of	38	B2
Thakhek	38	A2
Thal	42	C7
Thala La = Hkakabo Razi	41	C11
Thallon	63	A4
Thames	64	B6
Thames →	11	F7
Thane	43	K8
Thanh Pho Ho Chi Minh	38	B3
Thanjavur	43	P11
Thar Desert	42	F7
Tharad	43	G7
Thargomindah	63	A3
Tharrawaddy	41	J10
Thásos	23	D5
Thaton	41	J11
Thaungdut	41	E10
Thayetmyo	41	H10
Thazi	41	G11
The Alberga →	62	A2
The Frome →	62	A2
The Great Divide = Great Dividing Ra.	61	E8
The Hague = 's-Gravenhage	14	B3
The Hamilton →	62	A2
The Macumba →	62	A2
The Neales →	62	A2
The Pas	69	C9
The Rock	63	C4
The Salt L.	62	B3
The Stevenson →	62	A2
The Warburton →	62	A2
Thebes = Thívai	23	E4
Theebine	63	A5
Thermaïkós Kólpos	23	D4
Thermopylae P.	23	E4
Thessaloníki	23	D4
Thessaloníki, Gulf of = Thermaïkós Kólpos	23	D4
Thetford	11	E7
Thetford Mines	71	D3
Thevenard	62	B1
Thiel Mts.	96	C2
Thiers	13	D5
Thiès	53	F2
Thika	57	E7
Thimphu	41	D7
Thionville	13	B7
Thíra	23	F5
Thiruvananthapuram = Trivandrum	43	Q10
Thistle I.	62	C2
Thívai	23	E4
Þjórsá →	8	C1
Thomas, L.	62	A2
Thomasville, *Ga., U.S.A.*	83	D6
Thomasville, *N.C., U.S.A.*	83	B7
Thompson	69	C10
Thompson's Falls = Nyahururu	57	D7
Thrace	22	D6
Three Hummock I.	62	D3
Three Points, C.	53	H5
Thunder Bay	71	D2
Thung Song	38	C1
Thunkar	41	D8
Thüringer Wald	14	C6
Thurles	11	E3

Name	Page	Grid
Thurso	10	B5
Thurston I.	96	B2
Thysville = Mbanza Ngungu	56	F2
Tian Shan	34	B3
Tianjin	35	C6
Tianshui	35	C5
Tiaret	52	A6
Tiber = Tevere →	20	D4
Tiberias, L. = Yam Kinneret	46	C4
Tibesti	54	D2
Tibet = Xizang Zizhiqu □	34	C3
Tibooburra	62	A3
Tiburón, I.	84	B2
Ticino →	20	B2
Tiddim	41	F9
Tidjikja	53	E3
Tidore	37	D3
Tien Shan = Tian Shan	34	B3
Tientsin = Tianjin	35	C6
Tierra de Campos	18	A3
Tierra del Fuego, I. Gr. de	95	G3
Tiétar →	18	C2
Tiflis = Tbilisi	25	E5
Tifu	37	E3
Tighina	17	E9
Tigre →	90	D4
Tigris = Dijlah, Nahr →	47	E6
Tigyaing	41	F11
Tijuana	84	A1
Tikamgarh	43	G11
Tikhoretsk	25	D5
Tikiraqjuaq = Whale Cove	68	B10
Tikrit	46	D5
Tiksi	30	B10
Tilamuta	37	D2
Tilburg	14	C3
Tilos	23	F6
Tilpa	63	B3
Tilsit = Sovetsk	24	B1
Timaru	65	F4
Timbuktu = Tombouctou	53	E5
Timimoun	52	C6
Timiris, Râs	53	E2
Timişoara	16	F5
Timmins	71	D2
Timok →	22	B4
Timor	37	F2
Tinaca Pt.	36	C3
Tindouf	52	C4
Tingo Maria	91	E3
Tinnevelly = Tirunelveli	43	Q10
Tinogasta	94	B3
Tínos	23	F5
Tintinara	62	C3
Tioman, Pulau	39	D2
Tipongpani	41	D10
Tipperary	11	E2
Tīran	44	C2
Tirana	22	D2
Tiraspol	17	E9
Tire	23	E6
Tirebolu	25	E4
Tiree	10	C3
Tîrgovişte = Târgovişte	22	B5
Tîrgu-Jiu = Târgu-Jiu	17	F6
Tîrgu Mureş = Târgu Mureş	17	E7
Tirich Mir	42	A7
Tírnavos	23	E4
Tirodi	43	J11
Tirol □	14	E6
Tirso →	21	E2
Tiruchchirappalli	43	P11
Tirunelveli	43	Q10
Tirupati	43	N11
Tiruppur	43	P10
Tiruvannamalai	43	N11
Tisa →	22	B3
Tisdale	69	C9
Tisza = Tisa →	22	B3
Tit-Ary	30	B10
Titicaca, L.	91	G5
Titograd = Podgorica	22	C2

Titule

Titule	57	D5	Toora	63	C4	Trangie	63	B4
Tivaouane	53	F2	Toowoomba	63	A5	Trani	20	D6
Tívoli	20	D4	Topeka	75	F7	Transantarctic Mts.	96	C3
Tiwi	45	F4	Topolobampo	84	B3	Transilvania	17	F7
Tizi-Ouzou	52	A6	Torata	91	G4	Transilvanian Alps =		
Tjirebon = Cirebon	39	F3	Torbalı	23	E6	Carpaţii Meridionali	17	F7
Tlaxiaco	84	D5	Torbat-e Heydārīyeh	44	C4	Trápani	21	E4
Tlemcen	52	B5	Torbat-e Jām	45	C5	Traralgon	63	C4
Toamasina	59	H9	Torbay □	11	F5	Trasimeno, L.	20	C4
Toay	94	D4	Tordesillas	18	B3	Traun	15	D8
Toba Kakar	42	D6	Torgau	15	C7	Travemünde	15	B6
Tobago	87	D7	Torino	20	B1	Travers, Mt.	65	E5
Tobelo	37	D3	Torit	55	H5	Travnik	20	B6
Tobermory	10	C3	Tormes →	18	B2	Trébbia →	20	B2
Tobías Fornier	36	B2	Torne älv →	8	B10	Třebíč	16	D2
Toboali	39	E3	Torneå = Tornio	8	E12	Trebinje	20	C7
Tobol →	29	D7	Torneträsk	8	B9	Treinta y Tres	94	C6
Toboli	37	E2	Tornio	8	E12	Trelew	95	E3
Tobolsk	29	D7	Tornquist	94	D4	Tremp	19	A6
Tobruk = Tubruq	54	B3	Toro, Cerro del	94	B3	Trenque Lauquen	94	D4
Tobyl = Tobol →	29	D7	Toroníios Kólpos	23	D4	Trent →	11	E6
Tocantinópolis	92	D4	Toronto	71	D3	Trento	20	A3
Tocantins □	93	E4	Toropets	24	B3	Trenton	77	D8
Tocantins →	92	C4	Tororo	57	D6	Tres Arroyos	94	D4
Tocumwal	63	C4	Toros Dağları	46	C3	Três Lagoas	93	G3
Tocuyo →	90	A5	Torre de Moncorvo	18	B2	Tres Montes, C.	95	F1
Todeli	37	E2	Torre del Greco	21	D5	Tres Puntas, C.	95	F3
Todos os Santos, B. de	93	E6	Torrejón de Ardoz	18	B4	Três Rios	93	G5
Togian, Kepulauan	37	E2	Torrelavega	18	A3	Treviso	20	B4
Togliatti	24	C6	Torremolinos	18	D3	Triabunna	62	D4
Togo ■	53	G6	Torrens, L.	62	B2	Trichinopoly =		
Toili	37	E2	Torrent	19	C5	Tiruchchirappalli	43	P11
Toinya	55	G4	Torreón	84	B4	Trichur	43	P10
Tojikiston = Tajikistan ■	29	F8	Torres Vedras	18	C1	Trida	63	B4
Tojo	37	E2	Torrevieja	19	D5	Trier	14	D4
Tok-do	33	E2	Tortosa	19	B6	Trieste	20	B4
Tokala	37	E2	Tortosa, C.	19	B6	Triglav	20	A4
Tōkamachi	33	E6	Torūd	44	C3	Trikkala	23	E3
Tokanui	65	G3	Toruń	16	B4	Trikora, Puncak	37	E5
Tokarahi	65	F4	Tosa-Wan	33	G3	Trindade, Bolivia	91	F6
Tokat	46	B4	Toscana □	20	C3	Trinidad, Cuba	86	B3
Tokelau Is.	65	K13	Toshkent	29	E7	Trinidad, Uruguay	94	C5
Tokmak	29	E8	Tostado	94	B4	Trinidad, U.S.A.	80	A1
Tokushima	33	F4	Tosya	46	B3	Trinidad & Tobago ■	87	D7
Tokuyama	33	F2	Totma	24	A5	Trinity →	81	E6
Tōkyō	33	F6	Totten Glacier	96	A12	Trinity B.	71	D5
Tolaga Bay	64	C8	Tottenham	63	B4	Trinity Range	72	F4
Tolbukhin = Dobrich	22	C6	Tottori	33	F4	Trinkitat	55	E6
Toledo, Spain	18	C3	Toubkal, Djebel	52	B4	Tripoli = Tarābulus,		
Toledo, U.S.A.	76	D4	Tougan	53	F5	Lebanon	46	D3
Toledo, Montes de	18	C3	Touggourt	52	B7	Tripoli = Tarābulus, Libya	54	B1
Toliara	59	J8	Toul	13	B6	Trípolis	23	F4
Tolima	90	C3	Toulon	13	E6	Tripura □	41	F8
Tolitoli	37	D2	Toulouse	12	E4	Trivandrum	43	Q10
Tolo, Teluk	37	E2	Toummo	54	D1	Troglav	20	C6
Toluca	84	D5	Touraine	12	C4	Trois-Rivières	71	D3
Tomakomai	32	B7	Tourane = Da Nang	38	A3	Troitsko Pechorsk	28	C6
Tomar	18	C1	Tourcoing	13	A5	Trollhättan	9	D8
Tomaszów Mazowiecki	16	C4	Touriñán, C.	18	A1	Tromsø	8	B9
Tombouctou	53	E5	Tournai	14	C2	Tronador, Mte.	95	E2
Tombua	58	B2	Tournon-sur-Rhône	13	D6	Trondheim	8	C8
Tomelloso	18	C4	Tours	12	C4	Trondheimsfjorden	8	C8
Tomini	37	D2	Towada	32	C7	Trout L.	68	B7
Tomini, Teluk	37	E2	Towada-Ko	32	C7	Trouville-sur-Mer	12	B4
Tomsk	29	D9	Towang	41	D8	Troy, Turkey	23	E6
Tonantins	90	D5	Townsville	61	D8	Troy, Ala., U.S.A.	82	D5
Tondano	37	D2	Towa-Ko	32	B7	Troy, N.Y., U.S.A.	77	C9
Tonekābon	44	B2	Toyama	33	E5	Troyes	13	B6
Tonga ■	65	L13	Toyama-Wan	33	E5	Trucial States = United		
Tonga Trench	65	L13	Toyohashi	33	F5	Arab Emirates ■	44	F3
Tongareva	65	K15	Toyooka	33	F4	Trudovoye	32	B3
Tongchuan	35	C5	Toyota	33	F5	Trujillo, Honduras	85	D7
Tonghua	35	B7	Tozeur	52	B7	Trujillo, Peru	91	E3
Tongking, G. of = Tonkin,			Trá Li = Tralee	11	E2	Trujillo, Spain	18	C3
G. of	35	D5	Trabzon	46	B4	Trujillo, Venezuela	90	B4
Tongoy	94	C2	Trafalgar, C.	18	D2	Truk	64	J10
Tongsa Dzong	41	D8	Trail	69	D8	Trundle	63	B4
Tongue →	74	B2	Tralee	11	E2	Truro, Canada	71	D4
Tonk	42	F9	Trancas	94	B3	Truro, U.K.	11	F4
Tonkin, G. of	35	D5	Trang	38	C1	Truskavets	17	D6
Tonle Sap	38	B2	Trangan	37	F4	Trutnov	16	C2
Toompine	63	A3				Tsangpo = Brahmaputra →	41	F7

Tsaratanana 59 H9
Tsarevo = Michurin 22 C6
Tselinograd = Astana . . . 29 D8
Tsetserleg 34 B5
Tshabong 58 D4
Tshane 58 C4
Tshela 56 E2
Tshikapa 56 F4
Tshwane = Pretoria 59 D5
Tsiigehtchic 68 B6
Tsimlyanskoye Vdkhr. . . . 25 D5
Tsinan = Jinan 35 C6
Tsinghai = Qinghai □ 34 C4
Tsingtao = Qingdao 35 C7
Tskhinvali 25 E5
Tsna ➤ 24 C5
Tsuchiura 33 E7
Tsugaru Str. 32 C7
Tsumeb 58 B3
Tsuruga 33 F5
Tsuruoka 32 D6
Tsushima 33 F1
Tsuyama 33 F4
Tsyelyakhany 17 B7
Tual 37 F4
Tuamotu Is. 65 L16
Tuamotu Ridge 65 M17
Tuao 36 A2
Tuapse 25 E4
Tuatapere 65 G2
Tubarão 94 B7
Tübingen 14 D5
Tubruq 54 B3
Tubuai Is. 65 M16
Tucacas 90 A5
Tucson 79 D7
Tucumcari 80 B2
Tucupita 90 B6
Tucuruí 92 C4
Tucuruí, Reprêsa de 92 C4
Tudela 19 A5
Tudmur 46 D4
Tuguegarao 36 A2
Tui 18 A1
Tukangbesi, Kepulauan . . 37 F2
Tuktoyaktuk 68 B6
Tukuyu 57 F6
Tula 24 C4
Tülak 45 C5
Tulare 78 B3
Tulcán 90 C3
Tulcea 17 F9
Tulchyn 17 D9
Tulita 68 B7
Tullamore, Australia 63 B4
Tullamore, Ireland 11 E2
Tulle 12 D4
Tulsa 81 A6
Tulua 90 C3
Tumaco 90 C3
Tumatumari 90 B7
Tumba, L. 56 E3
Tumbarumba 63 C4
Tumbes 90 D2
Tumby Bay 62 B2
Tumeremo 90 B6
Tumkur 43 N10
Tump 42 F3
Tumpat 38 C2
Tumu 53 F5
Tumucumaque, Serra . . . 92 C3
Tumut 63 C4
Tuncurry 63 B5
Tundzha ➤ 22 D6
Tungabhadra ➤ 43 M11
Tunguska, Nizhnyaya ➤ . 30 C6
Tunguska,
  Podkamennaya ➤ 30 C7
Tunis 54 A1
Tunisia ■ 54 A1
Tunja 90 B4
Tunuyán ➤ 94 C3

Tupelo 82 B3
Tupinambaranas 90 D7
Tupiza 94 A3
Tupungato, Cerro 94 C3
Túquerres 90 C3
Tura 30 C8
Turabah 47 C5
Türän 44 C4
Turayf 47 E4
Turek 16 B4
Turfan = Turpan 34 B3
Turfan Depression =
  Turpan Hami 34 B3
Türgovishte 22 C6
Turgutlu 23 E6
Turhal 46 B4
Turia ➤ 19 C5
Turiaçu 92 C4
Turiaçu ➤ 92 C4
Turin = Torino 20 B1
Turkana, L. 57 D7
Turkestan = Türkistan . . 29 E7
Turkey ■ 46 C3
Türkistan 29 E7
Türkmenbashi 29 E6
Turkmenistan ■ 29 F6
Turks & Caicos Is. ☑ . . . 87 B5
Turku 9 C10
Turnagain, C. 64 D7
Turneffe Is. 85 D7
Turnhout 14 C3
Tŭrnovo = Veliko Tŭrnovo 22 C5
Turnu Mägurele 22 C5
Turnu Roşu, P. 17 F7
Turpan 34 B3
Turpan Hami 34 B3
Turukhansk 30 C6
Tuscaloosa 82 C4
Tuscany = Toscana □ . . . 20 C3
Tuticorin 43 Q11
Tutóia 92 C5
Tutong 38 D4
Tutrakan 22 B6
Tuttlingen 14 E5
Tutuala 37 F3
Tutuila 65 L13
Tuvalu ■ 64 K12
Tuxpan 84 C5
Tuxtla Gutiérrez 85 D6
Tuy = Tui 18 A1
Tuz Gölü 46 C3
Tūz Khurmātū 46 D6
Tuzla 20 B7
Tver 24 B4
Tweed Heads 63 A5
Twin Falls 73 E6
Twofold B. 63 C4
Tyachiv 17 D6
Tychy 16 C4
Tyler 81 C6
Tyre = Sür 46 D3
Tyrol = Tirol □ 14 E6
Tyrrell ➤ 62 C3
Tyrrell, L. 62 C3
Tyrrhenian Sea 21 E4
Tyumen 29 D7
Tzaneen 59 C6
Tzukong = Zigong 35 D5

U

U.S.A. = United States of
  America ■ 67 F10
Uatumã ➤ 90 D7
Uaupés 90 D5
Uaupés ➤ 90 C5
Ubá 93 G5
Ubaitaba 93 E6
Ubangi = Oubangi ➤ 56 E3

Ubauro 42 E6
Ube 33 G2
Úbeda 18 C4
Uberaba 93 F4
Uberlândia 93 F4
Ubon Ratchathani 38 A2
Ubort ➤ 17 B9
Ubundu 57 E5
Ucayali ➤ 90 D4
Uchiura-Wan 32 B7
Udagamandalam 43 P10
Udaipur 43 G8
Udaipur Garhi 40 D6
Udgir 43 K10
Udhampur 42 C9
Údine 20 A4
Udmurtia □ 28 D6
Udon Thani 38 A2
Udupi 43 N9
Uele ➤ 57 D4
Uelzen 14 B6
Ufa 29 D6
Ugab ➤ 58 C2
Ugalla ➤ 57 F6
Uganda ■ 57 D6
Ugljan 20 B5
Uibhist a Deas = South Uist 10 C3
Uibhist a Tuath = North
  Uist 10 C3
Uige 56 F2
Uinta Mts. 73 F8
Uitenhage 59 E5
Ujjain 43 H9
Ujung Pandang 37 F1
Ukhrul 41 E10
Ukhta 28 C6
Ukraine ■ 25 D3
Ulaanbaatar 35 B5
Ulaangom 34 A4
Ulaanjirem 35 B5
Ulan Bator = Ulaanbaatar 35 B5
Ulan Ude 30 D8
Ulcinj 22 D2
Ulhasnagar 43 K8
Uliastay = Ulyasutay . . . 34 B4
Ulladulla 63 C5
Ullapool 10 C4
Ullŭng-do 33 E2
Ulm 14 D5
Ulmarra 63 A5
Ulster □ 11 D3
Ulubat Gölü 23 D7
Uludağ 23 D7
Ulungur He ➤ 34 B3
Uluru = Ayers Rock 60 E5
Ulutau 29 E7
Ulverstone 62 D4
Ulyanovsk = Simbirsk . . 24 C6
Ulyasutay 34 B4
Umala 91 G5
Uman 17 D10
Umaria 40 F3
Umarkot 43 G6
Umbrella Mts. 65 F3
Ume älv ➤ 8 C10
Umeå 8 C10
Umera 37 E3
Umm al Qaywayn 44 E3
Umm Lajj 47 F4
Umm Ruwaba 55 F5
Umnak I. 69 C3
Umniati ➤ 59 B5
Umtata = Mthatha 59 E5
Umuarama 93 G3
Una ➤ 20 B6
Unalaska 69 C3
Uncia 91 G5
Underbool 62 C3
Ungarie 63 B4
Ungarra 62 B2
Ungava, Pén. d' 70 B3
Ungava B. 70 C4

155

Ungeny = Ungheni 17 E8
Ungheni 17 E8
Ungwana B. 57 E8
União da Vitória 94 B6
Unimak I. 69 C3
United Arab Emirates ■ . 44 F3
United Kingdom ■ 11 D5
United States of America ■ 67 F10
Unnao 40 D3
Unst 10 A6
Ünye 46 B4
Upata 90 B6
Upemba, L. 57 F5
Upington 58 D4
Upper Hutt 65 D6
Upper Volta = Burkina
 Faso ■ 53 F5
Uppsala 9 D9
Uqsuqtuuq = Gjoa Haven . 68 B10
Ur 47 E6
Ural = Zhayyq → 29 E6
Ural 63 B4
Ural Mts. = Uralskie Gory . 28 D6
Uralla 63 B5
Uralsk = Oral 24 C7
Uralskie Gory 28 D6
Uray 29 C7
Urbana 76 D1
Urbino 20 C4
Urbión, Picos de 19 A4
Urcos 91 F4
Urdzhar 29 E9
Urfa = Sanliurfa 46 C4
Urganch 29 E7
Uribia 90 A4
Urla 23 E6
Urmia = Orümiyeh 46 C6
Urmia, L. = Orümiyeh,
 Daryācheh-ye 46 C6
Uroševac 22 C3
Urubamba → 91 F4
Uruçara 90 D7
Uruçuí 92 D5
Uruguai → 94 B6
Uruguaiana 94 B5
Uruguay ■ 94 C5
Uruguay → 94 C5
Ürümqi 34 B3
Usakos 58 C3
Usedom 15 B8
Ush-Tobe 29 E8
Ushant = Ouessant, Î. d' . 12 B1
Ushibuka 33 G2
Ushuaia 95 G3
Usman 24 C4
Uspallata, P. de 94 C3
Uspenskiy 29 E8
Ussuriysk 32 B2
Ust-Aldan = Batamay . 31 C10
Ust-Ilimpeya = Yukta . 30 C8
Ust-Ishim 29 D8
Ust-Kamenogorsk =
 Öskemen 29 E9
Ust-Kuyga 31 B11
Ust-Olenek 30 B10
Ust-Port 28 C9
Ust-Tsilma 28 C6
Ust Urt = Ustyurt Plateau . 29 E6
Ústí nad Labem 16 C2
Ústica 21 E4
Ustinov = Izhevsk ... 28 D6
Ustyurt Plateau 29 E6
Usu 34 B3
Usumacinta → 85 D6
Usumbura = Bujumbura . 57 E5
Uta 37 E5
Utah □ 73 G8
Utiariti 91 F7
Utica 77 C8
Utrecht 14 B3
Utrera 18 D3
Utsunomiya 33 E6

Uttar Pradesh □ 42 F11
Uttaradit 38 A2
Uummannarsuaq = Nunap
 Isua 70 C6
Uusikaupunki 9 C10
Uvat 29 D7
Uvinza 57 F6
Uvira 57 E5
Uvs Nuur 34 A4
'Uwairidh, Ḥarrat al .. 47 F4
Uwajima 33 G3
Uyuni 91 H5
Uzbekistan ■ 29 E7
Uzerche 12 D4
Uzh → 17 C10
Uzhgorod = Uzhhorod . 17 D6
Uzhhorod 17 D6
Užice 22 C2
Uzunköprü 22 D6

V

Vaal → 58 D4
Vaasa 8 C10
Vác 16 E4
Vach = Vakh → 29 C8
Vadodara 43 H8
Vadsø 8 D13
Vaduz 13 C8
Vahsel B. 96 B5
Vaigach 28 B6
Vail 73 G10
Val-d'Or 71 D3
Valahia 22 B5
Valandovo 22 D4
Valcheta 95 E3
Valdai Hills = Valdayskaya
 Vozvyshennost ... 24 B3
Valdayskaya
 Vozvyshennost ... 24 B3
Valdepeñas 18 C4
Valdés, Pen. 95 E4
Valdez 69 B5
Valdivia 95 D2
Valdosta 83 D6
Valença 93 E6
Valença do Piauí 92 D5
Valence 13 D6
Valencia, Spain 19 C5
Valencia, Venezuela .. 90 A5
Valencia □ 19 C5
Valencia, G. de 19 C6
Valencia de Alcántara . 18 C2
Valencia I. 11 F1
Valenciennes 13 A5
Valentim, Sa. do 92 D5
Valera 90 B4
Valjevo 22 B2
Vall de Uxó = La Vall d'Uixó 19 C5
Valladolid, Mexico ... 85 C7
Valladolid, Spain 18 B3
Valle de la Pascua ... 90 B5
Valledupar 90 A4
Vallejo 72 G2
Vallenar 94 B2
Valletta 21 G5
Valls 19 B6
Valognes 12 B3
Valona = Vlorë 23 D2
Valozhyn 17 A8
Valparaíso 94 C2
Vals, Tanjung 37 F5
Valsad 43 J8
Valverde del Camino . 18 D2
Van 46 C5
Van, L. = Van Gölü .. 46 C5
Van Gölü 46 C5
Van Rees, Pegunungan . 37 E5
Vanadzor 25 E5

Vancouver, Canada ... 69 D7
Vancouver, U.S.A. 72 D2
Vancouver I. 69 D7
Vänern 9 D8
Vangaindrano 59 J9
Vännäs 8 C9
Vannes 12 C2
Vanrhynsdorp 58 E3
Vantaa → 9 C11
Vanua Levu 64 L12
Vanuatu ■ 64 L11
Vapnyarka 17 D9
Varanasi 40 E4
Varangerfjorden 8 A11
Varaždin 20 A6
Varberg 9 D8
Vardak □ 45 C7
Vardar = Axiós → 23 D4
Varese 20 B2
Varna 22 C6
Varzaneh 44 C3
Vasa Barris → 93 E6
Vascongadas = País
 Vasco □ 19 A4
Vasht = Khāsh 42 E2
Vasilevichi 17 B9
Vasilkov = Vasylkiv . 17 C10
Västerås 9 D9
Västerdalälven → ... 8 C8
Västervik 9 D9
Vasto 20 C5
Vasylkiv 17 C10
Vatican City ■ 20 D4
Vatnajökull 8 C2
Vatra-Dornei 17 E7
Vättern 9 D8
Vaupés = Uaupés → .. 90 C5
Vawkavysk 17 B7
Vaygach, Ostrov 28 C6
Vedea → 22 C5
Vega 8 B8
Vegreville 69 C8
Vejer de la Frontera . 18 D3
Velebit Planina 20 B5
Veles 22 D3
Vélez-Málaga 18 D3
Vélez Rubio 19 D4
Velhas → 93 F5
Velika Kapela 20 B5
Velikaya → 24 B2
Veliki Ustyug 24 A6
Velikiye Luki 24 B3
Veliko Tŭrnovo 22 C5
Velikonda Range ... 43 M11
Velletri 20 D5
Vellore 43 N11
Venado Tuerto 94 C4
Vendée □ 12 C3
Vendôme 12 C4
Venézia 20 B4
Venézia, G. di 20 B4
Venezuela ■ 90 B5
Venezuela, G. de ... 90 A4
Vengurla 43 M8
Venice = Venézia ... 20 B4
Venkatapuram 40 H3
Ventotene 21 D4
Ventoux, Mt. 13 D6
Ventspils 24 B1
Ventuarí → 90 C5
Ventura 78 C3
Venus B. 63 C4
Vera, Argentina 94 B4
Vera, Spain 19 D5
Veracruz 84 D5
Veraval 43 J7
Verbánia 20 B2
Vercelli 20 B2
Verde → 95 E3
Verden 14 B5
Verdun 13 B6
Vereeniging 59 D5

Verga, C. 53 F3
Verín 18 B2
Verkhnevilyuysk 30 C10
Verkhniy Baskunchak 25 D6
Verkhoyansk 31 C11
Verkhoyanskiy Khrebet . . 31 C10
Vermont □ 77 C9
Vernon, *Canada* 69 C8
Vernon, *U.S.A.* 80 B4
Véroia 23 D4
Verona 20 B3
Versailles 12 B5
Vert, C. 53 F2
Verviers 14 C3
Veselovskoye Vdkhr. 25 D5
Vesoul 13 C7
Vesterålen 8 B9
Vestfjorden 8 B8
Vesuvio 21 D5
Vesuvius, Mt. = Vesuvio . . 21 D5
Veszprém 16 E3
Vettore, Mte. 20 C4
Vezhen 22 C5
Viacha 91 G5
Viamão 94 C6
Viana 92 C5
Viana do Alentejo 18 C2
Viana do Castelo 18 B1
Viangchan = Vientiane . . . 38 A2
Vianópolis 93 F4
Viaréggio 20 C3
Vibo Valéntia 21 E6
Vic 19 B7
Vicenza 20 B3
Vich = Vic 19 B7
Vichy 13 C5
Vicksburg 81 C8
Victor 43 J7
Victor Harbor 62 C2
Victoria = Labuan 38 C5
Victoria, *Canada* 69 D7
Victoria, *Chile* 94 D2
Victoria □ 62 C3
Victoria, L., *Africa* 57 E6
Victoria, L., *Australia* . . 62 B3
Victoria, Mt. 41 G9
Victoria de Durango =
    Durango 84 C4
Victoria Falls 59 B5
Victoria I. 68 B8
Victoria Ld. 96 B14
Victorica 94 D3
Vicuña 94 C2
Vidin 22 C4
Vidisha 43 H10
Viedma 95 E4
Viedma, L. 95 F2
Vienna = Wien 15 D9
Vienne 13 D6
Vienne → 12 C4
Vientiane 38 A2
Vierzon 12 C5
Vietnam ■ 36 A3
Vigan 38 A2
Vigévano 20 B2
Vigia 92 C4
Vigo 18 A1
Vijayawada 40 J3
Vijosë → 23 D2
Vikeke = Viqueque 37 F3
Vikna 8 C8
Vila de João Belo = Xai-Xai 59 D6
Vila do Bispo 18 D1
Vila Franca de Xira 18 C1
Vila Nova de Gaia 18 B1
Vila Real 18 B2
Vila-real de los Infantes . . 19 C5
Vila Real de Santo António 18 D2
Vila Velha 93 G5
Vilagarcía de Arousa 18 A1
Vilaine → 12 C2
Vilanculos 59 C7

Vilanova i la Geltrú 19 B6
Vileyka 17 A8
Vilhelmina 8 C9
Vilhena 91 F6
Vilkitskogo, Proliv 30 B8
Vilkovo = Vylkove 17 F9
Villa Ahumada 84 A3
Villa Ángela 94 B4
Villa Bella 91 F5
Villa Bens = Tarfaya 52 C3
Villa Cisneros = Dakhla . . 52 D2
Villa de María 94 B4
Villa Dolores 94 C3
Villa Hayes 94 B5
Villa María 94 C4
Villa Mazán 94 B3
Villa Montes 94 A4
Villa Ocampo 94 B5
Villacarrillo 18 C4
Villach 15 E7
Villaguay 94 C5
Villahermosa 85 D6
Villajoyosa 19 C5
Villalba 18 A2
Villanueva de la Serena . . 18 C3
Villanueva y Geltrú =
    Vilanova i la Geltrú . . . 19 B6
Villarreal = Vila-real de los
    Infantes 19 C5
Villarrica, *Chile* 95 D2
Villarrica, *Paraguay* . . . 94 B5
Villarrobledo 19 C4
Villavicencio 90 C4
Villaviciosa 18 A3
Villazón 94 A3
Villena 19 C5
Villeneuve-d'Ascq 13 A5
Villeneuve-sur-Lot 12 D4
Villingen-Schwenningen . . 14 D5
Vilnius 24 C2
Vilyuy → 31 C10
Vilyuysk 31 C10
Viña del Mar 94 C2
Vinarós 19 B6
Vindhya Ra. 43 H10
Vineland 77 E8
Vinkovci 20 B7
Vinnitsa = Vinnytsya 17 D9
Vinnytsya 17 D9
Viqueque 37 F3
Virac 36 B2
Viramgam 43 H8
Virden 69 D9
Vire 12 B3
Vírgenes, C. 95 G3
Virgin Is. 87 C7
Virginia □ 77 F6
Virginia Beach 77 F8
Virovitica 20 B6
Virudunagar 43 Q10
Vis 20 C6
Visalia 78 B3
Visayan Sea 36 B2
Visby 9 D9
Višegrad 20 C7
Viseu, *Brazil* 92 C4
Viseu, *Portugal* 18 B2
Vishakhapatnam 40 J4
Viso, Mte. 20 B1
Vistula = Wisła → 16 A4
Viterbo 20 C4
Viti Levu 64 L12
Vitigudino 18 B2
Vitória 93 G5
Vitória da Conquista 93 E5
Vitoria-Gasteiz 19 A4
Vitsyebsk 24 B3
Vittória 21 F5
Vittório Véneto 20 B4
Viveiro 18 A2
Vize 22 D6

Vizianagaram 40 H4
Vladikavkaz 25 E5
Vladimir 24 B5
Vladimir Volynskiy =
    Volodymyr-Volynskyy . . 17 C7
Vladivostok 32 B2
Vlissingen 14 C2
Vlorë 23 D2
Vltava → 16 C2
Vogelkop = Doberai,
    Jazirah 37 E4
Vogelsberg 14 C5
Voghera 20 B2
Vohimarina = Iharana . . 59 G10
Vohimena, Tanjon' i 59 K9
Voi 57 E7
Voiron 13 D6
Vojvodina □ 22 B2
Volga → 25 D6
Volga Hts. = Privolzhskaya
    Vozvyshennost 24 C6
Volgodonsk 25 D5
Volgograd 25 D5
Volgogradskoye Vdkhr. . . 24 C5
Volkhov → 24 A3
Volkovysk = Vawkavysk . . 17 B7
Volochanka 30 B7
Volodymyr-Volynskyy . . . 17 C7
Vologda 24 B4
Vólos 23 E4
Volovets 17 D6
Volozhin = Valozhyn 17 A8
Volsk 24 C6
Volta, L. 53 G6
Volta Redonda 93 G5
Volterra 20 C3
Volturno → 20 D4
Volzhskiy 25 D5
Vóriai Sporádhes 23 E4
Vorkuta 28 C7
Voronezh 24 C4
Voroshilovgrad = Luhansk 25 D4
Voroshilovsk = Alchevsk . 25 D4
Vosges 13 B7
Vostok I. 65 L15
Vouga → 18 B1
Voznesensk 25 D3
Vrangelya, Ostrov 31 B15
Vranje 22 C3
Vratsa 22 C4
Vrbas → 20 B6
Vršac 22 B3
Vryburg 58 D4
Vryheid 59 D6
Vukovar 20 B7
Vulcan 17 F6
Vulcaneşti 17 F9
Vulcano 21 E5
Vulkaneshty = Vulcaneşti . 17 F9
Vung Tau 38 B3
Vyatka = Kirov 28 D5
Vyatskiye Polyany 24 B7
Vyazma 24 B3
Vyborg 28 C3
Vychegda → 28 C5
Vychodné Beskydy 17 D5
Vylkove 17 F9
Vynohradiv 17 D6
Vyshniy Volochek 24 B3
Vyškov 16 D3

W

Waal → 14 C3
Wabash → 76 F1
Waco 80 D5
Wad Hamid 55 E5
Wad Medanî 55 F5
Waddington, Mt. 69 C7

Waddy Pt.	63	A5
Wadi Halfa	54	D5
Wafrah	47	E6
Wager B.	70	B2
Wagga Wagga	63	C4
Waghete	37	E5
Wah	42	C8
Wahai	37	E3
Waiau →	65	E5
Waibeem	37	E4
Waigeo	37	E4
Waihi	64	B6
Waihou →	64	B6
Waikabubak	37	F1
Waikari	65	E5
Waikato →	64	B6
Waikerie	62	B2
Waikokopu	64	C7
Waikouaiti	65	F4
Waimakariri →	65	E5
Waimate	65	F4
Wainganga →	43	K11
Waingapu	37	F2
Waiouru	64	C6
Waipara	65	E5
Waipawa	64	C7
Waipiro	64	C8
Waipu	64	A6
Waipukurau	64	D7
Wairakei	64	C7
Wairarapa, L.	65	D6
Wairoa	64	C7
Waitaki →	65	F4
Waitara	64	C6
Waiuku	64	B6
Wajima	33	E5
Wajir	57	D8
Wakasa-Wan	33	F4
Wakatipu, L.	65	F3
Wakayama	33	F4
Wakefield	65	D5
Wakkanai	32	A7
Wakool	63	C3
Wakool →	62	C3
Wakre	37	E4
Wałbrzych	16	C3
Walcha	63	B5
Wałcz	16	B3
Wales □	11	E4
Walgett	63	A4
Walgreen Coast	96	B1
Walla Walla	72	C4
Wallachia = Valahia	22	B5
Wallal	63	A4
Wallaroo	62	B2
Wallis & Futuna, Is.	64	L13
Wallowa Mts.	72	D5
Wallumbilla	63	A4
Walvis Bay	58	C2
Wamba	57	D5
Wamena	37	E5
Wamulan	37	E3
Wana	42	C6
Wanaaring	63	A3
Wanaka	65	F3
Wanaka, L.	65	F3
Wandoan	63	A4
Wangal	37	F4
Wanganella	63	C3
Wanganui	64	C6
Wangaratta	63	C4
Wangary	62	B2
Wangerooge	14	B4
Wangiwangi	37	F2
Warangal	43	L11
Waratah	62	D4
Waratah B.	63	C4
Warburton	63	C4
Ward	65	D6
Ward →	63	A4
Wardha	43	J11
Wardha →	43	K11
Warialda	63	A5
Wariap	37	E4
Warkopi	37	E4
Warner Mts.	72	F3
Warracknabeal	62	C3
Warragul	63	C4
Warrego →	63	B4
Warren, Australia	63	B4
Warren, U.S.A.	76	C4
Warri	53	G7
Warrina	62	A2
Warrington, U.K.	11	E5
Warrington, U.S.A.	82	D4
Warrnambool	62	C3
Warsa	37	E5
Warsaw = Warszawa	16	B5
Warszawa	16	B5
Warta →	16	B2
Waru	37	E4
Warwick	63	A5
Wasatch Ra.	73	F8
Wash, The	11	E7
Washim	43	J10
Washington	77	E7
Washington □	72	C3
Washington, Mt.	77	B10
Wasian	37	E4
Wasior	37	E4
Waskaganish	71	C3
Wasserkuppe	14	C5
Watampone	37	E2
Waterbury	77	D9
Waterford	11	E3
Waterloo	75	D8
Watertown	77	C8
Waterville	77	B11
Watford	11	F6
Watling I. = San Salvador I.	86	B5
Watrous	69	C9
Watsa	57	D5
Watson Lake	68	B7
Watsonville	78	B2
Wattiwarriganna Cr. →	62	A2
Watuata = Batuata	37	F2
Watubela, Kepulauan	37	E4
Wau = Wâw	55	G4
Wauchope	63	B5
Waukegan	76	C2
Waukesha	76	C1
Wausau	75	C10
Wauwatosa	76	C2
Waverley	64	C6
Wâw	55	G4
Wâw al Kabīr	54	C2
Waxahachie	81	C5
Wayabula	37	D3
Waycross	83	D6
Wazirabad	42	C9
We	38	C1
Weda	37	D3
Weda, Teluk	37	D3
Weddell I.	95	G4
Weddell Sea	96	A4
Wedderburn	62	C3
Wee Waa	63	B4
Weiden	15	D7
Weifang	35	C6
Weimar	15	C6
Weipa	61	C7
Weir →	63	A4
Wejherowo	16	A4
Welkom	59	D5
Wellesley Is.	60	D6
Wellington, Australia	63	B4
Wellington, N.Z.	65	D6
Wellington, I.	95	F1
Wellington, L.	63	C4
Wels	15	D8
Welshpool	11	E5
Wemindji	71	C3
Wenatchee	72	C3
Wenchi	53	G5
Wenchow = Wenzhou	35	D7
Wendesi	37	E4
Wensu	34	B3
Wentworth	62	B3
Wenut	37	E4
Wenzhou	35	D7
Weri	37	E4
Werra →	14	C5
Werrimull	62	B3
Werris Creek	63	B5
Weser →	14	B5
Wesiri	37	F3
West Bengal □	40	F7
West Beskids = Západné Beskydy	16	D4
West Falkland	95	G4
West Fjord = Vestfjorden	8	B8
West Ice Shelf	96	A11
West Palm Beach	83	F7
West Pt.	62	C2
West Virginia □	76	E5
West Wyalong	63	B4
Westall Pt.	62	B1
Westbury	62	D4
Westerland	14	A5
Western Australia □	60	F3
Western Dvina = Daugava →	24	B1
Western Ghats	43	N9
Western Sahara ■	52	D3
Western Samoa = Samoa ■	65	L13
Westerwald	14	C4
Westland Bight	65	E4
Weston-super-Mare	11	F5
Westport, Ireland	11	E2
Westport, N.Z.	65	D4
Westray	10	B5
Wetar	37	F3
Wetaskiwin	69	C8
Wetzlar	14	C5
Wevok	69	B3
Wexford	11	E3
Weyburn	69	D9
Weymouth	11	F5
Wha Ti	68	B8
Whakatane	64	B7
Whale →	70	C4
Whale Cove	68	B10
Whales, B. of	96	B16
Whangamomona	64	C6
Whangarei	64	A6
Whangarei Harb.	64	A6
Wheeling	76	D5
White →, Ark., U.S.A.	81	C8
White →, Ind., U.S.A.	76	E2
White Cliffs	62	B3
White I.	64	B7
White Nile = Nîl el Abyad →	55	E5
White Russia = Belarus ■	24	C2
White Sea = Beloye More	8	B13
Whitecliffs	65	E4
Whitehaven	11	D5
Whitehorse	68	B6
Whitemark	62	D4
Whitianga	64	B6
Whitney, Mt.	78	B3
Whittlesea	63	C4
Wholdaia L.	68	B9
Whyalla	62	B2
Wichita	80	A5
Wichita Falls	80	C4
Wick	10	B5
Wickham, C.	62	C3
Wicklow Mts.	11	E3
Wieluń	16	C4
Wien	15	D9
Wiener Neustadt	15	E9
Wiesbaden	14	C5
Wilcannia	62	B3
Wildspitze	14	E6
Wilhelm, Mt.	61	B8

Name	Map	Grid
Wilhelm II Coast	96	A11
Wilhelmshaven	14	B5
Wilkes-Barre	77	D8
Willandra Creek →	63	B4
Willemstad	87	D6
William Creek	62	A2
Williams Lake	69	C7
Williamsburg	77	F7
Williamsport	77	D7
Williamstown	63	C3
Williston	74	A3
Willunga	62	C2
Wilmington, *Australia*	62	B2
Wilmington, *Del., U.S.A.*	77	E8
Wilmington, *N.C., U.S.A.*	83	B9
Wilpena Cr. →	62	B2
Wilson	83	B9
Wilsons Promontory	63	C4
Wimmera →	62	C3
Winchester	11	F6
Wind River Range	73	E9
Windau = Ventspils	24	B1
Windhoek	58	C3
Windsor, *Australia*	63	B5
Windsor, *Canada*	71	D2
Wingham	63	B5
Winisk →	71	C2
Winnipeg	69	D10
Winnipeg, L.	69	C10
Winnipegosis L.	69	C9
Winona	75	C9
Winston-Salem	83	A7
Winterthur	13	C8
Winton, *Australia*	61	E7
Winton, *N.Z.*	65	G3
Wirrulla	62	B1
Wisconsin □	75	C10
Wisła →	16	A4
Wismar	15	B6
Witbank	59	D5
Wittenberge	15	B6
Wkra →	16	B5
Włocławek	16	B4
Włodawa	17	C6
Wodonga = Albury-Wodonga	63	C4
Wokam	37	F4
Wolfsberg	15	E8
Wolfsburg	15	B6
Wolin	16	B2
Wollaston, Is.	95	H3
Wollaston Pen.	68	B8
Wollongong	63	B5
Wolverhampton	11	E5
Wondai	63	A5
Wongalarroo L.	63	B3
Wŏnsan	35	C7
Wonthaggi	63	C4
Woodenbong	63	A5
Woodend	63	C3
Woodland	72	G3
Woodroffe, Mt.	60	F5
Woods, L. of the	69	D10
Woodstock	71	D4
Woodville	64	D6
Woolamai, C.	63	C4
Woolgoolga	63	B5
Woomera	62	B2
Worcester, *S. Africa*	58	E3
Worcester, *U.K.*	11	E5
Worcester, *U.S.A.*	77	C10
Workington	11	D5
Worms	14	D5
Worthing	11	F6
Wosi	37	E3
Wou-han = Wuhan	35	C6
Wousi = Wuxi	35	C7
Wowoni	37	E2
Wrangel I. = Vrangelya, Ostrov	31	B15
Wrangell	69	C6
Wrangell Mts.	69	C5
Wrath, C.	10	B4
Wrexham	11	E5
Wright = Paranas	36	B3
Wrigley	68	B7
Wrocław	16	C3
Września	16	B3
Wu Jiang →	35	D5
Wuhan	35	C6
Wuhsi = Wuxi	35	C7
Wuhu	35	C6
Wukari	53	G7
Wuliaru	37	F4
Wulumuchi = Ürümqi	34	B3
Wuntho	41	F10
Wuppertal	14	C4
Würzburg	14	D5
Wutongqiao	34	D5
Wuwei	34	C5
Wuxi	35	C7
Wuyi Shan	35	D6
Wuzhong	35	C5
Wuzhou	35	D6
Wyandotte	76	C4
Wyandra	63	A4
Wyangala, L.	63	B4
Wyara, L.	63	A3
Wycheproof	62	C3
Wyndham, *Australia*	60	D4
Wyndham, *N.Z.*	65	G3
Wynyard	62	D4
Wyoming □	73	E10
Wyong	63	B5

X

Name	Map	Grid
Xaafuun	49	E5
Xai-Xai	59	D6
Xainza	34	C3
Xalapa	84	D5
Xangongo	58	B3
Xankändi	25	F6
Xánthi	22	D5
Xapuri	91	F5
Xátiva	19	C5
Xi Jiang →	35	D6
Xiaguan	34	D5
Xiamen	35	D6
Xi'an	35	C5
Xiang Jiang →	35	D6
Xiangfan	35	C6
Xianggang = Hong Kong □	35	D6
Xiangquan He = Sutlej →	42	E7
Xiangtan	35	D6
Xiao Hinggan Ling	35	B7
Xichang	34	D5
Xigazê	34	D3
Xing'an	35	D6
Xingu →	92	C3
Xining	34	C5
Xinjiang Uygur Zizhiqu □	34	B3
Xinjin = Pulandian	35	C7
Xinxiang	35	C6
Xinyang	35	C6
Xique-Xique	93	E5
Xisha Qundao = Paracel Is.	38	A4
Xixabangma Feng	40	C5
Xizang Zizhiqu □	34	C3
Xuanhua	35	B6
Xúquer →	19	C5
Xuzhou	35	C6

Y

Name	Map	Grid
Ya'an	34	D5
Yaapeet	62	C3
Yablonovyy Khrebet	30	D9
Yacuiba	94	A4
Yadgir	43	L10
Yahuma	56	D4
Yakima	72	C3
Yakovlevka	32	A3
Yakumo	32	B7
Yakutat	69	C6
Yakutsk	31	C10
Yala	38	C2
Yalinga	56	C4
Yalong Jiang →	34	D5
Yalova	22	D7
Yalta	25	E3
Yam Ha Melah = Dead Sea	47	E3
Yam Kinneret	46	D3
Yamagata	32	D7
Yamaguchi	33	F2
Yamal, Poluostrov	28	B8
Yamantau, Gora	29	D6
Yamba	63	A5
Yâmbiô	55	H4
Yambol	22	C6
Yamdena	37	F4
Yamethin	41	G11
Yamma-Yamma, L.	62	A3
Yamoussoukro	53	G4
Yampil	17	D9
Yampol = Yampil	17	D9
Yamuna →	40	E3
Yamzho Yumco	34	D4
Yana →	31	B11
Yanbu 'al Baḥr	47	F4
Yanco Cr. →	63	C4
Yandoon	41	J10
Yangambi	56	D4
Yangch'ü = Taiyuan	35	C6
Yangjiang	35	D6
Yangon = Rangoon	41	J11
Yangquan	35	C6
Yangtse = Chang Jiang →	35	C7
Yangtze Kiang = Chang Jiang →	35	C7
Yanji	35	B7
Yanqi	34	B3
Yantabulla	63	A4
Yantai	35	C7
Yanykurgan = Zhangaqürghan	29	E7
Yaoundé	56	D2
Yapen	37	E5
Yapen, Selat	37	E5
Yaqui →	84	B2
Yar-Sale	28	C8
Yaraka	61	E7
Yaransk	24	B6
Yaremcha	17	D7
Yarensk	28	C5
Yari →	90	D4
Yarkand = Shache	34	C2
Yarkhun →	42	A8
Yarlung Ziangbo Jiang = Brahmaputra →	41	F7
Yaroslavl	24	B4
Yarram	63	C4
Yarraman	63	A5
Yarras	63	B5
Yartsevo	30	C7
Yaselda	17	B8
Yasinya	17	D7
Yass	63	B4
Yatağan	23	F7
Yathkyed L.	68	B10
Yatsushiro	33	G2
Yavari →	90	D4
Yavatmal	43	J11
Yavoriv	17	D6
Yawatahama	33	G3
Yazd	44	C3
Yazd □	44	C3
Yazdân	45	C5
Yazoo →	81	C8
Ye Xian = Laizhou	35	C6
Yebyu	41	K12
Yecla	19	C5
Yedintsy = Edineț	17	D8

Yegros	94	B5
Yei	55	H5
Yekaterinburg	29	D7
Yekaterinodar = Krasnodar	25	D4
Yelarbon	63	A5
Yelets	24	C4
Yelizavetgrad = Kirovohrad	25	D3
Yell	10	A6
Yellow Sea	35	C7
Yellowhead Pass	69	C8
Yellowknife	68	B8
Yellowstone △	73	D9
Yellowstone ➤	74	B3
Yelsk	17	C9
Yemen ■	49	E3
Yenangyaung	41	G10
Yenbo = Yanbu 'al Baḥr	47	F4
Yenda	63	B4
Yenice	23	E6
Yenisey ➤	28	B9
Yeniseysk	30	D7
Yeniseyskiy Zaliv	28	B9
Yenyuka	31	D10
Yeola	43	J9
Yeovil	11	F5
Yerbent	29	F6
Yerevan	25	E5
Yermak	29	D8
Yershov	24	C6
Yerushalayim = Jerusalem	47	E3
Yessey	30	C8
Yeu, Î. d'	12	C2
Yevpatoriya	25	D3
Yeysk	25	D4
Yezd = Yazd	44	D3
Yiannitsa	23	D4
Yibin	35	D5
Yichang	35	C6
Yichun	35	B7
Yıldız Dağları	22	D6
Yinchuan	35	C5
Yingkou	35	B7
Yining	34	B3
Yinmabin	41	F10
Yishan	35	D5
Yithion	23	F4
Yiyang	35	D6
Yog Pt.	36	B2
Yogyakarta	39	F4
Yokadouma	56	D2
Yokkaichi	33	F5
Yokohama	33	F6
Yokosuka	33	F6
Yola	55	G1
Yonago	33	F3
Yonibana	53	G3
Yonkers	77	D9
Yonne ➤	13	B5
York, U.K.	11	E6
York, U.S.A.	77	E7
York, C.	61	C7
Yorke Pen.	62	B2
Yorkton	69	C9
Yos Sudarso, Pulau = Dolak, Pulau	37	F5
Yosemite △	78	B3
Yoshkar Ola	24	B6
Youghal	11	F3
Young	63	B4
Younghusband, L.	62	B2
Younghusband Pen.	62	C2
Youngstown	76	D5
Yozgat	46	C3
Ysyk-Köl	29	E8
Yu Jiang ➤	35	D6
Yu Shan	35	D7
Yuan Jiang ➤	35	D6
Yuba City	72	G3
Yūbetsu	32	A8
Yucatán □	85	C7
Yucatán, Canal de	85	C7
Yucatán, Península de	85	D7
Yuci	35	C6

Yugoslavia = Serbia & Montenegro ■	22	B3
Yukon ➤	69	B3
Yukon Territory □	68	B6
Yukta	30	C8
Yuma	78	D5
Yumen	34	C4
Yungas	91	G5
Yunnan □	34	D5
Yunta	62	B2
Yurga	29	D9
Yurimaguas	91	E3
Yushu	34	C4
Yuzhno-Sakhalinsk	31	E12
Yvetot	12	B4

Z

Zāb al Kabīr ➤	46	C5
Zāb aş Şagīr ➤	46	D5
Zābol □	45	D6
Zābolī	45	E5
Zabrze	16	C4
Zacatecas	84	C4
Zadar	20	B5
Zadetkyi Kyun	38	C1
Zafra	18	C2
Zagań	16	C2
Zagazig	54	B5
Zagorsk = Sergiyev Posad	24	B4
Zagreb	20	B6
Zāgros, Kühhā-ye	44	C2
Zagros Mts. = Zāgros, Kühhā-ye	44	C2
Zāhedān	45	D5
Zahlah	46	D3
Zaïre = Congo ➤	56	F2
Zaječar	22	C4
Zakhodnaya Dzvina = Daugava ➤	24	B1
Zākhū ➤	46	C5
Zákinthos	23	F3
Zalaegerszeg	16	E3
Zalău	17	E6
Zaleshchiki = Zalishchyky	17	D7
Zalew Wiślany	16	A4
Zalingei	55	F3
Zalishchyky	17	D7
Zambeze ➤	59	B7
Zambezi = Zambeze ➤	59	B7
Zambezi	58	A4
Zambia ■	59	B5
Zamboanga	36	C2
Zamora, Mexico	84	D4
Zamora, Spain	18	B3
Zamość	17	C6
Zanesville	76	E4
Zanjān	46	C7
Zanjān □	46	C7
Zante = Zákinthos	23	F3
Zanzibar	57	F7
Zaouiet El-Kala = Bordj Omar Driss	52	C7
Zaouiet Reggâne	52	C5
Zap Suyu = Zāb al Kabīr ➤	46	C5
Zapadnaya Dvina = Daugava ➤	24	B1
Západné Beskydy	16	D4
Zaporizhzhya	25	D4
Zara	46	C4
Zaragoza	19	B5
Zarand	44	D4
Zaranj	42	D2
Zaria	53	F7
Zaruma	90	D3
Žary	16	C2
Zarzis	54	B1
Zaskar Mts.	42	C10
Zävareh	44	C3
Zawiercie	16	C4

Zāwiyat al Bayḍā = Al Bayḍā	54	B3
Zāyandeh ➤	44	C3
Zaysan	29	E9
Zaysan, Oz.	29	E9
Zbarazh	17	D7
Zdolbuniv	17	C8
Zduńska Wola	16	C4
Zeebrugge	14	C2
Zeehan	62	D4
Zeila	49	E3
Zeitz	15	C7
Zelenograd	24	B4
Zemun	22	B3
Zenica	20	B6
Žepče	20	B7
Zêzere ➤	18	C1
Zgorzelec	16	C2
Zhabinka	17	B7
Zhailma	29	D7
Zhambyl = Taraz	29	E8
Zhangaqazaly	29	E7
Zhangaqürghan	29	E7
Zhangjiakou	35	B6
Zhangye	34	C5
Zhangzhou	35	D6
Zhanjiang	35	D6
Zhanyi	34	D5
Zhaotong	34	D5
Zhashkiv	17	D10
Zhayyq ➤	29	E6
Zhdanov = Mariupol	25	D4
Zhejiang □	35	D7
Zhengzhou	35	C6
Zhezqazghan	29	E7
Zhigansk	30	C10
Zhilinda	30	B9
Zhitomir = Zhytomyr	17	C8
Zhlobin	17	B10
Zhmerynka	17	D9
Zhob	42	D6
Zhodzina	17	A9
Zhongdian	34	D4
Zhumadian	35	C6
Zhytomyr	17	C9
Zibo	35	C6
Zielona Góra	16	C2
Zigey	55	F2
Zigong	35	D5
Ziguinchor	53	F2
Zile	46	B3
Zillah	54	C2
Zimbabwe ■	59	B5
Zimnicea	22	C5
Zinder	53	F7
Zion △	79	B6
Zirreh, Gowd-e	42	E3
Zlatograd	22	D5
Zlatoust	29	D6
Zlín	16	D3
Zmeinogorsk	29	D9
Znojmo	16	D3
Zolochiv	17	D7
Zomba	59	B7
Zongo	56	D3
Zonguldak	46	B2
Zorritos	90	D2
Zouar	54	D2
Zouïrât	52	D3
Zrenjanin	22	B3
Ẓufār	48	D5
Zug	13	C8
Zugspitze	14	E6
Zumbo	59	B6
Zunyi	35	D5
Zürich	13	C8
Zuwārah	54	B1
Zvishavane	59	C5
Zwettl	15	D8
Zwickau	15	C7
Zwolle	14	B4
Żyrardów	16	B5
Zyryan	29	E9

Projection:Hammer Equal Area